THE RAUPŌ POCKET DICTIONARY OF MODERN MĀORI

THE RAUPŌ POCKET DICTIONARY OF MODERN MĀORI

P.M. Ryan

PENGUIN BOOKS
Published by the Penguin Group
Penguin Group (NZ), 67 Apollo Drive, Rosedale, Auckland 0632, New Zealand
(a division of Pearson New Zealand Ltd)
Penguin Group (USA) Inc., 375 Hudson Street, New York, New York 10014, USA
Penguin Group (Canada), 90 Eglinton Avenue East, Suite 700, Toronto, Ontario, M4P 2Y3
Canada (a division of Pearson Penguin Canada Inc.)
Penguin Books Ltd, 80 Strand, London, WC2R 0RL, England
Penguin Ireland, 25 St Stephen's Green, Dublin 2, Ireland (a division of Penguin Books Ltd)
Penguin Group (Australia), 707 Collins Street, Melbourne, Victoria 3008,
Australia
(a division of Pearson Australia Group Pty Ltd)
Penguin Books India Pvt Ltd, 11, Community Centre, Panchsheel Park, New Delhi –
110 017, India
Penguin Books (South Africa) (Pty) Ltd, Rosebank Office Park, Block D,
181 Jan Smuts Avenue, Parktown North, Johannesburg 2196, South Africa
Penguin (Beijing) Ltd, 7F, Tower B, Jiaming Center, 27 East Third Ring Road North,
Chaoyang District, Beijing 100020, China

Penguin Books Ltd, Registered Offices: 80 Strand, London, WC2R 0RL, England

First published by Reed Publishing (NZ) Ltd, 1999
This edition published by Penguin Group (NZ), 2009

Typeset by Pindar NZ
Printed and bound in Australia by Griffin Press

ISBN 978 014301192 7

A catalogue record for this book is available
from the National Library of New Zealand.

www.penguin.co.nz

CONTENTS

PREFACE – HE KUPU WHAKATAKI

Tēnā anō koutou katoa. Kia ora! Kia tupu! Kāti ngā mihi.
Greetings to all. Keep in good health. Continue to broaden your knowledge. That's enough greeting!

Ko te putanga tuarua tēnei o te *Puna Kupu Pēke.*

Here is the second edition of this Pocket Dictionary.

I ēnei rā he nui ngā hōtaka Māori e kitea ana i te Taonga Whakaata ki Aotearoa, e rangona ana rānei i te Reo Irirangi.

In these days there are dozens of TV and radio programmes in Māori.

E whakaaria tonu ana ngā kupu o te ao tawhito, ā, e kitea ana ngā taitara ātaahua, otirā, nō namata hoki.

Old words are being revived with new meanings all the time and flash titles from the ancient world are given to programmes.

Ko ēnei ngā kupu hou i roto i tēnei putanga.

These are the type of words added to this edition.

Kua tangohia atu ētahi kupu ruha nei, otirā ka kitea tonutia aua kupu i roto i te *Puna Kupu Nui o Raupō.*

Some obsolete words have been removed, but they can still be found in The Raupō Dictionary of Modern Māori.

Aroha nui
nā Pā Ryan

PRONUNCIATION OF MĀORI – KO TE WHAKAHUA KUPU

The main stumbling block for Pākehā, or anyone else who has not grown up hearing Māori spoken, is the pronunciation of the vowel sounds. Correct vowel sounds are absolutely essential and will only come easily after much practice, listening to the experts and, if possible, listening to ourselves on tape-recorders.

However, once the correct pronunciation is achieved, we can tackle new words with confidence because the pronunciation of each vowel is absolutely constant, apart from its length.

In this dictionary, a lengthened vowel is indicated by a macron over the vowel and it is most important to recognise this. For example, compare 'anā te hōiho – there is a horse' (anā = there) with 'he ana tēnei – this is a cave' (ana = cave). In some publications a double vowel is used instead: 'anaa te hooiho – there is a horse'.

The vowel *a* is pronounced as in the English *far*. Avoid all trace of the flat *a* such as in *hat*.

The vowel *e* is pronounced like the *ea* in *leather*. Avoid the double sound of the vowel as found in *hay* and *may*.

The vowel *i* is pronounced as in the Latin languages. It is equivalent to the vowel sound in the English words *me* or *he*.

The vowel *o* is pronounced as the English word *awe*. Avoid all trace of the English pronunciation of *oh!* This is the most abused vowel sound when one is learning Māori; take great care with it.

The vowel *u* is pronounced like the double *o* in *moon*. Avoid saying it like the *ew* in *few*.

When two vowels occur together, begin by practising each separately until you can speed up without spoiling the clarity of the vowels when they are run together, e.g. 'koe' should be practised as 'ko – e' until the vowels can follow each other smoothly.

The only consonants to worry about are the following:

r must not be rolled. It is pronounced quite close to the sound of *l* in English. The tongue is near the front of the mouth.

p is generally softer than in English, not an explosive sound at all.

wh is usually pronounced like *f*. In some districts it is spoken like an *h* (e.g. in Hokianga) and in others like a *w* (e.g. in Taranaki), in others again like *wh* in *when*.

ng is a softer sound than in English, especially with regard to the *g*. The sound is similar to the middle *ng* in *singing*.

Note that in this dictionary passive endings are given in brackets after the verbs, and alternatives of these are separated by commas.

A BRIEF GRAMMAR – PAPA WETEREO POTO

These are general rules with many local variants.

The verb

The verb form does not change in Māori. Changes of time, etc., are indicated by the particles used with the verb.

Simple statements

a. Past, present or future	—	use ka + verb, e.g. ka kai ia – he will eat, *or* he eats/he ate
b. Past only	—	use i + verb, e.g. i kai ia – he ate
c. Completed	—	use kua + verb, e.g. kua kai ia – he has eaten/he had eaten
Negatives of **a**	—	*kāhore + subject + e + verb, e.g. kāhore ia e kai – he will not eat
of **a** and **b**	—	kāhore + subject + i + verb, e.g. kāhore ia i kai – he did not eat
of **c**	—	kāhore anō + subject + kia + verb, e.g. kāhore anō ia kia kai – he has/had not yet eaten

*Kāhore can be replaced by other forms of the negative such as kāore; hore kau; kīhai (for past); e kore (future).

Continuous action

d. Past, present or future	—	use e + verb + ana, e.g. e kai ana ia – he is eating/was eating/will be eating
e. Present only	—	use kei te + verb, e.g. kei te kai ia – he is eating
f. Past only	—	use i te + verb, e.g. i te kai ia – he was eating
g. Habitual	—	use verb + ai, e.g. haere ai ia i ngā Mane – he goes on Mondays

Negatives of **d** — kāhore + subject + e + verb + ana
e.g. kāhore ia e kai ana – he is not eating

e and **f** — kāhore + subject + i te + verb
e.g. kāhore ia i te kai – he is not/was not eating

g — kāhore + subject + e + verb + ana
e.g. kāhore ia e haere ana i ngā Mane – he does not go on Mondays

Emphatic subject

h. Future — use mā + subject + e + verb
e.g. *you* will call – māu e karanga
John will call – mā Hone e karanga

i. Past — use nā + subject + i + verb
e.g. *you* called – nāu i karanga
John called – nā Hone i karanga

Negatives as **a** and **b** above.

Commands

E + verb (used with verbs of one or two syllables): E noho – Sit
Verb alone (with longer verbs): Waiata – Sing
Verb with passive ending: Noho*ia* – Sit (used when there is a subject of the verb, even when not expressed); Noho*ia* (te tūru) – Sit (on the chair)
Kia + verb (rather strong): Kia mōhio koe! – Understand!
Kia + adjective (rather mild exhortation): Kia pai! – Be good!
Me + verb (also rather mild): Me noho – Please sit down

There are also several words which are implicit commands, e.g.
Kāti! – That's enough! *or* Stop!
Anō – Say it again
Turituri! – (Tai Tokerau) Noise! (i.e. Be quiet!)
Hoihoi! – Noise! (i.e. Be quiet!)
Negative commands: use Kaua e + verb, e.g. Kaua e karanga – Do not call
Instead of Kaua one may use Aua or Kauaka. Instead of 'e' one may use hei.
Kei + verb, e.g. Kei noho – Be careful not to sit

Conditional (if)

Future — use ki te, *or* mehemea, *or* mena + verb
e.g. ki te haere mai koe – if you are coming

Past	—	use me i + verb, *or* mehemea i + verb e.g. me (*or* mehemea) i kai koe – if you had had a meal
Negatives: future	—	use ki te kore e.g. ki te kore ia e kai – if he doesn't eat
past	—	use me i kāhore e.g. me i kāhore ia i kai – if he didn't eat

Sentences containing only the verb 'to be'

English structure:	John is good.	The house was big.	Those are posts.
Māori formation:	Good/John	Big/the house	Posts/those
	He pai/a Hone.	He nui/te whare.	He pou/ērā.

Negative: use ehara i + subject, and change 'he' to 'te'. For example:

That house is not big	–	Ehara tērā whare i te nui
or	–	Ehara tērā i te whare nui

Passive verbs

The Māori verb is changed to the passive by adding a passive ending to it. These endings vary with each verb and have to be learned: they are all in the order of –tia, -ria, -ia, -ngia, -ina. If you cannot remember the correct version for the verb you want to use, put –ngia on it and it will be understood quite well. (In this dictionary, passive endings are given in brackets after the verbs.)

e.g. e kimi ana te tangata i te kurī	–	the man is looking for the dog
e kimihia ana te kurī e te tangata	–	the dog is being sought by the man

If a passive ending is used, the word 'by' which follows in English will have to be translated by the following: 'e' for people or animals, 'ki' for instruments.

After verbs formed from particles and adjectives (see end of this brief grammar) 'by' is translated by 'i' for people, animals and instruments.

With the past emphatic, 'by' is translated by 'nā', e.g. nā te taraka i tō te waka – the truck pulled the canoe.

The verb 'to have'

As there is no direct equivalent of the verb 'have', the following methods are used to express this meaning:

1. kei + subject, e.g. I have – kei ahau; John has – kei a Hone
2. he + possessive pronoun, e.g. I have a dog – he kurī tāku
3. kua whai + object, e.g. kua whai moni ahau – I have some money (kua whiwhi can be used in the same sense)
4. I will have, i.e. future is expressed by hei, e.g. I'll have the boat, *or* let me have the boat – hei ahau te poti
5. Past tense 'I had' may be understood using construction **2** (he + possessive pronoun) or one may say i + subject (e.g. i a au te mea – I had the thing)
6. whiwhi (+ ki), e.g. ka whiwhi motokā ia – he has a car, *or* ka whiwhi ia ki te motokā

Adjectives

In Māori the adjective is always placed after the word which it describes, e.g. he motokā whero – a red car.

Positive:	pai – good
Comparative:	pai ake, pai atu, pai kē, pai kē atu – better
Superlative:	pai rawa, tino pai – very good; te tino pai – the best

Adjectives in Māori do not stand alone – use 'he' or 'te' with them. In the comparative form, some adjectives add 'iho', e.g. kino iho – worse.

Cardinal Numerals

1 = Tahi	11 = Tekau mā tahi	100 = Rau, Kotahi rau
2 = Rua	12 = Tekau mā rua	200 = Rua rau
3 = Toru	13 = Tekau mā toru	300 = Toru rau
4 = Whā	20 = Rua tekau	1,000 = Kotahi mano
5 = Rima	21 = Rua tekau mā tahi	2,000 = Rua mano
6 = Ono	30 = Toru tekau	1,000,000 = Miriona
7 = Whitu	40 = Whā tekau	1,000,000,000 = Piriona
8 = Waru	50 = Rima tekau	
9 = Iwa	60 = Ono tekau	
10 = Tekau	70 = Whitu tekau	

Ordinal Numbers

Place tua- as a prefix from 1st to 9th, e.g. 1st = Tuatahi; 2nd = Tuarua; 3rd = Tuatoru . . . 9th = Tuaiwa.

Otherwise place Te in front of all numbers. For example, 11th = Te tekau mā tahi; 30th = Te toru tekau.

From rua to iwa – 'e' is used before numbers when speaking of things, e.g. e rua ngā whare – two houses; ngā whare e rua – the two houses. 'Toko' may be used prefixed to the number when speaking of people, e.g. tokorima ngā tāngata – there are five men.

To multiply, place the numbers side by side without any connecting words, e.g. 20 x 5 – rua tekau rima.

To say 'in ones', 'in twos', etc., place 'taki' before the number, e.g. takirua – in twos.

When asking how many are wanted, and giving the reply, use 'kia' – let it be, e.g. kia hia putu – how many feet? Answer: kia toru – (let it be) three.

Pronouns

Singular (one person)

Personal		**Possessive**		
			(one thing possessed)	*(several)*
I, me	au, ahau	my, mine	tōku, tāku	ōku, āku
you	koe	your, yours	tōu, tāu	ōu, āu
he, she, him, her	ia	his, her, hers	tōna, tāna	ōna, āna

Dual (two people)

Personal		**Possessive**		
			(one thing possessed)	*(several)*
we (you & I), us	tāua	our, ours	tō, tāua, tā tāua	ō tāua, ā tāua
we (he & I), us	māua	our, ours	tō māua, tā māua	ō māua, ā māua
you	kōrua	your, yours	tō kōrua, tā kōrua	ō kōrua, ā kōrua
they, them	rāua	their, theirs	tō rāua, tā rāua	ō rāua, ā rāua

Plural (three or more)

Personal		Possessive		
we (you & I), us	tātou	our, ours	tō tātou, tā tātou	ō tātou, ā tātou
we (they & I), us	mātou	our, ours	tō mātou, tā mātou	ō mātou, ā mātou
you	koutou	your, yours	tō koutou, tā koutou	ō koutou, ā koutou
they, them	rātou	their, theirs	tō rātou, tā rātou	ō rātou, ā rātou

In the possessives one has to choose between the 'o' form and the 'a' form. The list below will give you some idea of how to use the two forms.

When to use the 'o' or 'a' form

'o' form used with things inherited	*'a' form used with things produced by one's own effort*
qualities	
transport	movable property
clothing	food
relatives not mentioned in 'a' column; also with 'hoa'	tools
land, country, town, city	husband, wife, children, grandchildren, nieces, nephews
buildings	slaves, servants
water for drinking	activities
organisations to which one belongs	animals, not used for transport
nouns formed from adjectives, participles, intransitive verbs, and transitive verbs used in a passive sense	nouns formed from transitive verbs and used in an active sense

Note: There are alternative forms, with a shortened vowel (taku, tana) which can substitute for the singular possessives.

Local nouns (place or time)

The following nouns do not take 'te' or 'ngā' or any other definitive and cannot be qualified by an adjective. Note that this rule does not apply when the word is considered as a thing in its own right, and not just a place, e.g. tai – the tide, roto – the inside, muri – the rear.

runga	top	konā	that place (near you)
raro	bottom	korā	that place (away)
roto	inside	reira	that place (already mentioned)
waho	outside	tai	seawards
mua	front	tahaki	on one side, the shore
muri	rear	pahaki	near distance
waenga, waenganui *or* waengarahi	the middle	tawhiti	far off
		āianei	now, just now
tua (taitua)	the other side of a solid object	aoake	following day
tāwāhi (rāwāhi)	the other side (of sea, river, valley)	nahea?	what time (past)?
uta	inland (from the coast, shore from the sea)	inanahi	yesterday
hea, whea?	what place?	inapō	last night
kō	that place/time	tahirā	day after tomorrow, or day before yesterday
konei	this place	nehe, neherā onamata	long ago

The noun

In Māori there are three points to note about nouns:

1. Nouns do not change in the plural (though there are a few exceptions, including tamariki, matua and wahine). The plural is indicated by the words preceding the noun.
   e.g. te whare – the house, ngā whare – the houses
   tō koutou whare – your house, ō koutou whare – your houses

Sometimes when the indefinite article 'he' precedes the noun it can be ambiguous, meaning 'a' or 'some', e.g. he whare, which can mean either 'a house' or 'some houses'.

In such cases there are usually other words in the sentence to give the clue. Compare:

he whare tēnei with he whare ēnei
this is a house these are houses

2. A noun never stands alone as, for example, with the English 'roads', 'houses', 'trees'. In Māori these would be preceded by the indefinite article, e.g. he rori, he whare, he rākau.
3. Quite often a noun may be used as a verb, e.g. kōrero, he kōrero – a speech; e kōrero ana ia – he is speaking; e kōrerotia ana e te iwi – it is being said by the people.

Participles and adjectives used as verbs

Many adjectives can be used as verbs in Māori; if they are followed by an agent or instrument by which the action is done, the word 'by' is translated as 'i'. This applies also to the following:

mutu	ended	marara	scattered	pakaru	smashed
pā	struck	oti	completed	riro	happened
poto	all dealt with	whara	injured	pau	used up
whati	broken	ea	paid for	marū	bruised
mahue	left behind	tū	wounded	mau	fixed, caught
takoki	sprained	motu	snapped	rato	provided
mākona	satisfied	rūpeke	assembled		

KEY VOCABULARY – RĀRANGI KUPU MATUA

Seasons of the year – Ngā wā o te tau

spring	kōanga	**autumn**	ngahuru
summer	raumati	**winter**	hōtoke, takurua, makariri

Months – Ngā marama

January	Hānuere, Kohi-tātea	**July**	Hūrae, Hōngongoi
February	Pepuere, Hui-tanguru	**August**	Ākuhata, Here-turi-kōkā
March	Maehe, Poutū-te-rangi	**September**	Hepetema, Mahuru
April	Āperira, Paengawhāwhā	**October**	Oketopa, Whiringa-ā-nuku
May	Mei, Haratua	**November**	Noema, Whiringa-ā-rangi
June	Hune, Pipiri	**December**	Tīhema, Hakihea

Days of the week – Ngā rā o te wiki

In Māori, one always puts 'te' or another definite article in front of the day of the week.

Sunday	Rātapu	**Thursday**	Tāite, Rāwhā, Rāpare
Monday	Mane, Rātahi, Rāhina	**Friday**	Paraire, Rārima, Rāmere
Tuesday	Tūrei, Rārua, Rātū	**Saturday**	Hātarei, Rāhoroi
Wednesday	Wenerei, Rātoru, Rāapa		

Points of the compass – Ngā tōpito o te ao

north	raki, tokerau, raro	**east**	rāwhiti
south	tonga, runga	**west**	hauāuru, uru

Parts of the body – Ngā wāhi o te tinana

head	māhunga, mātenga, upoko	**finger**	matihao (and many dialect words)
neck	kakī		
throat	korokoro	**thumb**	kōnui
shoulder	pakihiwi, pokowhiwhi	**index finger**	kōroa
		middle finger	māpere (and many variants)
chest	uma		
breast	ū, uma	**ring finger**	mānawa
waist	hope	**little finger**	koiti
arm/hand	ringaringa	**toes**	matikara
elbow	tuke	**hair**	huruhuru, makawe
leg/foot	waewae		
thigh	kūwhā	**face**	kanohi, mata
hip	humu, himu	**forehead**	rae
heel	rekereke	**eyebrow**	kape
ankle	pona	**eye**	kanohi, karu
joint (in arm or leg)	pona, punga	**ear**	taringa
		cheek	pāpāringa
knee	turi	**nose**	ihu
back	tuarā	**lip**	ngutu
buttocks	tou, nono	**teeth**	niho
stomach	puku	**mouth**	māngai, waha
belly button	pito	**jaw/chin**	kauae
armpit	kēkē	**tongue**	arero
rib	rara	**beard**	paihau, pāhau

Colours – Ko ngā tae/kara

black	mangu, pango	**blue**	purū	**yellow**	kōwhai
green	kirīni	**grey**	pūmā, kerei	**brown**	parāone
red	whero	**sky blue**	kikorangi	**orange**	parakaraka, ārani
white	mā			**striped**	whakahekeheke

Personal names – Ingoa tāngata

Many Māori names are derived from English ones and it is quite common to hear a person referred to as Henry when the speaker is using English, and as Hēnare when he's using Māori. Here are some Māori equivalents of well-known names and names from New Zealand history:

Adam Ātama
Agnes Akinehi
Albert Arapeta
Alfred Arapeti
Alice Ārihi
Andrew Ānaru
Ann Ani
Anthony Ātoni
April Āperira
Benjamin Peniamine
Bernard Perenara
Bruce Puruhi
Caesar Hīha
Captain Kāpene
Cook Kuki
Caroline Karoraina
Catherine Katarina
Cecilia Hihiria
Charles Hāre
Charlie Tiāre
Charlotte Hārata
Christ Karaiti, Kerīto
Christian Karaitiana
Christopher Kiritopa
Conrad Kānara
Daniel Raniera
Dave Rewi
David Rāwiri
Diana Raiana, Tiana
Dorothy Tārati
Edward Eruera
Elizabeth Irihāpeti
Emmanuel Emanuera
Esther Ehetere
Ezekiel Ehekiera
Ezra Ētera
Fox Pōkiha
Francis Werahiko
Frazer Pareiha
George Hōri
Gerard Kereti
Goliath Koriata
Grey Kerei
Harry Hāre
Henry Hēnare
Holyoake Hōrioka
Isaac Ihaka
Isabel Ihāpera
Isaiah Ihaia
Jack(ie) Haki
James Hēmi
Jane Hēni
Jason Hahona
Jeremiah Heremaia
Jesus Hehu, Ihu
Joel Hoera
John Hone, Hoane
Joseph Hōhepa
Joshua Hōhua
Judith Hutita
Lawrence Raureti
Louise Ruiha
Lucy Ruihi
Luke Ruka
MacDonald Maketānera, Makere
Margaret Makareta
Mark Maaka
Marsden Mātenga
Martha Maata
Martin Mātene
Mary Mere, Maria
Mary Anne Mereana
Michael Mikaere
Moses Mohi, Moihi
Nicholas Nikora
Patrick Pateriki
Paul Paora
Peter Pita, Petera
Philip Piripi
Polly Pare
Queenie Kuini
Rachel Rāhera
Ralph Rau
Rebecca Ripeka
Richard Rihari
Robert Rāpata
Ruth Rutu
Samuel Hamuera
Sarah Hera
Selwyn Herewini
Searancke Hērangi
Solomon Horomona
Sophia Te Paea
Stephen Tipene/Tewano
Susan Huhana
Tasman Tahimana
Te Kooti Te Turuki
Theresa Terehia

Thomas	Toma, Tāmati	**Tregerthen**	Tirikatene	**William(s)**	Wiremu
		Victoria	Wikitoria	**Wilson**	Wirihana
Thompson	Tamihana	**Walter**	Waata	**Winston**	Winitana
Timothy	Timoti	**White**	Waiti		

New Zealand place names – Ingoa wāhi o Aotearoa

Some Māori place names do have obvious meanings but unless the circumstances under which a name was given are known, mistakes can be made. Many names have been shortened and altered during centuries of use and no one can even guess what they were originally.

Alexandra	Areketānara	**Feilding**	Aorangi
Ashburton	Hakatere	**Fiordland**	Rua-o-te-Moko, Whakataka-Kārehu-o-Tamatea
Auckland	Ākarana, Tāmaki-makau-rau	**Flaxmere**	Waiharakeke
Banks Peninsula	Hakaroa	**Galatea**	Kuhāwea
Bastion Point	Takaparawha(u)	**Gisborne**	Whatu-i-āpiti, Tūranga-nui-a-Kiwa
Bay of Islands	Teketetonga Peiwhairangi	**Great Barrier Island**	Aotea
Birkenhead	Kaimoeone	**Greymouth**	Māwhera
Blenheim	Wairau, Waiharakeke	**Greytown**	Kuratawhiti, Houhou-Pounamu
Bluff	Murihiku	**Hamilton**	Hāmutana, Kirikiriroa
Brown's Island	Motukorea	**Hastings**	Heretaunga
Cambridge	Kēmureti	**Hawke's Bay**	Matau-a-Māui
Canterbury Plains	Ngā Pākihi-whaka-tekateka-a-Waitaha	**Huntly**	Rāhui Pokeka
Cape Runaway	Whangaparāoa	**Invercargill**	Waihopai
Chatham Islands	Wharekauri, Rēkohu, Arekohu	**Katikati**	Ngā Kuri-a-Whārei
Christchurch	Ōtautahi	**Levin**	Horowhenua
Cook Strait	Moana-o-Raukawa	**Little Barrier Island**	Hauturu
Coromandel	Moehau	**Lower Hutt**	Awakairangi
Dannevirke	Taniwaka		
Dargaville	Takuira		
Dunedin	Ōtepoti		
Featherston	Kaiwaewae		

Masterton	Te Oreore
Mayor Island	Tuhua
Mercury Island	Ahuahu
Milford Sound	Piopiotahi
Mt Aspiring	Tititea
Mt Albert	Ōwairaka
Mt Cook	Aoraki, Aorangi
Mt Eden (hill)	Maunga Whau
Mt Eden (jail)	Mautīni
Mt Edgecumbe	Pūtauaki
Mt Egmont	Taranaki
Mt Hobson	Remuera
Mt Smart	Rarotonga
Mt St John	Te Kopuke
Mt Wellington	Maungarei
Napier	Ahuriri
Nelson	Whakatū
New Plymouth	Ngāmotu
New Zealand	Aotearoa, Te Ika-a-Māui, Niu Tireni
North Cape	Muriwhenua
North Head	Maunga Uika
North Island	Te Ika-a-Maui
Northcote	Onewa
Northland	Tai Tokerau, Te Hiku-o-te-Ika
Oamaru	Te Oha-a-Maru
One Tree Hill	Maungakiekie
Otago	Ōtākou
Palmerston North	Te-Papa-i-Oea
Poor Knights	Tawhiti Rahi
Poverty Bay	Tūranganui, Pawati Pei
Riverton	Aparima
Russell	Kororāreka
South Island	Te Waipounamu
Southern Alps	Ngā Puke Māeroero
Spirits Bay	Kapo Wairua
Stewart Island	Rakiura, Te Puka-a-Māui
Taupo	Taupō-nui a Tia
Tauranga	Tauranga Moana
Thames	Pārāwai, Hauraki
Three Kings	Tirikingi
Tikarau	Tihirau
Tokoroa	Kaokaoroa-o-Pātetere
Tolaga Bay	Uawa
Upper Hutt	Whakatiki
Wairoa	Te Wairoa
Wanganui	Whanganui, Wainui-ā-rua
Wellington	Pōneke, Whanganui-ā-Tara
Whangarei	Whangarei-terenga-parāoa

Overseas places – Kei tāwāhi

Afghanistan	Awhekenetana
Africa	Āwherika
Albania	Arapeinia
Algeria	Aratiria
Amazon	Amāhona
America	Amerika
Amman	Āmana
Andes	Ānihi
Ankara	Anakara
Antwerp	Anatepe
Arabia	Areipia
Argentina	Āketina
Asia	Āhia
Atlantic	Ranatiki
Australia	Ahitereiria
Austria	Āteria
Babylon	Papurona
Baghdad	Pākatata
Baltic	Paratiki
Bangkok	Pangakoko
Bangladesh	Pākaratēhi
Barbados	Pāpatohe
Bay of Bengal	Whanga Pēngara
Beijing	Peihinga
Belarus	Pērara
Belgium	Peretiamu
Bering Sea	Peringa Moana
Berlin	Pearīni
Bermuda	Pāmura
Bethlehem	Peterehema
Black Sea	Moana Pango
Bogotá	Pokotā
Bolivia	Poriwia
Bonn	Pono
Botswana	Poriwana
Brahmaputra	Paramapūtara
Brazil	Parīhi
Britain	Piritene
Brussels	Paruhi
Bulgaria	Purukāria
Burma	Pēma
Caledonia	Karetōnia
California	Karepōnia
Cambodia	Kamupōtia
Canada	Kānata
Cannes	Kanehi
Caribbean	Karipiana
Caspian Sea	Kāhipiana
Chile	Hiri
China	Haina
Colombia	Koromopia
Colombo	Koromo
Congo	Kango
Cook Islands	Rarotonga, Kuki Airani
Coral Sea	Moana Kutakuta
Croatia	Koroātia
Cyprus	Haiperu
Dalmatia	Tarara
Danube	Tānupe
Denmark	Tenemāka
Dominica	Tominika
Dublin	Tāperene
Ecuador	Ekuatoa
England	Ingarangi
Ephesus	Epehi
Estonia	Etonia
Ethiopia	Etiopia
Europe	Ūropi
Fiji	Whiti
Finland	Whinarangi
Flanders	Paranihi
France	Parani, Wīwī
Frankfurt	Parewhiti
Fukuoka	Whukuoka
Ganges	Kānehi
Geneva	Hinīwa
Germany	Tiamani

Ghana	Kāna	**Mekong**	Mekonga
Greece	Kariki, Kirihi	**Melbourne**	Poipiripi, Merepana
Guam	Kuamu		
Guinea	Kīni	**Memphis**	Mēpihi
The Hague	Te Hēke	**Mexico**	Mehiko
Hamburg	Hamupēke	**Montevideo**	Mangaata
Himalayas	Himāria	**Morocco**	Marako, Moroko
Hokkaido	Hokairo	**Moscow**	Mohikau
Holland	Hōrana	**Muscat**	Muhukata
Hungary	Hanaraki	**Nagoya**	Nakoya
Iceland	Tiorangi	**Namibia**	Namīpia
India	Inia	**Nazareth**	Nahareta
Indonesia	Initonīhia	**Nepal**	Nepōra
Iran	Irana, Pēhia	**The Netherlands**	Hōrana
Iraq	Iraka	**New Delhi**	Nūteri
Ireland	Airana, Airangi	**New Guinea**	Niu Kini
Israel	Iharaira	**New York**	Niu Iaka
Italy	Ītari, Itāria	**Niger**	Nāika
Jakarta	Tiakāta	**Nile**	Naera
Jamaica	Hamaika	**Norway**	Nōwei
Japan	Hapani, Nipono, Tiapani	**Nuku'alofa**	Nukuaroha
		Oman	Ōmana
Jeddah	Hera	**Osaka**	Ohaka
Jerusalem	Hiruhārama	**Oslo**	Ōhoro
Jordan	Hōrano	**Pacific Ocean**	Moana-nui-a-Kiwa
Kalahari	Karahāri		
Karachi	Karāti	**Palestine**	Paretaina
Korea	Kōria	**Persia**	Pēhia
Kuala Lumpur	Kuara Rūpa	**Philippines**	Piripīni
Laos	Rāopo	**Poland**	Pōrana
Lesotho	Teroto	**Polynesia**	Porinīhia
Liberia	Raipiria	**Port Louis**	Poi Ruihi
Libya	Ripia	**Port Moresby**	Poi Moahipi
Lima	Rima	**Port Vila**	Poi Whira
Lisbon	Ripene, Rihipane	**Port of Spain**	Poi o Paniora
London	Rānana	**Portugal**	Potukara
Luxembourg	Rakapuō	**Qatar**	Katā
Macau	Makau	**Riyadh**	Riata
Malaya	Mareia	**Romania**	Romeinia
Malaysia	Marēhia	**Rome**	Roma
Malta	Merita	**Russia**	Rūhia

Samoa Hāmoa
São Paulo Hao Pāora
San Diego Hanga Tieko
Santiago Hanatiāko
Saudi Arabia Hauri Arāpia
Scandinavia Te Hauraro o Uropi
Scotland Koterangi
Seattle Heātara
Seoul Houra
Shanghai Hangahai
Singapore Hingapoa
Slovenia Horowinia
Solomon Islands Ngā Motu Horomona
South Africa Awherika Tonga
Spain Peina
Sri Lanka Hira Rānaka
St Helena Hāto Hērena
St Kitts Hāto Kete
St Lucia Hāto Ruiha
Stockholm Tokoomo
Suva Huwha
Sweden Wītana
Switzerland Witerana
Sydney Poihākena
Syria Hiria
Taiwan Taiwana
Tanzania Tānahia
Tasman Sea Moana Tāpokopoko-a-Tāwhaki
Tehran Terāna
Thailand Tairana
The Gambia Te Kamopia
Turkey Whenua Korukoru
Tuvalu Tūwaru
Uganda Ukānga
Ukraine Ūkareinga
United Nations Te Kotahitanga o nga Whenua o te Ao
United States of America Te Hononga o Amerika
Uruguay Urukoi
Uzbekistan Uhipeketāne
Valletta Whāreta
Vanuatu Whenuatū
Vatican Watikana
Vietnam Whitināmu
Wales Wēra
Washington Wāhitāone

MĀORI TO ENGLISH

A

a recognition of person (used before names and pronouns)
ā indicates future time (e.g. ā te Mane/next Monday)
ā with regard to (e.g. ā-tau = yearly)
ā and, until, of, those of
ā + *noun* in form of (e.g. ā-wairua = in spirit)
ā + *plural pronouns* belonging to us/you/them (e.g. ā rāua + their/theirs)
ā-iwi national, racial, tribal
ā mate noa lifelong
ā muri ake nei hereafter
ā-rohe territorial, in districts, local
ā-tau annual, yearly
ā-tinana incarnate, in the flesh, in reality
ā ture institutional, legally speaking
ā waho exterior, openly, outwardly
aata altar
āe yes, agree
aha what, anything, what sort, thread
aha(-tia) what can be done, so what!
ahakoa although, in spite of, except, nonetheless
ahakoa he aha whatever
ahakoa pēhea any kind, no matter what
āhea when?, at what stage?
āhei can be done, bird snare, clavicle
āhere angel
ahi fire
ahi kā occupation rights, burning hearth
Āhia Asia
ahiahi evening, afternoon
ahikirīmi ice-cream
ahipihopa archbishop
aho thread, weft, chord, sine
aho rino steel wire
aho tātea spermatic cord
aho whēkau catgut
ahorangi enlightened teacher, guru, professor
ahu (*n.*) dimension of space
ahu (*v.*) cultivate, face towards, heap up
ahu atu get stuck in
ahu whakamua progressive, look forward
āhua + *adjective* fairly, quite, rather
āhua o nāianei status quo
āhua o te rangi weather, climate
āhua riri irritable, irascible
ahuahi smoke
ahuahu(-ngia) heap up, tend, earth up crops
āhuareka pleasant, delightful
āhuatanga condition, aspect, mechanism
āhuatanga-ā-iwi social policy

āhumehume petticoat, lingerie, underwear
ahumoana fishing industry, fish farming
ahunga generation, heap, bearing (maths)
ahurangi unsettled, paragon
ahurei chief, glow, splendid, unique
ahurewa sacred place, shrine
ahuriri fish similar to kahawai, weir, dyke
ahuwhenua hard-working, agriculture, land development
ai *connects sub clause, use after verb* which, where
ai *after verb to show habitual action*
ai(-tia) sexual intercourse, procreate
āianei today, soon, now, at present
āianei tonu immediately
aihe dolphin, driftwood
aihikirīmi ice-cream
aikiha handkerchief
āinga violence, driving force
āio peaceful, calm
Airangi/Airana Ireland
Airihi Irish
aitanga descendants
aitu sickness, mishap
aituā accident, nemesis, omen
aituā waka car crash
aka vine, climbing plant
āka ark
Āka a Noa/Noe Noah's Ark
aka kaikū N.Z. passionfruit, clematis
aka pirita supplejack
aka pōhue bindweed
aka tawhiwhi rātā vine
aka waina grape vine
akaaka fibre, roots
ākau shore, beach, riverside
ake upwards, -self (e.g. nāna ake/ he indeed did it)
ake (after adj.) more (comparative degree)
āke, āke, āke forever
akeake hopbush, wood for handles
akene perhaps
ākene soon
āki(-na) crash upon, slam into
akiaki coerce, red-billed gull
akiakitanga motivation
ākihau exhaust stroke
akinga force
akinga hiko electrical force
akinga tō gravity
ākiri(-tia) dismiss, reject, throw away
akitō slow, drag out
akitu vortex, close in on
ako(-na) learn, teach, train
akoako consult, practise
ākonga pupil, learner, disciple
akoraiti benzine lamp, pressure lamp
akoranga learning, lesson, study
akoranga karihi nuclear physics
āku my (*pl.*), mine (*pl.*)
ākuanei presently, shortly
ākuarā soon
akutō lagging behind, late
ama outrigger of canoe
āmai giddy, sea swell
amaia halo
amana almond
amapaea umpire
amarara umbrella
āmengemenge curled

ami odour, smelly
āmi(-tia) gather
amiami scented shrub
āmine(-tia, -ia) say amen, agree
amio wander, circle around
āmiomio giddy, spinning round
amo carved uprights
amo(-hia) carry on litter or shoulders, stretcher
amohanga food rack
amokapua leader, priest
amokura red-tailed tropicbird, red feather of chiefs
amorangi priest, carrier of god emblem
āmua future, hereafter
amuamu(-tia) grumble, complain, criticise
āmuri ake nei henceforth, future
ana cave, burrow, grotto, lair
ana (after verb) implies movement
anā take that!, there!
āna his/hers, just so!
āna koia certainly, exactly so
anahe alone, only, sole
ānahere angel, archangel
ānahere tamariki cherub
anake alone, only
anana! well well!
ānau curve, wander, restless
anei here it is
ānewa reel about, dizzy, listless
ānewanewa dazed, reel, totter
anga enamel, shell, confront
ānga driving force
anga mārō hardback (book)
anga whakamua progress
angaanga skull, skeleton, chief
angai north by northwest wind
anganui face towards, opposite
angarau tika structural accuracy
angiangi thin, loose, move freely, *Coprosma*
aniana onion
anihau gentle wind, zephyr
ānini headache, dizziness, dizzy
anipā anxious
anitirinamu *Antirrhinum*
āniwa bright, reckless, halo
āniwaniwa rainbow, halo, nebula, potato variety
anō again, yet, like, -self, as though
anō te + *adjective* exclamation of admiration
anu cold
anuanu cold, offensive
anuhe caterpillar, mackerel markings, sickly
ao(-hia) to scoop, suitable
ao ātea planet, outerspace
ao manaaki supportive environment
ao Māori Māori world
ao mārama the human world, world of light
ao rauropi biosphere
aoake next day, previous day
aorangi iti asteroid
aorere scudding cloud
aotea white cloud, variety of thistle
aotūroa world of light, nature
apa working group, slave
āpā not as if
apaapa level, stratum, mortar
apakura lament, dirge
āpānoa until
apārangi group of nobles, entourage
apareka asparagus
aparua doubled, row of posts

apataki supporters, customer base
aperikota apricot
apiapi crowded
āpiha officer, official
āpiha tautoko adjutant
āpiha tiaki i te huarahi traffic officer
āpiha uiui mō te tūpāpaku inquest officer, coroner
āpiti(-tia) accrue, connect
apitihana parliamentary opposition
apitireihana arbitration
apititū standing toe to toe, scuffle, lineout
apo grasping, mean
apoapo(-hia) entangle, collect, roll up
aponga stack, pile
āpōpō tomorrow
āporo apple
āporopaina pineapple
āpotoro apostle
apu(-a) cram into mouth, gobble
apū move as a crowd, mob
apuapu stuffed, palatable
apuhau squall, small gust of wind
apumatangi squall, gentle breeze
āpure local reserve, zone, computer field
ara pathway, system, grayling
ara(-hia) arouse, get up, rise
arā over there, namely
ara hīkoi pedestrian crossing
ara hipa passing lane
ara io nervous system
ara kaiwaewae walkway, pedestrian crossing
ara kōpae traffic roundabout
ara kūiti lane, narrow track, gorge
ara raro underpass, subway
ara runga flyover, viaduct
araara trevally
arahanga flight of steps, bridge, ladder
araheke stairs, gangway
ārahi(-na) guide, lead, train, teach
arahi tika discipline
ārai(-a) curtain, insulate, defence
ārai ahi fender, fire screen
ārai hapū contraceptive
ārai huarahi road-block
ārai kanohi face guard, face mask
ārai karihi nuclear deterrence
ārai makariri anti-freeze
ārai mamae anaesthesia, anaesthetic
ārai waha mouth guard
ārai werawera anti-perspirant
arakiore dreadlocks
ārama aluminium
aramoana path of the sea, tāniko pattern
aranga resurrection, Easter
ārangirangi apathetic, idle
ārani orange
Arapa Arab
arapiki stairs
arapoka tunnel
ararā! look there!
ararangi air-corridor
araroa corridor, passage
ararōau hīkoi railway crossing
arata lettuce
aratākaro maha multiplay bars
arataki(-na) lead, guide, point out
aratau contour line, runway, mode

aratuku radio airwaves, radio frequency
ārau block (volleyball), entangled
arawa type of shark
arawaru freshwater eel
arawhata ladder, bridge
arawhata tūnoa step ladder
are overhang, open
areare unsupported arch, concave
arearenga hollow, cavity
areinga cricket insect
aremiere honeycomb
arenga point of weapon
arepa alpha, Alps
arero tongue
arewhana elephant
ariā shadow, spirit manifestation
āria deep water
ariā nukupapa plate techtonics
ariari visible, clear, shining
ariki lord, noble, chief of chiefs
ariki tamaroa first-born male
ariki tapairu sovereign lady, royalty
arikiwi kiwi feather cloak
āriponga conduction
ārita over-eager, keen on
aritahi single crease, one fold
āritarita over-eager, touchy
aro heart, morpheme, suet, front
aro(-ngia) turn over, show interest
aro atu pay heed
aro mātao cold front (weather)
aroākapa row, rank, front row
aroaro presence, front of person
aroarorua vacillating, wavering
aroarotea pied shag
aroha(-tia, -ina) love, sympathise, relent, pity
aroha atu sympathy, sympathise
arohaki tremble, flap
arohanui compassion, devotion
arohata ladder, bridge
arohi(-a) explore, reconnoitre, examine
ārohirohi feel giddy, hover
aromahana warmth, springtime
aromaunga mountain face
aronga in the direction of, meaning of
aronga kē non-standard, opposite
aronui facing, inclination
aropā friendly greeting, peer group
aropereina aeroplane
arorangi heavenwards, straight
arotahi lens of eye, focus, contact lens
arotake evaluate, assess, review, analyse
arotakenga evaluation, assessment
aru(-mia) follow
aruaru keep following, court a girl
aruhe fern root, bracken
ata morning, shadow, computer icon
atā! how horrible!
āta slowly, carefully, gently, clearly
āta haere amble, cruise, soft-pedal
ata mārie good morning
āta noho live happily, sit quietly, quiet
ata pō early morning darkness
āta tiro(-hia) check, examine, inspect, scan
ata tū just after daybreak
āta tuku oblige
āta whakarite whānau family planning
āta whiriwhiri(-a) hand pick

ātaahua attractive, graceful, elegant
ataarangi shadow
ataata video cassette, visual image, catseye snail
ataata-rongo audio-visual
ātae! wonderful!
ātahirā day after tomorrow
ātahu love charm
Atama Adam
atamaha crystal
atamai disdain, ridicule
atamira stage, dais, mezzanine
ātamira admiral
atapō darkness before dawn
ata pongipongi daybreak
ātārangi shadow
atarau moonlight, moonbeam
āta rongo easy listening
atarua double vision, dim sight, myopia
atawhai(-tia) look after, merciful
atawhai tamariki childcare
atawhai, tamaiti - orphan child, adopted
ate liver, heart of hearts, edge of weapon
ate, tau o te - seat of emotions, darling
ātea space, clear, blank, off (cricket)
ateate(-nga) chest, bosom
āteha assessor
ātete oppose, resist, treat roughly
atewhanewhane liver
atewharowharo lungs
atewhatukuhu kidney
ati then
āti (*see* ngāti) tribe, descendant, aunt
atiati(-tia) huntaway, herd animals, repel
ātirikona archdeacon
atitirauhea wander hopelessly about
ato(-hia) thatch, fence about
atu away (comparative – pai atu = better)
atu anō i apart from
atu i as well as, in addition to
atua god, uncanny
ātua first, primary
atuapo mean, stingy
atuatanga divinity
Atutahi Canopus star, whitebait
atutai whitebait
ātute to elbow, jostle
au I, me, current, smoke
āu your (*pl.*), yours (*pl.*)
aū slope
au miha rough sea
au moana open sea
au te moe heavy sleep
aua those mentioned, herring
aua (hoki) don't know!
aua atu nevertheless, furthermore, further on
aua e do not
auaha symmetry, system, creative
auahatanga creativity
auahi smoke
auahi nui big smoke (i.e. city)
auātu never mind!
auau frequency, recurring, bark of dog
auē oh dear!, wail, cry, bleat
auētanga outcry
auhaha look for
auheke surf, climb down, short descent
auhi distress, burdened with
aukaha(-tia) to tie, the ties, string

aukati constraint, barrier
aukatinga stopboard, restriction, discrimination
aumanga vent, smoke-hole, chimney
aumihi(-a) long for, welcome
aumoe at ease, asleep
aunihi ounce
aunoa mechanical, automatic, default (computer)
aupaki sloping ground, close quarters, stillness
aupatu bundle
aupēhi(-a) squash, press down on, repress
aupiki climb, overcome
auporo cut short, industrial strike
aupuru cushion, protective pad
auraki turn to, hurry to
aurara clutch
aurere moan, groan
auroa lengthened
auroro slope
auru(-tia) break off, pluck, destroy
auta out! (games), edge forward
autaha to one side
autaia strange fellow, unfamiliar
autaki detour, roundabout
autāne brother-in-law of woman
aute mulberry bark
autō magnetic pull, tow behind
autō-ā-hiko electromagnet
autui cloak pin, brooch, safety pin
awa river, channel, canal of bone, mullet
awa hau nasal passage, sinus
awa ihu nasal passage
awa mimi ureter, urethra
awaawa valley, gully, creek, groove, ravine
awai heavy, sodden, drag in singing
a wai rānei anyone, someone
āwake next day
awakeri ditch, drain, gutter
awamate dry river-bed
awanga southwest wind, variety of flax
āwangawanga (*n.*) qualm, upset, distress
āwangawanga (*adj.*) uneasy, misgiving, irresolute
awanui trumpet shell
awatea daylight, diurnal
awe soot, white feather, straggling cloud
aweke perverse, idle, frivolous
āwenewene sweet, saccharine
āwhā storm, gale
awhe arm span measure, range
āwhea when
awhenga conquered people
awheo halo, nimbus
awhero hope, desire
āwheto lettuce caterpillar
awhi(-tia) embrace, cuddle, aid, help
awhiawhi(-tia) embrace
āwhina(-tia) help, abet, assist
āwhina-ā-moni monetary aid
āwhina-ā-ngutu lip service
āwhio(-tia) go round about, circuitous
āwhiotanga rara parallel circuit
āwhiotanga perimeter
āwhiowhio whirlwind, cyclone
āwhiowhio nuku whirlwind of earth
āwhiowhio rangi whirlwind of heaven

awhireinga embrace in spirit
awhitireinga embrace in spirit world
āwhitu feel hurt
āwhiwhiwhi resemble, approximate

E

e by (agent – after passive verb), eh!
e + *short verb* imperative of the verb
e + *numeral* precede cardinal numbers 2 to 9
e + *verb* **+ ana** expresses continuous action
e hia? how many?
e kī rā! you don't say!
e ko! girl! (exclamation)
e koe! serves you right!
ea paid for, avenged, done, appear as star
ea te mate death is avenged, death duties fulfilled
eā! express surprise
eara earl
ehara! look at that!, lo and behold! (surprise)
ehara . . . i not
ehara i te tika unworthy, unjustified
ehē! no!
ēhea? which ones?
ehu muddy water, discoloured
ehu(-a) bail water, exhume
ei! well now!
eka acre
ēkara eagle
ekareta escalator
eke(-ngia) climb, mount, thicken, rise
eke hōiho horse riding
eke ki uta come ashore
ekore will not
ekore e mate immortal
ekore e pīrau incorruptible
ekore e taea impossible
ekore e taea te tatau incalculable
ekore e taea te tutuki inaccesible
ekore e taea te whakamārama inexplicable
ekore e tango inalienable
eku ague, fever, malaria
emarara emerald
emepaea empire
emi assembled
emiemi be gathered, assemble
ēnā those near you
ene anus, flatter
ene (tōu ene) exclamation of contempt
eneene boot licking
ēnei these
enetinia engineer
engari but, however
engari rawa ia provided always
engē serves (them, you) right!
ēngia is that so?
eo louse
epa(-ina) throw, pelt, bowl, pitch
epaepa(-ina) throw, thunderbolt
epeepe remote relatives
ērā those over there
ēraka those (distant)
ērangi on the other hand, but
eremita hermit
ero septic, pus, to rot, emaciated
ētahi some

ētahi . . . ētahi some . . . others
ētahi atu others
ete jell, thicken of sauce
eti loathsome, feel disgust
etia as if, just like, how great
etieti horrible
eto thin
etoeto volatile
ewe placenta, afterbirth
eweewe blood relations

H

hā essence, breath, taste
hā whakaora rescue breathing, filtered air
hāpa harp
hae flower pollen
hae(-a) cut, split, jealous, shine
haeana(-tia) iron, press
haeana ngarungaru corrugated iron
haeana rāti harpoon
haeata dawn, ray of light, daybreak, laser beam
haeatatanga beam of light
haehae(-a) rip up, lacerate, catty, groove (carving)
haemata(-tia) growing strongly, chop up raw
haere(-tia) move, motion, depart, travel
haere atu go away, farewell, depart
haere hāngai direct approach
haere mā raro walk, hike
haere mai welcome, come here
haere noa iho ramble
haere rā farewell, adieu
haere tahi i accompany, escort
haere tonu play on (games), continue
hāereere stroll, travel
haerenga travel, journey, voyage
haetanga pollination
haetara envied, admired
hāhā(-ria) devastate land, catch breath
hahaetanga first gleam of light
hahake naked, unbecoming
hahaki ostentatious
hahana glowing
hahani cause shame, miss the point
hahari mollusc
hāhau(-ria) seek
hāhi faith, religion
hāhira carburettor
hāhore bare, simple
hahu(-a) dig up, disinter, take up
hahunga exhumation of corpse
hai ace (cards), pinch hitter
hai (hei) as, for, let it be
haiana hyena
haihana sergeant
haihana-meiha sergeant major
haika anchor
haikiha handkerchief
haikura high school
haina(-tia) sign
Hainamana Chinese
haipū(-tia) stack
haira scythe
hairo ace low (cards)
haka fierce dance, misshapen
hāka jug, groundsel
haka a Tāne-rore quiver of hot air
haka taparahi haka without weapons
hakahaka shallow, low, attract attention
hakakao godwit
hākari(-tia) dress the hair

hākari feast, gift, fish roe
hākaro(-a) dig trench
hake crooked, naked, grotesque
hākeke Jew's ear fungus
hakere depressed, cropped hair
hākerekere depressed, gloomy, crowd of people
haki flag, cheque, Jack
hakihaki scabby, itchy, sore, scabies
hakihaki kanohi acne
hākihi husky dog, arrogant
hakikoko shoulder blade, scapula bone, corner flag (sports)
hākinakina fun, sport, recreation
hakinono small kūmara
hakirara annoy, insult, insincere, shallow, light song
hakiri hear vague sound
hākirikiri nebulous, cryptic
hako monkey, ugly, clown
hākoakoa happy, puffin, skua
hakoko bent, concave, twisted
hākona second (of time)
hakorā red-billed gull, silver gull
hakorea lazy
hākoro old man
hākorukoru wrinkled
haku grieve, complain, kingfish, colic
hakuhakutai slapdash
hākui old woman
hakurā large groper, scamperdown whale
hākure lice, delouse
hakuturi, tini o te - birds
hama(-ia) hammer
hāmaka hammock
hāmama shout, open wide, cheer, free from, gaping
hāmanu ammunition
hamapaka hamburger
hamarara umbrella
hāmaremare cough
hāmeme mumble, grouse
hāmene-ā-tuhi writ
hamo back of head
hāmoemoe sleepy
hamumu speak softly, mutter, whisper
hāmumumumu incoherent
hamupaka humbug
hamuti, kimi - look for an excuse
hana glow, fine cloak, pink, painted red, pilot light
hanahana shine, garment, female sex parts
hanake grow, come on
Hana Kōkō Santa Claus
hānara sandal
hānarete hundredweight, 1 cwt
hanatu go forward, go away
hanaweiti hundredweight
hanawiti sandwich
hane unmentionable, rotten, shameful
hāneanea pleasant, cosy, armchair
hanehane putrefaction, decay
hānene exhale, blow gently
hanepī struck dumb
hanga(-ia) build, create, transform (maths)
hanga demeanour, utensil, construction
hangahanga frivolous, improvise
hangahou(-tia) reconstitute, remake
hāngai vice versa, athwart, comply
hāngai pū relevant, affect directly
hāngai tonu effective
hāngaitanga adequacy

hanganga creation, structure, function
hanga noa despicable, of little worth, small baskets of food
hangarau technology, joke, pretence, fool around
hangawai(-a) transform (maths)
hangehange Māori privet, nīkau tree
hangenge garfish, piper fish
hāngenge numb, powerless, listless
hangere half full
hāngi earth oven
hango shovel
hangohango planting stick
hangore flexible
hāngorungoru draped in folds
hāngū reticent, silent, dumb
hāngurunguru grumble
hani long club, speak ill of
hanihani scandalous
hānihi harness
hānihi paki buggy harness
hanimūnu honeymoon
hanumi engulfed, assimilated
hanuwiti sandwich
hao(-a) surround, catch in net
hao net, basket, mud eel
haohao chopsticks, small basket
haona horn
haora hour, howl
hāora oxygen
hapa crooked, mistake, supper
hapahāpai lift often
hāpāhi half-past
hāpai(-tia, -a) lift up, start song
hāpainga set off with loads
hapanga default, loss
Hapani Japan
Hapanihi Japanese
hāpara(-tia) shovel, slit, daybreak
hāparangi bawl, cheer
hāparu desecrate
hāpati sabbath
hape deformed, handicap
hapehape bandy legged, crooked
hāpeta nuisance, fed up
hapī earth oven, hāngi
hāpiapia sticky, sellotape
hāpine scrape flax
hāpiripiri viscous, sticky, clinging
hapori small clan, family group, class, community
hapū pregnant, sub-tribe
hāpua lagoon, valley
hāpuka groper fish
hāpuku groper fish, tiger beetle larva
hapūtanga obstetrics, pregnancy
hara sin, foul (sport), crime
hara hangahanga infringement
harakeke flax leaf
hārakiraki inconsistent, unreliable
harakore innocent, flawless
haramai come, welcome
haramaitanga incoming
haranga sin, crime
hārapa lead the way, gallop
harapaki slope, begin fight, crack fleas
harare bleary eyed, red sealing-wax
hararei holiday
haratau suitable, deft
haratū whakarawarawa violent crime
haratua(-ngia) dress planks, ripsaw timber
haratūtanga criminality
hārau grope for, light touch
harawene jealous

H

harehare rash, itch
hārere celery
hari happy, cheerful
hari(-a) take, carry, transport
harihari song to bring in food
haringa bliss
hāro(-a) scrape clean
harore mushroom, fungus
haruru heavy sound, rumble
Hāta Maria Holy Mary, Madonna
Hātana Satan, demon
Hātarei Saturday, Rāhoroi
hāte shirt, heart (cards)
hāte kēhi hard-case, funny, zany
hātepe procedure
hātepe(-a) split, straight flush
hatete chip heater
hau wind, gas, soul, famous, fraction
hau(-a) hit vigorously
hau-ā-papa natural resource
hau ārai ozone
hau āwhiowhio whirlwind
hau kōwhai fluorine
hau huripari typhoon
hau māori methane, natural gas
hau piro stuffy
hau tūmū headwind
hau whakarua northeast sea breeze
haua don't know, hit
hauā uki permanent disability
hauaitu freezing, wasted away
hauangi cool, airy
hauanu frigid, wintry
hauare saliva, to miss
hauarea insignificant, clumsy, cowardly
hauata accident, mishap
hāuaua drizzle, rainy
hauāuru west, west wind
hauhā carbon dioxide
hauhake(-a) dig up, harvest, reap
hauhanga frost
hauhapa outside tee (golf)
hauhau windy, whip, mudfish
hauhauā argon
hauhiko electrical fan
hauhiku tailwind
hauhō neon
hauhunga frost
hauhuri rotation
hauī liquid petroleum gas, L.P.G.
haukā condensed natural gas, C.N.G.
haukai feast
haukāinga true home
haukeke meddle, handle carelessly
haukino carbon monoxide
haukino waka exhaust fumes
haukoti(-a) interrupt, curtail, cut off
haukotinga impedance
haukū dew, damp, mildew
haukume(-a) pull, bias
haukuru hit volley, smash, spike (sport terms)
haumākū get wet, humidity
haumāmā helium
haumi join, alliance, canoe section
Haumiaroa guardian spirit of fern root
Haumiatiketike guardian spirit of wild food
haumiri caress, hug the shore
haumotu clammy
haumura flammable gas
haunga stink, foul smell
hāunga not only, besides, except
hauora healthy, in good spirits

hauora kararehe veterinary science
hauoratanga health
hauota nitrogen
hāupa cogwheel
haupapa(-ngia) ice, frost, flat surface
haupatu(-a) attack, hit, roof over
haupepe ambush, quiet
haupiro exhaust fumes
haupitonga southeast wind
haupoi hockey
hauporo cut off
haupū(-ria) heap, place in heap
haupuru penned in
hāura brown
hāurahina grey-brown
haurākau club (weapon), hockey-stick
haurangi drunk, maudlin
haurapa search for
hauraro north wind, capitulate
hauripo wind eddy
haurua hemisphere, half
hautai sponge, rain-cloak
hautai mangu stamp pad
hautau fraction (maths)
hautepe split off
hautō desk drawer, drag
hautope(-a) cut down
hautū guide, timing chant
hauture jack mackerel
haututū insubordinate, nuisance
hauwai hydrogen, damp
hauware saliva
hauwarea irrelevant, cowardly
hauwere dangling down
hauwhenua dew, land breeze
hawa chipped, smeared
hawahawa lichen
hāwato caterpillar
hawene jazz, tease
hawere slobber
hāwere hang down, pendulous
hāwhe(-tia) half, halve
hāwhe-kaihe half-caste
hāwhepāhi half past
hāwini servant
hāwiniwini shiver
he a, an, some
hē wrong, error, fault
he aha? what?
hea share, hare
hea? where?, when?
heahea sob, naive, facetious
heamana chairperson
hēhē false start
hei amulet, as a . . ., let it be for . . ., hay
hei aha (atu) never mind, what for?
hei mahi work to be done, duty
heihei hen, poultry
heipū on target, straight for
heira birthmark
heitara accusation, defame
heitiki greenstone pendant
heka fungus, mould
heke (*n.*) rafter, thigh
heke(-a) (*v.*) descend, migrate, dismount
heke pī beehive
hēkena support, second for boxer
hēkene moment of time, second
hekenga migration, voyage
hekeretari secretary, clerk
heketā hectare
heketanga incline, descent, migration
heketau (*n. and v.*) parachute
heketua lavatory, privy
hēki egg

H

heki kapu mussel dredger
hēko sago
hēkona second
hema female sex parts, taper down
hemahema bare, sexy suggestions
hēmana chairperson
hēmanawa breathless, disheartened
hemo die, in coma, consumed
hemokai starving, malnutrition
hemonga death, heart's desire
hemoreke hemlock
henekeriti centigrade
heneti cent
hengahenga girl, Māori privet
hēngia be mistaken for another
heni Tiapani Japanese yen
henimeta centimetre
heoi however, that's that!
heoi anō/oti that's all
hepapa zebra
hēpara shepherd
hepareta separator
hepeta sceptre
hēramana sailor
here(-a) tie, mooring line
here cherry
here mōwhiti ring binder
herehere prisoner
herenga tether, conditional
hereni shilling
herepū(-tia) tie in bundles, embargo
herepuru caulking
hererapa rubber band
heri jelly
heri(-a) take
herikopeta helicopter
hero cello
heru comb
hēteri sentry
hēti shed, hedge
hetiheti hoe
heu razor, eaves of house, weeds
heuheu (heua) shave, clear scrub, separate
hewa mistaken, fooled
hī(-ia) fishing, angling, shine
hia, te – nui/reka How big! How nice!
hia? how many?
hiahia(-tia) wish for, required
hiahia nui covet
hiainu thirsty, thirst
hiakai hungry, appetite
hiako skin, hide (leather), rind, tree bark
hiamoe sleepy, drowsy
hīanga (*n.*) deception, fishing, raising
hīanga(-tia) (*v.*) deceive, play around
hiato gathered, composite
hieke rain cape
hihi sun's rays, tentacles, plumes
hihī hiss, diarrhoea
hihi ata reflected ray
hihiko brisk, keen
hihiri(-tia) desire, motivate
hihō donkey
hihore strip, peel
hīti sheet
hika light fire by friction, girl
hika(-ia) kindle fire by rubbing sticks
hika, e – ! form of address to girl
hikā cigar
hika kikokiko masturbate
hikahika rub, chafe
hīkaka rash, malicious, incautious

hikareti cigarette
hikareti rauhea reefer
hīkaro(-hia) extract, infer
hiki asthma
hikinuku lurch
hikirangi lift heavenwards, move vigorously
hiko(-a, -ia) zigzag, snatch, shine
hiko electricity, flash of lightning
hiko karihi nuclear energy
hikohiko twinkle, dodge about, glint
hīkoi step out, plod, pace
hikoki stagger
hikonga huahuaki electrocardiogram
Hikonga Uira Electricity Corp. of N.Z.
hīkori endive
hiku tail, fullback, suffix
hiku timo scorpion
hikuawa head of river
hikuhiku lace fabric
hikurere blouse, shoulder cape
hikuwai source of river, light rain, reservoir
hīmene hymn
himeporo cymbal
himi singlet, undershirt, vest
himiporo cymbal
hīmoemoe acid, acidic
himu hip, carved gargoyle, main post
hina pale moon, grey hair
hīnaki eel-pot, trap eels
hinapōuri very dark, pathetic
hinatea pale grey
hinātore hazy light, phosphorescence
hīnau hīnau tree
hinauri dark grey
hine form of address to girl
Hine-ahu-one first woman, created from earth
Hine-i-te-iwaiwa patron of childbirth, muse of weaving
hine kōrako moon halo
Hine-nui-te-Pō Woman of the Underworld
Hine Rakatauri Deity of the flute
hinehou baby girl
hinengaro mind, heart, intellect, psychology
hinga(-ia) topple, be defeated, lose
hingareti singlet, undershirt, slip
hīnota synod
hinu oil, lard, lubricant
hīoi mint, skinny, pipit
hiore tail of animal
hipa pass by, jump aside, bye (sports draw)
hīpae lie across, broadside on
hīpae hēki/huamanu egg slice
hīpae ika fish slice
hīpane apron
hipi sheep, mutton
hipi toa ram
hipo hippopotamus
hīpoki(-na) cover, canopy
hira important, lavish, numerous
hīra shield, sealed off, hallmark
hirahira great, important, spread out
hīrairaka fantail
hiraka silk
hīrau trip up, entangle, implicate
hirāwhe giraffe
hīrere gush out, shower
hīri(-a) wax seal (stamp)
hiri/hihiri energetic
hirihiri(-a) recite spells, charms
hiripa slipper

H

hiriwa silver
hirou dredge net
hīta cedar
hitari sieve, strainer, collander
hītau short slip, apron
hītekiteki tiptoe
hītengi squat (weightlifting)
hīti sheet
hītimi glass-marble, game of marbles
hītoki hop
hītori history
hiwa cheerful, alert
hiwete civet cat
hiwi hill, hump, ridge, caret
hiwi(-a) jerk line
hiwihiwi kelpfish
hō shout, spade
hoa friend, spouse, partner
hoa mahi colleague
hoa takatāpui best man, mate, off-sider
hoa tāne husband
hoa wahine wife, mistress
hoa whawhai sparring partner, opponent
hoahoa(-ina) layout, architecture, diagram
hoake give, go on ahead
hōanga hinu oilstone, whetstone
hōanga huri revolving grindstone
hoari sword
hoatu give away, go away, add
hoe(-a) paddle, oar
hoe urungi tiller
hoeha saucer
hoeroa curved throwing weapon
hōhā bored, humdrum, monotony
hohere lacebark
hohipere hospital
hohō buzz, trickle, waterfall
hōhonu deep, depth, impressive, soulful, abstruse
hohoro quick, hurry, speed
hohou rongo make peace, conciliate
hoi deaf, earwax
hōia soldier
hoihere lacebark, skirt of bark strips
hōiho horse, yellow-eyed penguin
hoihoi noise, keep quiet!
hoipū blister
hoka ling fish, red cod
hoka stakes, run out net
hokahoka flap wings, stick in
hokahokai stretch, large stride
hōkai spasm, step smartly, ling fish
hōkakatanga sexuality
hōkeke Jew's ear fungus
hoki also, indeed, because
hoki (*n.*) fish, blue hake, whiptail
hoki(-a) (*v.*) return, repeat
hōkī hockey
hōkio messenger bird
hōkioi mysterious night bird
hoko + *numeral* multiply *numeral* by 20
hoko(-na) buy, barter, trade
hokohoko barter, reciprocal, retail trade
hokorari ling
hokorīhi hire purchase
hokowhitu war party (140 warriors)
Hokowhitu-a-Tū Māori Battalion
hōmai give me, us, provide
hōmiromiro tomtit, keen-sighted
honae small basket, wallet
hone (moana) swell of the ocean
hongi(-a) smell, press noses

hongihongi hākino glue sniffing
hōngoi brace, stay, prop
honi honey, nibble
honihoni scrape, sexual intercourse
honikoma honeycomb
hono(-a) join, link up, form network
hono maitai weld
honohono continue a line, graft
hononga link, network, relationship
hōnore honour, honourable
honu turtle
honu whenua tortoise
hōpa sofa
hōpane saucepan
hopanga scientific problem
hōpani saucepan
hōpara belly, thorax, paunch
hope waist, hip
hopēkē carry sack, carry on back
hōpēwai sodden, watery
hopi soap
hopohopo overawed, reverence
hōpua pool, lagoon
hopuhopu keep on catching
hōpuni camping
hōpuru mouldy
hora(-hia) spread out, lay tables, low-pitched roof
horahora disseminate, *Astelia* plant
hore not, emptiness, negative, bald
hore kau not at all, none
hōrete stone, type of drill
hori mistaken, misfire
horihori false, rubbish!
horo quick, differ
hōro hall, shawl
horoeka lancewood
horohoro remove ceremonial stricture
horoi(-a) wash, cleanse
horoinga ablution, hygiene
horokawa bulrush
horomatua expert of lower rank
horomi(-a) swallow, devour
horopeka bronze whaler
horopito pepper tree
horopū swallow whole
horopuehu vacuum cleaner
horowai waterfall, type of eel, suction pump
horowhenua erosion, landslide, avalanche
horu grunt, roar of ocean, slap of waves
hōrua go down, toboggan
horuhoru weep bitterly, grunt, fungus
hōtēra hotel, inn
hotete sphinx moth
hoto link, preposition, wooden spade
hōtoke winter
hotu sob, desire, welling emotion
hōtuku data
hotumanawa pulse
hou(-hia) bind together, make peace
houhou new, enter, feather
houanga interval of time, overtime
houanga rongo peace making
houhere lacebark tree
houhi lacebark tree
hounga a year ago, a year ahead
houru hole
hourua double canoe
houtapu genuine

hōutuutu rifleman
howaka beetle
hū shoe, earth subsidence
hū, noho - keep silent, sit still
hua fruit, egg, profit, lever
hua(-ina, -ia) give name to, guess, prise up
hua maitai pinchbar
hua paru fish roe, milt
hua rākau fruit, fish spawn
hua whenua vegetables
huahae catkin
huahua preserved birds, pimple, sketch, rails
huakanga naming
huaki(-na) open up, assault
huaki kēne can opener
huakitanga onset, onslaught
huakiwi kiwifruit, only child
huakore unprofitable
huamanu egg
huamata planting ritual, green salad
huamoni interest (finance), profits
huamutu lined whelk
huanga profit, name
huānga relative, main elements
huanga, nō whea te - whoever heard of
huangi cockle
huangō asthma
huanui road, pathway, perch trap
huaota botany, botanical
huapae skyline, rail, cross member
huapapa flat rocks
huaparu milt
huapī peas in pod
huarahi road, procedure, circuit
hūare saliva, stomach juices
huarere weather, meteorology
huarewa raised aloft, gallery
huarua double, two edged
huata spear, plant-shoots
huatahi only child
huataki raise, begin
huatau graceful, opinion
huatawa dark silica
huatea milt roe, childless
hue gourd
hūhā thigh
hūhē weary, embarassed
hūhi (*n.*) weariness, swamp
hūhi (*adj.*) closed off
huhu peel off, remove tapu, grub or beetle
huhū(-ngia) strike match, buzz, erupt
huhua numerous, abundant, free of tapu
huhua noa plentiful, galore, prolific
huhuti (hutia) (*see* huti) pull up, yank up
hui(-a) gather, meeting, add up
hui uiui mō te tūpāpaku inquest
huia huia bird
huinga set (maths)
huirapa flippers, webfoot
huirau fern root
huirua meet together, bend double
huka sugar, snow, lather, sucrose
hūka hook
huka + *numeral* almost, short of, lacking
huka hori saccharine
hukahuka froth, fringe of cloak, palisade
hukākapu hailstones
hukanga foam
hukapapa ice, frost, frosty

hukarere snow, sleet, wind-driven foam
huke(-a) excavate, to bolt, uncover
hukehuke cheeky, idiotic, dig around
hūkeke staggering
hūkeri waves breaking
hūkerikeri stormy
huki(-a) avenge, transfix on spit
hūkui rub, scrub, handle of digging stick
hūmārie peaceful, beautiful, pleasant
hūmārietanga beauty, charm, allure
hūmarika inoffensive, gentle
hume(-a) bring to a point, taper off
humehume frill, lacy
humi abundance, plentiful
humu hip bone, hum
huna(-ia) conceal, hide, lay waste
hunahuna unexplained, undetected
hunaonga son-in-law, daughter-in-law
hunarei (*see* hungarei) father/mother-in-law
hunga people, down (fluff), decayed, faded
hunga mate deceased
hunga o ngā moutere Pacific Islanders
hungahunga fluff, nap, finely divided
hungarei father-in-law, mother-in-law
hungawai father-in-law, mother-in-law
hunu ray of sun
hunuhunu(-a) to singe
hūnuku family, shift house
hūoro murmur of wind
hupa soup
hūpana spring up, springboard, recoil
hūpane head gesture
hūpē mucus, catarrh
hūpeke bend, jump, vault
hūpenupenu mashed
hūpiro stinkwood
hūpoki (*see* hīpoki) cover up
hura(-hia) uncover, unveil, begin to flow
hura kōhatu unveil gravestone
hurahanga kōhatu unveiling memorial stone
hurahura(-hia) probe, search party
Hūrai Jew, Hebrew
hūrangi fly (insect)
hūrau interface
huri(-hia) revolve, turn, convert, innings
hūri jury
huri hiko generate electricity
huri kōaro turn anti-clockwise, turn inside out, topsy turvy
huri whakamua turn clockwise
hurihanga (*see* huringa) rotation, corner, conversion
hurihuri rolling, unstable, volatile
hurikōaro turn inside out
hurikōtua turn the back
huringa mutation, rotation, cycle
huripapa knucklebones (game)
huripara wheelbarrow
huripoki turn over, capsize
huripuru corkscrew
hurirapa horizontal turn, back to front, overturn

H

hurirere propeller
hurirua turn inside out, wrong way round
huritau birthday, anniversary
huritua turn the back
hūrokuroku uninterrupted
hurori unreliable, stagger
huru undergrowth, coarse hair, feather, cloak
huruhuru feather, hair esp. pubic, fur
hurukurī dogskin cloak
hurungutu moustache
hururua wig, brushwood
huti(-a) pull up, fish
hutiwai bidibid
hūtō judo
hūtoi stunted, dishevelled
hūtu suit
hutukawa wreath of pōhutukawa leaves
hutupaoro rugby football
hūwai fat pipi, cockle
hūware spittle, saliva
hūwherei souffle
hūwiniwini goose-pimples

I

i by, from, than (indicates obj. of verb)
ī seethe, ferment, thrill
i + *verb* indicates past time (e.g. i noho = sat)
i ētahi wā at times
i mua formerly, before
ia he, she, him, her, each, every, indeed, current
ia pō, ia pō nightly
ia rā, ia rā daily
ia toto blood pressure, bloodstream
ia wiki weekly
iaia vein, tendon, vascular
iāri yard
iheihe scamperdown whale
ihi (*n.*) essential force, sun's ray, tendril
ihi(-a) (*v.*) separate, split, divide, strip off bark, hiss, dawn
ihi (*adj.*) awe-inspiring
īhi yeast
ihi me te wehi dignity and worth, wonder and awe
ihiihi awesome, dawn, feelers, plumes on prow
ihipani Marmite, Vegemite
iho (*n.*) umbilical cord, essence, contents
iho (*adv.*) downwards, immediately, thereupon, following
Ihowa Jehovah, Yaweh
ihu nose, prow, nozzle, snout
Ihu Jesus
ihumanea clever
ihumoana large jellyfish
ihupuku scrupulous, economical, fur seal
ihupuni dogskin cloak
ihuroa elephant's trunk
ika fish, victim
Ika-a-Māui North Island of NZ, Aotearoa
ika oneone amphibian
Ika-o-te-Rangi Milky Way
ikapahi assemble, gather together
Ikaroa Milky Way
ike lofty
ikeike high, altitude
Ikiiki Whenua Aotearoa Land Transport New Zealand
ikura haemorrhage
īmera e-mail, electronic mail
ina for, inasmuch, since, when, if
inā because of, when
inā tata nei recently
inahea? when? (past time)
inahi(-a) (*v. and n.*) scale fish
inaho dandruff, scurf, shrub
ināhoki because, since
ināianei currently, lately, today
inaina warm oneself
inakuanei just now
inakuarā recently
inamata formerly, suddenly, forthwith
inanahi yesterday
inanga whitebait, pale greenstone

inaoake two days ago, recently
inapō last night
inarapa rubber, eraser
inati! too much!, gross!, share of food
ine(-hia) measure, compare, gauge
inē?! really?!
ine hauroa mileage, odometer
ine hinu petrol gauge
īnei?! is that so?!
inemahana thermometer
inetohu graph
inewhenua geometry
Ingarihi English
ingiki (*see* iniki) ink
ingo (*v. and n.*) desire
ingoa name, nominal, title
ingoakore anonymous, nameless
īnihi inch, hinge
inihua insurance
inohi (*v. and n.*) (*see* unahi) fish scale
īnoi(-a) pray, plead, request
īnoinga prayer
inu(-mia) drink, tipple
io muscle, nerve, strand of rope
Io God
ioio muscular, hard
ioka yoke
iorangi cirrus cloud, god emblem
iota yacht
ipo darling, lover
ipu bottle, calabash, cup
ipuipu test tube, phial, hollow
ira full stop, life principle, freckle
ira tangata human life, mankind
irahiko electron
irakati dot
iramoe neutron, recessive gene
irāmutu nephew, niece
iratāne male gender
irawahine female gender
irawaru incest
iri spell to control at distance
iri(-a, -hia) hang, suspend
iri kākahu clothes rack, coat-hanger
iriiringa baptism
iringa koti coat rack, coathanger
iringatau wax-eye
irirangi, reo - radio wave, spirit voice
iro thread-worm, maggot
iroiro(-ngia) maggot infested
ita compact, tight, holdfast
itahirā day before yesterday
itarēte interest (money)
iti small, minimum
ito enemy, trophy of revenge
iwa nine
iwa tekau ninety
iweri hell
iwi tribe, bone, nation, strength
iwi maha multiracial
iwikore weak
iwingohe discouraged, listless
iwituararo backbone
iwituaroa backbone

K

kā(-ngia) burn, lit up
ka + *verb* narrative particle indicates start of action
kānga burning
kāta cart, waggon
kaea haka leader
kāea long wooden trumpet, bush hawk
kāeaea eye greedily, bush hawk
kāeo freshwater mussel, sea squirt
kaha strong, able, strength
kaha rawa almighty, powerful
kahakaha inner garment, waistcoat
kāhaki(-na) abduct, bolt (run off), fastener, strap, kidnap
kaharoa large dragnet, driftnet, large seine net
kahawai kahawai fish
kāheru spade
kahi wedge
kāhia N.Z. passion-vine, carved face
kahika white pine, chief (fig.)
kahikatea white pine
kahikātoa mānuka, red tea-tree
kahikawaka N.Z. cedar
kāhikuhiku tail of dart, upper trunk of tree
kāhiti gazette
kāhiwahiwa very dark
kaho batten, crossbar
kāho keg, cask, barrel
kāhore no, not, nil
kāhore anō not yet
kahotea aqueous humour (eye), type of greenstone
kahu(-ria) dress, caul, spirit of stillborn
kāhu kite, harrier-hawk, chief
kahu kaukau swimming togs
kāhui flock, swarm, herd
kāhukahuka running parallel, resembling
kahuki involuntary jump, startled, reflex movement
kahuku monarch butterfly
kahukura rainbow, red admiral butterfly
kahunga slave
kahupapa raft, tree platform, gib board
kahupeka linoleum, flax armour
kahurangi noble, precious jewel, pale greenstone
Kahurangi Dame (title)
kahurau long-sighted
kahurua myopia, short-sighted
kahuwae leggings
kai(-nga) food, eat, dine
kāī black pine, young white pine
kai + *noun* influencing (e.g. kai whenua/controlling land)
kai + *verb* indicates the doer of the verb (e.g. kai-hanga/creator)
kai-ā-kiko casualty
kai-ā-kiri flesh wound, civil war
kai paipa smoke tobacco

kai pārana barium meal
kai te + *verb* (expresses continuous tense, e.g. kai te mahi = is working)
kai timotimo entrée
kai whakakaha nutrition
kaiā steal, plunder
kaiakiaki taskmaster
kaiako teacher
kaiārahi leader, guide, sports official
kaiārai defender, guard (sport)
kaiatua black magic
kaiawa bush hawk
kaiāwhina helper, benefactor, assistant, second (boxing)
kaieke rider (person)
kaiepa pitcher (softball), bowler
kaihāhā destroyer
kaihana cousin
kaihanga creator, maker, builder
kaihāpai waiata cantor, choir leader
kaiharopia scaup, black teal
kaihau batsman
kaihaukai present of food
kaihautū leader, steersman, host (network)
kaihe ass, donkey
kaiherehere captors, carry to captivity
kaiheu barber
kaihī fisherman
kaihiki lifter, weightlifter, nurse, dandle
kaihiko electrician
kaihoahoa architect, designer
kaihoe rower, oarsman
kaihohou peacemaker
kaihoko salesman, vendor
kaihomai donor
kaihopu captive, catcher, fielder
kaihoro(-tia) glutton, gulp food, work fast
kaihuihui musterer
kaikā eager, impetuous
kaikaiwaiū betray, plotter, double agent
kaikākahu wearer
kaikape rugby hooker
kaikarakia prayer leader
kaikaro goal keeper, spell to turn aside magic
kaikaute accountant
kaikauwhau preacher
kaikawaka N.Z. cedar
kaikawe bearer, carrier
kaikāwhaki plunderer
kaikeri miner, digger
kaikiko vengeance, carnivore
kaikino cold-blooded, merciless
kaikohikohi collector
kaikōhuru villain, thug, murderer
kaikōmako fire-making tree
kaikōpere archer, Sagittarius
kaikore famine, starvation
kaikōrero speaker, announcer, advocate, narrator
kaikori jelly
kaikuia kikuyu grass
kaikuru bowler, striker (soccer)
kaikuti shearer, hairdresser
kaimakamaka knucklebones
kaimākutu sorcerer, witchdoctor
kaimanu N.Z. passion-vine
kaimaoa dry wood, no sap
kaimataara watchman, lookout
kaimātakitaki spectator, bystander, observer
kaimatire sentry
kaimatū chemist, pharmacist
kaimau carrier, bearer

kaimeke boxer
kaimiri uaua physiotherapist
kaimoana seafood
kaimōwhiti optician
kainga eat!
kāinga home, residence, village
kāinga noho home address, abode, address
kāinga rua o te Kāwanatanga High Commission
kāinga taiohi hostel
kaingākau popular, dedicated, cherish, enjoy
kaingaki cultivator
kainoho occupant, tenant, dweller
kaioma runner
kaiora fearsome, ominous
kaioraora cursing, derisive chant
kaiota uncooked, raw, fresh, herbivore
kaipāho broadcaster, conductor (physics), newsreader
kaipahua brigand, robber
kaipakihi business, concerns, businessman/woman
kaipani plasterer
kaipānui announcer
kaipaowe wanderer, loafer, rolling stone
kaipapa headwind, squall
kaiparaurehe junk food
kaipātari tempter
kaipatokupu typist
kaipatu batsman
kaipauna paymaster
kaipiko being fed by another
kaipirau dishonour a corpse, necrophilia
kaipiu maitai hammer thrower
kaipohau talk gibberish
kaipokepoke potter
kaiponu(-hia) withhold, possessive, venal, niggardly
kaipōti elector, voter
kaipuke sailing ship, liner
kaipuke rukuwai submarine
kaipupuri holder, owner
kaipūrākau storyteller
kairākau battle-hardened warriors, party of warriors
kairau prostitute, Vestal Virgin
kairauhī consul, protector, collector
kairēhita registrar
kaireka dessert
kairere whaitua astronaut, spaceman
kairerehuka skier
kairetireti tobogganist
kairipoata reporter
kairīwhi deputy, proxy, understudy, heir
kairomiromi physiotherapist
kairota linesman, sideline umpire
kairūri surveyor
kairutu judoist, judoka
kaitā printer (person), prime, important
kaitāhae thief, burglar
kaitaka fine flax cloak
kaitakaporepore gymnast, acrobat
kaitākaro player
kaitakawaenga liaison person, race relations conciliator
kaitakitaki avenger
kaitangata cannibal, cat's eye mollusc
kaitango receiver, buyer
kaitango rīhi lessee
kaitango-whakaahua photographer

K

kaitapere actor, actress
kaitātai moni cashier
kaitātaki rhythm leader
kaitātari selector, selection panel
kaitātari kaute accountant, auditor
kaitatau moni bank teller
kaitau bob for eels
kaitaua belligerent, warlike, militant
kaitautoko supporter, seconder, accomplice
kaitea kōkiri pacemaker (runner)
kaitiakitanga guardianship
kaitiki carrier
kaitīmata starter
kaitiri cursor (computer)
kaitirotiro inspector, investigator, observer
kaititiro spectator, eye witness
kaititiro o te ora sanitary inspector
kaitito artist, author, composer
kaitoa serves you right!, warrior
kaitohatoha distributor
kaitohe protestor
kaitohe mana wahine feminist
kaitohutohu sports coach, counsellor
kaitono claimant, petitioner, applicant
kaitonotono servant, waitress
kaitōrangapū politician
kaituhi author, clerk, scribe, marker
kaitui seamstress, tailor
kaituku traitor, informer, server, donor
kaituku rīhi lessor
kaitukuata film producer
kaitunu parāoa baker
kaitūpekepeke acrobat
kaitūrama gaffer (television)
kaitūtae spy
kaiure chant to remove tapu
kaiwaenga go-between, hindrance
kaiwaiata singer
kaiwarawara addict
kaiwaru scrubber (cleaner)
kaiwawao defender, referee, umpire, linesman
kaiwawao papa base umpire (sports)
kaiwawao tāpora plate umpire (softball)
kaiwea surveyor
kaiwehewehe wūru fleeco, sorter
kaiwero challenger, harpooner
kaiwhakaahua cameraman, photographer
kaiwhakaako teacher, coach, trainer
kaiwhakaatu commentator, witness
kaiwhakahaere administrator, MC, conductor
kaiwhakahau leader
kaiwhakahoki receiver (tennis)
kaiwhakairo carver
kaiwhakakapi assessor, appointee
kaiwhakakata clown
kaiwhakamahi executor
kaiwhakamahi rorohiko computer programmer, analyst-programmer
kaiwhakamāori interpreter, translator
kaiwhakamārie comforter
kaiwhakamātau instructor, examiner
kaiwhakamōhio education officer
kaiwhakangāwari appeaser

kaiwhakaora saviour, healer
kaiwhakapae complainant, plaintiff
kaiwhakapaepae return gift (food)
kaiwhakarato service provider, supplier
kaiwhakarite administrative officer, organiser
Kaiwhakariterite Book of Judges
kaiwhakarua related to both sides, swap sides
kaiwhakataetae competitor, athlete, contestant
kaiwhakatau umpire
kaiwhakatau kaupapa policy maker
kaiwhakatau manuhiri receptionist
kaiwhakatika pukapuka editor
kaiwhakaue steersman, helmsman
kaiwhakawā judge (of guilt), adjudicator
kaiwhakawā kōti whānau family court judge
kaiwhakawā mana iti justice of the peace
kaiwhakawai tempter, agent provocateur
kaiwhakawhānau midwife
kaiwhāki informant
kaiwhana kicker
kaiwhanga ambusher, bush-whacker
kaiwharawhara wing feather of albatross
kaiwhiore incest
kaiwhiriwhiri selector, judge, arbitrator
kaiwhiu prosecutor
kaiwhiwhi takuhe beneficiary
kaka clothing, fibre, line, handnet
kakā red hot, inflammation
kāka cork
kākā parrot
kākahi freshwater mollusc, mussel
kakaho blonde
kākaho jointed stem of reed, batten
kākahu moe pyjamas, nightdress
kākahu moenga bedclothes
kākahu taratara sackcloth
kākahu tauwhainga tracksuit
kākāiti parakeet
kākaka brown, stem of fern
kakama astute, cunning, alert, acumen, expert, proficient
kakamu blink, open and close
kākanapa gleaming, sea-green
kākano tini multi-cultural
kākano whakauru variegated, hybrid
kakapa quiver
kākāpō ground parrot
kakapōhai dragonfly
kakapu small food-container
kakara pleasant flavour, fragrance
kākaramea red-coloured, scented plant
kakaramū shrub
kākarauri dusk, dark, dimly visible
kākarepō bogey-man
kakari single combat, quarrel, rugby scrum
kākari combat, wrestle, hand-to-hand fight
kākāriki parakeet, green lizard, green colour
kakaro parry a blow

kakaru spongy matter
kakaru moana jellyfish
kakata chuckling, cracks, crevices (earth, skin)
kākata brown, rust coloured
kakati sting, zip, sour taste
kākati (katia) constricted, grip, chew, squeeze, tie in bundle
kākatikati chewy
kakato pluck, snap off, pleasant taste
kakau handle, stem, axle
kakau wīti straw
kakauri dusk
kakawa sweat, harsh
kake(-a) climb, ascent, overcome
kakenga ascension
kakere child's game, hammer-head shark
kaketū half-cocked position, lull in hostilities
kakī neck, black stilt
kakī mārō stubborn, thick-skinned, red-necked
kakū croak
kaku/kaku scrape, flax scrapings, rough cloak
kākura scarlet fever
kama quick, clever, eager
kāmaka boulder, rock, stone
kamakama quick, agile
kāmana crested grebe
kamareihana accommodation
kāmehameha priceless
kāmera camel, camera
kāmeta scarf
kamo eyelash, wink, eyeball
kamo ake effervesce
kamokamo marrow, cucumber, wink repeatedly
kamonga eyelash
kamorā green potato, spoilt by the sun
kamu munch, squash in hand
kamupene enterprise, company, business
kamupūtu gumboot
kāmura carpenter, joiner
kana stare wildly, bewitch
kanae mullet
kānahi jersey
kanakana stare wildly, lamprey
kanapa shine, gleam, radiant
kanape abate (of wind)
kanapihi cannabis
kanapu brilliant, flash (lightning), bright
kānara colonel, candle, Conrad
kane feel choked
Kanehiana Canadian
kāneihana carnation
kānekeneke move along
kanene cunning, sly
kanewaha! damn cheek!
kanewai creepy feeling
kānewha unripe, immature, doze, spell to make drowsy
kānewhanewha witchcraft, dozing
kanga(-a) to curse, swear
kānga corn, maize
kānga pāhūhū popcorn
kānga pirau fermented corn
kangakanga blaspheme, abuse, curse
kangarū kangaroo
kani(-a) (*v. and n.*) saw
kani tūtengi ballet
kānihi patch clothing
kanikani dance, ballet, jig, sciatica
kanikani kirikau stripper
kanikani pātōtō tap-dance

kanioro grind back and forth
kāniwha barb, barbed spear, notch
kano berry seed, ovum, species (type)
kanohi eye, face
kanohi ārai cataract of eye
kanohi, kāinga - view
kanopio kaleidoscope
kanoti cover-up fire
kānuka white tea tree
kanukanu ragged, dilapidated
kānuku engine clutch
kāo! no!
kao kūmara dried kūmara pieces
kāoa coral
kaokao rib, armpit, chevron
kaokaoroa chiton (mollusc), long-ribs
kaongaro straight section of palisade
kāore not, but (to express surprise)
kāore anō not yet
kāore i ārikarika what a lot
kāore i pūāwai retarded
kaoriki little bittern (extinct)
kaotia be denied
kapa copper, penny, team, panel of people
kapakapa flutter, locust, bird snare
kapamua forward player
kapamuri backline player, back row
kāpanapana scintillate
kāpara corporal, heartwood tōtara, resinous wood
kaparua second row
kāpata cupboard
kāpātāu but if
kape eyebrow, socket, long ladle
kape(-a) reject, separate out with stick
kapehau extractor fan, air extractor
kāpehu compass
kāpene captain
Kāpene Kuki Captain Cook, wild pig
kapeneihana compensation
kapenga passover feast
kapenga ture transgression
kapetā flutter, writhe, dogfish
kapetau move to and fro quickly, babble
kāpeti cabbage, kale
kapeu ear pendant of greenstone
kapewhiti come and go often, boring behaviour
kapi(-a) top off, close, bails (cricket)
kāpia kauri gum, ear wax, cellulose adhesive
kapiti crevice, join, radius bone
kapiti o te waewae fibula
kapo(-hia) snatch, flash
kāpō blind
kapohau parachute, windmill
kāpoi throw up (netball)
kapokapo hand signal, clutch, twinkle
kapokapowai(-tia) smoke, preserve head
kaponga tree fern, hut made of tree fern
kaporeihana corporation, incorporation
Kaporeihana Āwhina Hunga Whara Accident Compensation Corporation
kapowai dragonfly, water turbine

kapu cup, hollow of hand, cabbage tree, crayfish tail, scoop water
kapu piripiri afro haircut
kapua cloud
kapukapu sole, curl of wave, gush, gleam
kapunga handful, scoop with both hands
kāpūngāwhā sedge, hollow-stem sedge
kapuni natural gas
kāpunipuni assembly, compressed natural gas
kāpura fire, flashlight
kapuranga take by handful, sunrise
kapurangi rubbish, weed, bio-degradable
kaputī cuppa tea
kaputino cappuccino
kapuwae instep
kara colour, collar, flag
kara, e - to address a man
karā basalt
karae type of seagull
karaehe grass, tumbler, class, glassware
karaehe rae ryegrass
karaehe toroi ensilage
karahi minnow, business firm
karāhi glass
karahini kerosene
karahipi scholarship, bursary
karahiwi spur of hill, pink pāua
kāraho flooring, stage
karahū mudsnail
karahui congregate, gather
karaipiture scripture
Karaiti Christ
Karaitiana Christian
karaka clock, clerk, orange (colour), tree
kārakaraka crock pot
karakia religious service, prayer-chant
karama gram
karamea red ochre, caramel
karamū shrub, stinkwood
karamui swarm around
kāramuramu irregular meals, squeeze in hand
karanga(-tia) call, shout, related person
karanga-rua doubly related
karangahape shellfish, type of shellfish
kārangaranga repeated calls
karangatā not responding to call
karangatanga relationship, vocation, relative
kārangi restless, irritated, mound for whipping-top
kārangirangi intolerance, unsure
kārani gallon
karaone hoe, sovereign coin
karapa squint, glance
kāraparapa flashing light
karapēpē fizz, ferment
karapetapeta move quickly, scurry
karapetapetau wriggle, flutter
karapetau quaff, gulp, flutter
karapiti fasten side by side, sandwich
karapoi surround, be surrounded
karapoti(-tia) surround, be surrounded
karapotinga cage, safety cage
karapu club (cards), group, glove, northeast direction
karapuke small hill

kararaha wide and shallow
kararehe mammal, animal, beast
karatī small snapper
karāti karate, garage
karatiti(-a) peg down, bolt, pin
karatiwha deep black
kārau grapnel, shellfish dredge, comb, mesh gauge
karauna crown, to crown, diadem
karauria rock oyster
kārawa severely bruised
karawai freshwater crayfish
karawaka measles
karaweta filth, shit
karawhaea scarifier, harrow
karawhaiwhai stitch net, trap for net
karawheta struggle
karawhiti assemble, uneven, sporadic
karawhiu(-a) toss, throw, wheel round, thump
kare ripple, long for
kare, e – ! hello (usually to a man)
kāre not
kare-ā-roto sweetheart, emotions
kareao supplejack
kārearea bush hawk, duckweed, carving pattern
kārehu spade
karekare surf, rough sea, wavy, eager
kāreko calico
karemu bung
karengo smooth, edible seaweed
kareparāoa cauliflower
karēpe grape
karepū pukapuka bookshelf
karere messenger, herald
karere hiko e-mail
karere rāwaho foreign correspondent
karere rorohiko electronic mail
karere tuawhenua rural delivery
karere waea telegram
karetao toy jumping jack, puppet
kāreti college, carrot, carriage
kāretu scented grass
kārewa buoy, a float, water surface
kari(-a) dig, gash, rush like wind
kāri garden, card
kāri namanama credit card
kāri toka rock garden
karihi(-tia) fasten, sinkers, crunch, glance
karihi nucleus, nuclear, fruit stone, tooth, sinker on net
karihi tupu new tooth
karihika erotic, pornographic
kārikarika wisecrack, dig, sift
Kariki Greek
kāriki garlic, green
karimaranga cutting wind
karioi dawdle, linger, lie dead
karipapa adjoin, touch, sodomy
kāri pēke bank card
karipi slash, glance
kariri cartridge, pellets, shot, sail in fleet
kārito shoots of raupō
karituangi(-tia) dig deep
kariwhenua hoe
karo(-hia) evade, dodge, circumvent, save goal, pick out of hole
kārohirohi iridescent, shimmering
karoro gull
kāroti carrot
karu eye, iris, pulp
karu mōwhiti eye-glasses

K

karu nika steamed pudding
karukaru raggy, glare angrily
karukaru hipi facial eczema
kārupe shelf, ledge, mantelpiece
karuwai robin
kata(-ina) laugh, be laughed at
kata puku secretly amused
kāta cart
kātae excellent!
kātaha yellow-eyed mullet, herring
kātahi then
kātahi anō for the first time, only then
kātahi te . . . what a . . .! (express admiration)
kātahi tonu only just
katakata ludicrous, funny, mirth
katamarani catamaran
katamu eat noisily
kātana carton
kātaroera castor oil
katate seagull
katau righthand side
katekate cape, shawl
katekihama catechism
katekita catechist
kātere accelerator
katero fermented potato
katete gull, move forward, lengthen
kātete leg length, custard
kati fastener, zip, close over
kati(-a) (*v.*) shut, bite, quit (computer)
kāti enough said, that's enough, stop it!, leave it
katikati nibble, shear, cut pack of cards
kātinara cardinal
katinga service hatch
katinga toto blood clot
kātipa constable
katipō poisonous spider, wasp
katipō kahurangi queen wasp
katira fishing rod, dowel, wand
katitohe throat ulcers, tonsilitis
katitoto blood clot
kato(-hia) pluck, flood tide, break off
katoa all, every, completely, total
kātoa tree mānuka
katoakatoa entire
kātoatoa loose weaving, shrunk, everybody inclusive
kātoretore glow dimly
Katorika Catholic
katote unstable (physics), shaking
kātote soft tree fern
kātua stock animals, adult, mare
kātuarehe crafty villain, clever
kau cow, only, naked
kau(-ria) swim, wade
kau (after verb) as soon as, just
kau aihe butterfly stroke
kau āpuru breaststroke
kau kiore backstroke
kau kūtētē dairy cow, milker
kau o te kanohi pupil of eye
kau, kāhore - not at all
kaua do not!
kauae jaw, curtain of defensive stockade
kauae mua elder brother/sister
kauae raro youngest child, earthly lore
kauae runga celestial lore
kauahi grooved block for firemaking
kauaka do not!
kauamo stretcher (to carry sick), litter

kauanga river ford, act of swimming, star – Canopus (towards dawn)
kauati rubbing block for fire production
kāuaua bush hawk
kauawhiawhi hug, cosy place
kauere scented plant, seaweed, pūriri tree, broken water
kaueti grooved block for fire-making
kauhanga open space, corridor, hallway
kauhanga riri battlefield
kauhanganui main council, open passage
kauhau sermon, preach
kauhimu gossip, spread rumours
kauhoa stretcher (carrying), drum up support
kauhoe swim
kaui(-tia) thread on string, shoelace
kauika pod of whales, lie in a heap
kaukau swim, bathe
kaukauranga swimming place, bathroom
kaumātua old man, elder, adult
kaumātuatanga old age, dotage
kaumingomingo chaotic, mixed up
kaumoana seaman, sailor
kaunati fire stick
kaunenehu murky
kaunihera council
kaunoni wriggle
kaunoti firestick
kauoro(-hia) grind, lapidary, scrubbing brush
kauoti grooved block for fire-making
kaupae rung, trestle, level, step
kaupane head, top end, head position in haka
kaupapa strategy, level floor, philosophy
kaupapa whiti bad luck
kaupare(-a) resist, deflect, shade eyes
kaupare atu avert
kaupe hanging loose
kaupēhi suppress, keep down
kaupeka branch, stick, rung, footrest
kaupekapeka branch
kaupoai cowboy
kaupoki cover up, turn over
kauraho vulva (labia majora)
kauranga ford, crossing
kaurehu obscure
kaurerehu dim, dark, gloomy
kauri kauri tree, gum, tattooing powder
kauriki little
kaurori(-hia) stir, stagger
kāuru tree top, river head
kāuru niho crown of tooth
kauruki smoke, haze
kāuta cooking shed, kitchen
kautahanga empty
kautāhoe swim across
kautangatanga swift movement
kaute account, count, bill, score
kautere float about, go in a group
kautetanga book-keeping
kautete, matā - primitive saw
kautorohī appear suddenly
kautū wade
kautuku bittern
kauwae jaw
kauwae raro lore of earthly things, lower jaw

kauwae runga lore of heavenly things, upper jaw
kauwhata food racks, spirit-medium, recite genealogy
kauwhau preach, sermon, recite genealogy
kauwhiti winch, part omitted
kauwhitiwhiti katydid, grasshopper
kawa protocol, acid, pepper tree
kawa-pēke saddlebag, cover-sack
kāwai lineage, tentacle, category
kāwai rangatira nobility
kawaka N.Z. cedar, furrow
kawakawa pepper tree, dark greenstone
kāwana governor
Kāwana-Tianara Governor-General
kāwanatanga government
kawari common whelk
Kāwari Calvary
kawariki cyan, swamp plant, parakeet, green lizard
kawatau debate at length
kawau great cormorant, varieties of cormorant, spear shaft, handle
kawau hake crankshaft
kawau mārō attack in column formation, haka movement
kawau moeroa driftnet fishing, permanent bird and fish traps
kawau pū chief
kawe(-a) carry, fetch, bring
kawe kē change
kawe, whiri - basket handle
kawekawe tentacle, tendril, fringe, freight
kāwekaweka lanky, rambling speech
kawekē change direction
kawenata covenant, testament
Kawenata Hou New Testament
Kawenata Tawhito Old Testament
kawenga luggage, opening ceremony, cartage
kāwetoweto gradually taper
kāwhaki(-na) take by force, make a break for it, kidnap
kāwhe calf
kāwhena coffin, casket
kāwhi coffee
kāwhi pēhia espresso
kawikawi marblefish
kawiri(-tia) twist, wring, strand of rope
kāwiriwiri intertwine
kawiti decrease in width, taper, dwindle
kawititanga wrist
kāwitiwiti tapered, narrowing
kē already, different, another, shriek
kea mountain parrot, bedsore
keha turnip, smelly, pale person
kehakeha stink
kehe marblefish, edible tuber of orchid, odd number
kēhi gas, case, crate, casing
keho apex, white frost, noisy fart, vulva (labia minora)
kēhua ghost, synthetic, Jack (cards)
kei in, at, located in, with
kei + *verb* don't, may it not be, lest
kei a + *name* *name* has it, according to *name*
kei hea? where is?, where are?

kei tawhiti remote
kei te + *verb* shows continuous action
kei te hinengaro self-motivating
kei whea? where is?, where are?
kekakeka filamentous algae, ear fungus
keke cake, obstinate
kekē crack noise, creak, rustling noise
kēkē armpits, quack, different, in another line
kēkēao overcast, gloomy
kekeno seal, sea lion, look around
kēkerengū stink-bug
kekerepō blind, bizarre carving
kēkerewai green beetle
kēkēwai freshwater crayfish, blue damselfly
keko squinting, peering, wink
kēmihi chemist, pharmacist
kemokemo wink, blink
kēmu game, match
kēna tin can
kēna nehu aerosol
kenakena Adam's apple, stare wildly
Kenehi Genesis
kēnepenihīni jerrycan
kenepuru mud, silt
kēneti genitals
keneturio centurion
keno seal, sea lion, night, underworld
keo ice, shooting target, squint, screech
keo pū ice-block
keokeo peak, summit
kepa lanyard
kera wēra orca, killer whale
kerehunga fuzz, lint, nap, soufflé
kerei grey
kereiti crate
kerekere, pōuri - extremely dark
kerekereao supplejack
kerēme claim
keremutu cut short, end suddenly
kerepeti playdough, malleable clay
kerepi sod, clod
kerēpi grape
kerēpiwhurūtu grapefruit
kerepō blind
kerepuru sodden earth
kererū pigeon
keretao puppet
keretoa heavy clay
keretū heavy clay, thwart of canoe
kerikeri digging, unearthing, violent rush
kero aim, point at, blink, injured
kerokero sight along gun-barrel, blink often
kete basket, kit, bag, womb
kete aronui basket of knowledge, arts and lovemaking
kete kapurangi rubbish bag
kete tūātea basket of knowledge, evil
kete tūāuri basket of knowledge, ritual
ketekete cheer on, click tongue to chivvy along
kēti gate
kēti pāpuni sluice gate
ketu(-a) digging stick, probe ground, turn of tide
ketuketu delve into, rugby ruck
ketunga poaka rooting place
keu(-a) pull trigger, trigger
keu o te whēkau appendix

kewa southern right whale, be extinguished, skin trouble
kēwai freshwater cray
ki to, at, with, into, against
kī(-a) tell, speak, full, key
ki te mea if
kī tūturu declare
ki uta shoreward, terra firma
kia let (*express a wish*), when, so that, until
kia ahatia? what can be done?
kia hiwa rā attention!
kia ora hello!, thanks!, may you have health
kia pērā anō ditto
kia tapu not negotiable
kia tau keep still, be alert
kīaka calabash, gourd, litre
kīanga act of speaking, expression (maths), phrase
kīanō not yet
kiato assembled, compact, repository
kīato canoe thwart
kiekie climber
kiha gasp, sigh
kīhai not, *negative in past time*
kīhau ghost, sail-spreader
kihi kiss, murmur
kihikihi cicada, locust, smooch
kīhini kitchen
kikī crowded, tight
kīki gig
kiki whenua cicada
kikihi rustling noise
kīkiki idiot, mad
kikikiki stutter, jabber
kikimo shut eyes
kikini(-tia) pinch, sharp pain, peppers
kīkino bad, wicked, ugly
kīkino koe e hoa! you're not so bad!
kikipounamu katydid
kīkītara tree cicada
kiko flesh, tissue
kikoha sharp, pointed
kikohunga gangrene, puffiness of wound
kikokā swelling around wounds
kikokiko flesh, tissue, self, kernel
kīkōpū bellyful
kikorangi sky blue, deep blue
kikorua double vision, twofold
kimi(-hia) look for, search, derive, evaluate, find
kimihanga quest
kimikimi (kimihia) look for
kimo wink, blink
kōmutu calabash with lid
kina sea-egg, sea-urchin
kīnaki savoury tidbit (meal/speech)
kīnakinaki blender
kini(-tia) pinch, hurt feelings
kinikini nip off, skirt, nibble
kino bad, vice, evil, malignant
kiokio edible fern, tall cabbage tree
kiore rat, mouse, rodent
kiore moana seahorse
kiorere buck (horse)
kioriki little bittern (extinct)
kipa spur, hasty
kīpūrena brimful
kira rough, prickly
kīrea exhausted land
kīrehe animal, dog
kīrera squirrel
kiri skin, leather, self (person), pelt
Kirihimete Christmas

kirikā fever
kirikau naked, leather
kirikira chinchilla
kirikiri sand, gravel, pebble, stoney
kirikiritona blear-eyed
kirikiti cricket (game)
kiri mangu negro
kirimate chief mourners
kirīmi cream, palamino horse
kirimini agreement
kirimoko skin-deep, superficial
kiringutu plot endlessly
kirīni green
kiripaka bronze, flint, tree bark, pork crackle
kiripiro inhospitable, bad tempered
kiripōhatu gravel
kiritai epidermis, wetsuit
kiritangata inner defences
kiritapu unwed, hymen
kiritea paleface, white races, Caucasian
kiriūka leathery, firm, unwavering
kiriwai inner skin, dermis, mānuka beetle
kiriwera sad person, depressed
kiriweti fanatic, hot-tempered, jealous
kiriwetiweti ghastly, gruesome
kiriwhenua pickaxe
kiriwhero redskins, red-faced
kiro kilo
kiromita kilometre
kita tight, intense, bright colour
kitā guitar, chirp of cicada
kītahi laconic, taciturn, terse
kite(-a) see, find, recognize, witness
kitekite see, see often
kitemea if, should it happen
kiwa wink, dark, sad
kīwaha colloquialism, idiom, phrase
kiwakiwa dark, gloomy, sad, fern
kīwhi disc
kiwi national bird, inhabitant of New Zealand
kiwikiwi grey, fern
ko as for, with regard to
kō (e kō!) girl!, young lady!
kō digging stick, engine choke, there!, bird song
kō(-ia) dig, plant, echo
kō atu further over, beyond
kō mai this side (of object), over here
koa happy, jubilant
koā please, it's a fact
koaea choir
koanga happiness
kōanga spring, planting time
kōangi cool, diarrhoea
kōangiangi breeze
kōanu chilly
kōara(-tia) split, crack, force open, bad omen
kōaro overturned, inside out, upside down
kōata glass, quarter
kōataata slide (transparency), translucent, reflection
kōateate spleen
koati toa billy goat
koati uwha nanny goat
kōau great cormorant, types of shag
kōau pongāihu nose flute
kōauau flute, bull kelp
kōawa valley, watercourse

kōawaawa gully, valley, grooved
koe you (one person)
koē screech
koea brilliant, lizard, long wooden trumpet
kōea setsquare, square
koehu muddy water, variety of shark
kōehuehu misty
kōeke level, cold, old man
koeke(-tia) grow old, mature
koeko coming to a point, spire, cone, taper
koekoeā long-tailed cuckoo
koemi flinch, wince
koero sickness, thaw, rot, menopause
koha donation, gift, parting message
kōhae(-tia) enjoy, long for, shine
kōhaki(-na) take by force
kōhamo back of the head
kōhamuhamu whisper
kōhanga nest, nursery, maternity house
kōhanga reo language nest, Māori pre-school
kōhao hole, socket, cavity
kōhao hiko power point
kohapa crooked, lame
kōhari cress, mashed food, nominate
kōhatu stone
kōhatu whakakai gem
kōhatu whakamaharatanga gravestone, headstone, memorial stone
kohe gabble, tree, passion vine
kohea? where?, clear, open
kohekohe cedar tree, long for, climbing vine
kōhengi light breeze, desire
kohepu kohekohe flowers
kohera twitch of limbs (omen), jerking of limbs
kohera split open, shine, enthralled
kōhere pound fern root, cake of fern root flour
kōheri beat, whisk, horse mackerel
kohete(-tia) scold, quarrel, reprove
kōheuheu fan
kohi(-a) collect, gather, trick (cards)
kohi, mate - tuberculosis
kōhihi stitch-bird, flit about
kohika infer, ancestor
kohikatanga inference
kohiko tinsel, twinkle, flash
kohiko(-tia) interject, flash
kohikohi collection, gather, opalfish
kōhikohiko erratic, heat haze, piecemeal
kohimako bellbird
kohimu whisper, gossip
kōhimuhimu whisper
kōhine girl
kohinu lure, tempt, deceive
kōhinu petrol
kōhiti pick out, appear, tattoo pattern
kōhiwi heartwood, base of canoe
kōhoi emaciated
kōhonihoni gnaw, nibble
kohu mist, concave, curse
kōhua boil, pot, camp oven
kōhue camp oven
kohuka foam at the mouth

kohuki about turn, worry, transfix on a spit
kōhukihuki show emotion, tress, frustration
kohukohu chickweed, moss, mist, curse
kohukohurangi alkaloid plant, Kirk's daisy
kohuku unfinished
kōhumuhumu whisper, murmur, cropped hair
kōhungahunga crushed, infant
kōhura sprout
kohurangi blue
kōhurihuri saplings
kōhuru(-tia) murder, treachery
kohuwai algae, underwater streamers
koi sharp, pierce with spike, headland, almost
koi (*see* kei) lest
koianā it is so, just that, isn't it?, that's all
koia rā! hear hear!
koiangi diarrhoea
kōihi split, open porch
koikoi prickles, thorn, staff sharp at both ends
koina that is, those are
koinā indeed it is!
kōina over there
koinaka that's why
koinei this is why
koineki this is why
koinga blade, point, spiny dogfish
kōingo strong desire, sorrow
koiora life, biological
koiota coyote
koira stare fiercely, look askance
koirā that's why
kōiraira spot, mark
kōiriiri wriggle, warm up
kōiro conger eel
koitareke N.Z. quail (extinct)
kōiti little finger/toe, weirdo, short length
kōiwi bone, corpse, so and so! (exclamation of disgust)
kōkā mother, ripe, grandparent
kōkai back
kōkako blue-wattled crow
kōkara true mother
kōkātanga maternity
kōkau incomplete, half-baked, skinny
koki angle, corner, bend, curve, small canoe
kōkī dawn chorus
kōkī poaka black pudding
kōkihi sprout, N.Z. spinach, container
kōkiri(-tia) charge forward, vault, rise together
kōkiri mana wahine feminism
kōkirikiri leatherjacket fish, go headlong, flash
kōkirikiriwhetū basket fungus
koko(-ia) scoop up, shovel, handnet, bay
kōkō(-ia) turn soil, fishing rod, tattoo
kōkō tūī, gurgle, cocoa
koko mihini bulldozer
koko parai spatula, fish-slice
koko tatakī humorist, joker, raconteur
kōkōhau breeze
kokohu hollow
kōkōmako bellbird
kokonga corner, recess, nook
kokonga ipu dipper, ladle

kōkopu native trout, giant kōkopu
kōkopurangi freshwater leech
kokori small bay
kokoroihe cockroach
kokoru bay
kōkota visa, direction mark, flattish mussel, pipi
kōkōtea hen tūī
kokoti ambush, interruption
kōkōwai red ochre, rouge, reddish brown
kōkuhu intruder, bastard child, insert
kōkura beetroot
kōmā whitish, ashen faced, creamy
kōmahi turn black, discoloured potatoes, fermented kūmara
kōmako bellbird
kōmāmā lightweight, soft, polystyrene
kōmanawa well up, spring of water, hydrant
kōmārohi strong
kōmaru canoe sail, overcast, solar
kōmata teat, areola, young shoot, sweetheart
kome chew
kōmeke comic book, fern root, cloak
kōmekemeke loosely coiled
komekome chew, move lips, tidbit
komeme withered, broken in, wrinkled
komenga chew
kōmihana commission
kōmihini engine choke
komingo curl, eddy, agitated
kōmiri(-a, -tia) grind, rub, knead with fingers
kōmiro whirling, twist
kōmiromiro tit
komiti committee
kōmore bracelet, bangle, taproot, shellfish
kōmoremore taproot
kōmou bank up fire
komu pātene buttonhole
kōmuhu whisper
komunio communion
kōmuri breeze, backwards, rub off
kōmutu lid of pot
kona cone, lower abdomen, nook
konā there near you, then
kōnae small basket, index file
kōnakinaki arise, well up
konani chewing gum
konape basket of food
kōnati lock hold (judo), strangle
konatu stir, mix, twinge, desire
kōnatunatu crumble (by hand), mince, stir up
konei here
kōneke sledge, slide along
kōnekeneke shuffle feet, make rustling noise
koneki here
koneti play darts
kōnewhanewha eyes closing, attention wandering
konga charcoal, burning ember, carbon
kongakonga chips, smash to bits, debris
koni move, here, thumb
koni atu more
kōnihi move stealthily, sneaky
konikoni move about
kōnini tree, edible berries of
kono small basket, bend, loop

konohete concert, recital, stage revue
konohi face, eye
kōnohi yearn for
konokono deep narrow container
konuhina magnesium
konuhono solder
kōnui thumb, big toe, 2 cm long
konuke bent
kōnukunuku bend
konukura copper metal
konumatā lead metal
konumohe aluminium
konuoi mercury
konupiere uranium
konupūmā calcium
konupūmura chromium
konurehu potassium
konutai sodium
konutai waihā caustic soda, sodium hydroxide
konutea zinc
konutuki radium
kooti (*see* kōti) court of law
kopa bent, lame, pass by, disappear
kopa satchel, briefcase
kōpā stiff with cold, congealed
kōpae circle, disc, floppy disk
kōpaepae diskette, plaited leaves to line umu (earth oven)
kōpaepae pūoro compact disc, CD
kopāina sunbather
kōpaki envelope, pillow slip, folder
kōpaki(-na) wrap, enclose, fold, lag pipe
kōpaki moe sleeping bag
kōpako back of the head, parietal bone
kopamārō portfolio, briefcase
kōpana(-ia) push, urge on, throb
kōpara bellbird
kōpare(-a) shade the eyes, blindfold, facemask, gift of food
kōparu bruise, sloppy, soggy
kōpata blob, droplet
kōpatapata droplets, pelargonium, geranium
kope baby's nappy, wrap, sanitary pad
kōpē(-ngia, -tia) squash, pulpy
kōpehupehu knock down, squash flat
kōpeke cold, winter, tuck up frog-like
kopēke back up (command to horse)
kōpenu squeeze, squash
kōpēpē mush, marrow, squeeze, pliable
kōpere sling (project with force), dart, rainbow, catapult, dash
kōpeti running noose
kopeū bra, brassiere
kopi shut, full stop, doubled over
kōpiha storage pit, pool
kōpiko meander, curved hoops for snares
kopikopi hand game, amusing freestyle/impromptu dance
kōpikopiko wander to and fro, meander
kōpio sphere, wind taken aback (nautical term)
kōpīpī weak, immature, frail
kōpiro fermented, marinated, intestines, soak, colon
kōpiupiu swing back and forth
kopu small freshwater fish, goby fish, large eel

kopū full to bursting, blister
Kōpū Venus
kōpū belly, womb, pregnant
kōpū tetere dropsy
kōpū waewae calf of leg
kōpua deep waters, deep pool, sinker
kōpuku fine cloak, swell, rounded, oedema
kōpukupuku rubella, buttercup, dappled
kōpuni in a group, dark colour, black cloak
kōpūpū blister
kōpura hole, blistered, kūmara tubers
kōpure patch of ground, clearing, spotty, spot
kōpurepure spotted, patchy, type of eel
kōpuru dark clouds, mouldy
kōpūrua swollen with dropsy, of two minds
kōputa albatross, heap
kōpūtahi blood-relations, combine, associate
kōputaputa sieve, pore of skin, fish bladder, strainer
kōpūwai grey mullet, watery
kora spark, sequin
korā over there
kōra goal, score, fuel
kōra rangi shrimp
koraha desert, open country, place to defecate
korakora ahi spark
kōrakorako pale ghosts, forest fairies
Korāna Koran
kōrapa wrong move (omen), long handled net
kōrapurapu grab, prehensile
kōrari flax esp. stem
kōrau turnip leaves, beet, tree fern
kōrawa agitated
kore (ka kore) nil, zero, trap, void, nought
kōrē nappy, sanitary napkin, absorbent moss
kore āhei not applicable (n/a)
kore atu not possible
kōrē paratiki plastic pants
kore rawa never, absolutely not
korekairama teetotaller, temperance
korekore waning moon, sterile, no activity
kōrekoreko fluorescent, dazzled
koremahi redundant
kōremu bilge plug
korenga absence
kōreporepo swampy
kōrere tap, gutter, spout
kōrerehu dusky
kōrero(-tia) speak, news, narrative, quotation
kōrero paki fairytale, legend, storytelling
kōrero pakiwaitara fairytale, legend, story
kōrero whakahīhī brag, skite
kōrerorero chat, conversation, discuss
koretaea unavailable
koretāke duty free
koretake useless, groundless, invalid, pointless
kōrewha blink eye, signal with eye
korewai drought

kori wriggle, play, physical exercise
kori, kai - jelly
kori tīraurau tea bag
korihi bird song
korikāwhe coffee bag
kōriki marsh crake, N.Z. quail (extinct)
korikori bestir oneself, exercise, get going
korikori tinana physical exercise, aerobics
korimako bellbird
kōrimurimu seaweed covered
koringa movement, wriggle
kōrino twist, curl
kōriorio(-tia) dehydrate, wizened
kōriparipa plough through water
kōripi(-a) slice, knife, paddle-stroke
kōripo eddy of water, whirl
kōriporipo ripple, swirling, eddy, ship's wake
kōriroriro grey warbler
korite in unison
kōrito heart of plant, blonde hair
kōritorito tousled hair, dreadlocks
koro sir, old man, desire
koro o te rore noose
koroa clover
kōroa forefinger
koroaha cheek tattoo
kōroaroa long
koroheke old man
koroheketanga old age
korohihī spurt up
korohū steam, boil
korohuhū boil liquid, simmer
korohunga in shreds, cloak with ornamental border
koroingo desire, yearn, welcome ceremony for newborn
koroirangi wayfarers, vagrants
kōroiroi wandering, confused, inattentive, deadly dull
koroiti little finger, little toe
korokē odd fellow, larrikin, guy, fellow, ironic
korokī chatter
korokoro loose, throat, taste buds, lamprey, turkey
koromāhanga noose, snare
koromatua big toe, thumb, Mayor, Mayoress
koromeke looped, crouch doubled up, bent
koromenge frown, crumpled
koromiko dysentery cure, hebe shrub
koronae hāngi leaves, broadside on
koroneihana coronation
korongenge deadened, paralysed
koroni colony
koronuke crooked
koropā doorbolt, wooden latch, sacred food
koropae leaves to line hāngi
koropeke crouch doubled up, bagged food
koropewa loop, arc of bow
koropiko pay homage, adoration
koropuku hidden, swollen, move cautiously
koropupū bubble, boil, poach (eggs etc.)
koroputa hole
kororā blue penguin, grey
kōrori stir up, warp, whisk
korōria glory, pomp, splendour
kororoa index finger

korotaha sideways, askance
korotangi storage pit, carved stone pigeon
korotao jumping jack
korotē(-hia) squeeze
korotiwha spot, inlay
korou desire, energy, purpose
koroua old man, clover
korowai tag cloak for chief
korōwha golf
korowhāwhā anchovy
korowhio whistle, blue duck
korowhiti bent round, hoop, jerk, whistle
koru spiral pattern, folded
Koru Aotearoa Air New Zealand
kōrua you two
kōruarua hole, rifle pits, trench
kōruhe puckered lips
korukoru turkey, wrinkle, parasitic plant, fold
kōrupe carving over doorway
korurangi galaxy
kōruru carved owl-face, cloudy
kota cockle shell, scraper, sawdust
kōtaha sling (weapon), sidelong
kotahi one
kotahitanga accord, coalition, unity
kōtamutamu chew, flap lips, flash continuously
kōtangitangi breeze
kōtare kingfisher, defence-stage of palisade
kotē(-hia, -tia) squeeze, squash, form of spell to bewitch
kōtea, kiri - albino
kōtere swelling, diarrhoea, runny, watery
koteretere o te ia toto low blood pressure
kōtero fermented kūmara or potato
kōtetetete chattering
koti(-a) coat, divide, cut across path (bad luck)
kōti court of law, goat, gorse
kotiate flat short club
kotikara fingernail, toenail
kotikoti divide up, cut in pieces
kōtimana thistle, Scot
kotimutu flask, small bottle, small calabash
kotinga boundary line, circumcision
kōtiotio prickly
kōtipatipa rifleman bird
kotipū cut off, cut short
kotire fishing rod
kotiri meteor, twitch during dream, in single file
kōtiro girl, wench
kōtiti deviate, detour, break racing lane, deviance
kōtiu north wind, swerve and dip of kite
kotiuru splitting headache
kōtiwhatiwha speckled, dispersed, spotted
kōtonga south wind, cold and miserable
kōtore anus, tail
kōtore moana sea anemone
kōtua turn the back, bad omen, token of respect, bad luck
kōtui lace up, interlaced, bind
kōtuke bent in a bow, arched
kōtuku rerenga tahi rare visitor
kōtureture chlamydia
kōtutu hand net, ladle, scoop water
kou knob, lump, bunch of feathers, clitoris

koua fish roe
kōua sprinkle rain, uprights of latrine beam
kouawai gall bladder, discharge from womb
kouka abyss, back of latrine
kōuka cabbage-tree
kōukauka kahawai fish
koukou morepork, cocoa
kōuku plaster-cast
kōuma breastplate, sternum, breastbone
kōunu out of joint, dislocated, pull out
kōura crayfish, gold, prawn
kōurarangi krill
kōuraura shrimp, bronze
kōuru top of tree, head of river
kōuru matangi puff of wind
koute gout
koutou you (*pl.*)
koutu peninsula, point of land
kōutuutu ladle water, dip up
kōwha female animals and plants, hen, mare
kōwae ako education module, unit of work
kowani(-a) scrape
kōwao clearing in bush, wild, untamed
kōwaowao overgrown, choked with weeds
kōwaro (*see* kōaro) upside down, blighted crops, shellfish
kowata transparent, broken twig signs
kōwatawata gleaming, tasty
kōwenewene casemoth
kowera glow
kōwerowero shoot out, begin to appear
kōwhai yellow
kōwhai ngutu kākā red kōwhai, kākā beak
kōwhai, mate - hepatitis
kōwhaikākonu brassy
kōwhaiwhai scroll painting on rafter
kōwhai(-na) pluck off, ready to pick, flash
kōwhaiwhai visual art
kōwhakiwhaki flash, tear off strips
kōwhanga nest, overcast sky
kōwhao hole
kōwhao, puku - dropsy
kōwharawhara split into strips, coastal *Astelia*
kōwhatawhata gleam
kōwhatu stone
kōwhāwhā flashing continuously
kowhera yawn, open up, lightning flash
kowheta wriggle, hasty, flounder about
kōwhetawheta writhing
kowhete quarrel, scold, mumble
kōwhetewhete whisper, argue
kōwheuwheu neap (minimal) tides
kōwhewhe split open, dried up
kōwhiri(-a) choose, whirl about, nominate
kōwhiti(-hia) sort by size, twitch
kōwhiti marama new moon
kōwhitiwhiti grasshopper, yellow cress, dancing water
kōwhiuwhiu to fan, winnow
kōwhiwhi small tree
kōwiri screw, wriggling, coil
kōwiriwiri wriggle, tortuous

K

kū coo, syllable, stillness, exhausted
kua + *verb* indicates completed action (e.g. kua whati = broken)
kua hai you're trumped
kua puta out (games), has emerged
kuaea quits, fulfilled
kūaha doorway
kūaka godwit
kūao young of animals, calf, lamb, puppy
kūao hōiho yearling horse
kūao kau heifer, calf
kūare stupid, ignorant, lack of understanding, senseless
kuha ragged, gasp, scraps
kūhā inner thigh, tree trunk, relation by marriage
kuhara edible grub, earthworm, cockle
kuhu(-a, -ngia) enter, go into, hide, put on clothes
kuhunga gate, entrance, political movement
kūī tiger beetle, cold, weak, stunted, ladybird
kuia old lady (e kui = form of address), matron
kuihana cushion
kuihi goose, fart, murmur, grey petrel
kuihipere gooseberry
kuini queen
kuinihi quince
kuira quilt
kūiti narrow space, constricted, confined, blind side (rugby)
kuka dry leaves, abortion
kūkā cinders, soot, clog, variety of mussel
kūkamo cucumber
kuki cook
kuku(-a) haunt, mussel, hold breath, tweezers
kūkū pigeon
kukume (kumea) pull, draw along, attract
kukume o te ao gravity
kukupā wood pigeon
kukuti (kūtia) bad influence, nip, restrict, contract, pinch
kumama long for, want, tasty
kūmara sweet potato
kūmarahou medicinal plant, rose-leaved anise, gum-digger's soap
kumau pliers
kume(-a) pull, asthma, adjustment slide
kume tōkena garter
kumekume pull out, extract, attract
kumemau zip-fastener, magnet
kumete wooden food bowl, casserole, trough
kumewaha horse's bit
kumi one fathom, six feet
kumikumi beard of mussel, white throat-feather
kūmore headland, stick out
kumu(-a) clench, stingy, anus, tail of bird
kumukumu gurnard
kūnatu kapurangi waste disposal unit
kūnatunatu mince
kunekune plump, rotund, plump piglet
kunene beg
kunikuni dark
kunuku skunk
kūoro grater, mouli, grinder
kūoro pīnikāwhi coffee grinder

kūpā belch, gasp, horse mussel, mildew
kupango dark coloured
kūpapa bend low, crouch, creep, traitor
kuparu John Dory fish
kūparu dirty
kupenga net, drape
kupere flow fast
kupiki cube, cubic
kupu text, word, message, remark
kupu āhua adjective
kupu tāpiri footnote
kupumahi verb
kupumahi huriaro passive verb
kupumahi ngoi active verb
kuputaka glossary
kuputohu participle, index, definite or indefinite article
kupuwāhi preposition
kura school, red feather, treasure
kura māhita teacher (male or female)
kūrae cape, headland, promontory
kurahaupō anti-cyclone, moon halo, lunar rainbow
kuratini polytechnic
kurī dog, animal, canine, hound
Kūri Australian Aborigine
kurī kerikeri terrier
kurī whakangau pig dog
kurikuri stinking, speargrass, wild spaniard
kuru mallet, ear pendant, greenstone, breadfruit
kuru(-a, -ngia) (*v.*) throw, hit, hammer, slam
kuru manawa precordial thump (heart restart)
kuru pounamu greenstone ornament
kuru taringa hammer of eardrum
kuru whengi shoveller, spoonbill, wading bird
kuru whiu penalty shot
kurupae (*n.*) beam, joist
kurupae(-tia) lie across, enfold, crouch, lurking, sheltering
kurupopo worm-eaten
kurutai hammer (athletics), salt
kūtai mussel
kuti(-a) draw together, cut, nightmare
kutikuti(-a) shear, shears, scissors, grayling
kutikutiroa shears
kutiriki aphid
kutu louse
kutukutu vermin, maggot, speckled greenstone
kutukutu-ahi delirium
kūwaha doorway, mouth
kūwao growing wild, of the forest
kūware stupid, oaf, obtuse
kūwata long for
kūwatawata chinks in palisade, light seen through chinks
kūwhā thigh, marriage dowry, relations by marriage, tree trunk
kuwharu pipi, cockle, edible grub
kūwhera legs apart stance

M

mā white, and (with numbers), concerning, by way of
mā and the rest (e.g. Hori mā = George and rest)
mā + *subject* the doer of future action, (emphatic future) *(see Brief Grammar)*
mā te wā till we meet again
māeke cold
maene easy, soothing
māeneene soft, smooth, itch, itchy
māero mile, channel, Milo drink
maero ngutu fire hydrant
maewa wandering
maha many, profuse, various
māha satisfied
māhaki calm, lowly, humble
mahana warm, temperature, heat
māhanga twins, snare, trap, cage
mahara(-tia) remember, consider, memory (computer)
māharahara worry, preoccupied
mahau verandah, pavilion
māhau for you (one person)
māhē sinker (fishing)
maheni smooth, bald, sleek
mahera open, mouth
mahere chart, map out
māhi mast, putrefy, ferment
mahi (*n.*) job, activity, trade, labour
mahi(-a) (*v.*) make, work
mahi atu! just do it!
mahi auau habitual action
mahi hīanga trick
mahi kē instead of
mahi matua major services
mahi noa self-acting
mahi rangahau research
mahi rapu pōti political campaign
mahi rerekē idiosyncracy
mahi tinihanga skylarking
mahi tiriwā shift work
mahi toi art
mahi whakahou restructuring exercise
mahimahi have sex, copulate
mahimanga workshop
māhina twilight
māhinahina hazy, dim light
mahinga kai cultivation, vege garden
māhita teacher, schoolmaster, schoolmistress
mahitareta/e magistrate
māhiti sort by size, cloak of dog-hair
māhoe whiteywood
māhoi, titiro - stare at
mahora spread out, give way
māhorahora freedom, open, sprawl, wide
mahore peeled
māhū gentle
mahua raised
mahue left behind, neglected, separated, derelict
mahue, mano - enormous number
mahuetanga superfluous
mahuki be startled, pulsate

māhuna head
māhunga head, hair
māhungahunga squashed to pulp
mahura uncovered
mahurangi kūmara flesh, Very Important Person
māhurehure chop up, thieving
māhuri growing, intermediate, sapling
māhuruhuru suckerfish, placid
mahuta jump, hop ashore
mai hither, clothing
maī sour, mataī tree, quiet
māia brave, hero, heroine, bravery, daredevil
maiaka(-tia) fasten with vines, thin
maiangi rise up, springy, weak
maiengi lifted up, weak
maihamo back of head
maihao finger, toe, claw, sprigs
maihara muscles, marshall
māihe railings, fence
maihea sinker (fishing)
maihi carved barge boards, mast
maihi(-tia) decorate, complete with carving
māika orchid tuber, kit for cooked food
maiki bad luck, migrate, incident
maikuku fingernail, toenail, claw, hoof
maimai haka of welcome (especially at tangi)
maimai aroha token of affection
maimoa pamper, parrot lure, nursing treatment
māio peaceful
maioha welcome, keepsake
maioro defended by rampart and fosses
māipi wooden spear, weapon
maira myrrh
mairangi lift, black maire
maire potent chant, weapon grade timber, cow-horn
maire, whare - tertiary education
maita bowl (heavy ball), bowls (game)
maitai iron, iron grating, beautiful
maiti little
maka mug, fish-hook
maka (-ia, -a, -ina) toss, throw, put in place, pass by hand
mākā wild, untamed, mark
maka māminga sell the dummy
mākahi wedge, split, gabble
makahinga fall
makamaka scattered, toss, bushman's mattress, recite spell
makao shark tooth pendant, sprout of taro
makara depart, arrive
mākara head
makariri cold, winter, chill, frigid
makatiti staple with pegs, split with wedges
makau wife, husband, darling, bent
makawe hair, mane, cilia, feud
makere drop/be dropped, ceased, leave
makere atu get rid of
mākete market, bazaar
māketoiho macintosh, raincoat
maki invalid, monkey
maki (as prefix) impetuous act, without consultation
mākī marquee
makihea sinker
makimaki monkey, ugly, skin disease
mākini serrated, jagged edge

makinui gorilla
makitaunu tease, deceive, riddle
makitohene uncalled-for insult
mako mako shark, shark's tooth, peeled
makoa (tai) low tide
makoha revealed, loosened, opened
mākohakoha soft-skinned, open minded, relaxed
makohu misty
mākoi shell, sharpened point, comb
makomako bellbird, wineberry, external remedy for rheumatism
mākona satisfied
makorea survivor
māku for me
mākū wet, damp, moisture, soppy
mākākū damp
mākura light red
mākurakura glowing, pink
mākutu bewitched, black magic
mākutu, tiro - stare, cast magic spell, accursed
mama percolator
māmā mother, lightweight
mamae pain, stress, hardship
mamaha steam
mamahu soothe
mamaku black-tree fern
māmangu black ink, jet black
mamao distant, distance, remote
mamaoa steam, cooked food, vapour
mamaru canoe-sail, lush growth, dark bank of cloud
mamate depressed
mamau hold (judo etc.), wrestling
māminga cunning, trick, deceitful
mamingo kata beaming with smiles
māmore bare, without branches
mamāoa atu furthest
mana integrity, charisma, prestige
māna for him/her, he will, she will
mana tangata human rights
mana tōpū incorporated society
mana tuku right to give
mana wahine women's right
manaaki(-tia) care for, entertain, show respect, hospitality
manaha open plain
manahau playful, cheerful
mānahenahe cleared country
manahua open like a flower
manaia carved beaked figures, seahorse, raft
manako(-hia) hope for, desire, set the heart on
manapōuri black stone
manarū ecstatic
manatā copyright
manatu anxious, sad, homesick
manatū authority, ministry
manatunga keepsake, heirloom, souvenir, memento
manauri dark coloured
manawa heart, breath, emotion, bowels
mānawa(-tia) welcome with pleasure, chanted prayers of blessing
mānawa ring finger, mangrove, prayer to keep good fortune
manawa kiore last breath
manawa popore considerate, attentive, careful
manawanui brave, patient, self-possessed

manawapā frugal, tight-fisted
manawareka satisfied, thrilled
manawarere impulsive
manawarū rapt, edgy, anxious
manawatū cardiac arrest, heart attack
manawawera angry chant, anger, frantic
manehau hen and chicken fern
manehu fern, scented plant
manene immigrant, migrant, pilgrim
manga stream, branch
mangā barracouta, spotted dogfish, gummy shark
māngai mouth, spokesman
Māngai Kāwanatanga Ambassador, High Commissioner
mangakino dredge for lake shellfish
mangamanga puzzling
mangamutu desolate, abandoned
māngaro floury, starch, ripe
mangaru mongrel
mangawai brook, stream
mangeao tree, flooring timber
mangemange creeper, bushman's mattress
mangeo itch, stinging, irritating
māngere lazy, lackadaisical
māngere hōnia lazy in extreme
māngina ephemeral, short-lived
māngiongio chilblain
mangō gummy shark, spotted dogfish
mangō ihunui broadsnouted shark
mangō pare hammerhead shark, kōwhaiwhai pattern
mangō pounamu great blue shark
mangō ripi thresher shark
mangō tara spiney dogfish
mangō ururoa great white shark
māngohe spongy, malleable
Mangoroa Milky Way
mangu black, swarthy
mangumangu ink, ugly
mania slippery, lubricate, brown gecko
mānia plain country, plateau
mānianía slippery
mānihi(-tia) constrict, flatten
manioro causing trouble, making a noise
maniua manure
mano thousand, large crowd, multitude
manomano horde, innumerable
manono shrub
manowai stream in flood
manu bird, kite
mānu to float, launch
manu aute kite of paper mulberry
manu tīoriori brave warrior, soloist
manuao man o' war, battleship
manuhiri guest, visitor
mānuka tea-tree
mānukanuka doubt, anxiety, fearful, worried
manukura chiefs in council
manurere aeroplane, kite
manutahi lean-to, single set of rafters
manutaki sentry, doyen, dean of university
manu-uku clay pigeon
manuware stupid, farcical
manuwhiri guest
maoa cooked, ripe
maoka cooked

M

maomao blue maomao, sweep fish
māori ordinary, natural, fresh
māori, wai - fresh water
māoriori at ease
Māoritanga Māori culture
māota dark green, chlorophyll, fresh food
māota, hau - chlorine
māpara resinous wood, pine resin
mapere marble, conscription, lottery
māpere middle finger, cutty grass, toss
mapi map, exude
māpihi personal adornments
māpo great cormorant
māpou red matipo(u)
māpouriki darkness
mapu mob, sigh, hum
mapu(-a) flow freely, mop up, pump
mara marinated, dirty, scraps
māra cultivation, garden, orchard
māra waina vineyard
mara, e -! old man!, dear me! (sarcastic)
marae area in front of meeting house, generous
marahea poor quality
marahihi molasses
maraka maracas
mārakerake clear, desert place, clearing in bush
marakihau sea-monster
Marako Morocco
marama moon, month
mārama informed, lucid, apparent
mārama noa self-explanatory
maramara wood-chips, bits
maramataka calendar
māramatanga awareness, explanation
maranga rise up, raise sail, begin
marangai east wind, stormy weather
mārangaranga spring up and down, arise
marara umbrella, scattered
mararī butterfish
marau topic, subject of sentence, syllabus
mārau fork, pronged stick, spiked dredge
marau-ā-iwi social studies
mare phlegm, cough
mare heihei whooping cough
mare motu whooping cough
marea many, commoners
mārehe stickler, fussy person
māreikura female supernatural being, noble lady
maremare cough, phlegm, catch a chill
maremare tai agar, jellyfish
mārena wedding, matrimony
mārenatanga marriage service, nuptials
marere free, extras, sundries (cricket), fall down
maretire martyr
marewa set out, raise up
mariao, mate - ulcer, sores
mārie peaceful, quietly, restful, appeased
marihi precious
mārika careful, exactly
mārika, āe - well well, you don't say!
Marikena American
maringi spilt, overflow, flux, slop
māripi carving knife

mārire quiet, gentle, discreet
maro(-hia) girdle, loincloth, sanitary napkin
mārō secure, stiff, headstrong
maro hukahuka gird loins for combat
mārō tonu straight on
mārohirohi brave, strong, valour
maroke dry, arid, parched
maromaro knickers, panties
mārōrō strong, able-bodied
maroro flying fish
marowae pantyhose
maru abundance, shelter, safety in numbers
marū bruised, crushed
mārū gentle, white tea tree
maruahiahi late evening
maruāpō aspiration, dream
maruhau windbreak
marumaru offering shade, sunshade
mata fresh, sharp blade, uncooked, eye
matā lead bullet, shotput, flint
mata ahutoru 3D surface
mata kai kutu warrior
matā tuhua obsidian
mataaho window, pure, bright
mataara attentive, vigilant, call of the watchman, witness
mataheu razor blade
mātahi autumn months
mataī mataī tree
mātai inspect, study, watch
mātāika first victim in battle
mātaitai seafood, tasting salty
matakahi wedge
matakana watchful, probation officer
matakawa distasteful
matakerepō blind
mātaki review, peek, watch
mātakitaki inspect, observe
matakite seer, second sight, intuition
mataku afraid, fear, scared, timorous
mataku apiapi claustrophobia
matakupenga belly fat, basket fungus, pockmarked timber
matakūrae headland
mātakutaku scarecrow
matamata point, top, sudden, source
mātāmua first-born child, primary
mātāmuri last-born child
mātangatanga hanging loose
matangerengere embarrassed, cramped, numb, red-faced
matangi wind, breeze
mātāngohi first victim
matangurunguru nervous, raising goose-bumps
mātāniho teeth marks
matanui open to the sun
mātao cold, frigid, infertile
mataora life cycle, alive, tattooing chisel
matapaki discuss, discussion
matapihi window
matapiko mean, stingy, miserly
matapō blind
matapo black shag, black teal
matapopore solicitous, caring for, retrench, guardian
matapōuri downcast, sad
mātāpuna source
matara unravelled, far away, rough, prickly
matāra watchful, alert

mātārae prominent headland, chief
matarau many-pointed fishing spear, polyhedron
matarehi mattress
matarehu hazy
matarekereke numb
Matariki Pleiades stars, northeast wind
matarua double-edged
matata fissure, crevice
mātātā shrub *Gloxinia*, fernbird
mātātaki challenge
matatara dam, weir
matatau competent, expert at, fully aware
matatiki resource, spring of water, headwaters
matatini complex
mātātoa fearless, vigorous
mātātuhi image, prophet, forecaster
matau hook, right hand side, sedge grass
mātau us, we
mātau(-ria) know, understand, skilful
mātauranga information, knowledge, education
mātauranga huaota botany
mātauranga kōhungahunga pre-school education
mātauranga koiora biology
mātauranga matū chemistry
mātauranga matawhenua geography
mātauranga noho-ā-iwi sociology
mātauranga tāuhu continuing education
mātauranga tikanga tangata anthropology
mātauranga whānui general knowledge
matawaenga undecided, dilemma
matawai stare at
mātāwai source, inspector, scanner
matawai roro brain scanning
matawaia brim with tears
mātāwaka ancestral canoe, ethnic origin
matawhāiti vigilant
Matawhānui Māori University Teachers' Association
matawhawhati unexpected, sudden
Matawhero Mars
matawī rushes
mate death, sickness, problem, defect
mate apokai bulimia
mate āraikore AIDS
mate ate kakā hepatitis
mate horokiwa muscular dystrophy
mate huka diabetes
mate hūkiki epilepsy, spastic
mate, i - died
mate iotanga paralysis
mate iotuarā polio
mate kikohunga gangrene
mate kōwhai hepatitis, yellow jaundice
mate, kua - dead
mate manawa coronary
mate Māori psychosomatic illness
mate mariao ulcer
mate moana lost at sea
mate moraru kupu dyslexia
mate ngōtahi bronchitis
mate paiori Parkinson's Disease
mate paipai sexually transmitted disease, gonorrhoea

mate pōrangi psychiatric disorder, mania, madness
mate pūira kehe mongolism, Down's syndrome
mate puku digestive disorder
mate pukupuku cancer
mate pukupuku taiawa cervical cancer
mate ringarau kleptomania, shoplifting
mate roma mimi cystitis, infection of urinary tract
mate rurutoto leukemia
mate toto tepekore haemophilia
mate warawara drug habit
mate wareware amnesia
mate weu whākau kākā appendicitis
mate whatukuhu genito-urinary disease
mate whawhati tata sudden death, emergency
matekai hungry, starve
matekiri puzzled, disappointed
matemate general ill-health
mātene mutton
matenga rawa death
mātenga head
mātengatenga cramped, numbed
matenui(-tia) desire
mateoha in love
materoto miscarriage, spontaneous abortion, stillbirth
matewai thirsty
māti matches, type of spear, fruit of kōtukutuku
mati whaiira decimal point, decimal place
mātia drive in stakes, wedge, spear, die away
mātiatia sand tussock
matihao sprig, cleats
matihe sneeze
mātihetihe sand fescue
matika stand up, fish-hook
matikao in bud
matikara finger, toe, fingernail, handspan
matike stand up, get up
mātiki mattock
matiko go down
matikuku finger, toe, claw, hoof
matimati fingers, toes
mātini, rua - nest in hollow tree
matiwani nail-file
mato growing well, crisp
matoe split open
mātohatoha spread around, divided up
matomato flourishing, agreeable
mātoretore coarse, rough
mātoro woo, stretch out
mātoru crowded
mātotoru thick, strong (e.g. tea), dense
mātou us, we
matū matter (science), chemical substance, fatty food
matū piere nuclear material
matua main stem, parent, first, army battalion
matua kēkē uncle
matua whāngai foster-parent
matuawhāpuku red cod, scorpion fish
mātuhi fern bird, needle, stitch
mātuhituhi bush wren
matuku white-faced heron
māturuturu trickle, distil
mātūtū convalescent, hospital ward
mau fixed, comprised, overtaken

M

mau(-ria) bring, carry, capture
māu for you
mau herehere prisoner, imprison
mau i te . . . caught by . . .
mau ki te . . . caught hold of . . .
mau kākahu wear clothes
mau pai caught on the full
mau rawa addicted
mau tangetange guilty, captured red-handed
mau taringa ear pendant
māua we two (not you), he/she and I, him/her and me, us
mauāhara hatred, abhor, loathing
mauāhua film negative
mauhere(-a) imprison, convict, prisoner
mauherehere arrested, accused
mauhoro contagious
mauī left-hand side, cat's cradle
māuiui tired, weary, unwell, sick
mauka dry
maukai take-aways
maukino(-tia) despise, ill-treat
maukoro shrub
mauku hen and chickens fern
maumahara remember, memorise
maumau waste
maunga mountain, act of carrying
maunga-ā-rongo peace-making
maunu drawn from belt, taken off
maunu(-hia) loosen, float
māunu bait, grey duck
maupoi held ball
maupū good catch
mauri life principle, special character
mauru eased, satisfied, quiet
maurua seam, join
mautere blotter
mauti vegetation, grass, fodder
Mautīni Mt Eden Prison
mawehe be separated
mawete loose
māwhaiwhai spider's web, cobweb
mawhara wide apart
mawharu muddy, boggy
māwhatu curly hair, ringlets
māwhe faded, pale colour, dogskin cloak
mawhera open, widespread
māwhero pink
māwhero tea pale pink
mawheto loosened
mawhiti leap, skip, glance
māwhiti white dogskin cloak
māwhitiwhiti grasshopper, hop about
me and (between nouns), if, with, added to
me te while
me te mea as if
me + *verb* please . . ., it is necessary to . . . (polite request)
mea thing, article, so and so
mea(-tia, meinga) say, do, think
mea tonoa requirements
mea tūtuki fait accompli, already done
mea whakatangi musical instrument
mea āpiti supplement
mēa mayor
mea, nō nā i te - because, the fact being, when
meake nei hereinafter
meamea used to giving orders, bastard
meha measure
mehameha set apart, lonely

meho untrue, rubbish
mēhua measure, meter, tape-measure
mei if, according to
meia mayor
meiha-tianara major-general
meinga be done, be thought, deemed
meinga ake turn on (power), switch on
meinga iho turn off (power), switch off
meka tawhiti handcuffs
mekameka chain, linking, rope ladder
meke(-a) punch, clobber
mekemeke box (fight), make a fist
mekore in a little while, a little more
mema member, cast of play
memeha dissolve, sickly, decaying, forgotten
memenga wither
mēnā if
menamena amendment
menemene smile, grin, grimace
meneti minute
mēnetia manager
menge withered
mēra mail
mere short flat club
merekara miracle
Meremere morning star in winter
Meremere Tū Ahiahi Venus in the evening
merengi melon
meroiti little, mini, insignificant
mētera medal, alloy
metemea as if
mīere honey, golden syrup
miha shoots of fern, descendant
Miha Catholic eucharist service, Mass
miha pakeke whale calf
miha, au - heavy sea
mihamiha put out shoots, start of growth
mihana mission
mīharo wonder at, incredible
mihi(-a) greet, admire, respect, congratulate
mihingare missionary, Anglican
mīhini machine, engine, motor
mīkara saw-tooth knife, serrated edge
mimi urine, urinate
mimingo wrinkled
mimingo kata beam from ear to ear
mimiti dry up, devalue, lessen
mina wish for, feel inclined, fancy
minamina long for
mine gather together
minemine assembled
mingimingi shrub juniper
mingo wrinkled, curled, crinkled
miniki mink
minita(-tia) minister, to minister, pastor
miniti minute (of time)
mira mill, myrrh, toothed, saw-edged knife
miraka milk
miraka tepe yoghurt
miri(-a) massage, rub, graze, tranquillise by touch
mirimeta millimetre
mirimiri fondle, stroke, traditional massage
miriona million
miririta millilitre
miriti millet

miro thread, twist thread, brown pine, filament
miromiro bubble, pied tomtit
mita pronunciation, idiomatic speech
miti(-kia) soak up, lick, lap, weapon-grade stone
miti moana backwash, ebbing tide, undertow
mīti meat
mīti paera stew
mitimiti lick, shellfish
mō for, about, apropos, in regard
mō te wā ad hoc, temporary
moa extinct bird
moa, mate-ā- dead as a dodo
mōaho sweet tasting, steeped in fresh water
moana lake, sea
moana, kei te - at sea
moananui ocean
moari swing, giant strides (game)
moata early
moe(-a) sleep, marry, doze
moe māori de facto marriage
moe nanu talk in one's sleep, troubled sleep
moe pō dream, daydream, diurnal animal
moe puku concubinage, de facto marriage
moe tāhae adultery
moehewa dream
moemiti praise, give thanks
moemoeā dream, fancy, hallucination
moenga bed, marriage
moeoneone bass, groper, type of grub
mohani sand down, chafe, fern root
mōhanihani smooth-faced, matt finish
mohe soft, supple
mōheuheu brushwood
mohimohi pilchard, mountain trout
mōhinuhinu varnish, glaze
mōhio(-tia) + ki know, intelligent, clever
mōhiti ring, spectacles
moho stupid, moron
mohoa up to now
mohoao hermit, uncouth
mōhou for you, about you
mōhua yellowhead (bird)
mōhukihuki thirst for, yearn for
mōhungahunga crumbling
moī call to pet animal, turn sour
moka end, bits, remains, caterpillar
mōkā muzzle animal
mōkai office assistant, pet slave
mōkau plain, undecorated
mōkehu white claystone, young fern fronds
mokemoke lonely, forlorn, secluded
mōkete mortgage
mōketekete express surprise, express annoyance
moki trumpeter fish, scented plant
mōki raft, surfing, toboggan
mōkī package, bundle
mōkihi sledge, parcel, move stealthily, raft
moko logo, tattoo, lizard, (short for) mokopuna
mokomoko head, skink, gecko, preserved head
mokopuna grandchild, young generation

mokoroa huhu bug, vegetable caterpillar, mainland
mokowhiti heartbeat, arrythmia, jump, herring
mokowhiti kakī carotid pulse
mokowhiti ringa wrist pulse
mōku for me
momi(-a) suck, draw on cigarette, enter with difficulty
momo species, batch, hereditary trait
momo āhuatanga wide spectrum
momohe soft, supple, gentle, kindly eyes
mōmona fat, fertile, obese, fond of
momori smooth, bare, bald, toothless
momotu(-kia) move away, set free, disconnect
momotuhi typeface, font
momou wrestle
mōna for him/her, about him/her
monaki monk
monamona joint (body), knot, knuckle
mōnehunehu misty, gentle rain, indistinct
monemone smooth
mongamonga crushed, smashed to bits, marrow (vegetable)
moni money
moni hua proceeds
moni iti petty cash
moni mātua principal sum
mōniania set teeth on edge
mono plug, caulk, spell to disable the enemy
monoa desire
monokuihi mongoose
mora mole (animal)
more headland, worn smooth, net value
mōrearea dangerous, dreary, gloomy
mōrehu survivor
moremore smooth, bald, open space
morihana carp, goldfish
mōrihariha disgusting, horrible
mōrikarika dirty, horrible, unpleasant
morimori(-a) handle carelessly, nurse infant, embrace
Moriori original Chatham Islander
mōro mulberry tree
moroiti (*see* meroiti) little, germ, microbe
moroki ongoing
moroki noa nei up to now
moruki supple
mōrunga lifted up, high up
mōtā mortar (gun)
motatau talk to oneself, ventriloquist
mote suck, gasp
mōtea wan, pale
mōteatea poems, laments, apprehensive
motēra motel
moto(-kia) punch
mōtoi ear ornament, gape, stare
motokā car
motopaika motorbike
motorore lorry, truck
motu island, cut off, broken off
motu(-hia, -kia) to separate, wound, snap, cut
motuhake private, special, extra, independent
motuhuka iceberg

motukā car
mōtukutuku lice
mōu for you
moua mower
mouku fern
moumou waste, to no purpose
mōunu bait
moutere island
mōwai calm sea, gentle, moistening
mōwhiti spectacles, goggles
mōwhititahi monocle
mū silent, draughts (game)
mua in front, formerly
muanga first born, eldest
muera mule
muha savage, belligerent
muhani faded, insult
muheama museum
mūhika music
muhukai inattentive
mūhuki blunt
mui(-a) swarm around, infest
muimui small
muka flax fibre
mūkiore muskrat
muku(-a) wipe, cloth, erase, rub, delete
mumu tāniko pattern, boisterous wind, brave warrior
mūmū complain, chafer beetle, depressed
mumura flare, glow
mumutawa ladybird
muna(-ia) gossip, tell secretly, darling
mura o te ahi front line, heat of the battle
muramura smoulder
mūrau famous, byword
mūrere clever, cunning
muri after, behind, kitchen area, north, breeze
muri ahiahi twilight thoughts
murihau breeze
mūrihi muesli
murikōkai back of the head
murimanu secondary wife
murimuri aroha nostalgia
muringa last born, afterwards
muritai sea-breeze
muriwai backwater
muru(-a) wipe, pluck, plunder, absolve
murunga remission (of penalty)
murunga hara absolution, pardon, remission (justice)
mutu finished, cease, end, finish
mutu anō that's all
mutu, ka - also
mutumutu cut short, mutilate, stump of limb
mutunga end, ultimate
mutunga kore eternal, infinite

N

na now then, d'ya see (common interjection)
nā from, belonging to, by way of, satisfied, rested
nā wai? who did it?, who owns it?, who is responsible?
nā wai tāu?! who told you?! (sceptical)
naenae mosquito, out of breath
naeroa mosquito
nahe alone
nahea? when?
nāhi nurse
naihi knife
naihi piko clasp knife, jackknife
nairona nylon
naka over there by you
nākahi snake
nakonako decorate, anxious thoughts
nāku mine, my own, belonging to me
nama debt, number, invoice
nama waea telephone number
namu sandfly, birthmark
nāna belonging to him/her
nanahi yesterday
nanakia clever, cunning, treacherous, fierce
nanamu tingle, irritate, smart, glitter
nanao (naomia) lay hold of, search inner wisdom, reach down
nanapi cling to, tweak
nanati throttle
nanekoti nanny goat
nanenane goat, rotted kūmara
nanī wild turnip, noisy, Māori cabbage
nao(-mia) lay hold of
naonao midge
nati(-a) nut, to pinch, choke, strangle
nāti headstrong, untamed
natinati encircle with rope, squeeze
natu(-a) scratch, stir, rip out
nāu your, yours
nau mai welcome
nauhea rascal
nawe complaint, on tenterhooks, scar
nē? isn't it? (implies question)
nēhā? isn't that so?
nehe long ago, old man!
neherā ancient times, time immemorial
nēhi(-tia) nurse, to nurse
nehu(-a) bury, dust, powder
nehunga burial
nei here, this (connected with person speaking)
neinei spiderwood tree, stretch, waggle
nekeneke manoeuvre, shift up
neketai neck-tie
neketana nectarine
neketarini nectarine
neneti toy dart

nenewha doze off, sun set
nēra nail
neti net, a dart
netipaora netball
netipōro netball
newha doze
niao gunwale, edge of instrument
niho tooth, gear (engine), point
niho rei canine tooth, eye tooth, tusk
niho roa tusk, fang
nihomeka sprocket
nihoniho incompatible, quarrelsome, shoots
nīkau palm
niko(-a) put rope around, coil about
ninihi steep, sneak along, neap tide
niti toy dart, knit
niu tell future, ceremonial pole, dress timber
niupepa newspaper
niwha resolute, bold, barb
nō of, belonging to
nō namata time honoured, from ancient times
noa free from tapu, spontaneous
noaiho quite, just, only, mundane
nohanga seat, sitting place, session
nōhea? from where?
nohi nosey, forest herb
nohinohi small, petty, wee
noho(-ia) sit, live in, remain
noho-ā-iwi race relations
noho aukati dock (of courtroom)
noho hītengitengi squat
noho hū inactive
noho whiu sin bin
nohoanga seat, habitation, reservation
nohoia occupied
nohopuku fast from food, silent, tacit, inertia (science)
noke worm, small
nōku my, mine
nōna his, hers
nōnahea? when?
nōnāianei just now, modern, up to date
nōnakuanei little while ago
nonakuara little while ago
nōnamata long ago
nōnānahi yesterday
nōnānoanei just recently, from then
nōnaoake day before yesterday
nonapō last night
nōnatahirā day before yesterday
none consume, waste, nun
noni crooked, bend, hook, vegetable oil
nono buttocks, bum, vagina
nonohi small (*pl.*)
nonoke wrestle, struggle, scrum
nōtemea because
noti (nōtia) tighten headrope, strangle, contract
nōu yours
nōwhea? where from?
nui amount, big, many, size, volume
nui, ka - adequate, enough
nui noa atu more than sufficient
nuinga majority, quantity
nuka(-ia) deceive, trick
nukarau(-tia) deceive, outwit, sly, trick
nuke margin indent, crooked
nuku(-hia) move up, increase, indent, nature
nukuhanga extension

nukunuku atu deport
numi(-a) pass behind, fold, pleat
numi raima cement-mixer
nunui big (*pl.*), large size
nunumi to disappear, pass behind, destruction
nūpepa newspaper

NG

ngā the (*pl.*)
ngā (ngāngā) to breathe, inhale, beak
ngaehe rustling noise, murmur
ngaeke crack, rip
ngāekieki discharge liquid
ngaengae heel, umbilical cord, wheeze
ngāeo freshwater mussel, Cook's Turban shellfish
ngaere to quiver, roll, soft, ripe
ngaeroa mosquito
ngahau games, entertain, enjoyment, jovial, happy
ngahere forest
ngahora spread out, laid out
ngāhorohoro to fall, be plentiful, fall bit by bit, plus
ngahuru autumn, harvest abundance, ten
ngahurutanga decade
ngāi title of tribe
ngāi tāua we the people
ngaingai empty shells, sob, bivalve (shellfish)
ngaio coastal shrub, toothache remedy
ngākau heart, sentiment, vitals
ngākau kōpae disk drive unit
ngākau kōpaerua double disk drive
ngākau pakeke heartless, cruel
ngākau pūremu lust, prurient, concupiscence
ngākaukore apathy, fainthearted
ngākaunui keen, proud, close to the heart
ngakeke creak
ngaki(-a) cultivate, dig, avenge
ngaki mate seek vengeance
ngaki taru pull weeds
ngaki- (prefix) intensifier (e.g. ngakimōwhiti = jump suddenly, ngakihōhoro = dash needlessly)
ngākihi limpet, rock oyster
ngakinga garden plots, cultivation
ngako grease, fat, suet, essence
ngako kau tallow
ngakototo cholesterol
ngaku shred, strip
ngakuru drop off, set (of fruit)
ngana be eager, persevering
nganga fruit stone, hailstone, core of boil
ngāngā gasp, breathe heavily
ngangahau zealous, active
ngangana glowing red, bluster
ngao adzed timber, palate
ngaoki creep, crawl
ngaoko itch, budge, tickle
ngaore smelt fry, succulent
ngāpara resinous wood for torches
ngārahu black dye, war dance, commander, take counsel
ngarangara ice-plant
ngārara reptile, bacteria, computer virus
ngārara moroiti germ, microbe

ngare(-a) send, close relative
ngārehu ash, cinders
ngaro lost, missing, absent, blowfly
ngaro noa self-defeating
ngaromanga disappearance, destruction
ngaru wave of sea, corrugation
ngaru taitoko tidal wave
ngarue (ngāruerue) shake, wave
ngaruiti microwave (oven)
ngata satisfied, fulfilled, snail
ngātahi jointly, together
ngātata split open
ngatete crackle
ngāti . . . people of . . . (used with tribal name)
ngau(-a) bite, gnaw, infect
ngau whiore incest, inbreeding
ngāueue to shake, quiver
ngaungau erode, teething ring, chew
ngautuarā back-biting, libel
ngāwari easy, lenient
ngawē yelp
ngawhā bloom, discharge
ngāwhāriki hot pools, boiling springs
ngawhewhe torn, worn out, exhausted
ngawhi be punished, suffer penalty
ngawī yelp
ngē noisy, screech
ngehe kelpfish, marblefish
ngeingei extending
ngene tuberculous cyst
ngenge weary, tired, fatigued
ngengere grunt, snarl, whine
ngengeti cicada shell
ngeri chant with actions, rough cloak, rap
ngeungeu squirm, writhe
ngia like, to be alike
ngiha burn, igneous
ngingiha burn, combustion
ngingio withered, cackle
ngira needle
ngita secure, fixed, thorn
ngoengoe screech
ngohe lithe, tender, agreeable
ngohi fish (general term)
ngohi moana whale (general term)
ngoi strength, energy
ngoikore weak, frail, passive
ngoikoretanga defect, flaw, shortcoming
ngoingoi crawl, old lady, creep
ngoio asthma, whistling sound
ngōiro conger eel
ngōki creep
ngonga beaten, crushed
ngongengonge deformed
ngongo suck, dimple, siphon, sinus
ngongohā snorkel
ngongohau jib-sail, bow of canoe
ngongopuata pipette
ngongore blunt, gummy
ngongoro snore, snort
ngore pompom cloak, entice, soft
ngorengore rubbery, young eel, smelt
ngoru slack, hanging in loops, worm-like
ngorungoru, pēpē - mashed thoroughly
ngota atom, piece, fragment
ngotangota iratuki radio isotope
ngōtata ion
ngote(-a) suck, suction, little bit
ngotewai syringe

ngoto permeate, head, poke deeply, click
ngōungou mature, fully ripened, well-cooked
nguha fierce, fight, rage
ngungu graze, ricochet, overt, tree
ngūngū devour, dumb person
ngunguru rumble, grunt, groan
nguru flute, grunt, chant/prayer for a successful marriage
ngutu lip, beak, mouthpiece
ngutu pare wry-bill
ngutu pārera flintlock musket, type of flax
ngutu pī babbler, gasbag, tattler
ngutuawa river mouth, estuary
ngutungutu gossipy, tasty, heated exchange
nguture blunt, sea fish, used, secondhand
ngututawa green beetle

O

o of, belonging to
ō fit in space, provisions, struggle into
oati(-tia) oath, take an oath, pledge
oha last words, inheritance, greeting, generous
ōhākī dying speech, legacy
ōhanga cradle, family home, economics
ohaoha economics, generous, plentiful
ohi childhood
oho wake suddenly, be aroused, alarmed
ohomauri be startled
ohonga surprise, shock
ohorangi christening, dedication
ohorere suddenly, emergency, spark off
ohotata sudden
ohu(-a) working bee, crowd around
ohu-ā-iwi iwi authority
Ohu Kaimoana Fisheries Commission
Ōhua half moon
oi muttonbird, tremble
ōi quicksands, shout
oinga childhood
oioi shake gently
oka machete, dagger, butcher knife
okaoka stab repeatedly, split off, lay fish open
oke(-a) squirm, struggle, eager
ōkena organ (musical instrument)
okeoke struggle, restless, writhe, small shark
okewa halo, rainbow spectrum
oki oak tree
ōkiha bullock, ox, barren sow
oko bowl, receptacle, basin, dish
oko whakaroto stethoscope
okooko parry a blow, cradle in arms
ōku my, mine
oma(-kia) to run, escape, scoot
oma tutuki home run
oma wawe going too soon (racing)
omanga running race
omaoma track for racing
omaoma-a-Tōhē marathon
omareta omelette
omoomo gourd
ōna his, hers
onāianei of present time
onamata of ancient time, historic
one beach, sand, earth, soil
onehunga alluvial soil
onekura poor soil
onemata dark volcanic soil, topsoil
onematua loam
oneone earth, soil, land, beach
onepunga light poor soil
onepū sand
onetai sandy, volcanic soil
ōnewa greystone, stone club

onga vibrate, shake about, churn
ongaonga edible nettle, irritated, sandfly, lacebark, dog-tooth pattern
onioni wriggle, sexual intercourse
ono six
ono(-kia) to plant
opa(-ina) throw, pelt
ōpapa mineral
ope working group, company
opeti crowded
opuru cram, stuff, gorge, overcrowded
ora alive, well, satisfied, servant, slave
ora matomato in best of health
oraiti barely escaped, safe on base
oranga health, welfare, safety, sanitation
oranga ake destiny
oranoa barely escaped
orapito escape danger
ōrau percent
ore poke with rod, drill, quiver, alarmed
oreore shake, fidget, incite, vibrate
orewa tawapou tree
ori to wave, agitate
oriori sleep-time chant, lullaby, rhythmical chanting
ōrite even number, equal, dead heat, weighing scales
ōriwa olive
oro(-hia) echo, eerie sound, phoneme
oro rangi portable player
orokotīmatanga very beginning
oruoru second-hand, swampy
ota(-ina) eat raw food, scraps, otter
ōta order
otaota herbs, garbage, weeds
ōti oats
oti atu gone for good
oti te pure purged
otiia but, however
otimira oatmeal
otinga solution of problem, rounding off
otirā but, however
otitōriama auditorium
ōu your, yours
ōuenuku rainbow
oumu oven
ouou few
owha last words, inheritance
ōwhiro new moon

P

pā (-ngia, -hia) touch, infect, tag (game), block up
pā stockaded village, stockade
pā, e – ! term of address to male elder, Father, Sir etc.
pā kahawai spinner
pā ki relating to, touching on, relevant, affect
pā mai impact
pae(-a) lie across, cast ashore, arrive in numbers
pae ara kerb, pavement
pae maunga mountain range, massif
pae ū goal line
pae whiu sinbin
paeārau shipwrecked
paeata line of symmetry, mirror line
paekaha gums
pāeke speaking order – locals first, innings
paekete pikelet
paekiri narrow flat space, beam, layer of skin
paekura lost property, flotsam
paemanu collar-bone, thwart of canoe, bird perch
paemate mourners
paenaena sunbathe, comfortable slipper
pāeneene bask in sun
paenga threshold, cross-piece, stranding
paeoru disco
paepae orator's bench, panel
paepae āwhā threshold, door-step
paekuru anvil
paepae maitai anvil
paepae para rubbish bin
paepae pēpi potty
paepae porotio ice-cube tray
paepae poto doorsill, front step
paeparu mudguard
paera(-tia) boil
paerata pilot
Paerau limbo, hundred horizons
paerewa arch of foot, achievement standard
paeroa southeast, range of hills
paetahi beginner's level
paetini poison
paewae door-sill
paewai driftwood, batten, jaw/shoulder bone, noble person
paewhenua expanse of land, weeds
pahaki short distance away
pāhanahana blush, glow, use red ochre
pāhao fish trap, windbreak
pāhau beard, whiskers
pāhauhau windbreak
pahawa smeared
paheke slip, ornamental threads, brush past
pāhekeheke unstable, ill-founded, slippery
paheko combine
pahemo pass by, miss

pahi bus, coach, ended
pahī group of visitors, camp
pāhi boss, pass, purse, parcel
pāhia(-tia) slap, mash
pāhihi passenger, passageway, corridor
pāhīhī dribble, spring of water
pahika gone further, exceed
pahiketepaoro basketball
pāhiko power station
pahinipi parsnip
pahiri parsley
pāhiwihiwi uneven, in ridges, kelp-fish
pāho broadcast, spread news
pahoa kākahu fashion designer
pāhoahoa back of head, headache
pahora exposed, spread out
pāhorehore scraped clean
pāhoro capture by storm
pahū hooter, wooden gong, explode
pahū hauwai hydrogen bomb
pahū karihi nuclear bomb
pāhua rob
pahūaketanga blow out
pahuhu slip off, speedy
pāhūhū to pop corn, bombardment
pahuka foaming
pāhuki brushwood-fence
pahupahu bark, emit
pahure come into sight, pass by
pahūtanga bombardment
pai good, excellence, quality, virtue
pai(-ngia) to like, approve, agree, bless
pai ai which is preferred
paia, whare - health clinic
paiaka root of tree
paihamu opossum
paihana pheasant, poison, basin
paihau beard, wing, projecting sides, winger
paihau, ika - catfish
paihautea lush undergrowth
paiheneti percent
paihere bundle, tie up, bind, compress, set
paiheretanga binding, book-binding
paihona bison
paikaka home-brew beer
paikea humpback whale
Paimārire religion of Te Ua, peaceful virtue
paina pine
pāinaina sunbathe, warm oneself, bask
paināporo pineapple
painga advantage, attribute
paipa pipe, hose
paipa ngongo syphon
paipai venereal disease, skin trouble
paipai ruaki bilious
paipapūroa blowpipe
Paipera Bible
paipōro piebald
pāiti to tip, low impact
paitini poison
paka dried food, bugger, weather-beaten
paka(-tia) quarrel, cook
pākā reddish, scorched
pāka box, park
pāka hiko electric battery
pākaha power stroke, press-stud
pākai protective screen
pākai-ahi fireplace
pākākā brown, dark orange, seal

pakake minke whale, kelp, weaving pattern
pakanga war, battle, campaign, hostilities
pākano seed pod, pine cone
pakapaka baked dry, belligerent, pork crackling, crisp
pakara smack lips, crow
pakarā unacceptable, out of place
pakari mature, self-assured, fully operational
pakaru broken, torn, wrecked
pākaru(-a) gush out, break out
pākarutanga breakdown, wreck, smash
pākati dog-tooth pattern
pakau wing, kite
pākaurua stingray
pakawai driftwood
pākawe shoulder strap
pakē ripping sound
Pākehā non-Māori, European
pākeho limestone, white clay
pākehokeho slippery
pakeke elder, adult, difficult, hard
pākeke follow on (sport)
pākēkē grate, scrape, sizzle
pakepake to grate
pakepakehā ghostly people, weird
paketai moana driftwood, flotsam
pākete bucket, packet
pāketi spaghetti
pakewa slip of the tongue, wandering, lonely
pākewakewa stumbling speech, syphilis
paki(-a) to slap, tap, narrative, kilt, buggy
pakiaka root of tree
pakihau fan, wing, fin
pakihi business, dried up, at lowest ebb
pākihi dig for roots, barren country
pākihikihi shallow
pakihitanga lowest tide
pakihiwi shoulder, ell cloth measure
pakihore shiftless, idle
pakikau wing, fin, cloak
pākiki inquisitive, nosey
pākikini pain, ache
pakimaero fairy story
pakini apostrophe, nip, nick, notch
pākini sting, sudden pain
pākinikini sore, hurt, spasm
pakipaki applause, dried head, dried food
pakipaki (pākia) to clap, keep in line
pākira bald, mistaken
pakiri te kata burst into laughter
pakitara wall, gossip, tell tales
pakitea dandruff
pakitua put behind one
pakituri, haere - go on foot, walk
pakitōne buckthorn
pākiwaha boastful, pectoral fins, windbag
pakiwaitara fairy story, scandal, fiction, mythology
pakiwara naked, scantily dressed
pakiwhara naked, venereal disease
pakō bang, blistered, pop
pakohe slate, dark grey
pakohu cavity, gap, chasm
pakoke random, pointless, aimless
pakoki toss up and down, distort

pakoko statue, dried up
pākoko childless
pakoko haere wander aimlessly
pakoro barren
pākoro store, storeroom
pākoromauti silo
pākoukou shoulder blade
paku matter in the eye, dried, scab, least bit
pakū explosion, resound, beat
pākūhā marriage gift, honeymoon
pakupaku small
pākura swamp hen, pūkeko, red sky, bad omen
pākuru percussion stick, rap, hit
pākūwhā marriage gift
pāmamae grieved, remorse, distress
pāmamao distant
pāmu farm
pāmu wēra sperm whale
pana spasm (omen), impetus
pana(-a, -ia) to shove, dismiss, send off (sports)
pana penihini petrol pump, bowser
pana tahi odd number
pana tamariki bring to birth, give birth
panahau pump
panana banana
panatahi odd number
pane head, header, postage stamp
pane kuini postage stamp
pane uruwhenua visa
panekākā rough in appearance, country bumpkin
paneke score, move forward, overtake
panekoti skirt, petticoat
panenehu fern
panga(-a, -ina) to throw, pass ball, aim at
panga puzzle, riddle
pānga effect, impact, dividend
panga kuti lawn mower
pangahono jigsaw puzzle
pangakupu crossword puzzle
pāngarau mathematics
pāngia e te mate ill, aegrotat
pango black
pangopango dark coloured
pangore immature, toddler
pangu punch, stopper, bung
panguru bass voice, gruff
pani(-a) orphan, smear
panihi punch (tool), make a notch, nick, cut
panikakā mustard
panikena mug, pannikin
panio banjo
Pāniora Spanish
panipani(-a) spread
panoho pole for punting
pānui(-tia) read aloud, advertise
pānui whakaata teletext
pānuitanga advertising
panuku move on, golf putter, scroll through
pānukunuku toboggan
panunu slide
pao(-a) beat, ditty, smash (tennis)
paoa smoke, struck
paoho alarmed, on alert
paoka fork, skewer
paopao(-a) hatch out, hit, tenderize, strip off bark
paora ball
paorangi thunderclap
paoro(-tia) crash into, echo
Pāpā Pope, father

papā(-ngia) explosive noise, impact
papa plank, base, field
Papa Atawhai Department of Conservation
papa autō magnetic field
papa pounamu calm
papa pukapuka bookshelf
papa pūkura badminton court
papa tākaro adventure playground, playing field
papa tiriwae stepping stone
papa toiake hip-bone
papa tupu/tipu Māori land in freehold title
papa waka car park
papa wetereo grammar book
papahoro unstable land, fall
pāpahu porpoise
papaī speargrass
papaihore buttocks
papakāinga original home, home base
papake whale meat
pāpaku shallow
papaku otaota grass grub
papakupu dictionary, glossary
papakura red glow, ominous sign, insect
papamā whiteboard
papamāene asphalt, silk, smooth surface
papamahi desk top, work station
papamuka linen, fibreglass
papanga layer, fabric, site, stratum
papangarua quilt, duvet
pāpango dark, black teal
papanui platform in tree, cloud ceiling, palm of the hand
pāpapa eggshell, husk, bran
papapātua food container
papapuata glass slide
paparaho deck
paparahua kitchen bench
pāparakauta public house
paparawhi clipboard
pāpāringa cheek (face)
paparite level, coplanar
papata ripples, cockroach, swarm
papatahi first base, first floor
papatairite level surface, flat surface
papatipu land with Māori title, ancestral home
papatoiake pelvis
papatua uncultivated soil
Papatūānuku Mother Earth
papatuhi tau numeric keyboard
papatuhituhi blackboard
papatupu land with Māori title
papi blind, puppy
papu pump
pāpuni dam, plug, staunch blood
pāpura purple
papāroa scarce
papī ooze, leak
para slime, small bits
para to clear bush
para, whai - have guts, plucky
pārae open country, shelter
paraehe prize
pāraerae sandal of flax
pāraha metal tool, computer tool
paraha something flat, pikelet
parahanga rubbish, jumbled
parahau justification (science), defence
paraheahea ugly, helpless
parāhi brass
parahou fern root
parahuka(-tia) strip

P

parahuti quick
parai(-tia) to fry, flapjack, frying pan
pārai screen, push back
paraihe prize, brush
paraikete blanket
paraire bridle, Friday
paraiti blight
paraka jersey, block
parakai scraps, eel-weir
parakaraka reddish kūmara, orange stone
parakete booty, plunder
paraketu scavenge
parakimete blacksmith
parakipere blackberry
parakipīhi pilot whale
parakitihi practice, rehearsal
parakuihi breakfast
parama plumber
paramanawa refreshments
paramino palamino horse
paramu plum
pārana barium
parangia overcome by sleep
parani brandy, brand, verandah
parani(-tia) brand
pārao pharaoh
parāoa bread, flour, whale, whalebone weapon
parāoa kinikini dumpling
parāoa parai scone
parāoa rewena yeast bread
parāoa takakau damper bread
parāone brown
parapara offal, excrement
pararahi flat area
pararāwaha mutter
pararē shout, bawl
pararehe shout
parareka variety of potato
pararutiki paralytic
parata whirlpool demon
paratai current, tidal drift
parataniwha spreading plant
paratau semen, roe
paratawhiti orchid
paratē maize
paratiki plastic
paratinaku loiter
paratohe fry of snapper
paratūtae sewage
paratī spurt, squelch
paratī atu depart
pārau(-a) seize, enslave
parau(-tia) plough, tell lies, disloyal
parauri dark colour, dark skinned
parawaha spit, bits of food
parawai cloak with decorated border
parawera burnt-off land, south wind
parawhenua flood, tsunami
parawhiti radiation
pare(-a) discard, banish, headband, carved lintel
pāre barley
pare taua green-leaf headband
parehau air resistance
parehua balcony, terrace
pārekareka pleasant, comical, recreation, spotted shag
parekohu overcast, darken
parekura battlefield, bloodbath
Pāremata Parliament
Pāremata Kotahitanga o ngā Iwi o te Ao United Nations
pāremoremo stammer, hesitate in speech
parenga river bank, protection
pārengarenga leggings

parengo red seaweed
pareone mudbanks
parepare defences, palisade, gills, shin pads
pārera mallard, grey duck
pārerarera plantain, young godwit
paretai riverbank, washboard
paretao fern
parete Brussels sprouts
pārete spurs, tow
pāreti porridge
pāreti waiwai gruel
pari bodice, cliff, high tide
pari-uma bra
pariha/parihe parish
pāringa handball
paripari(-a) buffet, precipitous
parirau wing
parito heart of plant
paritū steep, sheer
pāroherohe relaxed, shrivelled
paroiwi bone
paronga furlong
pārongo stethoscope, information
parore mangrove fish
pāroro threatening clouds, howling noise
paru mud, dirt, sordid
paruparu dirty, sludge
parure drooping, listless
paruru compact, close together
pāruru windbreak, shaded
paruwhatitiri basket fungus
pasī pai drenched (northern dialect)
pata butter, grain, drop of water
pātahi common denominator, clean-sweep
pātai(-a) ask, question
pātaitai quibble, small flatfish
pātaka storehouse, cupboard
pātaka keo freezer
pātaka mātao fridge
patamiraka buttermilk
pātangatanga banana-like fingers of tāwhara vine
patapata drip, raindrops, tentacles, parallel lines
patapātai(-hia) interrogate, quiz, quizzed
pātara bottle
pātaritari amuse, entice, tease, provoke
patatē cracking noise, seven-finger
pātātea contraceptive diaphragm
patatō rattle, knock over
pātaua submersed, rain damaged
pātea fine cloak, body armour
pātehetehe short
pateko immobile, static
pātene button, batten
pātengitengi vegetable crisper
pātere flow, rhythmical chant
patero cracking sound
pātero fart
patete(-tia) accelerate, rub against grain
pātētē creaking noise
pati coax, bludge
patī splash
pāti party, patch
patiha badger (animal)
pātīmata ignition (engine)
pātiotio rock borer shellfish, frozen over
patipati flatter, praise
pātītī meadow grass, tomahawk
pātito sores on crown of head
pātitotito whale barnacle
patō pestle, cracking sound, spread

patoa scrublands
pātohe untilled ground, fallow
patopato typewrite
patoti cut notch, cut furrow
pātōtō knock, tapping
patu weapon, beater, bat, racquet
patu(-a) beat, ill-treat, slaughter
pātū wall, boundary, screen wall
patuero antiseptic
patuheni venereal disease
pātuhi key (typewriter, etc.)
pātuhi muku delete key
pātuki(-tia) piston, heartbeat, beat, jab, thrust
pātukituki knocking
patungaro flyswat, canoe plumes
patupaiarehe fairy, nymph
patupatu batter, pulsate
pātura banjo
pātūtū shelter (*n.*), protection, dogskin cloak
pau used up, eaten up, extinct, gone
pau ngā tau years have passed
pau te hau winded, exhausted
pāua fishhook of pāua shell, abalone
paukena pumpkin
pauku cloak rolled as shield
pauna(-tia) pound (lb.), weigh, impound
paunga rā whitu week-end
paura(-tia) powder
pāura glow
paute spout
pawa smoke, bird or rat snare
pāwera hot, scared
pawharu packhorse crayfish
pāwhera dried fish, rape, self-exposure
pawhero reddish hair
pāwhiri selector button, click
pē mushy
pea perhaps, pair, pear, bear (animal)
peara pearl
peau turned away
peha proverb, wisecrack, husk, peelings
pēhanga press, look down, heap, pressure
pehapeha boast
pēhea somehow, manner
pēhea? what about?, how?
pēhea, me - what must be done?
pēhi(-a) press down, weigh down
pehipaoro baseball
pehipehi(-a) ambush, porpoise, threshold, toilet seat
peho hoot of morepork, morepork
pehopeho(-ria) draw in mouth of bag
pehu(-a) cursor, ball of cooked taro
pei spade, bay horse
pei(-a) drive out, push, shove, banish
pei ki raro relegate
peihana basin, pheasant
peipei sod of earth
peita paint
peita paraihe paint brush
peka branch, turn aside to visit
pēka baker
peka atu sidetrack, divert
pēkana bacon
pekanga side road, side stream, branch line
pekapeka bat, carpet shark
pekaputa off-ramp
pekauru on-ramp
peke jump, limb, appendage

pēke(-tia) back up, reverse a vehicle
pēke sack, bag
pekengaru surfing, wave jumping
pekepeke jump, limbs
pekepeke haratua daddy-long-legs
pekepoho first born child
pekerangi outer palisade, screen, ozone layer
pekerapu bankrupt
peketua burden, centipede
pekī chirp, twitter
pēnā like that, in that case
penapena(-tia) conserve, protect
pene pen, pencil, penny
pēne band, sheep pen
penehīni benzine, petrol
pēnei like this, if so
pēneti bayonet
penihana pension
pēniho toothpaste
penopeno smelly
penu squashed flat
penu(-a) smear, squash
penupenu squashed flat, masher, mashed
pepa paper, pepper
pepa heketua toilet paper
pepa hōanga emery paper
pepe butterfly
pepeha proverb, motto
pēpeke frog
pēpepe butterfly
peperiki aphid, slater
pēpi baby
pera pillow, whale blubber
pērā like that
perakēhi pillowcase
perawīti bail of wheat
pere bell, sail, arrow
pēre bale, pail, bucket
perori swerve, dodge
peru nut, snort, apoplectic, eaves
peruperu potato, dance with weapons
petapeta worn out, rags, all at once
peti(-a) bet, heap up
pēti bed, spades (cards)
petipeti gamble, jellyfish
peto used up
peu smash (tennis), bird trap
pewa arc, curved
pēwera bevel
pēwhea? how?
pī(-a) treat with disdain
pī bee, pea, chick
pī kanohi corner of eye or mouth
pī tauira DNA molecule
pī, titiro - side glance, look from corner of eye
pia spear, beer, first stage pupil
piaka young shoots of mangrove
piako empty, hollow
piana piano
pīari abnormality, hunchback
pīata shine, bright
piau iron axe, tomahawk
piha butcher, gills of fish
pihanga window
pīhao(-a) surround
pihapiha gills, ripple pattern
piharau lamprey
pihareinga grasshopper, outlaw
piharoa chopper, sheet metal
pīhau inflatable dinghy, quiet fart
pihe song of grief with gestures
pihei wax ear
pihepihe girdle
pihi(-a) split, chop, horn
pīhi block of land

pīhi pīni bean sprout
pihikete biscuit, cookie
pihipihi waxeye
pīho skite, boaster
pihoi deaf, inattentive
pīhoihoi N.Z. pipit, ground lark
pihona antler
pihongi sniff
pīhono hyphen
pīhopa bishop
pīhopatanga diocese
pīhore(-hia) rip off, peel
pīhuka gaff, fish hook
pika comma, pixel
pikao peacock
pīkaokao rooster
pīkara ampersand
pīkari chick
pīkari, wahine - lesser wife
pīkaru discharge from eyes
pīkau(-ngia) carry on back
pīkaunga burden
piki(-tia) climb, step over (bad omen)
pīki fig
pikiarero roof of mouth, climbing plant
pikīni bikini
pīkini billycan
pikiniki picnic
pikipiki jungle gym, climb over
pikirangi plant, heavenward
pikitanga ascent
pikitia pictures (films), movie
piko(-a) stoop, comma, curve
pikopewa hook and eye
pikopiko winding about, fern fronds
pikopoto warped
pikoro piccolo
pikorua double quotation marks
pinaki weeding tool
pīnati peanut
pinātoro Strathmore weed
pine close together, pin
pine whakairi drawing pin
pinepine little
pīngao golden sand sedge
pingawi sagging
pingohe supple, floppy
pīngongo shrink, deflate
pīngore flexible, weak, buckling
pīni bean
pīnohi poker, tongs
pinono beggar, dependant
pīoi see-saw, song of revenge
pioka/e shark, lemonfish
pīokaoka strip off
piopio thrush (extinct), provoke
pīoraora agitate
piori annoying, teasing
pīoriori song
pipi cockle
pipī ooze, gush out, smear
pipiha snore, spout (whale)
pīpihi storm
pīpipi shallow, brown creeper
Pipiri cling together, June (month)
pīpīwai damp, swampy
pīpīwharauroa shining cuckoo
pīpoi breakdance
pīra legal appeal
pīrakorako twinkling
piramiti pyramid
pirangi(-tia) desire, want, need
pirara separated, wide apart, branching
pīrata glisten, keen, sharp
pirau extinguish, decompose
pire bill, pill
pīrere fledgling, to migrate, flyer

piri cling, hide, thick felt, protector
piri ka piri press near, close quarters
piriahi couch potato
piriawaawa leech
pirihi priest
pirihi kōrana imam
pirihimana policeman
pirihō fleecer/fleeco
pirihono linger near
pirikahu burr, bidibid
pirimia prime minister
piringa shelter, sanctuary, asylum
piringi kāta spring cart
piriniha prince
pirinitete princess
pirinoa parasite, mistletoe
piriona billion
piriota billiards
piripiri huddle together, velcro
piripoho baby, suckling, last-born infant
piripono loyal
pirita supplejack, mistletoe
piriti bridge, priest
piritoka limpet
piriwai mayfly
piriwheke prefect
piro(-ngia) odour, try (rugby), intestines
pīroiroi entangled
pīrori bowl ball, roll dice
pīrorohū bumble bee
pita horse's bit
pītaketake nestling
pītara pistol, beetle
pītari incite
pitau frond, perforated spiral, black tree fern
pītau pīni beanshoot, green bean
pītawitawi sag, floppy
piti join, place side by side
pīti beet, trounce
pitihana petition
pītiti peach
pito navel, end, terminal
pito ake positive wire
pītoa feijoa
pitoi(-tia) tie in bunch
pitoiti almost
pītoitoi robin
pitopito kōrero notes
pītore expose buttocks in rude gesture
pitototo blood relation
piu(-a) swing, toss, skip
piu maitai hammer throw
piukara bugle
piupiu flax skirt, oscillate
piuta solder
piwa beaver (animal)
pīwa fever
pīwa rūmatiki rheumatic fever
piwaka dollar sign
pīwakawaka fantail
piwhera hāte beaver hat
pīwhetū asterisk
pō night, realm of death
pō mataara vigil
pō rākaunui full moon
pō whenua midnight
poa food, bait, smouldering
Poa Boer
poai boy
poaka pig, pork, pied stilt
pōānanga clematis plant
pōangaanga skull
pōānini dizzy
poapoa(-tia) lure, entice, stained, seduce
poari board, council

pōāritarita hectic, rushed
poataniwha bush with aromatic leaves
pōātinitini dizzy
poau puzzled, bewildered
pōauau stupid, at a loss, disorientated, schizophrenia
pōhaha split open
pohane lewd insult, rude
pōhara impoverished, pauper
poharu morass, mud hole
pōhatu stone
pōhauhau mistaken, confused
pohe apathy, torpor, withered, blind
pōhēhē(-ngia) think mistakenly
pōhēhē kino bloomer, blunder
pōhekaheka mouldy food
pohewa vision, in trance
pōhi boss, post
pōhimāhita postmaster
pōhiri(-tia) welcome
poho chest, stomach, bosom
pōhoi ear ornaments
pohongawhā heartburn
pohū bang, bomb, explosion, dynamite
pōhuatau correct word
pōhue bindweed
pōhuehue wire vine creeper
pōhūhū cloudy, infested, bunched together
pohūtanga bombshell
pōhutu splash
pōhutukawa tree, N.Z. Christmas tree
pohūwai torpedo
poi(-a) ball, sphere, swing the poi
pōī swarm about
poihuka snowball
poipātū squash (sport)
poipoi(-a) twirl, knead, nurture
pōito fishing float, water wings
poka(-ina) operate, gut fish, dig grave
poka ara tātea vasectomy
poka raho emasculate, castrate
poka tata short cut
pokahū hollow in ground
pōkai(-a) assembly (esp. Tainui), ball of string
pōkaiwhenua pioneer, rover, trek
pōkākā stormy, heat capacity
pokanga surgery
pokapoka pierce with holes, docking knife, imperfect
pokapū centre-spot, bulls-eye
pokapū wira axle
pōkare stir liquid
pōkarekare ruffle, rough water
poke green vegetables, dirty
poke(-a) haunt, knead, work as a mob, swarm over
pōkē dark, morose, black cloud
pōkeka poetic saying or chant, rough cloth, rain-cape
pokekore immaculate, perfect
pokenga kneading of dough
pōkeno murky
pokepoke knead, mix with water
pōkere purple
pokere noa thoughtless, foolhardy
poki (pōkia) cover, knee-cap
pokiha fox
pokihiwi shoulder
pokipoki rat-trap
poko hole, extinguish, beaten
pokohiwi shoulder
pokokōhua boil your head (the ultimate curse)
pokorokoro grayling

pokorua ant, larynx, cavity
pokuru throw, scent
pōkurukuru lumpy
pona cord, knot, joint
pona(-ia) tie a knot, tether
pōnānā rush about, flustered
ponaturi sea-ghosts sleeping on shore
pongere smoulder, dusky, stifling
pōngia overtaken by darkness
pongipongi(-a) shadowy, stupid, breeze
pōnitiniti bewildered, giddy
poniu marsh cress
pono truth, valid
pononga servant, slave
pōnotinoti stunted
popo(-tia) rotten, flyblown
pōpō papaya, lullaby chant
popoa sacred food
pōpōhue climber, morning glory
popoia flywheel, handle of basket
pōpokatea whitehead
popoki (pōkia) cover, kneecap, infested
pōpokorua ant, freezing, hole
popona expand, bud, form a knot
pōporo breadfruit tree, borer-eaten
popoti surround, rough basket
popou(-a) pour in/out
popowhatitiri fungus
pora big canoe, coarse cloak, block
pora matanui low-pitched roof
pora, tangata - foreigner, stranger
pōrae trumpeter fish
pōrahurahu awkward, annoying, grievance
porai ake step aside
poraka block, frock, frog, jersey
pōrakaraka ball of red earth, red ochre
pōrangi(-tia) hectic, crazy
porara having gaps, spread out
pore faint, slip off, cut short, toss during sleep
pōre de-horned
pōrearea bother, nuisance
pōrewarewa illogical, senseless
pori dependant, supporter, crease in skin
pōria bone necklace bead
Porinihia Polynesia
pōriro bastard, illegitimate
porito pole (physics)
poro(-a) cut short, log, truncated
pōro ball, stunned
poroaki farewell
poroāwhio discus
porohau gout, dropsy
porohaurangi drunk, drunkard
porohehio procession
porohete prophet
porohewa with a bald patch
porohita circle, wheel, centre circle (sports)
poroiwi bones
poroka block, frog
poropeihana probation
poropiti prophet
poroporo purplish, black nightshade, breadfruit
poroporo(-tia) cut short, mauve
poroporoaki farewell, closing ceremony
pororaru disturbance, distracted
pōrori slow, stupid
porotaka round, circular, draughts
Porotehana Protestant

porotehe insult (to one's virility)
porotītaha ellipse
porotiti disc, wheel, whizzer toy
porotītīwai phosphorescence
porou eager
porowhā oblong
porowhā rite square
porowhita(-ngia) round, circle
porowhiu(-a) pitch ball, throw away, trash
porowini province
pōrutu flute, splash
pōtae hat, cap, hood
pōtae mati thimble
pōtaka spinning top
pōtangotango very dark
pōtari snare, running noose
pōtata near
pōteretere drift about, float
pōtete tied up, draw string, talk a lot
pōtēteke somersault
poti boat, cat
pōti(-tia) vote, election
poti koko dredge
pōti motuhake by-election
pōtiki last-born, youngest, runt, infant
potipoti moth, sandhopper
pōtitanga election, referendum, plebiscite
poto short, all fixed up, succinct, brevity
potopoto short
pōtuki pestle, beater
pōtuki(-a) hit, throb, baton
pōturi deaf, slow, pig-headed
pou pole
pou(-a) fix in ground, establish
pou-ā-haokai feast of seafood
pou maitai derrick
pou niho dentist
pou rāhui boundary marker
Pou Tokerau North Pole
pou tokomanawa centre pillar
Pou Tonga South Pole
pouahi pillar of fire
pouaka box, fescue
pouaka hukapapa fridge
pouaka whakaata TV screen, computer screen
pouākai giant mythical bird
pouaru widow, widower
pouāwai degenerate person
pouawhi probation officer
pouhawaiki ship's rat, plant
pouihi battens
poukoki stilts
poumāhita postmaster
poumuri fullback
pounamu greenstone, bottle
pounga plunging in, eclipse
poupou steep, posts, in-laws
poupoutanga o te rā noon
pourā date stamp
pourangi platform shelter, date stamp
pourapa rubber stamp
pourewa tower
pourewa hinu oil rig
pōuri dark, sad
pōuriake stand aside, get out of the way
pōuriuri gloomy, melancholy, murky, subdued lighting
poutāhuhu thematic paragraph, upright post
poutaka platform on post, work bench
poutama steps pattern
poutāpeta post office
poutiriao zodiac

poutini star Rigel
pōuto(-a) fishing float, cut off
poutoko stilts, halfback
poutoti stilts
poutū vertical, on high (sun/ moon), stack up
Poutū-te-rangi March, star Altair
poutuki baton, hit, goal attack, skittle
pouwaiwai rotor, propellor, fan
pouwaka box, carton
pouwhenua long club
pouwhiwhi tangled up
pōwhiri(-tia) welcome, invitation
powhiro expert, specialist
pōwhiwhi intertwined, convolvulus, tangled
pū(-ngia) lie in a heap, bundle up
pū centre, gun, armament, clever person
pū hiko power supply, electrical battery
pū hurihanga rotation, centre point
pū kāea war trumpet
pū korokoro larynx, pharynx
pū kotahi full house of cards
pū mōtā mortar (gun)
pū ngote drinking straw, feeding tube
pū pukapuka book case
pū rarangi alphabet
pū repo cannon
pū rongowaipiro breathalyser
pū taiao science
pū tame tommy-gun
pū tongamimi urinary catheter
pua seed, flower, bud
pūahi dogskin cloak, cigarette lighter
puaki tell, emerge, disclose
puakoro loose, slack
pūāmua front vowel
pūānanga clematis plant
pūangi balloon, cool breeze
puango hollow, empty
puano vertigo, acrophobia, wren
pūao dawn
puapua wreaths, female parts, shield of rolled cloth
puare(-tia) open, hole, vowel
puarere thistledown, parrot
puaretanga vent
pūaroha real sympathy
puata clear, transparent
pūataata transparency
pūau quick, ripples, gourd
puāwai(-tia) flower, blossom
puawānanga bush clematis
puea avenged, rise to surface
pūeaea sudden short thunderstorm
puehu dust, muddy water
pūeru skirt
puha full, carving knife, overflowing
pūhā sow-thistle
pūhaehae envious
pūhana glow
pūhanga root, basis
pūharakeke flax clump
puhau lightweight
puhera envelope, bushel, paper bag
puhi virgin, bunch of feathers, Virgo
puhi(-a) to shoot, blow, adorn oneself, betroth
puhi ariki canoe streamers
pūhihi sun ray, feeler, comet tail
puhikura skin rash
puhina leftovers of crop

pūhina grey
puhipuhi bunch of hair, puff
puhitai billow, wave of sea
pūhoi slow, deaf
pūhore scarce, bad luck hunting
puhoro sea net, scroll pattern
pūhuka snow, wintry weather
pūhuki blunt, dull
pūhunga reserve, put on one side
pūhuruhuru hairy
pūhutihuti shaggy, unkempt
puia volcano, geothermal spring
pūia be shot, fired
puihi pussy
pūihi antennae, feelers, wild
pūioio burly, muscular, knotty grain
puka card, brochure, form
pukā eager, jealous
puka whakauru enrolment form, entry form
pūkāea long wooden trumpet
pūkaha engine, flax scrapings, energy
pukahu abundant, spongy
pūkahukahu lungs, breathing
pūkai(-ria) crowd together, lie in a heap
pūkei(-tia) lie in a heap
pūkākā burning fiercely
pūkaki source of river
pūkana stare wildly, grimace
pūkano fallopian tube
pūkanohi eye, knot in timber
pukapuka book, lungs, documents
pukapuka namawaea telephone directory
pukapuka rārangi kupu lexicon, thesaurus
pukapuka taki kupu dictionary
pūkarakara redolent, fragrant, marinate
pukarau pūtea deposit slip
pūkarukaru *Medusa* (jellyfish), small waves
pukatea laurel
pūkawa bitter taste, reef of rocks
pūkawa-ā-tai continental shelf
puke hill, swell up, flood
pukehina belly of net
pūkei lie in a heap
pūkēkē armpit
pūkeko swamp hen
pūkenga lecturer, professional
pukepoto dark blue earth
pukepuke hilly, rough, dune
pukerae peninsula, headland
pūkeri rush violently, cut swathe
pūki bookie
pūkiki stunted, undersized
pūkirikiri large basket for gravel
pūkohu mist, misty fog
pūkohukohu moss
pukoko lichen
pūkōrero oratory
pūkoro sheath, pocket
pūkorokoro throat, windpipe
pukoru skirt pleat, drape
pūkorukoru gather up folds, rotten wood
puku abdomen, centre circle, secret, computer drive
puku te rae frown, livid with rage
pukuaroha sympathy
pukukai greedy
pukukata hilarious, laughter
pukumahara thoughtful, caring, memory
pukumahi active, industrious, energetic

pukunui greedy, glutton, dotterel
pukupā barren
pukupuku lumpy, pelargonium
pūkura badminton, shuttlecock
pukuriri angry, anger, irritable, grumpy
pukutākaro playful
pukuwhenewhene boil (sore), tree cancer
pūmā grey, whitish, grizzled
pūmahana warmth
pūmahara wistful, nostalgic, thoughtful, memory
pūmahi verbal particle
pūmāhu steamy, muggy weather
pūmanawa breathe deeply, ability, computer software
pūmaoa rotten, overripe
pūmau permanent, reliable, definite article
pūmotu chemistry element
puna spring of water, resource
puna koromahu sauna
puna kupu thesaurus
pūnaha system
punanga refuge, secluded
punarua second wife, in pairs
punawai artesian well, pond
pune spoon
pune toha serving spoon
punga anchor, joint, odd number, eel trap
pūnga origin, centre, object (grammatical)
pūngāwerewere spider's web, spider, type of net
pūngao energy
pūngao hiko electrical energy
pūngao karihi nuclear energy
pūngao matū chemical energy
pūngao moe potential energy
pungapunga pumice, bread made from pollen
pungarehu ash
pūngāwhā sulphur
pūngawī bagpipes
pūngohe slack cord
pūngoi calory
pūngorungoru sponge
pūnguru worn away, blunt, tuba
puni camp, blocked up
pūniho gums
punipuni brood, litter, driftwood leaves
pūnitanita thistle
punua young animal/bird, calf, kitten, small size
punuhuki blunt
pūnui nearby, fern, cabbage
pūnuki blunt
pūoho startle, timer, buzzer, siren
pūoko hihiani radar detector
puoro sing, sing bass, timbre of voice
puoto tin can, cylinder, container, kitchen sink, basin
pūpā belch, gorged with food
pūpakapaka conch shell trumpet
pūpara plaited
pūpara, tātua - sporran, belt purse
pupirikana publican (biblical tax collector)
pūponga hunched up
pupū boil up, well up
pūpū periwinkle, winkle, bundle
pupuha whale spout, gasp for breath
pupuhi (pūhia) blow, shoot, swelling
pupuni lurk, crouch
pupuri (puritia) hold, save to memory

pupuritanga tenure
pupuru grip, pulpy
pūputa blister
pūpūtai foam, sea spray
pūpūtanga frequentative, sum total
pūputu at short intervals
pūpūwai shark, soggy
puraka pullover
pūrākau myth, story
purapura seed, seed potatoes
purapura whetū weaving pattern of stars
pūrara plaited
pūrārangi alphabet
purari bloody
purata clear, very calm
pūrata contrast
pūrātoke glow worm, phosphorescence
pure(-tia) ritual to remove tapu, purge
pūrehurehu butterfly, moth
pūremu(-tia) adultery, promiscuous
pūrena brim-full
purenga decontamination, dough
purepure patchy, new potato
pūrere device, motor
pūrere arotahi focus device
pūrere ataata video recorder, V.C.R.
pūrere horoi washing machine
pūrere horoi rīhi dishwasher
pūrere rorohiko computer hardware, computer
pūrere tuitui sewing machine
pūrere tukuata film projector
pūrere whakaahua photocopier
pūrerehu cirrus clouds
pūrerehua red admiral butterfly
pūrewa float
purewha mussel
puri(-tia) hold, keep
puri pepa paper clip
purimau mechanical jig, vice
puringa grip, handlebars
purini pudding
puritanga grip, handle, knob
pūrohu roll up clothes
pūroku rumpled clothing, wrinkled
pūrongo report, policy statement
pūrongo pēke bank statement
pūrongo waipiro breathalyser
pūrongo pūtea financial statement
pūrongorongo tell news
pūrori knob, handle, pommel
pūrorohū whizzing sound
pūroto stagnant, inside centre
purotu handsome, transparent, delightful
pūrourou saddle-back
puru(-a) plug, stuff into, pulped vegetables
purū blue
pūru bull
puru hipi bloat
puru taiawa tampon
pūrua pair, computer backup
puruhau air valve
puruhekaheka musty
puruhi flea
purūkamu bluegum tree
puruma(-tia) broom, sweep
pūrunga superscript
purupuru(-a) block crevices, blockage, changing
pururua dense foliage
purutu blunt
puta opening

puta(-ina) appear, release, move onwards
puta-auahi exhaust muffler, chimney
pūtahi crossroads, bull's eye
pūtaiao science
pūtāihu nostril
pūtaitai shoveller duck
pūtake base, purpose, root (maths)
pūtanetane belch, retch
putanga exit, appearance, edition
pūtangitangi paradise duck, harmonica
putaputa pitted
pūtara sea shell trumpet
pūtaratara prickly bush
pūtātara trumpet with wooden mouthpiece
pūtawa large potato
putē stare wide-eyed
pūtea haki cheque account
pūtea penapena investment, deposit
pūtēhue gourd personified
pūteketeke crested grebe
pūtenetene knobbly
pūtī(-tia) cross-grained timber
pūtia butcher
pūtihitihi close cropped hair
pūtiki knot together, unite
pūtimutimu covered in tree stumps
pūtiotio rough, prickly
putiputi flower
pūtoi tie in bunch, order (biology)
pūtoki undersized
putoko slug
pūtongatonga southeast
pūtōrino flute
pūtoti stunted
pūtoto raw meat, haemoglobin
pūtōtō door knocker
putu lie in a heap, depth
pūtu boot, 1 foot length
putupaoro football
putuputu frequent, dribs and drabs
pūtūtae-whetū phosphorus
pūtāruru crowded together
pūwāhi mathematical point
pūwerewere spider, hyperbola
pūwero syringe
pūweru skirt, cloak, clothing
pūwhā sow-thistle
pūwhara fighting platform
pūwheki(-tia) hampered
pūwhenua(-tia) to settle on land
pūwhenua storage basement, dwarf
pūwhero reddish, noble, chiefly
puwheto small, mock
pūwhewhero reddish
pūpūrangi kauri snail

P

R

rā by way of, day, sun, sail (of fabric)
Rāhoroi Saturday
rāhuritau birthday
Rātapu Sunday
rā tō setting sun
rā tū midday
Rātuarima Friday
Rātuarua Tuesday
Rātuatahi Monday
Rātuatoru Wednesday
Rātuawhā Thursday
rā whakahoki return date, due date
Rā Whānau o te Kaiwhakaora Christmas Day
Rāapa Wednesday (recent)
rae brow, headland
raenga roa peninsula
raha extended, open
rāhana sunshine, sunny
raharaha (*adj.*) spread out
rahi size, enough
rāhia engaged, wed
Rāhina Monday (recent)
rahinga size, point (type size), amount, quantity, dimension
rāhipere raspberry
rahirahi thin, weak
rahirahinga temple of skull
rahiri(-tia) welcome, admire
rāhiri line of people, rope
rāhui(-tia) 'no trespass' sign, embargo
rahurahu bracken, meddle with
rāia (interjection) isn't it
rāihe enclosure, animal pen
raihi rice
raima cement, mortar
raina line
rainei (place after alternative) or, either
rāinga animal pen
raiona lion
rāiti light
rāiti mua headlight
rāiti muri tail-light
raiwhara rifle
raka agile, lock, over there!
raka(-ina) lock up, entangled
rākai decorate oneself
Rakamaomao 'Mr. Wind'
rakaraka scratch, rake, over there!
rākau tree, weapon, wood
rākau āporomaki acmena
rākau kahupapa plywood
rākau karihi nuclear armed
rākau pokepoke rolling pin
rākau whira violin bow
rākaunui full moon
rake clump of trees, barren land
rākete racquet, rocket
raki north, lucky
rakiraki duck (barnyard)
raku scrape
rakuraku rake, scratch
rama rum, lantern
rama pātiki flounder fishing by torchlight
ramamua headlight

ramamuri rear light
ramarama pepper tree
ranea plentiful
rānei (after alternative noun) or, whether
ranga sandbank, shoal of fish
ranga(-a) weave, perform ritual
rangahau(-a) research, survey
rāngai elevated
rāngai ika shoal of fish
rangaki seek revenge
rangapū partnership, company
rangaranga lift, weave, paddle
rangatahi new fishing net, modern youth
rangatira chief, landlord, noble
rangatiratanga chiefly power, sovereignty, realm
rangatū in ranks, fine cloak
rangawhenua planet, Mars
rangi sky, weather, tune, day
rangi waiata melody
rangiahua great
rangimārie peace, peaceful, relief
rangiora sign of life, ragwort
rangirangi(-a) beat time
rangiriri smelt
rangirua in two minds
rangitahi temporary, transient
rangitaro delayed
rangitoto lava, scoria
rangitupu scaffolding
rango blowfly, roller, overgrown land
rangona heard
rāno from then on
ranu(-a) mix, juice, gravy
rāoa choked
raorao grassland, fairway
raoriki buttercup
rapa stern post, oar blade
rapa(-ngia) look for, stick to, flash
rāpaki(-tia) girdle, sash, kilt
rapanga searching, maths problem
raparapa carved ends of barge-boards, in doubt
Rāpare Thursday (recent)
rape buttocks tattooing
rāpea (adds emphasis) indeed, really
rāpeti rabbit
rapi rabbi
rapi(-a) to scratch, to claw
rāpihi rubbish, recycling bin
rapirapi(-tia) scratch, claw
rāpopoto short-list, summary, gathered
rapu(-a) look for, squeeze, detect
rara rib, clause (grammar), school of fish
rarā roar, repercussions, echoes
rārā (rāngia) grill, twig, brushwood
rarahi big size, quite big
rarahu (rahua) handle roughly
raraku scrape
raranga plait, weave, direction, row (rank)
rārangi line, list, stripe
rārangi ira dotted line
rārangi pūrite concurrent (lines)
rārangi tū meridian, longitude
rārangi ūpoko table of contents
rārangi weherua bisector, median of triangle
rarapa (*see* rapa) clinging, seek
rarapi clutch, grasp
rarata tame, soothe, docile
rarau gather up, grope, catch, settle
rarauhe bracken, fern root

R

raraunga data, citizenship, statistics
rarawa swamp
rarawe clasp tightly, easy to get
rarawhi grasp, hug, embrace
rare sweets, lolly, toffee
rari plentiful, pot mitt, ling
rarihi radish
Rārima Friday
raro bottom, under, north, below, beneath
raru(-a) trouble, preoccupied
raru i a . . . confused by . . .
Rārua Tuesday
rarunga loss (game)
raruraru trouble, problem, be in trouble
rata doctor, tame
rātā tree-vine
rata kararehe veterinary
rātaka diary, journal
Rātana religion of Rātana, lantern
rāti harpoon, lunge forward
rātihi radish
Rātini/Ratina Latin
rato served, supplied
rātō west
ratonga service to public, service delivery
ratonga ahi fire service
rātou they (more than two), them
Rātū Tuesday (recent)
rau hundred, leaf, oar blade
rau(-a) confuse, entangle in net
rau ara network
rau ārai sepal of flower
rau aroha signs of love, head-dress of leaves
rau kakara herb
rau kapurangi rubbish bin
rau matatiki artesian bore
rau mā whitu army, crowd of warriors
rau mita hundred metres
rau pūtea deposit slip
rau tuawhiti thallus of leaf
rau uira lightning
rāua they (two only)
rāua ake themselves
rāua tahi both of them
rauako allot garden sections
rauamiami mixed herbs
rauangi thin, delicate
rauangiangi tissue paper
rauaruhe bracken, fern root
rauata overhead projector
rauawa canoe topsides
rauemi income, resources
rauemi-ā-whānau family income
rauemi ako teaching material
rauemi katoa total
rauemi moroiti-ā-whānau guaranteed minimum family income
rauemi rauata overhead resources
rauemi tapeka-ā-whānau gross family income
rauemi tuhi textual material
rauemi tūturu authentic resource
rauemi tūturu-ā-whānau actual family income
rauemi whakaahua illustrative material
rauene smooth edged
rauhanga trickery, cunning
rauhea marijuana
rauhī(-tia) protect, hold
rauhī kōkā women's refuge
rauhītanga guardianship
rauhuia herb
rauika assembly, heap

rauiri intertwine
raukaha capacity
raukai food container
raukai keo freezer bags
raukakai human sacrifice
raukaraka greenstone
raukataura muse of music
Raukatauri goddess of the flute
raukatauri fern, drooping spleenwort
Raukawa Cook Strait
raukawa aromatic plant, branches as sign of mourning
raukeke pull about carelessly
raukena of unknown paternity
raukikini spice
raukirikiri sand-pit
raukōiri callisthenics, physical training
raukoti disturb, meddle
raukūmara shrub
raukura feather, grey mullet
raumaewa wander about
raumahara puzzled
raumahehe small kōkopu
raumanga fern, pantry
raumangu small plant
raumarie trevally
raumaroke dry
raumata mesh, net (geometry)
raumati summer
raumoa silvery sand grass, variety of flax
raumutu top edge of canoe sides
rāuna round
raunaha arrange
raunaha ata arrange icons
raunaha aunoa automatically arrange
raunga enclosure in letter, condiment set
raungaiti desolate, compressed
raungāwari supple
raunui species of eel, wide
raununui wide, variety of eel
rauora rescue
raupā chapped, cracked skin
raupane/raupani frying pan
raupapa (*n.*) flat ground, in order, healed over, sequence
raupapa (*v.*) organise
raupapa auheke descending order
raupapa hiahia order of preference
raupapa mahi procedure
raupapa paheko BODMAS (maths)
raupapa tāpiri arithmetic sequence
raupapa tohu tangi music scale
raupapa tono computer program
raupapa upane sequence
raupapa whakarea geometric sequence
raupapa whakaari drama series
raupāpapa bran flakes
rauparaha greater bindweed, pōhue creeper
raupatu(-tia) seize land, conquest
raupeka in doubt
raupeti black nightshade
raupī(-tia) nurture, cherish, cover over
raupine repair by darning, pull draw-string
raupō bullrush
raupōhā filo pastry
rauponga spiral pattern
raupua petal
rauraha(-tia) scattered, come into flower
raurākau shrub, rangiora shrub

R

raurangi another time
raurangi, waiho mō - leave it for now
raurauraunga datasheet
raurau foliage
raurau tuhi writing pad
raurawa car boot
raureka deceitful, aromatic leaves
raurēkau grass, shrub
raurenga kidney fern
rauriki pūhā, sow-thistle
rauroha extended, strew about
rauropi organism, ecology
raurōroa coarse pūhā
rauru plaited cord, umbilical cord
Rauru-kī-tahi inventor of carving, man of few words
rauru motu runt, puny child
rautahi serene, childless person
rautaki strategic, strategy
rautami glean root crop
rautanga degree
rautangi scented oil, shrub
rautao(-ngia) wrap food in leaves
rautau century, centenary
rautāwhiri large shrub
rautini shrub
rautipu revenge killing
rautītapu, uri o te - descendants of nobility
rautītapu plume
rautoha expenditure
rautū sharp keel
raututu N.Z. sole, yellow-belly flounder
rauuru hair
rauwaka allot garden sections
rauwene object of criticism
rauwhare thatch
rauwhero reddish brown
rauwiri(-tia) interweave, wickerwork fence, weir
rauwiringa kaiao eco system
rawa chattels, door latch, choke
rawa (after adj.) the most
rawa ahumahi industrial plant
rawa-ā-motu national assets
rawa pūmau fixed assets
rawa-ā-tangata human resource
rawa atu/ake very, eventually (after verb)
rawa māori natural resources
rawa mārena matrimonial property
rawa neke movable property
rawa, pai - best, quite, very
rawa taiao natural resource
rawa whakanao industrial plant
rawa whenua natural resource
rawahanga trouble making
rāwāhi abroad, over sea/river
rāwaho outsider, foreigner
rāwaho whakaaro travelling expenses
rāwai fish
rawaka abundant, enough
rāwakiwaki feeling of hopelessness
rawakore beggar, destitute
rāwaru blue cod
rawe excellent, comical
rawe(-a) wrap, tie around, extend in all directions
rawehoi fraud, cheat
raweke(-tia) molest, interfere, fool around, handle
raweke ira genetic engineering
raweke pūtea embezzlement
raweke rākau woodwork

raweke, tangata - smart fellow, capable
rawetukutuku firmly set, immovable
Rāwhā Thursday
rāwhānau birthday
rāwhara canoe sail
rāwhara pukunui spinnaker
rawharawha agitate
rāwhera(-tia) raffle
rawhi(-a) snatch, basket, peg
rawhipepa paper clip
rawhipuka bulldog clip
rāwhiti east
rāwhitu week, Sunday
rāwiki weekday
Rāwiri David, Common Prayer
rē! look! (exclamation), take note!
rea flourish
rea hou fresh growth
rēanga growth
rearea young vegetation, spring growth
rearea, me te - how beautiful!, superb!
rehe expert, professional
rehea confused
reherehe buttocks, long-finned eel
rēhia recreation, circus
rehione legion
rēhita register
rehu misty spray
rehu(-a) render drowsy
rehu aka scouring powder
Rēhua Antares (star)
rehunanu heroin, narcotics
rehunga anaesthesia
rehutai sea-spray
rehuwai vapour
rei tusk, ivory, jewel
rei(-a) rush upon
rei puta neck pendant, tusker
rei, niho - eye-tooth
reihi race
reimana layman, laity
Rēinga, Te - Spirits Bay
rēinga place of leaping, spring-board
Reipa Labour Party
reira there, then
reiti rates
reka sweet, tasty
rekareka itching, exciting
reke butt end, hairpin, knob
rēkena leggings
rekereke heel
rekoata recorder, record
rēmana lemon
reme lamb
remu hem, tail feather
rena(-a) distend, stretch out
Reneti Lent
renga overflowing, meal mash, pollen
rengarenga N.Z. spinach, fritter, crushed
reo voice, language
reorua bilingual
repata leopard
repe gland, type of potato, rock oyster, elephant fish
repera leper
reperepe elephant fish, tattooed buttocks
repi rape plant
repo swamp, cannon
rera thigh, leather
rēra rail, banister
rera, mā te - you're all talk
rere abruptly, waterfall, diarrhoea
rere ahiahi evening star
rere kōkiri swoop down

rere tūpou dive headfirst
rere, waha - all mouth
rerehau glider, sail plane
rerehua beautiful
rerekē different, alter direction
reremai basking shark
rerenga take off place, sentence (grammar), escapee
rererangi aeroplane, aviation
rererangi tupua U.F.O.
rererere dash about, diarrhoea
reretopa helicopter
rērewē railway
reri ready, available
rērihi lettuce
reta letter
retareta maniac laughter
reti skateboard
rēti rent, rates
rētia reindeer
retieta radiator
rētihi lettuce
retihuka skiing
rewa float, defrost, ship's mast
rewarewa N.Z. honeysuckle
rēwena leaven
rēwenakore unleavened
rēwara level (tool)
rēwera devil
rewha eyelid, eyebrow
rewharewha flu, epidemic, fresh-water eel
rewherī(-tia) referee
rī dish, screen
ria protection, pad
rīanga room-divider, wind-break
riha nit, louse egg
rihariha louse
rīhi dish, lease
rihīti receipt
rika impatient, to squirm
rikarika angry, dithering
riki small, minor
rīki rugby league
rīki leek, onion
rikiriki spring onion, exceeding
rīkona deacon
rikoriko twilight, twinkle
rima five, pentathlon
rīmiti remit
rimu red pine, seaweed
rimurapa bull kelp
rimurēhia eel grass, seaweed
rimurei sphagnum moss
rimurimu green seaweed, moss, mildew
rīnena linen
ringa arm, hand
ringaringa knucklebones, fingers, hands
Ringatū religion ('upraised hand')
ringawera marae caterer, kitchen helper
ringi(-hia, -a) pour, spill
rīngi ring, dial
rino iron, twisted cord
rinoringa handcuffs
rinorino rhinoceros
rio withered, wrinkled
ripa ridge, edge, furrow
ripanga table (list)
rīpeka(-tia) crucify, crucifix
rīpeka passionfruit
rīpeka piko swastika
Rīpeka Whero Red Cross
rīpekanga cross-roads
rīpene ribbon, tape cassette
rīpene ataata video cassette
rīpene reo audio tape
ripeneta repent
ripi(-a) cut, slice off, frisbee
ripiripi cut open, skim surface

ripo eddy, spread in waves
rīpoata report
riporipo ripple, whirlpool
rīrapa maze
rīraparapa tangled, covered with fibre
rire deep water
rirerire cricket (insect), grey warbler, shimmering heat
riri(-a) angry, combat, be irate
riri tarāwhare civil war, family conflict
riria lily
ririka impatient, wriggling about
ririki small, minor, few
ririko twilight
riringi(-hia, ringia) pour, spill
ririno whirlpool
ririo withered, wrinkled
riro hei become
riro i obtained by
riro kē become, change to
riroi twisted, bent
rita litre, evil spirit
rītaha italics, slope
ritania litany
rite alike, drawn game
rite pū identically equal
rite, te - relationship, comparison
ritekore inequality
ritenga custom, meaning, similarity
rito heart of plant, central leaf, head
ritua disjointed, separated, divide
riu valley, groove, bilge
riua gone missing
rīwai potato
Rīwaiti Levite, disciples of Prophet Rua
riwha broken, chipped
rīwhi delegate, substitute, successor
rō in, low card, stick insect
roa long, tall
roaka abundant
roanga continuation
rōau beam
rōera royal, regal
roha spread, untidy, expand
rōha rose (plant)
rohe(-a) margin, boundary
rohe haukae strike zone
rohe kararehe zoo
rohe moana territorial waters
rohe pānuku putting green
rohe pōti electorate
rohe pou tokerau north pole
rohea weary, unkempt, bored
rohekore unlimited
roherohe separate, mark boundary
rohi parāoa loaf of bread
roi knotted, knot
rōia lawyer, barrister, solicitor
roimata weeping, teardrop
roimata toroa tukutuku pattern
roiroi(-a) tie up
roiroi whene dwarf, little person
rokiroki calm after the storm, exhausted
roko a bit extra (used with negative)
rokohanga came unexpectedly, came across
roku going down, weakening
rōku log
roma stream, channel, deluge
romi squeeze
ronarona struggle
rongo (rangona) hear, sense, smell

R

Rongo-mā-Tāne god of peace and agriculture
rongo matua big toe, thumb
rongoā medicine, healing drug
rongoā pani ointment
rongoā paturopi antibiotic, penicillin
rongoā rehu general anaesthetic
rongoā whakakaha tonic
rongomatua thumb, big toe
rongomau peace, peacekeeping
rongona heard
rongonui(-tia) famous
rongopai gospel
rongowaha muzzle
rōnihi launch
rōpā slave, lodger
rōpā, whare - community house, club house
rōperi strawberry
ropi body, rope, body language
ropi(-a) cover
ropiropi care for
rōpū group, gang
rōpū taki task force
rōpū tono delegation
rōpū tōrangapū political party
rora lay out
rōrā weak, poor quality
roraha spreading, extended
rōrahi volume (science)
rore snare
rōreka sweet, harmonious, melodious
rori (*see* rorirori) road, stupid, sea slug, staggering about
rōrī tie up, knotted
rōria Jew's harp, fastened
rōriki small
rorirori ridiculous, clumsy, awkward
roro brains, central computer unit
rōrō keep going
roro wheua bone marrow
rorohiko computer
rorohuri foolish, vertigo
roroi grated kūmara, fern root
rorokore brainless
roromi (romia) to squeeze
rorotu hypnosis, hypnotise
roru pinched with cold
rota lottery
rōtāne stick insect
rotarota sign with hands, sign language
roto the inside, lake
roto rawa inmost
rotu(-a) put to sleep, knock out, hypnotic
rou long forked stick
rou kākahi dredge for kākahi (shellfish)
rourou small basket
rū shake, earthquake
rua two, hole
ruahine old woman
ruaki vomit, nausea
ruānuku wizard
ruarangi big, sturdy
ruarua few
Rūaumoko god of earthquakes
ruha ragged, worn out, rags
ruhi weak, confused
Rūhiana Russian
rui(-a) sow seed, shake, sprinkle, brandish
ruirui(-a) shake up and down
rūkahu false, blustering
ruke(-a, -hia) throw away, pour out, dispose of
rukiruki (intensifier) extremely

ruku(-hia, -tia) plunge, dive for, rush along
rūma room
rūma kai dining room
rūma karakia chapel
rūma moe bedroom
rūma noho lounge, parlour
rumaki(-na) submerge, drown, bury
rūmātiki rheumatism
rūmene amass, assemble, convene
runa ribbonwood, tangle herb
rūnā(-a) pull together, draw-string
rūna earthquake, simplify (maths)
rūnanga(-tia) assembly, debate, discuss in assembly
runga upwards, top, south
runga atu in addition
Runga Rawa Almighty God
rūpahu to tell lies, bluster
rūpapa rhubarb
rupe pigeon, door lintel, spring trap
rupe(-a) agitate, treat roughly
rūpeke all assembled, all taken care of
rupi ruby
ruranga visitor, stranger
rure(-a) to shake, wave, scatter
rurenga castaway
rūri measuring ruler
ruriruri amorous chant, lurch
ruritai sea shanty
ruru morepork, knucklebones
rūrū(-hia, -tia) handshake, wield, shake
ruruhau silverbeet
ruruku(-tia) diving, draw together
rūrūtaina in panic
rurutu fall like tears
rūtene lieutenant
rutu(-a) shake, jolt, tackle
ruturutu bump along, judo
rūwai useless
Rūwaimoko earthshaker god, Vulcan
ruwha rag, worn out
rūwhenua seismic activity

R

T

tā(-ngia) print, strike
tā pigment dye, quill
tā (possessive) the . . . of
Tā Sir
tā moko tattoo
tā te tikanga normal, typical
taara dollar
tae colouring, sap
tae(-a) arrive, attain
tae atu ki as far as
tae noa ki including, as far as
taea done, captured, possible, carried out
tāekaeka stripes
taekamo mascara
taeke(-hia) set snare
taenga arrival
tāeo clump of kiekie
tāepa hanging, dangling
tāepaepa dangling
taera sexual longing
taero grow weak
taewa potato, foreigner
tāewa dangle
taha side, bypass
taha, i te - at the side
tahā calabash
taha tangata personal
taha toi art
taha whakahaere operational base
tāhae(-tia) steal, cheat
tahaki to one side
tahanga naked, empty
tāhapa go past, askew
taharangi skyline, listless, frostfish
taharua both sides
tahataha steep bank
tahatai seaside, coast
tahatika riverside, coastline
tahatū skyline
tahe abortion, menstrual
tāhei(-tia) wear necklace, set snares
tāhei perch bird-trap, collarbone
tāheke rapids, sheer slope
tāhere bird spear, cloud covering
tāhere(-tia) tie up, ensnare
tahi one, unique
tahi(-a) sweep, dust, smooth
tahi rīwai/taewa peel potatoes
tahia para refine
tāhiko electrical
tāhinga sloping, tilting over
tahirā one day ahead
tahiti distant, unfamiliar
tāhiti spring trap
tahito ancient, old
tahiwi heartwood, hull
tahora(-tia) spread out, display
tahora wilderness, uncultivated
tāhora gather fruit
tāhore variety of potato
tāhorehore denuded, shorn, deaf
tāhoro(-a) havoc, create havoc
tahu lover, suitor, darling
tahu(-na) burn, cook, ignite
tāhuhu table of contents
tahu ki te ahi cremate, incendiary, incinerate

tahua heap of food, fund of money
tāhuhu ridgepole, ancestral line, ministry
tahumaero epidemiology, wasting sickness
tāhuna tara gathering of chiefs
tahuri turn round, overthrow
tahuti run off, scuttle off
tahuti mai! welcome!
tai sea, tide, salty
tai hauāuru west coast
tai rāwhiti east coast
tai tamatāne west coast
tai tamawahine east coast
tai timu ebb tide
Tai Tokerau Northland
tai tonga south
taia washed by tide
taiā neap tides
taiaha long club
taiaho laser
taiahoaho bright, sparkling
taiaki hormones
taiaki huka insulin
taiaki whakatupu growth hormone
taiākotikoti wear away, frayed
taiama dry white clay
taiāmiki roam
taiāniwhaniwha tsunami
taiao universe, wide world
taiapa (*see* taiepa) fence, hurdle, brackets
taiapo(-hina) lullaby, carry in one's arms
taiapu(-tia) attack with force
taiari(-tia) crush, repel
taiaro para rubbish skip, bin
taiaroa weary, basket, enemy's head
taiatea nervous
taiawa canal, cervix, cockle
taiāwhio encircle
taiepa(-tia) fence, bracket
taiharahara short supply, humble oneself
taiheke descend, rapids
taihere fastening, draw-string
tāihi(-tia) cut in two
tāiho heartwood
taihoa soon, wait a while
taika tiger, horse
taikaha persistent pressure, bold print
taikākā heartwood
taikaumātua middle-aged person
tāiki plaited basket, trellis, rope for snares
taikiri (expresses surprise) dear me!
taikiu thank you
tāiko black petrel, leprosy, sandalwood
taikōhatu hāngi stones
taikuia middle-aged woman
tāima time
taimaha (*see* taumaha) heavy, stressed
taimāmā lightweight
taimana diamond
taina (*pl.* tāina) (*see* teina) young brother of male, young sister of female
tāinanahi yesterday
tāinaoake day before yesterday
tāinawhea? when was it?
tāingoingo speckled
tainoka broom
taiohi youth, teenager
taiope as a group

T

taipakeke middle-aged
taipara volley
taiparapara machine gun
taipō typhoid, devil
taipo, mangumangu - goblin, spook (insult)
taipohū dynamite
taipū heap, sandhill
taipua banks of cloud
taipuehu dustpan
taipuru clog up, hamper
tairanga raised up
tairangi(-tia) stir, mix with water
tāiri be suspended
tairite equal, on a level with
tairo thornbush
tairua valley, hollow
tairutu dangerous tackle
taitā snag
taitāhae young man, teenager
taitai brush, first fruits
taitai(-a) wash, brush, tapu removal ceremony
taitakoto lie prostrate
taitama young man
taitamāhine young woman
taitamaiti child
taitamariki young person
taitamarikitanga adolescence
taitapa edge, periphery, border
tāitarihā day before yesterday
Tāite Thursday
taitea pale, sapwood
taitōkai sexual abuse, incest
taitua other side of object
taituarā security, best man
taiwhanga waiting room, wait for, site
taiwhatiwhati bivalve shellfish
taiwhenua land, district
taiwherū worn out
taka(-ina) fall down, prepare food, flat note
taka noa all around
taka porepore gymnastics
takapa(-ria) mat, spread mat
takapau wharanui legitimate children
takapiri stay close
takapōkai wrapped up
takapore vertical turn, flip
takaporepore acrobatics
takapū belly, uterus
takāpui homosexual friend, soulmate
takarangi stagger, feel dizzy
takarape sunset shell
takarepa(-tia) lacerate
tākaro(-hia) play, game, sport
takaroa slow, late, overdue
takarure nag, flap the lips, grumpy
takataka tumble, traverse
takatakahi trample, pedal, be disrespectful
takatakatū prepare
takatāpui bosom friend, companion of same sex
takatū prepared, ready
takatūpou plummet headlong
takawaenga liaison officer, negotiator
takawai damp, humid, quartz
takawairore spinning disc toy, favourite
takaware dawdle
takawhiti hustle, rush
takawiri corkscrew, to screw
take cause, base, topic, reason
take(-a) originate, initiate
takē missing, not available
tāke tax, levy

tāke hokohoko goods and services tax, G.S.T.
take taharua biculturalism
tākeke entangle, make loops
tākeketanga mesh
takenga mai background, source, basic facts
takere hull, keel, sea bottom
taketake base (support), well-founded
taki(-na) begin, musical beat, challenge
tāki(-na) place to one side
taki + *numeral* in groups of . . .
Taki o Autahi Southern Cross
takiaho string, to thread fish
tākiri(-tia) sudden departure, dawn, pull upwards
takirua in twos, doubles (sport)
takitahi individual, singles
takitai coastline
takitaki picket fence, screen
takitaki(-na) tease, seek revenge, recite
takitaro in a little while, in a moment
takitini in crowds, plural
takitūtū in file, stand to attention
takiura sacred food for rituals
takiura, whare - university, place of sacred learning
takiwā area, zone, time
takiwā rerenga T.V. channel
takiwhā pēpi quadruplets
takiwhenua roam
takō worked loose
takoha taxes, keepsake
tākohu vapour, shrouded in mist
takoki strained, sprained
tākoko shovel
tākopa doubled up, folded
takoto(-ria) lie down, arm span
takotoranga resting place, position, layout
tākou red ochre
taku/tāku my (one item), mine
takuhe benefit, bursary, grant
takuhe hauā invalid benefit
takuhe koremahi dole, unemployment benefit
takuhe pani orphan's benefit
takuhe tamariki family benefit
takuhe tūroro sickness benefit
takuhe whānau family support
takurua winter, star Sirius
tākuta doctor
tākuta kararehe veterinarian
tākuta mate pōrangi psychiatrist
takutai sea coast
takutaku recite, intone
tama son, boy
tama heihei rooster
tamāhine daughter, girl
tamahou baby boy, new potato
tamaiti child, boy
tamaiti atawhai stepchild, adopted child
tamaiti tohu prodigy
tamaiti whāngai adopted child
tāmaoa cooked
tamarahi talk big
tamariki children, childish
tamarikitanga childhood
tāmaru(-tia) cloud over
tamatāne young man
tāmau(-tia) love, betrothed
tamawahine daughter, east coast, gentler element
tame pū tommy-gun
tametame smack the lips
tāmi(-a) smother, press
tāmiro twist thread

tamomo fontanelle, hollow
tāmore taproot, projecting point
tāmuimui(-a) swarm, gather in numbers
tamumu drone of insects, buzz
tāmure fish, snapper, erotic dance
tāmutumutu intermittent
tana ton, tonne
tāna his, her, tonne
tānakuru spanner
tānapu(-tia) to trump (cards), rear up
tane(-a) belch, choke
tāne husband, male
Tāne Mahuta guardian spirit of the forest
tāne moe tāne homosexual man
tāne moe wahine heterosexual
tānetanga masculine sex
tānga hard copy, publication
tānga manawa draw breath
tāngaengae umbilical cord, prayer at birth
tāngahangaha spotty, banded wrasse
tangai bark of tree, peelings, neck vertebra
tāngākai bird's crop
Tangaroa guardian of the sea, Neptune
tangata (*pl.* tāngata) person, people
tangata hara accused (legal), sinner
tangata haratā mōrearea dangerous criminal
tangata kaipakihi businessperson
tangata oruoru pedlar
tangata whenua local people, aborigine, native
tangatanga loose, probationer
tangetange consumed, immediately
tangetange, mau - guilty, caught red-handed
tangi(-hia) wail, mourn, birdsong
tangihanga mourning
tangipātua pretend to cry
tangiwai fine clear greenstone
tangiweto cry like a baby
tango(-hia) grasp, take away, extract
tango atu and then, take away, subtract
tango tāoke detoxify
tangohanga taking away, holding
tangotango handle often, acquisitive
tāngoungou fully ripe
tanguru gruff voice, deep sound, green cockchafer beetle, coastal tree daisy
tāniko embroidered border, braid, tapestry
taniwha water monster, powerful person, ogre
tānoa(-tia) look down on, despise
tanoi twisted ankle
tanoni sprained, twisted
tanu(-mia) bury, plant
tanuku crumble, disintegrate
tanumanga burial
tanumi disappear behind
tao spear, javelin, lance
tao(-na) cook on fire
taokete brother-in-law of man, sister-in-law of woman
tāone town, city, municipality
taonga property, treasure, apparatus
taonga whakanui reo microphone
taopuku cook in a bag

tāora towel
taoroa long spear
tāoru spongy, putrefying
taotahi single-pointed spear, single line of ancestry
taotao latticework, sarking
taotātea spermatozoa
taotū wounded, hit, struck
tapa margin, edge
tapa(-hia) cut, recite, nominate, claim
tāpae(-tia) stack up, offer, gift
tapahanga surgical operation, cross section
tapahi(-a) slice, operate surgically
tapairu honoured lady, first-born female
tāpaki lining of leaves for hāngi
tapamaha many-sided, polygon
tapanga label, caption
tapaono hexagon
tāpaora simplify ceremonial
tāpapa stoop, lie face down
tāpara double, long for
tāparaha pastry
taparahi berserk, bravado
tāparepare fenced in
taparima pentagon
tapatahi folded, single fold
tapatapa incantation, claim by name
tapatapahi(-a) cut in pieces
tapatoru triangle
tapatoru pīataata prism
tāpatupatu wallop, give hiding
tapawaha cheek tattoo
tapawhā quadrangle, oblong
tapawhā rite square
tapeka turn aside, vinyl
tāpeka(-tia) roll up clothing, muffle up
tapeke cumulative, sum total
tāpena(-tia) offend against tapu
tapenākara tabernacle
tapere amusement (house of)
tāperu glower, pout, contort
tapetape talk continuously
tapi(-a) patch, criticise, forelock
tāpi(-tia) smear on, dress wound
tapī hāngi, earth oven
tāpia cellulose
tāpihapiha whale's blowhole
tapiki(-tia) grip, fold up, fish guts
tāpiri(-tia) add, join, assist
tāpiritanga addition, additive, appendix
tapitapi touch of colour, criticise, patch up
tāpoa(-ina) smoke out vermin
tāpoi sightseeing, tourism
tāpōkere swarms of workers
tāpora cook in small baskets, hessian
tapore footprint, impression in sand
tāpore to make calm, tranquillize
tāpōrena tarpaulin
tāporepore weaken, sag
tapou depressed, bowed down
tapu sacred, confidential, taboo
tāpu tub
tapuae footprint
tāpui(-a) mark ownership, fasten in bundle
tāpuke(-tia) bury
tapukōrako red hawk
taputapu utensil, equipment, instrument, goods
tapuwae spoor, footprint
tara apex, thorn, sexually aroused
tara(-a) irritate, stir up
tāra dollar

tara-ā-whare, mate - die a natural death
tara iti area to left of door, tern
tarahae quarrel, envious
tarahī diarrhoea, showery weather
tarahiti trustee
tārahu heat up oven, heating element
tarai try, score, attempt
tārai(-a, -tia) shape timber, hollow out
taraipāta whaler's try-pot, cauldron
taraipiunara tribunal
taraire tree
taraiti tern
taraiwa(-tia) to drive, driver
taraka truck
tarakeha screech
tarakihana tractor
tarakihi type of fish, locust, cicada
tarakona dragon
tarakore spiritless
tarakupenga sand-dune, *Coprosma* plant
tarāmaui lancewood
taramea scented grass, perfume extract
taramengemenge crinkly, kinky
taramoa brambles, bush lawyer
taramore skinny, shrivelled
taramu drum, tram, tympanum
taramutu dorsal fin
taranui paspalum
tarānui Caspian tern, place of honour
taraongaonga tree nettle
tarapake crab louse, tick
tarapeke(-tia) spring up, jump
tarapepe wiggle, quiver
tarapī thin fibre, streak, squirt
tarapiki criss-cross
tarapō ground parrot, kākāpō
tarapouahi shawl, rug
tarapu stirrup, strap
tarapunga gull-jackie, red-billed gull
tararua double pointed, divided in two
tarata lemonwood, White Terraces
taratara coarse, barbed, jagged, picket fence
taratarawai dyspepsia, heartburn, reflux
taratutū menacing, ferocious
tarau trousers, pants
tarau tāngari jeans, dungarees
taraute trout
tārawa swell of the sea, hang
tarawene complain, find fault, whine
tarawera small fern, shrimp
taraweti(-tia) alien, horrible, treat as enemy
tarawewehi frightening, make blood run cold
tarawhai hurry, rush, stingray
tarāwhe draught horse
tarawhete chatter
tarawhiti netball goal, basket (basketball)
tarawhiti(-tia) enclose, encircle
tare(-a) dangle, send, transmit
tāre doll, kewpie, moppet
tare te haki raise the flag
tāreha red ochre
tārehu cover, secretly, black tattoo dye
tārei hollow out, carve, shape
tāreke small sharp tool, quail
tarenga bench, shelf, transmission

tārenga cover over
tarepa short of a number, dangling
tāreperepe buttocks, ragged edge
tārera defiant grimace
tārere spurt out, overflow, swing
taretare ragged, moth-eaten
tārete wūru yarn fibre
tārewa hanging up, sinking sun, unpaid debt
tari office, study, department, ministry
tari(-a) fetch, take, encourage
tari tākuta doctor's surgery
tāria wait for
tāriana boar, stallion
taringa ear
taringa kurī flapjack
taringa noa deaf, obstinate
taringa rākau obstinate
tarioi delay
taritari ope recruit
tariwai robin, xylem (botany)
taro bread plant
tārohe(-a) set limits to
tārona(-tia) strangle, hang by the neck
tārore(-a) tangle, noose-snare
taru grass, weeds
tārū(-a) severe, agitate
tāruarua duplicate, repeat
tāruke hurry, crayfish pot, avenge
tārukenga exterminate, massacre
tarukino illegal drug
tāruru crowded, tempt, afraid
tāruturutu jerk, stumble, cripple
tata near, close to
tatā bail water, bailer
tātā stalk, shin bone, smash
tata ake nei impending
tātaku recite slowly
tātāmi (tāmia) press down, smother, hold in place
tatanga approach, nearing
tatangi jingle, rattle
tātara conch shell trumpet, rough cloak
tātarakihi locust, cicada
tātarāmoa briar, brambles
tatari loiter, moratorium, pause
tātari(-tia) grade, sift, sieve
tatari (tāria) wait
tātari kaute audit
tātari kounga quality assurance
tatau(-ria) count, door, enumerate, classified index
tātau we, us (inclusive)
tatauāmoa casual acquaintance
tataunga statistic
tātāwhāinga tournament
tātea semen, sperm
Tatimana Dutchman, Dutch
tātou we, us (inclusive)
tatū settled, to land, at ease
tātua(-tia) put on belt, apron
tātua pūpara belt purse
tātua raho jock-strap
tāturi earwax
tau tidy, year, season, sweetheart
tau(-ia) shut, settle down
tau(-ria) number
tāu your, yours
tau, kia - settle down
tau-ā-ira decimal number
tau koki angle parking
tau kōpae pair of compasses
tau oti whole number
tau otinga solution (maths)
tau paroro castanet
tau pūtea financial year
tau te mauri peace, peace-making
tau te whakaaro make up mind

T

tau whakarara parallel parking
taua that mentioned already
taua(-tia) to attack, war-party, expedition
tauā in mourning
tāua we two, you and I, you and me
taua muru war party, plundering party
tauanga Book of Numbers, statistics
tauapo hug, carry in arms
tauārai(-tia) insulate, screen off
tauaro directly, opposite
tauawhi enfold, hug, cling
tauera towel
tauhanga lie in wait, arithmetic
tauhara odd number
tauheke old man, descend
tauhena rākau bonsai tree
tauhere(-a) bind, co-ordinate
tāuhi sprinkle
tauhinganga down
tauhinu cottonwood
tauhōkai stretch limbs, skate, rising of moon or star
tauhokohoko buying and selling
tauhou strange(r), wax-eye, novice
tāuhu taurite parallel bars
tauhunahuna hide and seek
tāuhutahi horizontal bar
taui sprained, slack tide, recede
tauihotauihu bow figurehead
tauine measuring ruler
tauira senior student, role model, pattern
tauiwi late arrivals, gentile
taukapo snap card game, twinkle
taukari dig, dibber
taukawe handle
tāuke disconnected, separate
taukehe odd number
taukiri! how horrible!
tāukiuki ancient
taukoro large hamper
taukoru distended, swollen
taukumekume pull in opposite directions
taukuri dear me!
taumaha heavy, weight, important
Taumāhekeheke o te Ao Olympic Games
taumaihi upright support, lookout post
taumanu thwart of canoe, collar-bone
taumārere building ties
taumārō thick, stubborn
taumarumaru shady
taumata brow of hill, orator's bench
taumata tangata hostage
taumau engaged to be married, fiancé
taumauri composure, serenity, caution
taumua front part
taumutu abrupt, spur of the moment
taunaha claim, child betrothal, pre-order
taunga co-ordinates, landing place
taunga ika fishing ground
taunga manurere airstrip, aerodrome, tarmac
taunga poti dock, wharf
taunoka shrub, broom
taunu(-tia) jeer at, scoff at
tauomaoma race, track event
tauonioni sexual intercourse

taupā obstruction, hymen, shepherding (rugby)
taupae ridge
taupaepae escort visitors
taupahī camp, place for camping
taupaki smack, 'snap' card game
taupare to block, hinder
taupata coastal shrub
taupatu match (sport)
taupatupatu compete, rally (tennis), debate, rhythmic
taupiri intimate, clasp, adhere
taupiripiri arm-in-arm, clasp round the waist
taupoki(-na) cover, turn over
taupoki wira hubcap
taupū heap, index (maths)
taupua float, support oneself, lay ambush
taupua, kāinga - temporary refuge
taupuhipuhi hold someone up, give helping arm
taupūmau sweetheart
taupunipuni hide and seek, secret rendezvous
taupurupuru hold someone up, scrum
tauputu lie in heap, mode
taura rope, cord, string
taura katete extension cord
taura kikī tight rope
taura marohi cable
taura ngaiaku nylon cord
taura rere flying fox
taura rino steel cable
taura tieke measuring tape
taura whiri cord of many strands
Taura Whiri i te Reo Māori Māori Language Commission
tauraki dry in the sun, dehydrator
tauranga anchorage, landing pad
tauranga poti marina, harbour
taurangi variable, algebra, temperamental
taurapa sternpost of canoe
taurarua occult, sorcery
taurekareka slave, scoundrel, prisoner of war
taurekereke tied in knots, entangled
tauremu creel, fish basket
taurewa no fixed abode, fugitive
taurewarewa dawdle, straggle
tauri (kōmore) wristlet, anklet, decorative band
taurima entertain, adopt, care for
taurite equivalent, match up
tauriterite balance, equilibrium
taurua even number, double canoe
tautahi only child, odd one, first person (grammar)
tautangata foreigner
tautapa give command, nominate
tautari upright rods in latticework
tautau pendant, hang suspended, howl
tautauā coward, faint-hearted
tautauhea commoner, hoi polloi
tautauira sample
tautauwhea low-born, coward, lazy
taute repair, quarrel, bring to maturity, grieve
tauteka brace, carrying pole, barbell
tautētete feint, sleight of hand, sell dummy
tāuteute concerns, allocate, be engrossed
tautiaki look after

T

tautika level, straight, direct, even
tautimai welcome!, haere mai!
tautohe persevere, argue, dispute
tautohetohe wrangle
tautōhito skilled, genius, expert
tautoko(-na, -tia) to support, promotion
tautuhi define, pinpoint, specify
tauwehe(-a) to separate, factor (maths)
tauwehewehe discrimination
tauwera towel
tauweru hang in clusters, grape-like
tauwhāinga apunga monopolistic competition
tauwhāinga contest, matchplay
tauwhanga wait for, ambush
tauwhare overhang, jut out
tauwhena dwarf, small, pygmy
tauwhere(-a) bind
tauwherū tired
tāuwhi sprinkle, spray over
tauwhiro watch over, be on guard
tāuwhiuwhi sprinkle, spray, cover
tauwhiwhi knotted, fasten up
tauwi spray
tawa tree, spear-making timber, purple
tawa uho, para - fruit of tawa tree
tāwae separate, trample flat
tāwaewae disentangle, open out
tāwāhi other side of valley, overseas
tāwaho breeze off the sea
tawai silver beech
tāwai ridicule, canoe shell
tāwaka large shark, grey duck, quail
tāwakawaka keyboard
tāwara pleasant flavour, taste
tawari exhausted, hanging by a thread
tāwari forest tree tāwari, appeal against land claim
tawatawa hardwood, oar, fern, mackerel
tāweka hindrance, come across suddenly, tangle
tāweko threadbare, willy away (rugby)
Tāwera Venus in morning sky, charred
tāwere odd number, redundant
tāwerenga remainder
tāwerewere dangling
tāwēwē sound with plumb line, dangle
tawhā boundary line, diameter, calabash
tawhā burst open
tawhai silver beech
tāwhai stretch out, travel, mimic
tāwhana curved contour, spring trap, stance legs apart
tāwhanawhana rebound
tāwhangawhanga bay, stretched out, headlong
tāwhao brushwood, scraps, flotsam
tāwhara taste, vine, fruit of kiekie
tāwharau(-tia) bivouac, booth, cover
tāwhārua gouge out, valley
tāwhe travel around, fluff
tawhera wide open, leaf
tāwheta writhe, dangle
tāwhi suppress feelings
tāwhio(-tia) go around, tour
tāwhiri fan, air freshener, tree

Tāwhirimātea god of winds and storms
tāwhirowhiro food processor
tawhitawhi to delay, hesitate
tawhiti distance, distant
tāwhiti snare, rat-trap
tawhiti, kei te - wonderful!
tāwhiuwhiu twirl around
tāwhiwhi entangled, entwined
tāwiri cowardice, white rock shell
te (indicates singular) the
tē not (forms negative with verb), rude noise
tē rongo refused to listen
tea white, clear
tēhea? which?
tēhimeta decimetre
teihana station
teina (*pl.* tēina) younger brother of boy, younger sister of girl
teitei high, altitude, clearance
teka(-ina) tell a lie, urge on, throw dart
teka mārika unbelievable
tekau ten, tenth
tekau mā rua dozen, jury, Ringatū Holy Day
teke female vulva
tekehi deck
tekihana section
tekoteko figurehead, gargoyle
temani thimble
temepara temple (building)
tēnā that (near you)
tēnā koa! come now
tēnehi tennis
tēnei this
tēneki this
tenetene uvula
tēneti tent
tenga goitre, Adam's apple, bird's crop
tēpara stable, staple
tepe clot, congeal
tepetepe gossip, prancing about, jellyfish, blood clot
tēpu table
tēpu huri turntable
tēpu patopato keyboard
teputeihana deputation
teputi deputy
tera saddle
tērā that (away from us)
terapēke saddlebag, pack
tere quick, speed, sail swiftly, school of fish
terehu bottle-nosed dolphin
terei dray
tereina train
terenga swimming pool, velocity
teretere flow, brown gecko
tereti slate
Terinita Trinity
tero backside, anus
teroi pickled pūhā and mussels
tētahi/tētehi a, one, a certain
tētahi atu another, alternative
tetē gnash the teeth, strain
tētē grey teal, young fronds, figurehead
tetēā gnash teeth
tetekō gobbling noise
tētēkura chief, fern, Prince of Wales feather
tetepe congeal, jell
tētere swollen, trumpet
tetere whete moss
tetetete teeth chattering
tētēwai grey teal, watery eyes
tetipea teddybear

tewe foetal membrane, fermented juice
tewha, ngutu - chattering, mouthy
tewhatewha long axe-shaped club
tī tea, stick game, cabbage tree
tī kouka cabbage tree
tī raurau tea leaves
tia(-ina) steer, stick in
tiā jar
tia, e - like, as if, my dear!
tiaho shine, radiate, sparkle
tiaka jug
tiakarete chocolate
tiaki(-na) look after, jack (cards)
tiakitanga treatment, maintenance
tiamana chairman
tiamu jam
tianara general (military)
Tiapani Japan, Japanese
tiaparani chaplain, padre
tiāti judge
tiatia stick in
tiāwhe chaff
tīehu(-tia) stir up mud, splash
tīeke saddleback, measure, tape measure
tiemi see-saw, unsettled
tīemiemi lurch up and down
tiepa hanging loose, spell to catch birds
tīere scent, jelly
tīhae(-a) to rip, tear
tīhaehae piercing
tīhāhā rant, rave, act like maniac
tīhāhā, noho - sit with legs apart
tī hāte T-shirt
tihe to sneeze
tihei (exclamation of approval) long live!
tīheru bail water, tote water
tihi apex, topknot, maximum
tīhi cheese
tihingo dingo
tihirau multipeak
tīhohe giggling, snigger
tīhoi disobedient, split up, deviate
tīhoihoi boisterous, rowdy
tīhoka drive stakes, make windbreak
tīhore(-a) split, peel, skin
tiiti deeds (legal)
tika correct, authentic, rights
tikanga meaning, custom
tikanga rua two-tier system
tikanga, whai - important
tīkaokao rooster, fowl
tīkapakapa stir, flick over with stick
tīkape rebuff, hook shot, lament
tīkaro(-hia) tear out, scoop out, peck out
tīkera kettle, radiator
tīkera kānoa automatic kettlejug
tiketike high, height, important
tiki neck pendant, primal human
tiki(-na) retrieve, go to fetch
tikihope torso
tikinare dictionary
tīkiti ticket, tab
tikitiki topknot, diadem
tiko(-na) shit, excrement
tikoatua puffball fungi
tīkohi(-a) gather carefully
tīkohu scoop out, excavate
tīkoki wobbly
tīkoko(-a) scoop up, bulldoze
tīkorikori vibrant
tikotiko diarrhoea, the runs
tikowhatitiri basket fungus
tima steamer, beak, garden hoe
tīmaramara scraps

tīmata(-tia) begin, initiate
tīmatanga/tīmatatanga beginning, matrix
timere(-a) chimney, flue, to funnel
timo (*see* tima) peck
tīmohu asthma, wheezing
timopene pen nib
timu low tide, ebb tide, muscular spasm, coccyx
timuaki senior chief, head person
timutanga low tide
timutimu tail
tina dinner, fixed
tina, kia - make firm!
tina pō supper
tinaku to garden, germinate, tubers
tinana body, oneself, chassis
tinei(-a) turn off power, quench
tīneinei all set to go, off balance
tingotingo mottled, spotted
tīngoungou lump, moth chrysalis
tini many, tin, plenty
tini(-a) caulk
tīni chain, change, fetters
tīnia overcome by emotion
tinihanga trick, fraud, cheat, gimmick
tinimete tinsmith
tinimoutere archipelago
tino very, absolute, main, real
tio oyster, very cold, frozen, bird cry
tīoi quiver, shake
tīoioi sway, shake from side to side
tioka chalk, stab
tioki jockey
tīonioni wiggle, flutter
tiori wave a banner, on show
tīoriori, manu - decoy bird, brave warrior, solo singer
tioro to tingle, scream
tiotio rough, prickly
tipa scallop
tīpae lie across, deflect water into mouth
tīpaki crack fleas
tīpakopako pick up pieces
tīpapa lie down
tīpare headband
tīpāta teapot
tipatipa fake, off course
tipi(-a) glide, skim along
tipi haere make short trips
tipihori curved, waning moon
tipitaha variable, erratic
tipiwhenua roaming, vagabond
tīpoka summarise, make a beeline for
tīpokapoka fish, cockabully
tipoko perish, rot, extinguished
tīpona(-tia) to knot
tipu(-a) grow bigger, new growth, bud
tipua devil, foreign, strange
tipuaki top of head
tipuheke decay, deteriorate
tipuna ancestor, grandparent
tiputipu bulge, tumour
tira in line, touring party, pole
tīra deal, hardened steel
tīraha lie face up, out of plumb
tīrairaka fantail
tīrangaranga strewn about
tīrangi shaky, insecure
tīrapa giraffe
tīrara wide apart, spread out
tīrau digging stick, paddle sideways
tīraumoko bastard

tīraurau tea leaves, tea bags
tirawhetū constellation
tīrengirengi bounce up and down
tīrepa insulation
tīrewa rails, scaffolding
tiri(-a) scatter seed, share out
tirihou nosedive, swoop down
tirikara treacle
tiripara soccer
tiripou sky diver, bungy jump
tirira messenger
tiriti treaty
tiriwā(-tia) plant wide apart
tiriwae grapevine (aerobics)
tiriwhana arched over, curved
tiro(-hia) (*see* titiro) look, check, peep
tiro whānui survey, overview
tirohanga view, survey
tirotiro inspect, oversee
tīrou(-a) sharp stick, fork
tītaha wobble, tilt, italics, lunge
titaka unsteady, wobble
tītaka rotate
tītakataka turn over and over, fantail
tītama(-tia) to dawn, light up
tītari(-a) scatter, share
tītaritari scatter, distribute
titi(-a) peg, tee, ray of light
tītī mutton-bird, squeak
titiko watersnail
titiro (tirohia) look at, perspective
titiro tata short-sightedness
tītītai rhythmical rowing chant, fugleman
tītitipounamu bush wren, rifleman
tititorea stick-game
titiwai glow-worm, overhang
tītīwainui petrel, fairy prion
tito invent story, compose
tītōhea infertile, exhausted land, stony land
tītohu reveal, diploma
tītoi mock, masturbate
tītoki N.Z. ash, red dye, axe
tītoko(-na) pole-spreader, fend off, sail sprit
tītokotoko(-na) keep away, spreader
tītongi peck, nibble
tītore split, separate, torn
tiu(-a) swing, restless, stew
tiuperi jubilee
Tiuteronomi Deuteronomy
tiuti duty, tax
tiutiu thrush
tīwae split up, separate
tīwaha shout, yell
tīwai trunk, canoe hull, stabiliser
tīwakawaka fantail
tīwanawana dishevelled
tīwani sandpaper, file
tīwara split, separate, can opener
tīwata fence, palisade
tīwatawata palisaded
tīwāwā widely spaced
tīwē screech
tīweka vagrant, footloose, digressing
tīwēwē noa immoderate
tiwha bald spot, washer, pāua eyes
tīwhao wander
tīwharawhara split open, stereo sound
tiwhikete certificate
tīwī television
tō(-ia) drag, conceive, sunset, stove
tō kāpuni gas stove
toa store, warrior, stud animal

toa kaipakihi entrepreneur
toanga heroism
tōanga trailer
toangi/toengi west
toanui shearwater, black petrel
toatoa tree
toe left over, remaining
toemi hand-net
toene fish roe, fish yolk, setting sun
toenga balance, residue, remnant
toetoe sedge grass, pampas grass
toha(-ina) deal cards, distribute
tohanga handout
tohatoha(-ina) to distribute, sharing
tōhau dew, sweat, condensation
tohe(-a) persist, argue, contention, persevere
tōhē thief, mean, miserly
toherere(-tia) running knot, tie
toheroa shellfish
tohetake dandelion
tohetea waste land, exhausted
tohi(-a) purification ceremony, select
tōhi(-tia) toast, toast speech
tōhī stockpile
tohipa deflect, miss target
tohitū direct, straight
tohorā southern right whale
tohoraha southern right whale
tōhou your, yours
tohu sign, emblem, musical clef
tohu(-ngia) reprieve, preserve, identify
tohu kī key signature, pin number, inverted commas
tohu mai our reference
tohu manatārua copyright symbol
tohu paerua master's degree, post graduate degree
tohu paetahi bachelor degree (B.A., B.Sc., etc.)
tohu pātai question mark
tohu tangi musical note
tohu tō macron
tohu tuhituhi punctuation
tohu wā timer
tohu wānanga tuarua master's degree
tohu wānanga tuatahi university bachelor degree
tohu wānanga tuatoru doctorate
tōhua egg yolk, full moon
tōhuka sugar-cane
tohukī takitahi single quotation marks
tohumātao fridge dial
tohunga expert, specialist, priest, artist
tohunga ahurewa highest class of priest
tohunga hauora health professional
tohunga mākutu wizard (black magic)
tohunga whiriwhiri connoisseur
tohungatanga prowess, quality, expertise, competence
tohurau degree Celsius
tohurehe golf handicap
tohutohu instruction, indicate, brief (legal), coach
tohutua degree Fahrenheit
tohutuku accreditation
toi art, tap root
toī ear-splitting
toi whenua original inhabitants, native people
tōihi stride, split, tendrils of plants
tōiki heartwood, tiger shark

toimaha (*see* taimaha) heavy
tōingo smart (clothing), desirable
toiora well-being
toipoto close together
toirua rifleman, wren
tōiti little finger/toe
tōitiiti dainty, petite
toitoi jog, trot smartly, pied-tit
toitoi tuna catch eels with bob of worms
toitoi waka keep paddlers in time
toitū permanent, entire, trot
toitupu indigenous
toka rock, bedrock, firm, solid
toka ātea meteor
toka manawa satisfied
tokai floor or trellis supports
tōkai copulate
tōkai-kore asexual
tokakawa steam, damp, sweat
tokanga large basket, closed container
tokanui boulder
tokānuku man of importance
tōkari(-tia) cut notch, cut off, ebb tide
tokatoka venereal disease
tōkawa antelope
toke worm, uvula, lobe, clitoris
tōkeke equity, justice, fairness, impartial, stubborn
tōkena stocking, sock
tōkena pirikiri tights
tokerangi death-watch beetle, percussion sticks
tokerau northern, autumn
tōkere castanets, clappers, death-watch beetle
toki axe, adze
toki kāta dog cart
tokitītaha axe
tokitoki totally, placid, dabchick, brown duck
toko pole
toko(-na) to pole, to punt
tokohana hiccough
tokohia? how many people?
tokomaha population, numbers
tokomanawa central post, mainstay
tokomauri hiccough, fall in love
tokonui thumb, big toe
tokonuku gear lever
tokopā indigestion, belch
tokopuaha belch, burp
tokorangi crane (machine), levers, death watch beetle
tokorau absent, at a distance, divorce
tokorera forked
tokorima quintet
tokoroa lean, lanky
tokorua two people, game of singles
tokotoko walking stick
tokotoko tao non-infectious disease
tokotoko wae crutch
tokotokorangi epidemic, infectious, infection
tokotoru trinity, trio, trilogy, threesome
tokouru west wind, the west
tokowae crutch support
tokowhā quartet, four of a kind, doubles
tōku my, mine
tāmairangi dew
tōmato tomato
tōmina desire, wish for
tōmiti dehydrate
tomo cave

tomo(-kia) enter, assault party, marriage negotiation
tomokanga entrance, lobby, gateway
tōmua early, forefront
tōmuri afterwards, late comer, latter
tona corn (on foot), wart
tōna his, hers, its
tōnana warts
tonanawe lag behind
tōnapi turnip
tonatona nodule
tone knob, handle
tōneke trolley, trundle
tonga south, south wind
tōngāmimi bladder
tongarewa translucent greenstone
tongatonga blemish, wart
tongi spot, fertiliser, speck, dot
tongi meroiti microdot
tongitongi mottled, spotty
tōnihi move cautiously, sneak up
tonini clitoris
tono(-a) demand, command
tono kaupare non-molestation order
tono whakahauora S.O.S.
tonotono bossy
tonu still, straight away
tōnui thumb, big toe, prosperous
tōnuitanga prosperity, heyday
topa soar, fly, field event
topaki hover, flutter
tōpana force (science)
tōpanatanga units of energy
toparapara game of tag (tiggy)
tōpata in tiny bits
tope(-a) cut down, new fern growth, smear with paint
tōpeka transverse, diagonal
tōpiki plaiting
tōpito extremity, end, district
tōpū total, all together, couple, association, paired off
tōpuku swollen, rounded, stuffing
tōpuni camp, dogskin cloak, saturate, close together
tōrangapū politics
tore(-a) arouse, excite sexually
tore pia immature girl
tōrea oystercatcher
torehapehape rough texture
tōrehe fishing net, variety of eel
toremi drown, disappear
torengi disappear, set of sun
torepuku neap tide
tōrere infatuated, burial cave
torete snap (weak fibres), harsh call
toretore inflammation, anus
torewai tearful, mussel
tori cat, scratchy
tōrino wafted sound, squeeze-bag
tōrino, pū - trumpet
toro(-na) visit, stretch out, grow, explore
toroa albatross, drawer
tōroa middle finger
torohē examine, marauding party
toroheke sand-growing shrub
torohere tie up, capture
torōhi knickerbockers
torohihi diarrhoea
torohū huddled up, secret, potential
toroi fermented pūhā and mussels, brush teeth
toroihi bud, sprout, cheeky, insolent
toromi drown
toromiro brown pine

torōna throne
toronga distant relative, dole out, extension
torongi disappear, set of the sun
toropā creeping plant, spread
toropapa lie flat, fragrant shrub
toropona trombone
toropuke hillock
tororaro wire-vine
torore trolley
tōrori home-grown tobacco
tororua double movement
torotī spurt out
torotika straight, inflexible
torotoro stretch out hands, vanguard
torotoro, aka - creeper used for binding
torouka raw, promontory
toru three
toru papanga three-ply
toru tekau kore 30–love (tennis)
tōrua twofold, duet
torutoru few, rare
toruwae tripod
tōtaha tied around
tōtara tree, shrub, moss
tōtata hurry
tote salt
totepita saltpetre
toti limp
tōtika straight, just
tōtiti sausage
totitoti limp along
toto blood, bleed
tōtō pull
toto ora arterial blood
tōtōā bad-mannered
totoa wae hape silly mid-on (cricket)
totohe (tohea) persist, argue
totohi split, cut up
totohu sink, founder
totoke conger eel
totokore bloodless
totope abbreviate, cut short, sharp edge
tōtōpū meticulous, pain-staking
totoro stretch out, droop
totoroene N.Z. jasmine
tōtoroie grey warbler
tōtoropuku slyly, furtively
tōtoru vinyl, threefold, triple
tōtōwai robin
tou buttocks, anus, bird-tail
tōu your, yours, stove
tou(-a) dip, plant, dunk, immerse
tou(-a) ahi kindle flame
tōu ake kāinga self-addressed
toua te paranga controlled burn
touapo insatiable, grasping
tourepa unstable, wandering
toutou(-a) sprinkle, dunk, droop, dangle
toutouwai robin
touwhero baboon, red bum
tōwene/toene set of sun
tū(-ria) stand, stop, occur, hurt
tū (as prefix – tones down meaning) rather, quite
tū atu withstand
tū tangata self-reliance
tua back, beyond
tua(-ina) to cut down
tuā(-ina) to name, magic spell
tūā (as prefix) moderately
tua + *single digit* ordinal number, first, second etc.
tua atu after, besides
tūahiahi evening
tuahine (*pl.* tuāhine) sister (of male)

tuahiwi cervical vertebra, ridge, shoal
tūāhu shrine
tūāhua kind of, sort of
tuahuru shaggy, hairy
tūāhuru muggy weather, stuffy
tūai skinny, thin, lean
tuaina twine
tuaitara dorsal spines
tuaiwi backbone
tuakana older brother of male, older sister of female
tuakau poor fern root, barren land
tuaki(-na) gut fish, disembowel
tuakiri personal identity, wall of house
tūākiri wounded, flesh wound, set of game
tūāmanomano of many strands
tuangi N.Z. cockle
tuanui roof, ceiling, harsh, overhanging
tūao casual work, travel visa
tūāoma trotting pace, leg of journey
tuaono sixth
tūāpae horizon
tūāpaka steel, hard material
tūāpapa flat rock, platform, dais
tuapeka pretend, cheat
tūāpō night work
tuapōkere purplish, violet
tuāporo block of wood, log
tuapuke knoll, mound
tuapuku round cord, swelling, tumour, lump
tuarā backbone, ally, defender (sport)
tūārai screen, curtain, concealment
tūāraki north, north wind
tūārangi from afar, ancient, outer space
tuararo backbone
tuarāwharau thatched roof
tuari steward, barman
tuarongo back wall of house
tuāru west, west coast
tuarua second, twice, deputy, runner-up
tuatahi initial, first, foremost, primary
tuatangata that certain person, hero
tuatara ancient reptile
tuātara dorsal spines
tuatea pale, anxious, evil
tuatete spiny, rough, hedgehog
tuatini bronze whaler shark
tuatinitini of many strands
tuatoru third, third man
tuatua shellfish, ridge of hill
tuaukiuki old, traditional
tuauri ancient, ritual, indigo
tuauriuri ancient, open sea
tuāuru west coast
tuawahine subject of tale, 'our heroine'
tuawaru eighth, plaited rope
tuawhenua mainland, interior, rural
tuawhitu seventh
tueke swag, rucksack, gear
tūemi item
tuere blind eel
tuha spit, distribute
tūhāhā unique
tūhāngai bestride, open out
tūhawaiki leprosy
tuhāwiri shiver
tuhera open
tuhi(-a) write, sketch, stitch

T

tuhi whenua cartography
tuhi whika notation
tuhinga kupu rapa search warrant
tuhira wish for, wishful thinking
tuhituhi(-a) write, draw, stitch
tūhonohono bind, interlocking
tūhoro kai greedy
tūhourangi clumsy, boorish
tūhua obsidian rock
tuhui paspalum grass
tui(-a) to thread, stitch, bind
tūī parson bird
tuiau flea
tuinga suture, seam
tūingoa derived noun, pronoun
tuiri a drill, tremble
tuitui(-a) to stitch, panel decoration
tuituinga needlework
tūkaha strenuous, hasty, impulsive
tūkari(-tia) heap up, spade, lusty, eager
tuke elbow, angle
tuke(-a) nudge, jerk
tukemata eyebrow, tāniko pattern
tūkeri scouring wind
tuketuke funnybone, angular, to prod
tuki(-a) challenge, rhythmical chant
tukinga impact
tūkino cold-hearted, wicked, damage
tūkino(-hia, -tia) abuse, ill-treat
tukitanga implementation
tukituki (tukia) batter, knock to pieces
tukorou desire
tuku(-a) pass, surrender, send, betray
tuku hē no ball, service fault
tuku iho let down, lower, unload
tuku-ā-kaka transmit by fibre optics
tuku mana devolution, give permission
tuku tūranga resign
tukumaru shady, overcast
tukunga offering, handing over
tukupapa(-tia) lay out flat, prostrate
tukuperu pilot whale
tukupoi turnover
tukupoto cut short, short stop
tukupū overcast, misty
tukurou desire
tukurua repetition, recycle
tukutahi synchronised attack, joint
tukutuku(-ria) ornamental panels
tukutuku, manu - kite
tukuwai hydrant, transpiration
tuma challenge, threat
tūmanako hope, objective, expect, trust, wish
tūmanakotanga ahurea cultural expectations
tūmārō hard, stiff
tūmatakuru thorny bush, briar, speargrass
tūmatarau stingy, magic
tūmatatenga worried, grief-stricken, moody
Tūmatauenga god of war, man personified
tūmau servant, steady
tumeke panic, shaken, alarm, startle
tumere chimney, funnel

tūmingi juniper, kidney medicine
tūmoko personal name
tūmomo sort, type, brand
tūmoremore stripped bare, hairless
tumu stump, wicket, block of wood
tūmū head wind
tumuaki principal, dean
tumutumu stump
tuna eel
tuna hakaheke silver-belly eel
tuna korokoro lamprey
tunewha drowsy
tunga toothache, tooth decay
tūnga position, wound, status
tūnga wahu grass grub larva
tungāne brother of female
tungaroa back section of house
tungatunga beckon
tungi (tūngia) set alight, ignition
tungitungi kindling
tungongo chrysalis, to dry up
tūngou nod, beckon
tūngoungou chrysalis
tūnguru eroded, blunted
tunu(-a) roast, grill
tunu puku roast whole
tunuhuruhuru ill-treat, bad-tempered
tunutunu scared
tuohu bow the head, stoop
tūoi thin, skinny
tūoma hurry, jog on the spot
tūoro monster
tupa spring of trap, scallop
tūpae lie across
tūpākihi shrub, skin healing
tūpana handspring, bounce, bouncy, springy
tūpanapana throbbing, dribble (basketball)
tūpapa bench, pub bar
tūpāpaku corpse, cadaver
tūpara double-barrelled gun
tūpare shade eyes with hand, headband
tūpari cliff face
tūparu decorated panelling
tūpato cautious, economical, foresighted
tupehu irate, make a fuss
tupeka tobacco
tūpeke jump, high jump (sports)
tūpekepeke jump about
tupenu squashed flat, stubborn
tupere pout, mountain daisy, shark
tūpererū quail (bird), make whirring noise
tūpoki cover, capsize
tūpou stoop, bow in reverence
tūpoupou elders, nodding
tūpourangi steep place
tupu(-ria) develop, increase, social status
tupu, whakaheke - treat with disrespect
tupua demon, magician
tūpuhi storm, thin
tupukaha rampant
tūpuku inertia
tupuna (*pl.* tūpuna) ancestor, grandparent
tupunga evolution
turaki(-na) overpower, overthrow, depose
tūrama illuminate, restless, alert
tūranga position, identity, role
tūrangawaewae domicile, home, home turf
turapa to spring, rebound

T

ture law, justice system, rule, statute
tūrehu fairy, ghost
tūrehutanga winking
tūrēiti late
turi knee, fence-post, deaf, stubborn
turihaka bow-legged
turipa tulip
turipēpeke with knees bent
turipona knee-joint
turipū weak in the knees
turituri noise, shut up!
turiwhati knees bend, red-breasted dotterel
turiwhatu slow, banded dotterel
tūroa well-established, continual
turori stagger, totter, wobble
tūroro sick person, shellfish
tūroro torotoro outpatient
tūrotowaenga midnight
tūru chair, stool
tūruhi tourist
turuki(-tia) go by short stages, supplement
turuma lavatory, long-drop
turupeke somersault, head over heels
turupou(-tia) insert a pole
turuturu drip, establish, fixed
tūtae dung, shit, turd
tūtae atua puff balls, edible mushrooms
tūtae kākā buttercup
tūtae kēhua basket fungus
tūtae kererū Māori jasmine
tūtae kiore N.Z. eyebright
tūtae kōau celery
tūtae kurī dog shit, type of grass
tūtae ruru green beetle
tūtae whatitiri basket fungus
Tūtaenui Marton
tūtahi painted with, stand alone
tūtāhinga leaning over
tūtai spy, scout
tūtakarerewa psychological tension, apprehensive
tūtaki(-na) meet, shut door/lid, encounter
tūtakitanga social intercourse, rendezvous
tūtakitanga ahurea cultural intercourse
tūtakitanga hoa kura school reunion
tūtakiwā place name
tūtanga portion, equity
tūtara slander, gossip
tūtara kauika school of whales
tūtārere straggle
tūtata near
tūtaumaha a spell
tute(-a) to shove, nudge, elbow
tūtehu restless
tūtei sentry, spy, backstop
tute roa rolling and wriggling
tutetuke jostle with elbow
tutetute hustle, shove
tūtika self-respect, law-abiding, upstanding
tūtira stand in line, single file
tutu(-a) soak, preserve in fat, shrub
tutū impudent, stand up, stirred up
tūtū be established, standing in row
tūtūā low-born, worthless
tutuki reach limit, conclude, succeed
tūtuki (tukia) bump, stumble, crash

tutukitanga achievement, fulfilment
tutuku depart
tūturu real, authentic, permanent
tuuta atlas neck joint
tūwaewae guest, war dance
tūwai bony, skinny, gaunt
tūwara can-opener
tūwatawata, pā - hedge enclosure
tuwha(-ia) spit, distribute
tuwhenge wrinkled
tūwhenua leprosy
tūwhiti(-tia) expel, lever up
tūwiri tremble, drill, aghast

U

ū(-ngia) firmly ground, breast
ū pohe hit wicket, own goal
ū tonu unmoved
ua when (ua tae = on arrival)
ua muscle, neck of cloak
ua(-ina) (*v.*) rain, caught in rain
ūā isn't it?, please don't
ua nganga hailstone
ua whā quadriceps
ua whatu hailstones
uaki(-na) open, shut, slide open
uanga tāpui company, firm, occupation
uapare pass the buck, deflect criticism
uāpo inclement weather
uara(-tia) value, long for, need
uaratanga aim, objective, needs
uaua difficult, sinew, laborious
uauawhiti shooting pain, twinge
uawhatu hailstones, dogskin decoration
ue(-a) thrust, shake, steer with paddle
ueke rough, hardened
uene snivel, moan, whine
Uenuku rainbow personified
uepū squad, group, caucus
ueue (uea) shake, stir up
uha female, female partner
ūhanga goal-post fixtures, goal area
uhi cover, yam, tattoo needle
uhi(-a) put on
uho umbilical cord, core, essence
uhu numb, cramped
uhumanea clever
uhunga lament, mourning ceremony
ui(-a) ask questions
ui ake at a later date
uira lightning
uiui inquire, interrogate
uiuinga interview
uka blood clot, euchre
ūkaipō alma mater, mother
ukanga density
ukarere ukulele
uki olden times
ukiuki full-time work, continuity
uku(-a) wash, clay soap
ūkui(-a) wipe, tea-towel, erase
ukupapa all taken care of, wipe out
ukupara smear all over, smudge
ūkura gleaming, glowing red
uma breast, chest, lap of person
umanga business, career
umanga kāpura fire brigade
umere cheerful shout, applause
umu oven, earth oven
unahi scale of fish, parabola
unahiroa will o' the wisp, comet
unaki eunuch
unga(-a) dispatch, eject, expel
ūnga landing place, target
ūngutu butt together, dovetail
uniana union (trade)
unikanga unicorn
unu(-hia) remove, withdraw, doff hat

unu(-mia) (*see* inu) to drink
unua(-tia) join two canoes, double
upane in rank, crest of hill
upoko headline, chapter, heading
upoko, tōu - (exclamation) you fathead!
upoko mārō frozen ground, insensitive
upokohue pilot whale, Hector's dolphin
upokokororo grayling, mastermind
upokorua ant
ura reddish brown
ūranga landing place
ure penis, courage
ure ngaua you poor lot!
uretū progenitor, forebear
ureure fire-stick, kiekie fruit
uri descendant, offspring, dark green
uriuri dark, of short duration, negotiator
uru head, chief, grove of trees
uru(-a) ki enter, participate, qualify
uru mai transition, participate
uru, ngā - (*see* huru) hair
uruao fry of cockabully, winter
uruhanga gust of wind
urukehu light haired
urumaranga ambush, surprise tactic
urunga rudder, pillow, transition
urungi(-tia) rudder, setting sun, to steer
uruora helper, partner
uruoro microphone
urupā cemetery, tomb
urupare response, answer, feedback
urupounamu enquiry
urupū painstaking, persevering
urutā outbreak of epidemic
urutapu virginal, pure, untouched
urutira dorsal fin
urutomo(-kia) enter, poach, invasive
uruuru join, urge on
uruwehi be in awe of, anxious
uruwhenua passport
uta shorewards, landwards
uta(-ina) put, load, go aboard
utanga burden, luggage
utauta equipment, appliance
utiuti niggle, fuss, hen-pecked
utu cost, price, compensation
utu(-a) take revenge, dip water, charge fee
utukore gratis, free
utunga expenses incurred
utunui expensive, de luxe, invaluable
uwha female animal, calm, gentle
uwhango indistinct, misty
uwhi yam
uwhi(-a) to spread out, to cover
uwhiuwhi(-a) sprinkle, irrigate, spatter, cover

W

wā place, time, opportunity
wā kāinga true home
wā kati deadline
wā, ā tōna - ultimately, in time
wae foot, leg
waea phone call, telegram
waea mamao toll call
waea pūkoro cell phone
waea tawhiti toll call
waea tuhi telex
waea whakaahua fax
waekura umbrella fern
waenga middle, among, centre
waenganui among, average, medium, centre
waenganui pū dead centre, central
waengapū dead centre
waengarahi centre
waere(-a) clear away
waerehe wireless
waerenga clearing, field
waero tail
waeroa mosquito, long leg (cricket)
waetea runner, fleet of foot
waetea-a-Tōhē marathon runner
waewae foot, leg, paw, mast stay
waewae tapu stranger, newcomer
waha mouth, nozzle, entrance, voice
waha(-ngia) carry on the back, lift up
waha rere blatherskite, loquacious
wahahuka bragging, skite
wahaika short club
wahanga load, burden
wāhanga zone, section, chapter
wahangū dumb, mute, tight-lipped
wahanui hoop-net, vociferous
wahapū articulate, eloquent, estuary
waharoa gateway to pā
wāhi(-a) to break, cleave, pull apart
wāhi place, location, little (before noun)
wāhi tapu cemetery, reserved ground
wāhi tuku issues desk, service court
wahia/e firewood
wāhikai cafeteria, canteen
wahine (*pl.* wāhine) woman, wife, female
wahine kairau callgirl, prostitute
wahine moe puku de facto wife
wahine takāpui gay woman, lesbian
wāhiruatanga gap
waho outside, out at sea
waho, kei - outside, outdoors
wahu sundew, ice-plant
wai water, liquid
wai (as prefix) synchronised action, salvo
wai? who?
wai inarapa latex
wai ira hormone

wai rākau liquid manure, natural medicine
wai rēmana lemonade
wai rongoā tonic
wai tātea semen
wai tōhua custard
wai toto serum, lymph
waia accustomed to
waiapu flint shard, kilt of fine flax
waiari small kūmara, chirp
waiariki hot springs, thermal water
waiaruhe sourness
waiata(-tia) sing, chant, song poem
waiata-ā-ringa action song
Waiata o te Motu National Anthem
waiata maioha theme song
waiate bile
waiaua Hector's dolphin
waihanga ritenga mould
waihape change course, go about, tack
waiho hei be regarded as
waihoki similarly, also, furthermore
waihonga sweet juice from plants
waihuka makawe hair mousse
waiira hormone
waikamo tears
waikanaetanga peace, calm, equilibrium
waikari ditch
waikauri tattoo ink, tattooed
waikeri ditch, irrigation canal
waikohu steam, haze, fog
waikū dew
waikura rust, corrosion, corrode
waikure mangrove
waimaero debility, weak
waimangu ink
waimāori fresh water
waimarie quiet, luck, meek, inauspicious
waimate premonition, hereditary disease
waimatū amniotic fluid
waimatua source
waimeha wishy-washy, insipid
wāina wine, gourd
wainamu aversion to certain foods
waingōhia simple, pleasant, easy
Wainui mother of heavenly bodies
waioha greeting, expression of appreciation
waiora health, viola, well-being
waipapa growth
waipara dregs
waipawa brittle timber, cooking stones
waipera viper
waipia glue
waipipi urethra
waipiro liquor, alcohol, booze
waipū reddish, deep water, salvo
waipuke(-tia) flood, deluge, spate, upsurge
waipuna spring of water, water-well
waiputa waste pipe, drainpipe
wairākau natural medicine
wairangi excited, reckless
wairanu gravy, ketchup, sauce
wairau bruised, potato peel
Wairehu star appearing during December
waireka lemonade, soft drink, tasty, calm
wairewa liquid solution

wairoro brains
wairua attitude, mood, spirit, soul, moss
wairua hihiko innovative
wairua Māori Māori perspective
wairua motuhake unique identity
wairua nēnene humour
wairua pīnono attitude of dependency
Wairua Tapu Holy Spirit
wairuhi tired, exhausted
waitai brine, salt water
waitākiri spasm, twitch
waitara hailstones, pipe dream
waitau decay, grow faint, immature
waiti wēra southern right whale
waitohu(-ngia) mark, appoint, brand, logo
waituhi painting (art), ink, water trough for bird trap
waiū milk, of the family
waiū atua N.Z. gloxinia
waiū korikori junket
waiū tepe yoghurt
waiuku fine clay, soap
waiwai soaked, sodden, essence
waiwai pū volley of gunfire, barrage, cannonade, salvo
waiwaiā lovely, exquisite
waka canoe, vehicle, container
waka ama outrigger canoe
waka ātea space capsule
waka ātea kōpiko space shuttle
waka hari transport
waka hari hinu oil tanker
waka huia treasure box
waka kōpikopiko ferry
waka mania hau hovercraft
waka niho gearbox
waka noho caravan
waka rerehau glider
waka taua war canoe
waka taura cable car
waka tētē ocean-going canoe
waka tīwai simple dugout
waka tōrua articulated truck
waka tūroro ambulance
wākāinga true home
wakapīhau centipede
wakarā yacht
wakarererangi aeroplane
wakareretai seaplane
wāke to walk
wākena wagon, trolley
wakewake in a hurry, restless
wākihi wax
wāku my, mine
wana bud, sprout, ray of light, thrill
wāna his, hers
wāna anō (sympathetic exclamation) that's his/her nature
wana mai come into operation
wana take one trick (card game)
wānanga learning, seminar, discussion
wānanga, whare - university, wise informant
wanawana fearsome, to bristle, shiver
wanawana, tū te - become excited, get one's hackles up
wanea content, settled in mind
wani(-a) comb the hair, skim over
waniwani glide, bitchy, unkind, friction
wao forest, jungle
waoriki buttercup
wāpi wasp

wāpu jetty, wharf
wara indistinct sound, rustle, rumour
warati warrant
warawara yearning, craving, ravenous
ware ignorant, tasteless, sticky sap, oakum
ware noa off guard
warea occupied with, overcome by, oblivious
warehenga kingfish
warehou trevally
wareware(-tia) forget, forgetful, forgotten, useless
warihi waltz
wāriu value
waro coal, carbon, deep hole, charcoal
warou swallow
waru eight, peelings, planer
waru(-hia) scrape, shave, scuff
waru, e - pū! not at all!
waru, te rā o te - time of scarcity
warutīhi cheese grater
wāta slowly, carefully
wāta kirihi watercress
wāta merengi watermelon
wātaka timetable
wātara wattle
wātea free, clear, not busy, vacant
wāteatanga availability
wātene warden
wati watch
wāu your, yours
wāua subject of rumour
wawa rushes
wawā rumble, scattered, roaring noise
wāwāhi (wāhia) wrench, spanner, split open with blast
wāwahi rua scattered
wawana fierce
wawao defend, console
wawara indistinct sound
wawata daydream, desire, wishful thinking
wāwau quarrel, make noise
wawe early, quick, soon, punctual
wē squeak, squeal, liquid, middle
wē parāoa whale oil
wehe(-a) divide, enraptured, delighted with
wehenga division, compartment, tributary
wehenga mārena divorce
weherua divide, bisect, diameter
wehewehe(-a) separate out, sort out, divorce
wehi fear, awe, terrible, formidable
wehikore daring
wei whey
weiweia sub-standard, N.Z. dabchick
weka wood-hen
wekeweke sow-thistle, tentacles
weku(-a) catch hold of, scrape, snag
wene envy, grumble, shoot of gourd
wenerau object of criticism or envy
wenewene gourd, flute holes, moth
wepu(-a) whip, lash
wepuwepu beat frequently
wera(-ngia) hot, burnt, heat, set alight
werakore fireproof
werawera sweat, hot, heat, perspiration
were hang up, barnacle, bird's wattle

weri(-a) put out feelers, penetrate the mind
weriweri vile, creepy, repugnant
wero(-hia) stab, inject, challenge
werowero pierce repeatedly
weru garment, cloth, tassel
wētā weta, cave weta
wete(-kia, -kina) untie, set free, extricate, unwind
Weteriana Wesleyan, Methodist
wetewete untie
wetiweti disgusting, horrible
weto turn off, knock out, be extinguished
weto, tangi - cry-baby
weu strand of hair, tuft, appendix
weu whēkau appendix (anatomy)
wēwē yelp
wewehe love-struck, lovelorn
weweia N.Z. dabchick, low-born
wewete untie, set free, extricate, unravel
wī chase, play tag, tussock, rushes
wī epa cricket bowling crease
wihara whistle, weasel
wihiki whisky
wiki ripple, fuse wire
wiki week, Sunday
wini window, to win, variety of kūmara
winika vinegar, acetic acid
winiwini shudder, terror
wīra wheel, willow
wīra takahurihuri winch
wiri drill, screw, auger, muscular tremor
wiriwiri shiver, twist, quiver, tremble, quiver hands
wirou (*see* whiro) osier, willow
wītā outer defence
wīti wheat
witipiki Weetbix
wīwī tussock, rushes, recoil
Wīwī French, France
wīwī wāwā through thick and thin, no fixed abode
wiwini to shudder
wiwiri thread of screw
wōnati walnut
wopatu wombat
wūru wool
wuruhēti wool-shed
wuruhi wolf

WH

whā four
whā putanga i te tau quarterly
whaaki(-na) admit, confide, confess
whae, e - ! lady!, madam!
whaene mother, aunt
whāereere sow, mare, dam
whai string game, stingray, skate
whai(-a) follow, go in search of, court
whai + *noun* possessing (e.g. whai hua = fruitful)
whai kōrero make a speech, oration, rhetoric
whai kupu talk seriously
whai rawa opulent
whai takenga claim, interests (concerns)
whai taonga rich, affluence, wealthy
whai tikanga momentous, crucial, formal, meaningful
whai tikanga rawa indispensable
whai wāhi opportunity, participate, consultation
whai whakaaro think, reflect on
whaiā obsessed, bewitched, inure by karakia
whaiāipo sweetheart, beau, heartthrob, darling
whaiao daylight, world of light
whaiapu sharp stone
whaiaroaro personality, real self
whaiere(-tia) express outrage, revulsion
whaihanga(-tia) make, do, construct
whaimana valid
whāina(-tia) fine (penalty), forfeit
whāinga pursuit, following, removal of tapu
whāinga poto short-term objective, purpose
whāinga roa long-term objective, goal
whāinu share a drink, offer a drink
whaioro encounter
whaipainga benefit, food, sustenance
whaitaki lead, go to meet
whāiti constricted, narrow, condensed
whāiti noa limited
whaitiri thunder, white feather headdress
whaitohu place a seal on, mark
whaiwhai(-tia) to hunt, chase, court, pursue
whaiwhaiā(-tia) bewitch, witchcraft, hostile spirit
whaiwhakaaro tactful, considerate, forethought
whaka . . . (prefix) cause to do, towards
whakaae(-tia) approve, favour, agree
whakaaetanga permission
whakaeaea gasp for breath, try to get words out

whakaaetanga acceptance, contract, give green light
whakaahei access
whakaahu(-tia) pile up, upset, swell
whakaahua(-tia) diagram, make image, photograph, draw
whakaahuru cuddle, nuzzle up, warm
whakaaiai pollinate
whakaaio make peace, peacemaker
whakaako(-na, -tia) teach, instruct, coach, train, educate
whakaakoranga teaching, doctrine, training course
whakaanga approach, turn towards
whakaangaanga to ponder over, reflect on
whakaangi, tamaiti - stepchild, niece, nephew
whakaangiangi fly a kite, dive through the air
whakaara(-hia) arouse, motivate, inspire, erect, boot up
whakaaraara watchman's chant, recite
whakaare expose backside as insult, arched clouds
whakaari(-a) reveal, announce, drama
whakaariki! invaders!
whakaaro(-tia) think, opinion, feelings, concept
whakaaro heipū straight-laced
whakaaro nui wisdom
whakaaro rua bicultural
whakaaroaro consider
whakaaroha(-ina) pitiful, heart-rending, tear-jerker
whakaarokore careless, haphazard, thoughtless, indifferent
whakaata(-ria) reflect, reveal
whakaata paoro radar
whakaata raiti reflector
whakaataata exercise, gymnastic routine, reflect
whakaatamira spread on platform
whakaatu(-ria) indicate, present, show
whakaaturanga demonstration, stage play, computer field
whakaaturanga āpure computer field
whakaau sound asleep
whakaauraki mainstream, rehabilitate (justice)
whakaawa ford river, make a groove
whakaawaawa keep in trough of wave
whakaawe(-tia) dominate, influence, put out of reach, fade away
whakaawhiawhi(-tia) hug, cling together
whakaawhiwhi approximate, round figures
whakaea compensate, gasp, ritual prayer, come up for air
whakaeaea pant, lift from water, consolation, strive
whakaeatanga compensation, reparation
whakaeke(-a) attack, go up, ally, arriving visitors
whakaekeeke follow on the trot, arriving parties
whakaemi(-a, -tia) gather
whakaeneene annoy

whakaeneene, moe - sodomy
whakaero shrivel, condense, congeal, putrefy
whakaerotanga concentration of substance
whakaete force a passage, squeeze through, gatecrash
whakaetietinga spit with loathing
whakaeto dissolve, evaporate, vapourise
whakahā(-ngia) breathe, have a break, infuse, respire
whakahaehae mutilate, slash, sci-fi monster, scare
whakahaere organise, officiate, exercise rights, manage
whakahaere aroha charitable organisation
whakahaere kaimahi staff management
whakahaere tāngata personnel management
whakahaere whakangungu training scheme
whakahaerenga arrangements
whakahaka to make one dance
whakahakahaka menacing shape, loom threateningly
whakahako adorn oneself, put on adornments
whakahana brandish weapons, wield
whakahāngai adapt, reconcile, phenomenal
whakahāngū change to passive
whakahanumi admixture, digest, blender
whakahao to net, Hooker's sea lion
whakahapa leave destitute
whakahapū fertilize
whakahara to convict
whakaharahara huge, extraordinary
whakaharatau to practise speech or manual dexterity
whakahari delight
whakaharuru(-tia) make a roaring noise
whakahātea bleach
whakahau(-tia) give command, imperative (grammar)
whakahauhau to order, hurry, urge on
whakahauora(-tia) refresh, revive
whakahāwea(-tia) snub, discriminate unjustly
whakahē(-ngia) blame, lead astray
whakaheke ngaru surfing, ride the waves
whakaheke tupu insult, be disdainful, indignity, lose status
whakahekeheke striped
whakahemo eat up, consumed, dying
whakahemohemo attend death-bed, help at the death
whakahere(-ngia) offering to god, sacrificial gift, confine, bind
whakahī(-a) sneer, intone, lead a song, raise the pitch of song
whakahianga favourite
whakahiato co-ordinate, formulate policy
whakahīhī arrogant, officious, opiniated, smug
whakahīhiri encourage, assist, depend on
whakahiki elevate
whakahiko generator
whakahikohiko zig-zag

whakahinapōuri make sad
whakahinga cause to fall, defeat
whakahipa alter course, deviate, elude
whakahira boast, vainglorious
whakahoa be friendly with, associate with, affiliate
whakahoahoa play favourites, plan a building, make friends
whakahōhā make weary, bore, annoy
whakahohe energise, activate, enable
whakahoho alarm
whakahōhonu dig deep
whakahōia enlist, involve in military
whakahōnore honour, idolise, venerate
whakahore escape, refuse, despise, cast a line
whakahori(-a) disbelieve, reject
whakahoro(-a) let down, break down, free from tapu
whakahou(-tia) revise, modernise, update
whakahū hush, keep quiet, flow silently
whakahua(-tia) pronounce, recite
whakahuakitanga opening
whakahuri(-hia) reorientate
whakaī conceited, looking splendid
whakaihi(-a) betroth, set apart, dedicate, inspire
whakaihiihi encourage, exciting
whakaingoa give a name, appoint, identify, nominate
whakainu(-mia) to give a drink to
whakaio single file, steady
whakaioio strict, stern
whakaipo woo, cherish
whakaipurangi resource centre
whakairi(-a) hang up, charm absent person
whakairi kaka coat hanger
whakairinga impute misfortune
whakairo(-tia) carve, engrave
whakairo kōhatu sculpture
whakairoiro graphics, intricate work
whakaita hold firmly
whakakā light switch, turn on switch, kindling
whakakaha strengthen, reinforce
whakakaha anō recharge
whakakāhore veto, negative, delete, eliminate
whakakai earrings
whakakākahu to dress
whakakakara perfume, scent
whakakake overconfidence, give oneself airs
whakakāniwha notch, barb
whakakao gather
whakakapi(-a) fill up, substitute, shut
whakakapinga closure
whakakāpō act blind
whakakapokapo twinkle
whakakaporeihana incorporate
whakakarapoti sheath, surround
whakakarauna crown
whakakata amuse, laugh, skit, witty
whakakaupapa plan, establish, set up project, layout
whakakeko wink
whakakī(-ia) fill
whakakī anō refill
whakakikī tighten

whakakīkī tell, exhort
whakakiko(-tia) pretend, give body to, fill in dents
whakakiko, mahi - livelihood
whakakikokiko become human
whakakikorua cover with second skin
whakakino despise, ignore
whakakirihou plastic surgery
whakakite(-a) display, reveal
whakakitenga display, exhibition, Book of Revelations
whakakoekoe tickle, titilate
whakakōhao drill hole, make opening
whakakōhatu petrify
whakakoi sharpen, point, sharpener
whakakōingo crave, desire, mourn for, regret
whakakōnae file documents, put in basket/tray
whakakopa to clamp, wrap up
whakakōpaki wrap, fasten
whakakopenu turn the edge, crumple, squash
whakakopia excavator
whakakōpura shine, flicker
whakakorakora sprinkle, scatter
whakakore abolish (*see* whakakāhore), cancel, delete
whakakori tinana aerobics, physical exercise
whakakorikori stir up, arouse, shake
whakakorōria glorify, honour
whakakotahi unify, integrate, combine
whakakotiti(-tia) mislead, lead astray
whakakōwaowao choke
whakamā shy, embarrassed
whakamāhaki to calm
whakamahana to warm, heater, radiator
whakamahara remind, commemorate
whakamahere tangible plan, map making
whakamahi set to work, shape, to fashion, carry out
whakamāhorahora make feel at home, offer hospitality
whakamaiangi feel light, floating, prayer to lift up
whakamākūkū mouth watering, moisture
whakamāmā make easy, free from tapu, simplify
whakamamae torment, torture
whakamana authorise, empower
whakamanamana be happy, to thrill, exult, boast
whakamānawa to give honour to, to ask a blessing on
whakamanu change into a bird, mistrust
whakamaoko concealed, cringe
whakamāori translate, interpret
whakamārama explain, enlighten, justify, describe
whakamarara scatter, dispel
whakamārie pacify, appease, comfort, placate
whakamārō lengthen, draw out, stretch out hand
whakamārō waea fence strainer
whakamaroke dry, dehydrate, stunt growth
whakamārōrō fence strainer
whakamarumaru shelter, defend, shade

whakamataku menace, grisly, nerve racking, hair raising
whakamātao refrigerate, to cool
whakamatara dismantle, loosen, free, solve
whakamātaratara piercingly cold, freezing
whakamātau test, philosophy, experiment, study, examine, try out
whakamātautau attempt, inspect, evaluation, examine, examination
whakamate deadly, crave for, lethal, execute, deaden
whakamāturuturu dribble water, pour drop by drop
whakamemeke poliomyelitis
whakamenemene pull faces, grin from ear to ear, smile
whakamīharo surprising, astonishing, astounding
whakamihi acknowledge, congratulate, eulogise
whakamikiki point the toe
whakamine assemble, gather
whakaminenga assembly, congregation
whakamoe put to sleep, give in marriage, soporific
whakamōhio notify, tell, acquaint, insinuate, refer
whakamomoka deceive, win by cheating
whakamokeke secret, sullen, silent
whakamōkito minimise
whakamōmona fatten
whakamomori wait patiently, grieve deeply
whakamōwai be modest, shy
whakamua forward, retrospective
whakamui make swarm
whakamūmū silencer
whakamuri backwards
whakamutu finish, exit (computer), curtail, terminate, quit
whakamutunga final, end, last
whakanā lull, satisfy, bye in competition
whakanamunamu appear as a distant speck
whakanao produce, mint coinage, make, handle
whakaneinei peep at, move up, bob up and down
whakaneke shift
whakanekeneke mobile
whakanene tell saucy story, make laugh, play joke
whakangā have a rest, a breather
whakangahau amuse, entertain, encourage
whakangahoro to attack, charge
whakangaio deceive, trick
whakangaro destroy, make disappear, obliterate
whakangata appease
whakangau hunt with dogs, bite
whakangāueue move
whakangāwari soften, melt, tenderise, mitigate
whakangiha set fire
whakangohe weaken, soften
whakangoikore weaken, adulterate, ennervate
whakangongo kume asthma inhaler
whakangote suckle, lactation
whakangungu to train, protect, vaccinate, arm-shield
whakangutungutu stubborn, full of excuses

whakanihoniho throw up shoots
whakanoa free from tapu, make ordinary
whakanoho fix in place, give in marriage
whakanui enlarge, boost, dilate
whakaohiti warn, cautious
whakaoioi shake, jiggle
whakaoma hasten
whakaongaonga excite, goad, stimulate
whakaono sixth part
whakaopeti congregate, rally
whakaora cure, salutary, recover, resuscitate
whakaoranga remedial, salvation, therapy
whakaoranga-ā-rōpū group therapy
whakaoreore probe, move the body
whakaōrite equalise, equality, synchronise
whakaoti finish, solve (maths), accomplish
whakaotinga completion, last child, accomplishment
whakapā touch, match weapons, catch a sickness
whakapae horizontal
whakapae accuse, incriminate, hypothesis
whakapae teka slander, talk scandal, accuse falsely
whakapāhare neutralise (chemistry)
whakapāho broadcast
whakapahūtanga detonation
whakapākanga youngest child
whakapakari make mature, strengthen, develop, grow up
whakapākehā translate into English
whakapakeke be ill-treated
whakapakepake motivate, persuade
whakapakoko embalm, idol, statue
whakapane frank (postage stamp)
whakapāoho reo broadcast
whakapapa genealogy, cultural identity, Chronicles
whakapaparanga lineage, generation, laminate, layer
whakapapatipu solidify
whakaparahako despise, scorn
whakaparakore to sand
whakaparu defile
whakapati bribe, flatter, coax, persuade
whakapatipati flatter, soft-soap, suave
whakapau use up, squander, consume, exhaust
whakapau kaha concentration, expend all one's energy
whakapawera peril, trouble
whakapē squash, crush
whakapeau turn away, snatch away
whakapehapeha boastful, vain, bombastic, gloat
whakapeke fold up, hide onself, crouch
whakapiako empty out
whakapīata polish, glaze, irradiate
whakapiki increase, promote
whakapiko bend, drop hint that assistance is needed
whakapiri draw close, fasten, attach, join battle

whakapohane lampoon, mock, obscene gesture
whakapōhēhē confuse
whakapohū detonate, detonator
whakapōkaikaha work hard
whakapōkarekare disturb, muddy the waters
whakapono belief, faith, religion
whakapononga article of faith, creed
whakapōrearea darken, inconvenience, overcast
whakaporo abbreviate, bring to end
whakapoto abbreviate, abridge
whakapōturi slow-down
whakapouaru left desolate, widowed
whakapōuriuri look mournful
whakapowai smoke meat/fish
whakapū heap up, stack in layers, give round number
whakapua make smoke
whakapuaki announce, declaration
whakapuare open, make public, unfold
whakapūhoi decelerate, change down, block the ears
whakapuke surge, zeal
whakapuku surge
whakapūmau guarantee, emphasise, make permanent
whakapūmautanga sustainability
whakapuru upholster, stuff in, plug, shrimp net
whakaputa make come out, appear
whakaputa mōhio clever dick, know-all
whakarae, tumu - very high chief
whakarahi to enlarge, stretch out, enlargement
whakaranea elaborate, beautify
whakarangatira ennoble
whakaranu blend juices, make gravy/sauce
whakaraoa choke oneself
whakarapa affix, aloof, split open, bird net
whakarāpihi despise, make rubbish of
whakarāpopoto review, synopsis, résumé
whakarārangi to catalogue, lineout (rugby)
whakararata pacify, subdue, build good relationships
whakarare pass the buck
whakararo lower reaches of river, northward
whakararu be busy, hindrance, jeopardise
whakararuraru interference
whakarata pacify, friendly overtures
whakarato serve, provide
whakarau multiply, capture, prisoner
whakarauora save alive
whakarautanga multiplication
whakarawa to bolt, lock, boost
whakarāwai enhance, decorate
whakarea expand, multiply
whakarehu see a vision, dream, savoury
whakarei cast away, ornamented
whakareka make agreeable
whakarere excessive
whakarere, tua - long ago
whakarere abandon, suddenly, bequeath

whakarērea uninhabited, cast away
whakarerekē to change, amend, adapt
whakarerenga riddance
whakareri prepare
whakarewa slipway, solvent, defrost, launch
whakarewarewa war dance, show of force
whakarewatanga launching
whakarihariha barbarous, eyesore
whakaripa along the edge
whakaripanga tabulation
whakarite compare, decide, adjust, prepare
whakaritenga neighbour, restitution, pact, computer settings
whakariterite put in order, arrange, prepare
whakaritorito sprouting
whakaroa delay, lengthen, stretch
whakarōnaki slide down, glide, make level, make even
whakarongo listen, sensitive, submissive
whakarongoā prescribe
whakaropiropi hand game
whakarōpū to classify, to sort, grouping
whakaroto internal, inward
whakarua hollow in ground
whakaruhi exhausting, weaken, neutralise
whakarunga upwards, southward
whakaruru afford shelter
whakaruruhau shelter
whakatā relax, display, draw (sketch)
whakataetae competition
whakataha deflect, veer, put on one side
whakatahe abort, miscarriage
whakataka prepare, turn around, muster
whakatakariri angry, rile, get cross
whakatakataka move about, shake
whakatakē preference, mislead
whakatake mai result from
whakatakere bed of river, straggler
whakataki go to meet, recite, preface
whakatakitaki explain, fully
whakatakoha levy a fee, bond money
whakatakoto formate, stipulate, submit reports
whakatakoto kaupapa give blueprint, lay down policy
whakatamatama jeer, give oneself airs
whakatangitangi play an instrument, blow whistle, jukebox
whakatāpapa lay something flat, face down
whakatapu bless, consecrate
whakatara challenge, gossip
whakataratara gossip, irritate
whakatare hang, keen, intent upon, peer at
whakatārewa inconclusive, charge interest, unsettled
whakataritari incite, challenge, provoke
whakatata nearing, bring close
whakatatū settle

whakatau decide, diagnose, bark, simulate
whakatau kaupare non-molestation order
whakatau Tiriti Treaty settlement
whakataua depend on
whakataua te mate condemned
whakatauākī proverb, maxim
whakataumaha weight, barbell, heaviness
whakataunga compact, agreement, resolution
whakataurekareka enslave
whakataurite equalise, compare, put into perspective
whakatauritenga comparison
whakatautau theatrical play, charade, graceful movement
whakatāuteute bother, concern
whakatāwera postpone
whakatē drain out, squeeze out
whakateitei grow tall, enlarge
whakateka discredit, flying tackle
whakatekāinga homewards
whakatekateka resplendent, dart about
whakatenatena egg on, encourage
whakatene impromptu song, sing solo
whakatenetene annoy, quarrel
whakatēpara stapler
whakatepe conclude, complete
whakateretere accelerate, buoy up, sail, steer
whakatete quarrel, stubborn, unwilling, taunt
whakatētē to milk, to squeeze out
whakatētere to bloat, pour, make flow
whakatētete molest, annoy, pick a quarrel
whakatewhatewha investigator, inspector
whakatiaho illuminate
whakatika straighten, rectify, amend, correct
whakatiketike lift up high
whakatiki diet, fast from food
whakatiko laxative
whakatina fix, imprison, sharp birth-pains, restrain
whakatinana embody, mandate, implement policy
whakatipu grow, bring up, educate, nurture
whakatītaha go to one side, slant, tilt
whakatītaritari scatter
whakatō cultive, ambush, instil, impregnate
whakatoatoa defy, boast, disdain
whakatoe leave over, leftovers
whakatohatoha propagate
whakatōhi toaster
whakatoi cheeky, annoy, tease, retort
whakatoke attack by stealth, commando raid
whakatōkihi creep along
whakatopa soar aloft, hover
whakatopatopa give orders, monopolise, paternalistic
whakatōpū combine, unified, save up
whakatoro stretch out
whakatorouka troubled sleep
whakatotohu drown, submerge
whakatotoro offer, touch, palpate
whakatū brake vehicle, establish, practise, appoint
whakatū rākau weapon drill
whakatū riri uprising, warfare

whakatuapuku arch up
whakatuarā ally, support, go backwards
whakatūingoa identify
whakatumatuma act defiantly
whakatūpato cautious, to warn, suspicious
whakatūpehupehu fury, bluster
whakatuperu blow raspberries, sniff disdainfully
whakatūpou bar graph
whakatupu grow, breed, nurture, upbringing
whakatupuranga generation
whakaturi act deaf
whakatūtaki shut, close up
whakatūtehu to upset, stir up, agitate
whakatūtū set up, build, pile up, positioning
whakatūtūā degrade, make look silly
whakatutuki carry out, honour agreement
whakatuturi stubborn, disobedient
whakatāturu establish, definitive, verify
whakatuwhera to open
whakatuwheratanga opening ceremony
whakaū confirm, establish
whakauaua exert oneself, with difficulty
whakaupoko introductory verse
whakauru enlist, insert, implant, enrol
whakauruuru join in, enlist
whakautu answer, respond to, caress
whakawā judge, adjudicate, monitor, cut groove
whakawā wawe prejudice
whakawaha put on the back, load
whakawahi anoint with oil
whakawahine unmanly, effeminate
whakawai weapon drill, tempt, rehearse
whakawaireka to delight, indulge, please
whakawaituhi turn red, ceremony after birth
whakawākanga judgement
whakaware delay, distract
whakawareware cheat, to fool
whakawātea liberate, acquit, declare (cricket)
whakawāwā to plan, argue, examine, take advice, wrangle
whakawehe separate, estrange, lane divider (track races)
whakawehi frighten, scare, threaten
whakawera to heat
whakawere to hang up
whakaweti menace, threaten
whakaweto quench fire, shut down, switch off
whakawhaiāipo date a girl/boy, go steady
whakawhāiti compress, limit, specialise
whakawhānau give birth, obstetrics
whakawhānui extend, widen
whakawhārangi paginate, number pages
whakawhata hang up, put on high place

whakawhenua immovable, firmly grounded
whakawhenumi combine ingredients, mixed up, absorb
whakawhere persuade, ill-treat
whakawhero dye red
whakawherowhero pre-dawn hoot of the owl
whakawhetai give thanks, grateful, gratitude
whakawhirinaki trust in, fasten, lean against, rely on, get to know
whakawhiti cross over, carry across, transit, transplant
whakawhiu punish, sanction, bully
whakawhiwhi to award, endow
whakawiri tremble, wring, ill-treat
whakawiriwiri cruel, violent, pressurise
whāki confess, tell, disclose
whaki snatched, grasped, gather (fruit)
whakiinga waina vintage
whākoekoe tickle, make scream
whākorekore deny, make into nothing
whāmere family, nuclear family
whana kick, spring, rebel
whana kai tangata decisively rout enemy
whana kokoti ambush
whana porotete grubber kick
whana rere volley
whana taka drop kick
whana turuki conversion (rugby)
whana whakaū conversion (rugby)
whana whiu penalty kick
whanake spring up, cabbage tree, develop
whanaketanga childhood, days of youth
whānako theft, steal, robber
whānako-ā-tai aggravated robbery
whananga company of travellers
whānāriki sulphur, brimstone
whanatu go away, go forward
whānau give birth, family, genus
whānau ake nuclear family (mother, father, offspring)
whānau hāparangi Caesarian birth
whānau hou reborn
whānau kōarotanga breech birth
whānau mārama heavenly bodies
whanaunga blood relative, kindred
whānautanga birth, nativity
whanawhana dribble a ball, bend back and forth
whanga bay, span, astride, ambush
whanga ono cube
whāngai care for, adopt child, load gun
whāngai, matua - foster parent
whāngai, tamaiti - adopted child
whāngai hau first victim's heart (battle ritual)
whanganga arm-span measure
whanganui gulf, bay, harbour
whangawhāngai a spell, a charm
whango hoarse, distant murmur
whāngongo help to drink through straw
whāngote breast-feed, lactation
whano ready to go, lead, move
whanokē odd, strange, mischief

whanonga behaviour, conduct, discipline, field of study
whanowhanoā annoyance
whānui wide, width, Vega (star), liberal
whānuitanga range (extent)
whānuitanga tīwae column width
whānuku wide open, far distant
whao chisel, nail, perforate
whao(-whina) fill, put into, crowd into
whāō swallow whole, devour
whāomoomo ration, take care of, intensive care
whaowhao carve, whittle
whāpuku groper fish
whāpuni tent
whara accident, injured, physically handicapped
whārangi page
wharangi kura musk-scented shrub
wharangi piro *Olearia*, shrub
whāranu juice, stock, mix
wharanui spread wide
wharau lean-to, boatshed, pavilion, travel
wharauroa shining cuckoo
wharawhara *Astelia* plant
whare house, suit (cards)
whare, rongo ā - peace brought about by a woman
whare hākinakina sport stadium
whare herehere jail
whare hohohoko store
whare hokohoko pūtea stock exchange
whare karakia church
whare kōhanga maternity home
whare Kōrana mosque
whare kura school
whare maire house of learning
whare miere beehive, N.Z. parliament
whare paku toilet
Whare Pāremata House of Parliament
whare patu abattoir
whare pikitia cinema
whare pōtae house of mourning
whare punanga refuge
whare puni dormitory
whare rāiti hei tohu lighthouse
whare takaporepore gymnasium
whare takiura college of education
whare takotoranga taonga museum
whare tangata relation by marriage, womb
whare tapere theatre, community centre
whare tauā mourners
whare wānanga university
whare whakaatu taonga art gallery, museum
whare whakairo carved house
whare wīti barn
whareatua plant, mushroom
wharehenga kingfish
wharemoa hollow
wharerā acolyte, altar server
whārērea forsaken
whārewa lever
wharewhare housie, bingo, overhanging
whāriki carpet, mat, pathway made ready
whārikiriki carpeted
wharirū shake hands
whārite equalise, equation, measuring scales

whārite kore inequality, inequation
whārō stretch out, at full length
whāroaroa stretch
whārona giant strides, run, strut
whāronatanga stride
whārōrō stretch out, at full length
wharowharo scrape, cough, clear throat
whārua valley, footprint
whāruarua a hollow, excavation
whata shelf, platform, rack
whata kūaha door hinge
whata pouheni coat rack, cloakroom
whata wīti granary
whataamo stretcher, litter for carrying
whatarangi platform, stage
whātero stick out the tongue
whati broken, bankrupt, fracture
whati mai come on quickly
whati/whati(-a) flee, escape, break
whatīanga limb joints, biblical cubit, angle
whatinga take flight, departure, exit, rift
whatitiri thunder
whatitoka doorway
whatiwhati break off, broken
whātoro stretch out
whātōtō wrestle
whatu stone, pupil (eye), optics, weave
whatu whakanui microscope, zoom lens
whatu whānui wide-angle lens
whatuaro belly-fat of fish
whatukuhu kidneys, renal
whatumanawa emotions, feelings, kidneys
whatungarongaro disappear
whatura vulture
whaturama hernia, rupture
whaturei breastbone, sternum
whau 'cork' tree
whaupa gulp food
whāura fierce, ruddy
whāuraura bluster
whāurutau adapter
whauwhau N.Z. fig, mountain ribbonwood
whauwhi lacebark
whāwhā to touch, take in hand
whāwhā haere grope one's way
whawhai to fight, bout, conflict
whāwhai urgent, impatient, hurry
whawhai atu resist
whawhaki pluck, snatch
whāwhakou tree
whawhao(-whina) fill
whāwhārua hollow place, female ancestor
whawhati break, put to flight
whawhati tata sudden emergency, hit and miss
whawhe disturb, chatter
whawhewhawhe busybody
whē stick insect, caterpillar
whea, kei - mai! where else! (lucky), wonderful!
whea? where?
wheiao (whaiao) world of light
wheinga feud, enemy, old person
wheinu thirst
wheita wince
whēkau belly, colon, laughing owl
whēkau pae transverse colon
whēkau piko sigmoid colon
whekawheka swag, garment
wheke act wildly, octopus

whēke creak, squeeze
wheketere factory
wheketere tangoparu refinery
whekewheke scaly skin
whekī tree fern
whēkiki quarrel, tease
whēkite dazzled, haze
whekoki disfigured, contort
whēnako steal
whengo fart noisily
whengu snort, blow nose
whenu warp thread, webbing
whenua ground, country, region, placenta
whenua hāhā desolate land
whenumi eclipse, go into shadow
wheo to buzz, tingle
wheoro crashing noise, thunderous
wheowheo buzz, buzz off
whera spread, spread open
whērā (*see* pērā) like that, in the same way
Whērangi Uranus
whēranu murky, muddy
wherawhera fan out, spread out, open out
wheriko flash in the pan, glistening
whero red, orange red, arse, hoot of owl
wherū slow, inactive, mope
wheta struggle, dodge, writhe
whetau dodge, wriggle, reflex action
whetē stare wildly, glare at
whetereihana federation
whētero protruding, tongue out
whētētē stare wildly
whetewhete to whisper
whētiko mud snail
whetoko step, move along
whetowheto trivial, petty
whetū star
whētui fold, lapel
whētukituki throb, be shocked
whetūrangi shine like a star, appear above the horizon
whetūriki asterisk
wheu overgrown
wheua ngohe cartilage
wheuwheu feather moss
wheuwhi lacebark
whēwhē boil, ulcer, abscess, cyst
whēwhē kino carbuncle
whewhenga folds of skin, slack skin
whewheia enemy
whewhengi shrunken, wrinkled
whewhengu nostrils, snout, muzzle
whewheo hum
whewhera wide open, sit open-legged
whēwhero pink
whēwhī quail
whī be able
whia? how many?
whika arithmetic, number
whīkoi stride, march
whīnau tree
whio whistle, blue duck
whioi ground lark
whioioi shake, brandish
whiora viola
whiore tail
whiowhio whistle, hiss
whira violin, fiddle
whīra field, feelings
whira kaitā double bass
whira maihara field marshall
whiranui cello

whiri plait, twist rope, coil
whirinaki depend on, lean on, buttress, unite
whiringa heat (athletics), round (sport)
whiringa-ā-tau grey warbler
whirirua Mixed Member Proportional Representation
whirīti fridge, refrigerator
whiriwhiri judge, choose, plait, representative player
whiro rising moon, evil personified, willow
Whiro planet, Mercury, Pluto
whiro tangiweto weeping willow
whiroia N.Z. dabchick
whīroki thin, lean
whita firm, stable
whita(-ngia) fasten hook
whītau flax fibre, string, textile
whitawhita keen, quick, eager, urgent, burning briskly
whiti verse, crossing over, east
whiti hiko electric shock
whitianga joint, diameter
whitihoro hypnotise, bewitch
whītiki belt/girdle, loop, tie up
whītikiranga belt, loop, to tie up
whitinga o te rā sunrise
whitireia new moon
whitirua flail about
whitirua, taringa - daydreaming, inattentive
whito (*see* wheto) dwarf
whitu seven, heptathlon
whiu satisfied, penalty, muster animals
whiu tārewa indeterminate sentence (justice)
whiu teka play darts
whiu whakamuri backlash
whiuwhiu deal cards, toss about, wag, whisk
whiwhi ki gain possession of, to win
whiwhi moni cashflow, earnings
whiwhi painga enjoy rights
whiwhinga credit, obtaining
whiwhinga tāke revenue
whiwhinga tōmua mai prepaid income
whīwhiwhi entangled
whonokarawhe gramophone, record player
whoroa floor
whurū flu
whurupēke fullback (football)
whurūtu fruit
whutupaoro football
whutupaoro whakapā touch rugby

USEFUL PHRASES IN MĀORI – HE KUPU WHAI HUA

Swapping pronouns and names will give you a wide choice of handy sentences.

Meeting people

Greetings to one person

G'day, mate.	Kia ora, e hoa.
Hello, sir.	Tēnā koe, e koro.
Hello, madam.	Tēnā koe, e whae.
Good morning.	Tēnā koe; kia ora.
Good evening.	Tēnā koe; kia ora.
Nice to see you.	Ka pai te kite i a koe.

These are the traditional greetings. The actual time of day was not considered significant. Recognition ('That is *you*') was the important part of the message. However, many Māori have succumbed to the temptation to use borrowed sounds like 'mōrena' (morning) or words like 'ata mārie' (peaceful morning). At first these words were a joke but now even the elders think they are politically correct.

Northern Dialect

How are you?	Pēhea ana koe?
Very well.	Tino pai ana ahau.

Southern Dialect

How are you?	Kei te pēhea koe?
Very well.	Kei te tino pai.

Ngāti Porou

How are you?	Kai te aha koe?
Very well.	Kai te tino pai.

Greetings to two people

Hello you two.	Tēnā rā kōrua.
How are you?	Pēhea ana kōrua?
It's lovely to see you again.	Ka pai te kite anō i a kōrua.

Greetings to several people

Hello everyone.	Tēnā koutou katoa.
How are you all?	E pēhea ana koutou? Kei te pēhea koutou?

General greetings

Long time no see.	Tangata ngaro kua kitea.
Welcome.	Haere mai! Nau mai!
Let us hongi.	Homai tōu ihu.
Come and sit down.	Haere mai ki te noho.
Would you like a drink?	He inu māu?
How about a cuppa?	He inu tī māu?
Sure, that's nice.	Āe, ka pai tēnā.
No, I have to go.	Kāhore, me haere ahau.
That's all right.	Kei te pai.
Cheerio.	Haere rā.
Bye (to person staying behind).	Hei konei rā.
Don't get up.	E noho rā.
Be seeing you.	Ka kite anō.

Referring to a recent death

Sorry to hear about your grandfather.	Tēnā koutou i tō koutou koroua.
Sorry to hear about the misfortune (accident).	Tēnā koutou i tō koutou aituā.
Sorry to hear about Hinemoa.	Tēnā koutou i a Hinemoa.

Meeting people who don't know you

I am from Wellington.	Nō Pōneke ahau.
I am from Australia.	Nō Ahitereiria ahau.
What is your name?	Ko wai tōu ingoa?
My name is Henry.	Ko Hēnare tōku ingoa.
What are your parents' names?	Ko wai ōu mātua?
My father is George.	Ko Hori tōku pāpā.
He is a European.	He Pākeha ia.
My mother is Sue.	Ko Huhana tōku māmā.
She is Māori.	He Māori ia.
She is from the far north.	Nō Te Aupōuri ia.

For alternative country and personal names, see the lists on pages 19–24.

I'm looking for the marae.	Kei te kimi ahau i te marae, kei hea?
Do you know my family?	Kei te mōhio koutou ki ōku whanaunga?
I'm a newcomer here.	He waewae tapu ahau ki konei.

Personal

Welcome, friends.	Haere mai, e hoa mā.
This is my family.	Ko taku whāmere tēnei.
This is my husband Philip.	Ko taku tāne a Piripi.
I am Theresa.	Ko Terehia ahau.
These are our children.	Ko ēnei ā māua tamariki.
Three boys and three girls.	Tokotoru tama, tokotoru kōtiro.
Sir, how old are you?	E koro, e hia ōu tau?
I don't know.	Kāhore ahau e mōhio.
How old are you, old lady?	E kui, e hia ōu tau?
Just twenty-one.	Rua tekau mā tahi noa.
Where did you grow up?	I whea koe tupu ake ai?
I grew up in Northland.	I tupu ake au i Te Taitokerau.
Where do you come from?	Nō whea koe?
I am from America, from the U.S.	Nō Amerika ahau, nō te Hononga o Amerika.
She is from England.	Nō Ingarangi ia.
Those two are from Samoa.	Nō Hāmoa rāua.
They are from Japan.	Nō Hapani rātou.
Do you two belong here?	He tangata whenua kōrua?
No, we are visitors.	Kāhore, he manuhiri māua.
You are important visitors.	He manuhiri tūārangi koutou.
You have been welcomed.	Kua pōwhiritia koutou.
Now you are people of the land.	He tangata whenua koutou ināianei.
Let us speak of we and us.	Me kī tātou, tātou.
What is your occupation?	He aha tō mahi?
I'm a receptionist.	He kaiwhakatau manuhiri taku mahi.
I'm a primary school teacher.	He kaiako tamariki ahau.
I'm an estate agent.	He kaihoko whare taku mahi.
He's a policeman.	He pirihimana ia.
Those people are fishermen.	He kaihao ika ēnā tāngata.

The weather

The weather is not a general topic of Māori conversation; only if it is extreme. Weeping skies during a tangi are a good sign.

This rain is dreadful.	Tino kino tēnei ua.
Lovely weather for ducks.	He wā pai mō ngā rakiraki.
This rain is the sign of a chief.	Ko tēnei ua te tohu rangatira.
The day has turned out fine.	Kua paki te rā.
The sun is shining.	E whiti ana te rā.
It's really hot.	Te wera hoki!
It's very cold.	Tino kōpeke!
It's very misty.	Ka nui te kohu.
This is just a shower.	He kōpatapata noa iho tēnei.
The storm is coming.	Kei te haere mai te marangai.

Food

Are you feeling hungry?	E hiakai ana koe?
Yes, where is the dining room?	Āe, kei hea te whare kai?
Come and eat.	Haere mai ki te kai.
Would you like coffee?	He kāwhi māu?
Here is the dinner menu.	Anei te rārangi kai.
The hāngi food is very tasty.	Tino reka ngā kai hāngi.
What sort of food is in the hāngi?	He aha te kai kei roto i te hāngi?
There's mutton, pork and chicken.	Ko te mīti hipi, te mīti poaka me te heihei.
Can you cook it all together?	Ka taea te tao ngātahi?
Oh yes, with the vegetables too.	Āe, me ngā hua whenua hoki.
What do you have for breakfast?	He aha te kai mō te parakuihi?
Porridge, bacon and eggs are the most common.	He pāreti, he pēkana, he hēki ngā mea nui.
That is too much.	Te nui rawa o te kai.
Some eat pork and pūhā for breakfast.	Ko te parakuihi a ētahi he poaka, he pūhā.
What is this rotten corn I hear about?	He aha tēnei kānga pirau e rongo nei au?
It is not really rotten, it is fermented.	Ehara i te pirau, ēngari he kōpūwai.
Do the Māori like bread?	Pēhea ngā rohi parāoa, he reka ki te Māori?

No meal is complete without bread.	Ki te kore he parāoa ka hiakai tonu te Māori.
Māori people are very fond of flapjacks.	Ko te parāoa takakau he tino reka ki te Māori.
What's this potato bread?	He aha tēnei parāoa rīwai?
That is mixed with potato yeast.	Ka pokepokea ki te rēwena rīwai.
That is a favourite of mine.	Tina reka tēnā ki ahau.
What about seafood here?	Pēhea ngā kai moana o konei?
We love all the seafood – snapper, flounder, John Dory, eels, oysters, crayfish and so on.	Tino pai ki a mātou ngā kaimoana katoa – ko te tāmure, te pātiki, te kuparu, te tuna, te tio, te kōura, te aha, te aha.
What is the food of the chief?	He aha te kai a te rangatira?
The food of the chief is speechmaking.	Ko te kai a te rangatira he kōrero.

Prices and shopping

What is the value of the New Zealand dollar?	He aha te wāriu o te tāra Niu Tireni?
It's a third of the English pound.	He wāhi tuatoru o te pauna Ingarihi.
It's about half an American dollar.	Ko te hāwhe pea o te tāra Marikena.
How many Japanese yen to the Kiwi dollar?	E hia heni Hapani ki te tāra Niu Tireni?
I've forgotten but it is a lot.	Kua wareware ahau, engari he nui.
What is the price of Māori carvings?	He aha te utu o te whakairo Māori?
A couple of dollars for these little tourist pieces.	E rua tāra mō ngā mea iti nei mō te tūruhi.
Many hundreds of dollars, though, for the important works.	Otirā e hia rau tāra kē mō ngā taonga rongonui.
What is the price of a cinema ticket?	He aha te utu o te tīkiti pikitia?
This cinema costs twelve dollars before 5 p.m.	Tekau mā rua tāra te utu i mua i te rima karaka.
After 5 p.m. it's twenty dollars.	Rua tekau tāra i muri i te rima karaka.
What is the best place to shop?	Kei hea te wāhi hokohoko tino pai?
I like the markets.	Pai ki ahau ngā mākete.
Are there any fashion stores here?	Kei konei rānei ngā toa hoko pūweru o te wā?

Oh yes, the latest from Italy and France.
Āe, ko ngā momo katoa o Ītari, o Wīwī.

Let's go shopping for some trendy clothes.
Haere tāua ki te hoko pūweru ātaahua.

Spiritual values

Do the Māori people believe in God?
Kei te whakapono rānei ngā Māori ki te Atua?

Yes, for sure, but there are many denominations.
Āe mārika, engari he nui ngā karanga hāhi.

Do they say prayers before meals?
He karakia tā rātou i mua i te kai?

They won't eat till someone has said grace.
Kāhore rātou e kai, ki te kore he karakia whakapai kai.

The Māori won't start anything unless there is a blessing first.
Kāhore te Māori e tīmata te mahi, ahakoa te aha, ki te kore e mātua whakapaingia.

Tell me a Māori blessing.
Kōrero mai he karakia whakapai.

This is a grace before meals.
He karakia whakapai tēnei i mua i te kai.

Bless these foods, O God, for the health of our bodies.
E te Atua, whakapaingia ēnei kai hei ora mō ō mātou tinana.

Feed our souls with the bread of life.
Whāngaia ō mātou wairua ki te taro o te ora.

All things come from you. Amen.
Nāu hoki ngā mea katoa. Āmene.

Give me a prayer before a meeting.
Homai he karakia tīmatanga hui.

O God, we your servants make this prayer to you.
E te Atua, tēnei mātou āu pononga te īnoi nei ki a koe.

That you will be close to us at this time –
Kia tata mai koe ki a mātou i tēnei wā –

To help and guide us.
Hei āwhina, hei arataki i a mātou.

May your holy name be blessed in all that we do.
Kia whakakorōria ai tōu ingoa i roto i ā mātou mahi katoa.

You are God who lives and reigns for ever. Amen.
Ko koe te Atua e ora nei, e mana nei mō ngā tau mutunga kore. Āmene.

PROVERBS – HE WHAKATAUĀKĪ

1. Hōhonu kakī, pāpaku uaua.	Deep throat, shallow muscles. (Long on words, short on action.)
2. E moe i te tangata ringa raupā.	Marry a man with worker's hands.
3. He kōanga tangata tahi, he ngahuru puta noa.	Spring planting is lonely. Autumn harvest has many helpers.
4. Mā mahi ka ora (Ko mahi ko ora).	Work brings health (prosperity).
5. Mauri mahi mauri ora, mauri noho mauri mate.	Work makes you well.
***or* Tama tū tama ora, Tama noho tama mate.**	Laziness makes you sick.
6. Maramara nui a Mahi ka riro i a Noho.	Big chips from the worker's chisel reach those who sit around. (Lazybones get some of the benefits of the hard worker.)
7. Mā pango, mā whero ka oti te mahi.	If chief (Red) and worker (Black) pull together, the job is done. (Many hands make light work.)
8. He toa taua he toa pāhekeheke, he toa mahi he toa mau tonu.	A champion warrior's life is precarious, but a champion worker lives on.
9. Pō tūtata, ao pāhorehore.	United at night, scattered in the day. (A group plans together in the evening, but when dawn comes each goes his own way.)
10. He moana pukepuke e ekengia e te waka.	A choppy sea can be navigated. (Persevere.)
11. Tā te rangatira tana kai he kōrero, tā te ware he muhukai.	Speech is the food of a chief, the ignorant person is inattentive. (This is a play on the word 'kai'.)
12. He tangata kī tahi.	A man who speaks once. (A man of his word.)
13. Me he korokoro tūī.	With the throat of a bellbird. (An orator.)

14. Ko ngā rangatira o te tau tītoki.	Chiefs of the tītoki year. (Imitation chiefs. Anybody could look like a chief in those years when the red tītoki berries were plentiful.)
15. Waiho mā te tangata e mihi.	Let someone else sing your praises.
16. Whatu ngarongaro he tangata, toitū he whenua.	Man disappears but the land remains.
17. He matua pou whare e rokohia ana, he matua tangata ekore e rokohia.	The main (parent) pole in a house can always be found, but a human parent cannot always be found. (Similar to **16**.)
18. Papatūānuku te matua o te tangata.	Mother Earth is man's parent.
19. He tōtara wāhi rua he kai nā te ahi.	A totara split in two is food for the fire. (Unity is strength.)
20. He toa takitini taku toa, ehara i te toa takitahi.	My bravery was the bravery of many not just of one warrior.
21. Nāu te rourou, nāku te rourou ka ora te manuwhiri.	With your food basket and my food basket the guests will have enough. (May each contribute.)
22. Hokia ki ngā maunga kia purea koe e ngā hau o Tāwhirimātea.	Return to the mountains to be purified by the winds of Tāwhirimātea.
23. Tangata i akona ki te kāinga, tūnga ki te marae, tau ana.	A person trained at home will stand on the marae with dignity.
24. He puta taua ki te tāne, he whānau tamariki ki te wahine.	As warfare is to men, childbearing is to women.
25. Kia mau koe ki te kupu a tō matua.	Heed your parents' advice.
26. He iti rā, he iti māpihi pounamu.	Small indeed, but made of greenstone.
27. E iti noa ana nā te aroha.	Small gift, given in love.
28. Mate atu he tētēkura, whakaeke mai he tētēkura *or* **Hinga atu he tētēkura, ara mai he tētēkura.**	A leader falls, another rises. (Refers either to the figurehead of a canoe or to a tall fern in the forest.)
29. Ka hinga te tōtara i te wao nui a Tāne.	The tōtara tree has fallen in Tāne's great forest.
30. E tata mate, e roa taihoa.	Death is close compared to the latecomer.

31. **E mua āta haere, e muri tata kino.**
    The early ones go leisurely, the latecomers rush dangerously.
32. **Mate kāinga tahi, ora kāinga rua.**
    When one home is destroyed, you still have the second. (Have two strings to your bow.)
33. **Te wahine i te ringaringa me te waewae kakama moea, te wahine whakangutungutu, whakarerea atu.**
    The woman with active hands and feet, marry her, but the woman with overactive mouth, leave well alone.
34. **He ao te rangi ka uhia, he huruhuru te manu ka tau.**
    Clouds adorn the sky as feathers adorn a bird. (Original meaning: Dress correctly for the occasion. Modern meaning: 'Mā te huruhuru te manu ka rere' – Feathers [money] enable the bird to fly.)
35. **Ka pū te ruha ka hao te rangatahi.**
    The old net lies in a heap while the new net goes fishing. ('Rangatahi' has become synonymous with youth.)
36. **Ko te amorangi ki mua, ko te hāpai ō ki muri.**
    The carriers of God's emblems first, the carriers of food later. (God's worship first, worldly things later.)
37. **He harore rangitahi.**
    A one-day mushroom. (A flash in the pan.)
38. **He kura kāinga e hokia, he kura tangata ekore e hokia.**
    You may return to a treasured home, but not to a treasured person. (Similar to **17**.)
39. **He ihu kurī, he tangata haere, he mōkai manuhiri te puta noa.**
    The nose of the dog, the traveller, a visitor's pet has appeared. (The welcome traveller's presence is shown when his pet runs ahead and pokes his nose in the door.)
40. **Tangata takahi manuhiri, he marae puehu.**
    If a man insults a guest, his marae is dirty.
41. **He tao huata e taea te karo, he tao nā aituā kāore.**
    Human spears can be deflected, but not those of Misfortune (Death).
42. **Kia mahara ki te hē o Rona.**
    Remember the fault of Rona. (Rona is the woman in the Moon. She cursed the Moon and would not stop even when warned.)

43. **He kōtuku rerenga tahi.**	The white heron is a bird of one flight. (A rare visitor.)
44. **He toa piki rākau he kai nā te pakiaka.**	A champion tree-climber is food for the roots.
45. **He kūkū ki te kāinga, he kākā ki te ngahere.**	As a cooing dove is at home, so is a parrot in the forest. (Refers also to men who say nothing in discussion but are full of opinions afterwards.)
46. **He wahine, he whenua, ngaro ai te tangata.**	Men die because of land and women.
47. **He kokonga whare e kitea, he kokonga ngākau ekore e kitea.**	The corners of the house may be seen, but not the corners of the heart.
48. **Tūngia te ururua kia tupu whakaritorito te tupu o te harakeke.**	Burn the overgrowth to allow the flat shoots to show through.
49. **Tā te tamariki tana mahi he wāwāhi tahā.**	Children's work is breaking calabashes.
50. **Ekore e ngaro he takere waka nui.**	It will not be undetected, it is the hull of the canoe.
51. **He hokinga mate, he hokinga kāinga, he hokinga oneone.**	A sickly return, a return to home, a return to the soil. (A badly injured warrior just wants to return home.)
52. **He toka tūmoana he akinga nā ngā tai.**	A rock standing alone is lashed by the tides. (The tall poppy syndrome.)

Proverbs regarding certain tribes and areas – He pepeha

53. **ATI AWA**	
Ko Te Ati Awa o runga o te Rangi.	Ati Awa from heaven above. (Tamarau, one of the ancestors of Ati Awa, was a wairua.)
54. **TAURANGA**	
Ko Maunganui te maunga, ko Tupaea te tangata.	Maunganui is the mountain, Tupaea is the man.
55. **KAWERAU**	
Ko Pūtauaki te maunga, ko Rangitukehu te tangata.	Putauaki is the mountain, Rangitukehu is the man.

56. **NGĀTI KAHUNGUNU KI HERETAUNGA**	
Ko Kahuranaki te maunga, ko Te Hapuku te tangata.	Kahuranaki is the mountain, Te Hapuku is the man.
57. **WAIKATO**	
Waikato taniwha rau, he piko he taniwha, he piko he taniwha.	Waikato of a hundred monsters, at every bend a monster. (There are many tales of mysterious beings in the Waikato River, but here 'monsters' refers to the numerous independent chiefs.)
58. **TE ARAWA**	
Ko Te Arawa e waru pūmanawa.	The eight beating hearts of Te Arawa. (Te Arawa is a confederation of eight tribes descended from the eight children of Rangitihi.)
59. **Ko Te Arawa māngai nui.**	Arawa of the big mouth. (The Arawa people are famous for their oratory.)
60. **MAKETU, NGĀTI RANGITIHI**	
Ko Ruawahia te maunga, ko Mokonuiarangi te tangata.	Ruawahia is the mountain, Mokonuiarangi is the man.
61. **NGĀPUHI**	
Ngāpuhi kōhao rau, kai tangata.	Ngāpuhi of a hundred holes, man-eaters. (Ngāpuhi were not united but very fierce.)
62. **HOKIANGA**	
Hokianga whakapau karakia.	Hokianga which exhausts prayers. (Recalls the rivalry between chiefs Ruanui and Nukutawhiti, who used up all their spells in trying to defeat each other.)
63. **Hei kōnei rā, e te Puna o te Ao Mārama. Ka hoki nei tēnei, e kore e hoki anganui mai.**	Farewell, Spring of the World of Light; I am going home and will not return this way again.
64. **OHAEAWAI**	
Ka kata ngā pūriri o Taiamai.	The pūriri trees of Taiamai laugh, there's good news in the north.

65. HOKIANGA AND BAY OF ISLANDS

Ka totō te puna i Taumarere, ka mimiti te puna i Hokianga. Ka totō te puna i Hokianga, ka mimiti te puna i Taumarere.

When Taumarere's spring overflows, Hokianga's spring ebbs; when Hokianga's spring overflows, Taumarere's spring ebbs. (Hokianga to the west and Taumarere [Bay of Islands] to the east. What happens to one influences the other.)

66. TŪHOE

He kotahi nā Tuhoe ka kata te pō.

There is amusement in the underworld if only one Tūhoe dies in battle.

67. Tūhoe, moumou kai, moumou taonga, moumou tangata ki te pō.

Tūhoe, lavish with food, lavish with goods, lavish with men who fall in battle.

68. NGĀ RAURU

Rauru kī tahi.

Their chief, Rauru, was a man of his word.

69. NGĀTI POROU

Ko Hikurangi te maunga, ko Waiapu te awa, ko Ngāti Porou te iwi.

Hikurangi is the ancestral mountain, Waiapu is the river, Ngāti Porou is the tribe.

70. Waiapu kōkā huhua.

Waiapu of many mothers. (Ngāti Porou is always concerned for her children. Some say the proverb implies disunity.)

71. Ngāti Porou nukarau, he iwi moke, he whanokē.

Ngāti Porou, deceivers, lonely, but daredevils.

72. NGĀTI MARU

Tini whetū ki te rangi, ko Ngāti Maru ki te whenua.

As many as the stars in heaven, so numerous is Ngāti Maru on the earth. (Ngāti Maru were once very numerous in the Thames area and to the south of there.)

73. NGĀTI TŪWHARETOA (LAKE TAUPO)

Ko Tongariro te maunga, ko Taupo te moana, ko Te Heuheu te tangata.

Tongariro is the ancestral mountain, Taupo their own lake and Te Heuheu the paramount chief.

74. HAWKE'S BAY

Ko Heretaunga haukū nui.

Heretaunga of heavy dew-fall. (Heretaunga is very fertile.)

75. TARANAKI

Kāore e pau, he ika unahi nui.

It will not be eaten, that fish has big scales. (That fish [Taranaki] is too tough to eat.)

76. WHANGANUI

He muka nō te taura whiri a Hine Ngākau.

A thread from the woven rope of Hine Ngākau. (Many sub-tribes are her descendants from Wanganui, even north as far as Taumarunui.)

77. Ngā uri a Haunui-ā-Pāpārangi, nāna i taotao (takahi) te nukuroa o Hawaiki.

The descendants of Haunui-ā-Pāpārangi who trampled the length and breadth of Hawaiki. (Haunui was a courageous ancestor of the Wanganui people.)

78. AOTEA (but applicable to all)

Ekore e piri te uku ki te rino.

Clay will not stick to iron. (Do not pretend to be what you're not, because the clay disguise will fall off.)

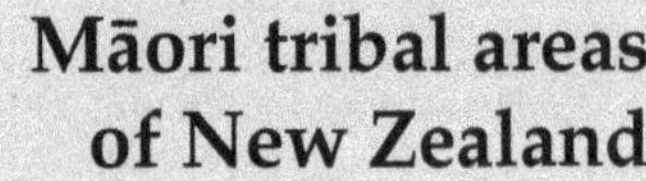
Māori tribal areas of New Zealand

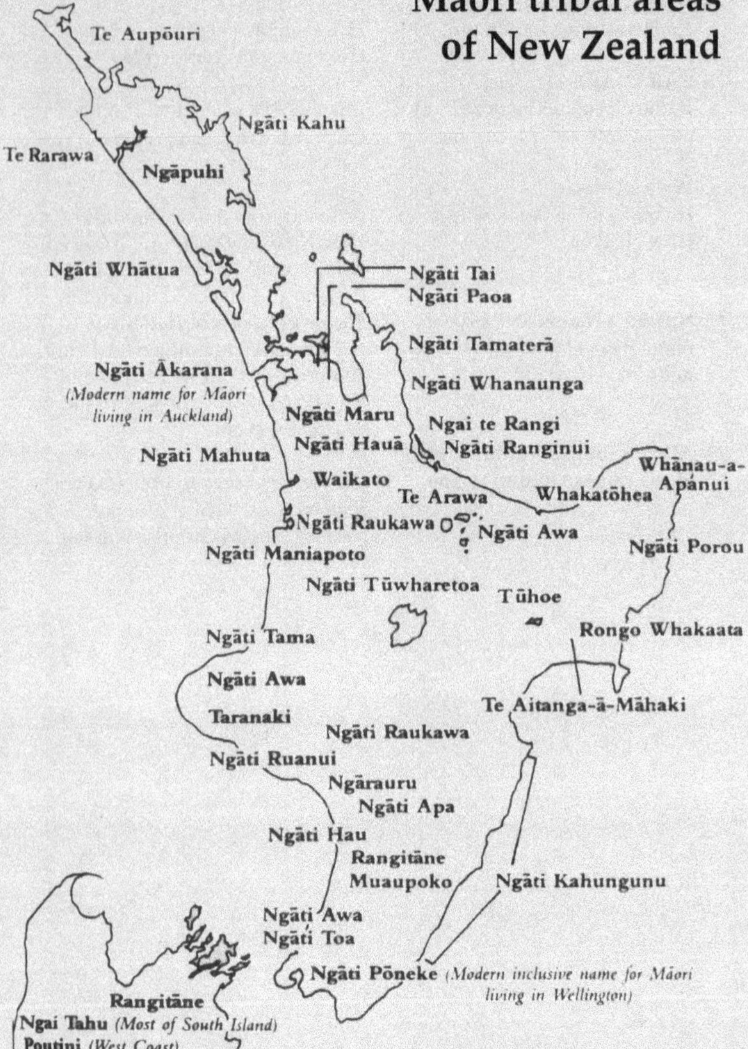

Te Aupōuri
Ngāti Kahu
Te Rarawa
Ngāpuhi
Ngāti Whātua
Ngāti Tai
Ngāti Paoa
Ngāti Tamaterā
Ngāti Ākarana
(Modern name for Māori living in Auckland)
Ngāti Whanaunga
Ngāti Maru
Ngai te Rangi
Ngāti Hauā
Ngāti Ranginui
Ngāti Mahuta
Whānau-a-Apanui
Waikato
Te Arawa
Whakatōhea
Ngāti Raukawa
Ngāti Awa
Ngāti Maniapoto
Ngāti Porou
Ngāti Tūwharetoa
Tūhoe
Rongo Whakaata
Ngāti Tama
Ngāti Awa
Te Aitanga-ā-Māhaki
Taranaki
Ngāti Raukawa
Ngāti Ruanui
Ngārauru
Ngāti Apa
Ngāti Hau
Rangitāne
Muaupoko
Ngāti Kahungunu
Ngāti Awa
Ngāti Toa
Ngāti Pōneke *(Modern inclusive name for Māori living in Wellington)*
Rangitāne
Ngai Tahu *(Most of South Island)*
Poutini *(West Coast)*
Ngāti Māmoe *(Far south)*

ENGLISH TO MĀORI

A

a/an he, tētahi
A.C.C. Kaporeihana Āwhina Hunga Whara
abalone pāua
abandon whakarere(-a)
abase whakaiti(-tia), whakahāwea
abate (sea) mauru, iti haere
abate (wind) kanape, māriri, mārie
abattoir whare patu mīti
abbreviate whakarāpopoto(-a)
abdomen puku, kōpū, tia
abet tautoko(-tia)
abeyance whakaupa, takaware, hiki, tārewa
abhorrent whakarihariha
abide by whai(-a), pono ki
ability kaha, pūmanawa
ablaze mura, mūrara, kā
able (can be done) taea, āhei
able (he is -) ka taea (e ia), e kaha ana
able-bodied mārōrō, mārohirohi
ablution block whare horoi
abnormal rerekē, tupua
aboard kei runga poti
aboard, load - uta(-ina)
abolish pēhi(-a), whakakāhore(-tia), whakahorohoro
abominable mōrikarika, weriweri
abomination mea whakarihariha
aboriginal tangata whenua, toi, taketake
aborigine tangata whenua, Kūri (o Ahitereiria), toi
abort whakatahe, whakamateroto
abortion tahe, materoto, kuka
about (almost) tata ki, tatangia
about (concerning) mō
about-face tahuri atu, tītaka
above kei runga, i runga, i runga atu/ake
above board tika, matanui
abrasive taratara, whakataratara
abridge whakapoto(-a), tāpoto(-tia)
abroad rāwāhi, ki tāwāhi, tawhiti
abruptly rere, ohorere, ohotata
abscess whēwhē, tuma, mariao
abscond rere, oma, paheke
absence korenga, ngaronga, kore
absent ngaro, matangaro
absent oneself takē
absent-minded wareware, muhukai, hinengaro makere
absolute tino, motuhake, pū, uara pū
absorb (soak up) mimiti, ngongo
abstemious ihupuku, nohopuku
abstinence papare
abstract (general) tikanga whānui
abstract noun kupu ingoa whānui
absurd heahea, wairangi, hohore
abundance ngahuru, huhua, ranea, huhuatanga
abundance, year of - tau humi
abundant huhua, rahi, tinitini, maha, tini
abuse (cursing) kangakanga

abuse (maltreat) raweke(-ngia), takahi(-a), tūkino(-tia)
abuse (wrongdoing) hara
abuse, sexual - raweke(-tia), kaitōkai
abuse, solvent - hongi kāpia, hongi wairou
abysmal koretake, raro rawa
abyss tōrere, poka tōrere, orunui, tomoau
academic taha mātauranga
academy kura motuhake
accelerate whakakakama, kātere, whakatere
accelerator (motor) kātere
accent (dialect) reo rerekē, mita o te reo
accent (stress) pei, tōnga
accept whakaae(-tia), tango(-hia)
acceptable tika, pai, wanea
acceptance whakaaetanga, manakohanga
access uru āhei, huarahi ki, whiwhi ki
accessible ka taea e te tangata
accessory (helper) kaitautoko
accessory item whakarawe, mea tāpiri, taonga tāpiri
accident aituā, mate whawhati tata, mea tūpono
accidental mea tūpono, aituā
acclamation umere
acclimatise waia ki te noho
accommodate whakanoho
accommodation whare noho, kāinga noho, kamareihana
accompany haere tahi i, haere hei hoa, haere i te taha
accomplice kaitautoko, hoa mahi, hoa hara
accomplish whakaoti, whakatutuki(-tia)
accomplished (done) oti, taea, ea
accomplishment whakaotinga, mea taea, mahi pai
according to e ai ki ngā kōrero, hei tā (mea)
accordingly nō reira, hoi, heoi, heoi anō
accordion kōriana
account pūkete, kaute, pire
account, bank - pūtea pēke
account for whakamārama
account, savings - pūtea penapena
account, of no - hauwarea
accountability whakatau tika
accountable to tū i raro i, papanga ki
accountant kaikaute, kaitātari kaute
accreditation tohutuku
acculturation whakamāori-ā-noho
accumulate kohikohi(-a)
accumulation whakaeminga
accuracy tikapūtanga
accurate tikapū, āta (mōhio)
accusation whakapae, heitara
accuse whakapae(-tia), whakawā(-tia)
accused, the - mauherehere, tangata e whakapaetia ana
accustom waia, taunga, whakawaia(-tia)
ace (cards) hai
ache mamae
achieve whiwhi ki, tae(-a), tutuki(-tia)
achievement whāinga hei tutuki, tutukitanga, taumata kua ekea

acid kawa, hīmoemoe, waikawa, mangeo, kakati
acknowledge whakamihi, whāki(-na), manako(-hia)
acne hakihaki, papata kiri
acolyte wharerā, kaiāwhina
acorn kano oka
acoustic pā ki te taringa, pai ki te whakarongo
acquaint whakamōhio(-tia)
acquire whiwhi ki, riro i a
acquisitive tangotango
acquit whakawātea(-tia), wete(-a)
acquit oneself well nanahu
acquittal wetenga
acre eka
acrid kikini
acrimonious mauāhara, whakatumatuma, pūtiotio
acrobat kaitūpekepeke, kaitārere
acrobatics takaporepore
across whakawhiti
across, lie - tīpae, hāngai, hīpae, kurupae, takoto whakapae
across valley/sea kei/i tāwāhi, rāwāhi
act (do) mahi
act (imitate) whakatau(-ria)
act (legal) ture
acting (pro tem) tūtei, whakakapi, rīwhi
action! mahi, tīmata!
action song waiata-ā-ringa, waiata haka, waiata kori
activate whakaoho(-ngia), tīmata(-tia), whakaharuru
active ngohe, whakahohe, mātātoa, kakama
active document tuhinga hohe
active object ahanoa hohe
active verb kupu mahi ngoi
active voice (grammar) reo hāpai
active window matapihi hohe
activist kaikorikori
activity mahi, hohe-ā-ringa, tūmahi
actor, dramatic - kaitapere, kaiwhakangahau
actress kaitapere wahine
actually engari koa
acupuncture werowero ngīra, ngīra whakaora
acute tārū, taruru, ihi, koi, matau
Adam's apple kenakena, tane o te kakī
adapt whakarite(-a), takatū(-ria), urutau
adaptation hurihanga, urutaunga
add tāpiri(-tia), āpiti(-tia), hono(-a), tatau(-ria)
add together huihui(-tia, -a)
addict kaiwarawara, kahunga mau rawa
addicted mau rawa, pūwaia ki
addiction waranga, pūwaiatanga
adding machine mīhini tātai/ōrite, kaitatau
addition tāpiritanga, roanga, whakanuinga ake
additional tāpiri
additive, food - matū kai
address (home) kāinga noho
address (speech) whai kōrero
address labels tapanga wāhitau
adept kaiaka, mātau, tautohito
adequate ka nui, hāngai ana, rawaka
adhere piri, pipiri, mau
adhesion piritanga
adhesive piripiri
adjacent i te taha, pātata, āta piri
adjective kupu āhua

adjourn hiki, waiho kia tārewa
adjudicate whiriwhiri(-a), whakawā(-kia), whakatau(-ria)
adjudicator kaiwhiriwhiri, kaiwhakawā, kaiwhakatau
adjust whakarite(-a), whakatika(-ina)
administer (run) whakahaere
administer (e.g. medicine) hōatu, whāngai
administration mana whakahaere
administrator kaiwhakahaere
admiral atamira
admire mihi(-a), whakamihi, titiro whakamīharo
admission tono
admit (let in) tuku(-a), whakahāngai
admit (confess) whāki(-na), whakapono(-hia)
adolescence taitamarikitanga, whanaketanga, taiohinga
adopted child tamaiti whāngai, tamaiti atawhai
adoption atawhai, whāngai, taurima
adoptive parents mātua whāngai, mātua atawhai
adore koropiko ki, tino aroha
adrift tere noa, kōrewa
adult kaumātua, pakeke, koeke, koroheke
adulterate whakangoikore, whakaranu, tūkino(-tia)
adultery pūremu, moe tāhae, tōkihi, hemahema
advance haere ake, haere ki mua, whakaeke, kōkiri arā anō
advantage take whai hua, pai, huanga
advent taenga mai
Advent season Aweneti
adventure mātātoa, haere māia
adventurer kiri māia
adverb kupu tūkē, hikumahi
advertise pānui(-tia)
advice kupu tohutohu, aki
advisable tika, whakaaro nui
advise tohutohu, whakatakoto kōrero
adviser whakaruruhau
advocate (*n.*) kaitautoko, māngai, kaiwawao
advocate (*v.*) taunaki(-tia), tautoko-ā-kupu
aerate panahau wai
aerial (antenna) hihi irirangi, pūhihi
aerial post pou irirangi, toko irirangi
aerobics whakakori tinana, haukori
aerodrome taunga manurere
aeroplane aropereina, manurere, wakarererangi
aerosol kēna rehu, rehu matūriki
aerospace ao ātea
affect pā ki, hāngai ana ki, pāpā, whakaawe(-a)
affection aroha, awe
affectionate mate oha
affidavit tuhinga kupu oati, oati-ā-pukapuka
affiliate whakahoa, whakakotahi, whakawhanaunga
affirm whakapūmau, whakakoia(-tia), whakaū(-ngia)
afflict pā(-ngia), karawhiu(-a)
affliction whakamamaetanga
affluence whai taonga, whai rawa, houkuratanga

afford whai moni (hei utu), tae(-a), whai rawa
afloat mānu ana, tere ana, rewa
afraid mataku, pāwera, wehi
Afrikaans reo Tatimana o Awherika, reo Poa
afro tūtū ngā makawe
after i muri, tua atu
afterwards i muri, a muri, tua atu, muringa
afterbirth whenua, ewe, rehuwhāerere
afternoon ahiahi
afterthought whakaaro taka noa
again anō
against ki, pā ki te taha
age taipakeke, pakeke, kaumātua haere
age, old - koroheketanga, kaumātuatanga
agency tari whakahaere, rōpū takawaenga
agenda hei mahi, kaupapa mahi, rārangi mahi, rārangi take
agent (rep.) māngai, kaikawe, pokapū, kairīwhi
aggression riri, pukuriri
aggressive taikaha, whakatuki
agile raka, ngāwari te tinana, koi, kamakama
agitate whakakorikori, rutu-a, whakaueue(-a)
ago ki mua
agony mamae nui whakaharahara
agree whakaae(-tia), rite, pai, whakaaro tahi
agreeable pai, reka, āhuareka, purotu
agreement whakaaetanga, whakaaro tahi
agreement, legal - kirimini, kirimina
agriculture ahu whenua, mahi whenua
aground ū ki uta, titi ki te onepū, pae, eke
ahead i mua, kei mua, e tū mai nei
aid awhi(-tia), āwhina(-tia)
AIDS (disease) mate āraikore, mate parekore
aim a blow panga, tū, whai(-a)
aim (purpose) whāinga, tino kaupapa
aim (to point) kero, whakakeko, whakakoi
aimless karore, āniwa, pakoke
air (atmosphere) hau, hauora, huinga hau
Air New Zealand Koru Aotearoa
aircraft wakarererangi
aircraft carrier manuao hari wakarererangi
airforce taua rererangi, tauarangi
airline kamupene rererangi
airmail reta rererangi, karere-ā-rangi
airport tauranga manurere, taunga rererangi
airship waka pūangi
airstrip taunga wakarererangi
airwaves irirangi, aratuku
airy hauangi pai, pongipongi, hākoakoa
alarm (startle) whakaoho, whakamataku, paoho
alarmed paoho, tūmeke, oho
alas auē
albatross toroa
albino rako, kōrako, kirikōtea
album pukapuka whakaemi

alcohol waipiro, waiwaihā
ale pia
alert kakama, hiwa, korita, tūmatohi
alert (arouse) whakaaraara
alias arā, ingoa kē, ingoa tango
alien tauiwi, nō te ao takiwā, manene
alienate (separate) whakawehe, tāpae atu, whakawātea(-tia)
alight (disembark) heke iho, tau ki raro, makere
align whakarārangi, whakahāngai(-tia)
alike rite, ōrite, taurite, pātahi
alive ora
all katoa
all around huri noa, huri
All Blacks Kapa Ōpango
alley ara whāiti, ara tuarongo
alliance haumi, hononga
allocate wehewehe, tohatoha
allocation pūtea i whakaritea
allot tohatoha(-tia), whakarato(-a)
allotment whakaratonga
allow tuku(-a, -na) ki, whakaae(-atia)
allow for whakaae(-tia), whakaaroaro
allowance (money) tāpaenga, utu
alloy pūhui konga, pūhui konganuku
ally (*n.*) kaitautoko, kaiāwhina
ally (*v.*) whakatuarā, uru ki roto, whakauru(-a)
almighty kaha rawa
almost tata(-ngia), wāhi iti nei, tata tonu, tōtahi
aloe aroe
alone anake, anahe, kau, nahe, tōtahi
along i, mā, atu
alpha ārepa
alphabet pūrārangi, tātai reta
alphabetise whakarārangi-ā-pū
already kē, noa
alright kei te pai
also hoki (after qualified word), anō
ALT key pātuhi ALT
altar āta, ahurewa, tūāhu
alter whakarerekē(-tia), whakakē
alteration whakarerekētanga
altered rerekē, whakahōu(-tia)
alternate huri atu huri mai, hokohoko, takirua
alternating current hiko kīnakinaki
alternative tētahi atu
alternatives ētahi atu huarahi
although ahakoa
altogether āpiti, kātoatoa, ngātahi
aluminium konumohe, ārama
always rite tonu, tonu, ake ake
am (express by word position e.g. a boy/me) he tama ahau
amateur utukore, ringarapa
amaze whakamīharo(-tia), whakaue
amazement mīharo
amazing whakahirahira, ka mau te wehi
ambassador māngai o te kāwanatanga
ambiguity rangiruatanga
ambiguous rangirua
ambition whakaeaea, tūmanako, tohe, hao nui
ambitious whakapai(-tia)
amble āta haere
ambulance waka tūroro

ambush aukati, kokoti, tauhanga, haupapa
amen āmine, āmene
amenable ngāwari, ngawhere, ngākau māhaki
amend whakatika(-hia)
amendment whakatikanga (ture), menamena
amenities taonga whakaahuru
American Marikena
amiable ngāwari, hoahoa, hūmarie, hūmārika
amid roto, rō
ammunition hāmanu
amnesia mate wareware
amnesty maungarongo, muru hara
amnion popoki, kahu
amoeba pūora huri kē
amok wairangi, pōrangi mārika, hōkeka
among i waenganui i, i roto i
amorous mate wahine, mate tāne, mateoha
amount nui, pupūtanga, rahi
amplifier whakanui reo, ranu reo
amplify tīwera, whakapāohoreo, whakawhānui(-tia)
amputate poro(-a), pororere
amuse whakangahau(-tia), whakakakata
amusement whakangahau, rēhia
an he
anaesthesia mahi ārai mamae, rehunga
anaesthetic, general - rongoā rehu
anaesthetist kairehu, kaiārai
analyse whakawā, tātari(-tia), arotake
analysis tātaritanga
anatomy hikohiko tinana
ancestor tipuna (*pl.* tīpuna), tupuna (*pl.* tūpuna)
ancestral land papatipu
ancestry whakapapa, tātai tupuna, kāwai tupuna
anchor (grapnel) punga, haika
anchor (moor) tau
anchorage tauranga, taunga (ūnga waka)
ancient onamata, o nehe rā
and ā, me, hoki (after word qualified)
anemone, sea - kōtore moana, humenga
angel āhere, ānahera
anger riri, pukuriri, riringa
angina hēmanawa
angle tuke, koki, konaki
Anglican Mihingare
angling hī ika
angry riri, tupehu, ongaonga, matawheke
anguish mamae nui, aurere, kohuki
angular tuketuke
animal kararehe
animate whakaoho(-tia), whakahauora(-tia)
ankle pona
ankle bone whatīanga raparapa
annex (take) kōhaki
annex (building) whareāpiti
annihilate whakakāhore(-tia), whakangaro(-mia)
anniversary huri tau, rā whakamaharatanga
announce pānui(-tia), whakapāho(-tia)
announcement pānuitanga
announcer kaipānui

annoy whakahōhā, whakatoi, whakatenetene
annoyance whanowhanoā
annoyed riri, hōhā, rikarika, whanowhanoā
annual ā-tau
annul whakakāhore(-tia)
anoint whakawahi(-a)
anonymous ingoakore, ingoamuna
anorexia whakatiki hārukiruki, mate whakatiki
another tētahi atu, tētahi anō, kē (after verb)
answer whakahoki(-a), whakautu(-a)
answer (maths) otinga, whakaō
ant pōpokorua, pokorua
antagonism mauāhara
antelope tia pihiroa, anaterope
antenna pūihi, pūhihi, pūtihi, rērehu
anthropologist kaimātai tikanga tangata
anthropology mātau o te noho tangata, mātauranga tikanga tangata
antibiotic rongoā paturopi
anticipate tūmanako(-tia)
antidote rongoā whakanoa
antifreeze ārai makariri
antiperspirant ārai werawera
antiquated hanga tawhito
antique nō namata, taonga tuauki
antiseptic rongoā horoi, patuero
antler pihona, pihi
anus nono, tero, whero, kumu, puta, kōtore
anvil paepae maitai, pae kuru
anxiety mānukanuka, āwangawanga
anxious māharahara, manawa popore, āwangawanga
any tētahi, ētahi, ia
anyhow ahakoa he aha
anyone awai rānei, he tangata
anything aha anō
anyway he ahakoa
anywhere hea rānei, ahakoa ki hea
apart wehe, motuhake, meha, ki tahaki
apart from atu anō i, hāunga, motuhake
apartheid noho wehewehe, tupu wehewehe
apartment whare noho
apathy pohe, ngākaukore, haumaruru
ape makimaki nui
apex tihi, tara, toi
aphid peperiki, weo, kutiriki, ngō
apologise pōuri, nā tōku hē, nāku te hē
apology kupu pōuri whakamārie hoki
apostle āpōtoro
apostrophe koru, pakini
apparatus taonga, taputapu, pānga
apparent mārama
apparition kēhua, whakakitenga wairua, mariko, kīhau
appeal īnoi(-a)
appear (come out) puta(-ina), whakaputa, urunga ake
appear in sky kōhiti
appearance āhua, pēhea, āhuatanga, putanga
append hono(-a), tāpiri(-tia)
appendicitis mate weu whēkau kakā, hiku whēkau kakā

appendix (anatomy) keu o te whēkau, weu whēkau
appetite hiakai, matekai, puku, mina
appetizing whakamākūkū, whakawaiwai
applaud (clap) pakipaki
applause umere, pakipaki
apple āporo
appliance utauta, taputapu, pūrere
applicable e pā nei ki
applicant kaitono
application (request) tautono, puka tono, tono mai/atu
apply dressing tāpi atu, tākai(-a)
apply for tono(-a), whakapātai(-tia)
appoint whakaingoa(-tia), whakatū(-ria)
appreciate whakaaro whakahari, whakamaioha(-tia)
appreciation maioha
apprehend hopu(-kina), mātau
apprehensive āwangawanga, mataku, hopohopo
apprentice tauira, ākonga, pia whakangungu
approach whakatata
approach direct haere hāngai
approach (path) ara, huarahi
appropriate tika, hāngai, ū
approval whakapai(-tia), whakaaetanga
approve whakaae(-tia), whakapai(-tia), whakatau(-ria)
apricot aperikota, pirikōti
apron maro, pini, hipane, taupaki
aptitude for matatau ki, mōhio ki, māiatanga
aquarium kauranga ika
aqueduct roma wai
arbitrary kei a wai te tikanga, pohewa
arc pewa, tāwhana, ānau, tīwhana, kape, piko
arch tāwhana, areare, tīwhana, kōpere
arch up whakatuapuku
archaeologist kaimātai whaipara tangata
archaeology mātau whaipara tangata, rangahau mea onamata
archaic tino tawhito, tuauri
archangel ānahere
archbishop ahipihopa
arched tiriwhana
archer kaikōpere
architect kaihoahoa, kaimahere
architecture hoahoanga, waihanga, hoahoa āhua whare
are express by word position (e.g. people/they = he tāngata rātou)
area wā, wāhi, takiwā, rohe
area chart tūtohi horahanga
area code waehere rohe
Area Health Board Poari Hauora-ā-rohe
arena papa hākinakina
argue tautohetohe, totohe, ngangare
argument tautohe, tohenga
arise ara, maranga, puta ake, kake
aristocracy Te Aitanga-a-Tiki, kāhui rangatira
arithmetic whika, tauhanga, tātai
ark āka
arm ringa, ringaringa
arm-in-arm taupiripiri
armchair nohoanga āhuru, nohoanga hāneanea

armed forces ope taua ārai hoariri
armpit kēkē, kaokao
army ope taua, hokowhitu
aroma kakara, mōkarakara
aromatic whakakakakara, tīere, tīare
aromatic leaves raureka, karamū
around ki tētahi taha, tawhio, rawhi
arouse whakaara, whakaoho
arrange whakarite(-a), raunaha
arrangements whakahaerenga, whakaritenga, whakanahanaha
array whakakākahu(-tia), huānga
arrears nama tārewa
arrest whakarau(-a), mau ki te pirihimana
arrival taenga, whakaekeeke
arrive tae(-a), whakaeke, tau
arrogant whakahīhī
arrow pere
arsenal pūtea rākaupū, whare matā, takapū
arson tutū ahi, tahu ki te ahi
art taha toi, mahi toi, toi
artery iaia mai i te manawa, uaua toto whero
artillery ngā pū
artist tohunga, pūkenga, kaitāri moko
artistic tohunga, rerehua
arts (and crafts) mahi-ā-ringa, kōwhaiwhai, haratau
as hei, pērā, anō, rite tonu
as far as tae noa ki, tae rawa ki, ahakoa
as if me he mea, me, anō he, anō nei
as soon as possible tere tonu, taro ake nei
ascending aupiki
ascension kakenga, whakareanga
ascent pikitanga
ash pungarehu, ngārehu
ash tree (N.Z.) tītoki
ashamed whakamā, matangerengere, numinumi
ashore ki uta, tahaki
aside ki tahaki, peka kē, ki te taha, whakaitu
ask pātai(-ngia), ui(-a), īnoi(-a), tono(-a)
asleep moe(-a)
asleep, sound - parangia
asparagus apareka, parakati
aspect āhuatanga, aronga, tirohanga
aspiration (ambition) hiahia, pīrangi, wawata
aspire hao, manawanui, ngākaunui(-tia)
ass kaihe
assailant kairuhi
assassin kaikōhuru
assemble hui(-a), whakamine(-a)
assembled emi, rūpeke, whakakao
assembly rūnanga, hui, whakaminenga
assent whakaae(-tia), whakaaetanga
assess āta whakatau, arotake, wāriu(-tia)
assessment āta whakataunga, aromatawai
assessor kaiwhakakapi, āteha
asset hua, taonga
assignment mahi i tonoa, wehenga mahi
assimilate hanumi, momi, whakawaimeha, horonga
assist āwhina(-tia), whakahirihiri, awhi(-tia)

assistance āwhinatanga
assistant taituarā,kaiāwhina,tāpiri
associate pāhono
associate (colleague) hoamahi, kaiāwhina
associate with whakahoa
association rōpū, tōpū
assortment tūmomo
assurance kī pono, kupu tūturu
assure whakatūturu
asterisk pīwhetū, whetūriki
astern ki muri
asthma kume, huangō, hiki
astonishing whakamīharo, tūmeke
astound tino whakamīharo, tumeke rawa
astray kotiti, ngaro, kaewa, paihore
astrologer kaititiro whetū
astrology wānanga kōkōrangi
astronaut kaipōkai-ātea, kairere whaitua
astronomer tohunga kōkōrangi
astronomy tātai arorangi, mātau kōkōrangi
astute kakama, mōhio, mūrere
asylum piringa, whare pōrangi
at kei, kai, ki
at large kei te wātea, nō ngā moka wātea
at once tonu iho, ināianei tonu
at sign (@) tohu 'kei'
athlete kaiwhakataetae
athletics kaiaka, kaipara
atlas pukapuka mapi, pukapuka mahere whenua
atmosphere hau takiwā, rangatea, rangi, ariā
atom ngota, kongakonga, kitakita, mākarokaro
atom bomb pahū karihi, pahū nukiria
atonement whakamārietanga, whakangāwari
atrocious tino hē, tino kino
attach whakapiri, whakamau(-a), āpiti
attack huaki(-na), whakaeke(-a), tuki(-a), kōkiri(-tia)
attack by stealth whakatoke
attain tae(-a), tareka(-tia)
attempt (try) whakamātau(-ria), whakatū(-ria)
attend to aro, mūtūtū, tae ki, tahuri
attendance tini i tae mai, taenga mai
attendant kaitiaki, kaitono, tūmau
attention, pay - anga te whakaaro, aro atu, mahara, whakarongo
attentive whakarongo pīkari, mataara, hihiwa, puakaha
attitude wairua, āhuatanga, waiaro
attract kumekume(-a), whakamanea(-tia), kukume
attractive ātaahua, manea
attribute painga, huanga
auburn ura
auction mākete(-tia), hoko kairapu
auctioneer reo hokohoko, kaimākete
audible pā ki te taringa, rangona ki te taringa, hīrea
audience hunga mātakitaki, whakaminenga
audio reo, ororongo
audio tape rīpene reo
audio-visual rongo-kite, ataata-rongo

audit tātari kaute, ōtitatanga
audit fees utu tātari kaute
audition whiriwhiringa, wā whakarongo
auditor kaitātari kaute
aunt whaea, āti, whaene
aura āniwaniwa
aural nō te taringa
aurora tahu nui ā rangi
Aurora Australis (Southern Lights) Tahunui-ki-te-rangi, Kurakura-o-Hinenui-te-Pō
Australian nō Ahitereiria
authentic tūturu, tino tika
author kaitito, kaituhi
authorisation whakamanatanga
authorise whakamana(-tia)
auto aunoa
autocorrect whakatika-aunoa
autograph hainatanga anō, waitohu
automatic noa, aunoa, hanga noa
automatic jug tīkera kānoa
automobile motokā
autonomy whiriwhiri mōna ake, mana motuhake
autumn ngahuru, tokerau
auxiliary kaiāwhina, tautoko, tāpiri
available reri, rite, wātea
available memory pūmahara wātea
avalanche horowhenua, horonga
avenge rapu utu, ngaki mate, takitaki, whakaea
avenged ea, pūea
avenger kaitakitaki, kairanaki
avenue huarahi marumaru
average kei waenganui, wawaenga
aviary whare rāihe manu
aviation whakahaere rererangi
avoid karo(-hia), pare(-a)
await tatari (tāria)
awake oho, whakaoho, whakaara
awaken whakaoho(-ngia), mataara
award (give) whakawhiwhi(-a)
award (trophy) paraihe, tohu pai
award wage papa utu
aware kakama
away noho atu
awe wehi, pāwerawera, wetiweti, wanawana
awe inspiring wanawana
awful kino te āhua
awl wirikoi
awning maru, kōmaru
axe toki, tokitītaha, panekeneke, piau
axle pokapū wīra, kakau wīra, pae wīra, uehā

B

B.A./B.Sc. degree Tohu Wānanga tuatahi, Tohu Paetahi
babble whawhe, kapetau
babbler ngutu pī
baboon maki touwhero
baby pēpi, tamaiti, kōhungahunga, pōtiki
bach wharau, kōpuha
bachelor takakau, whai tohu mātauranga
back, to the - ki muri, i muri
back of body tuarā
back, go - hoki
back, hold - pupuri (puritia), pēhi(-a), kuku(-a)
backbite ngautuarā, muhari
backblocks wāhi tūhāhā, wāhi mokemoke, tuawhenua
backbone tuaiwi, iwi tuararo, ua, tuakoko
backfire pohū ki muri
background papamuri
backline (sport) pae muri
backline players kapamuri
backlog whakaputunga
backslash rītahamuri
backstroke kau kiore, kau tīraha, kauhoe tīraha
backup pūrua, tārua
backwards whakatuarā, ki muri, komuri, whakamuri
backwash miti (o te moana), tai whakahoki
backwater muriwai
bacon pēkana
bacteria moroiti, kitakita, huakita
bad (evil) kino
bad (decayed) pirau
badge tohu
badminton pūkura
bag pēke, pūtea, pāhi
bag (paper) pākete, pūhera
baggage utanga
bagpipes pōrutu kotimana, pūngawī
bail water tā(-ngia), tatā, tīheru(-a)
bailer tātā
bailiff kaituku hāmene, pononga tuku hāmene
bait mōunu, māunu
bake tunu(-a), tao kai
baked beans pīni maoa
baker kaihanga parāoa, pēka, kaitunu parāoa
bakery toa hoko parāoa, hereumu
baking soda pēkana houra
baking tray paepae tunu, paetopī
balance (*n.*) pūrere whārite
balance (*v.*) tīemiemi
balance books whakarite(-a) kaute, whakataurite
balance (of money) toenga, kaute
balance (weights) ōrite, whārite, tūorite
balance of power mana ōrite
balance sheet ripanga (whārite) kaute, pūrongo tātai
balcony mahaurangi, parehua, nohoanga runga

bald pākira, porohewa, tīhore, moremore
bale pēre
ball paoro, poi, poikiri
ball bearing pōro kawe, poi kawe
ballast pēhi, tao waka
ballast, adjust - utauta
ballet kanikani tūtengi, ori hīteki
balloon pūangi, poihau
ballot pōti, pōtitanga, māpere, rawhara
ballpoint penepura, penepōro
ballyhoo kōrero noaiho, kōrero pōrangi
bamboo inanga
ban ārai(-a), rāhui(-tia)
banana panana, maika
band (head) tīpare
band (musical) pēne
band of people ope, pahī, tira
bandage takai(-a), tākaikai
bandit kaitahae, pihareinga
bang pahū, pao
bangle kōmore
banister rēra, rōau, taka
banjo panio, pātura, kūaho
bank account pūtea pēke
bank card kāri pēke, kāri putea moni
bank, money - pēke
bank, river - parenga, tahataha
bank teller kaitatau moni
banker kaitaupua moni
bankrupt pēkerapu, whati
baptise iriiri(-a)
baptism iriiringa
bar (gymnastic) tāuhu, tauteka
bar (law) pae ture
bar (pub) tūpapa
bar (rod) paepae, rēra, tūtaki
barb kāniwha, keka
barbecue rorerore, tunutunu-ā-waho
barbed wire pāpu waea
barber kaikuti makawe, kaiheu pāhau
bare (cleared smooth) mārakerake, moremore
barge (*v.*) pana(-ia)
barge (flat boat) waka papa, pāwai, pāti
baritone reo panguru, reo tamawae
bark (dog) auau, tautau, whakaparoro, pahupahu
bark (tree) hiako, kiri rākau, kiripaka
barley pāre, pārei
barnacle pātitotito, kōmāungaunga
barracks puni hōia
barracouta mangā
barrage waiwaipū
barrel (cask) kāho
barrel of gun ngongo, ongo
barren land hahore, tītōhea, pākeka, rake
barren female pukupā, pākoko, rautahi
barricade ārai(-a), pā(-ia), papatū, tāiha(-tia)
barrier aukati, aukatinga, pōreareatanga, tauārai
barrister roia
barrow huripara
barter hokohoko, tuopu(-tia)
base word kupu matua
base, softball - papa
baseball pēhipaoro
baseboard papa pūtake
bashful whakamā, konekone
basic tino kaupapa, waiwai

basin peihana, paihana, oko
basis pūtake, kaupapa
basket kete, kōnae
basket, large - tokanga, hao
basket, small cooking - pohewa, tāpora
basketball poi hao, pahiketepōro, poirawhi, poitūkohu
bass fish moeone
bass voice reo tāne hōhonu, reo nguru
bastard pōriro, tīraumoko, tama meamea
bat (animal) pekapeka
bat (sport) rākau, haurākau
bat (strike) pao(-a), patu(-a), hahau(-tia)
batch momo, rourou
bath tāpu kaukau, kauranga
bathe kaukau (kauria), whakakaukau(-ria), toutou(-tia)
bathroom rūma kaukau, kaukauranga, kauranga
batsman kaihau, kaipatu
battalion mātua, hokowhitu
batten pātene, kaho, pouihi
batter (beat) patupatu, mekemeke, pātukituki
batter (cooking) kiri parāoa, pokewai
batter (sport) kaipatu, kaihahau
battering ram rākau tukituki, poutukituki
battery (electric) pāka hiko, pūhiko, pātere, urukā, pēteri
battle (*n.*) riri, pakanga, whawhai, kakari
battle (*v.*) kakari
battlefield parekura, tāhuna, kauhanga riri
battleship manuao
baulk/balk ārai atu, tawhitawhi, kōrapa
bay whanga, koro
bay horse pei
bayonet pēneti, okapū
be ora, mauri ora
beach (*n.*) one, ākau, taha moana, tahatai, tāhuna
beach (*v.*) whakaū(-ria), tō(-ia) ki uta
bead poria, rei puta, kano
beak ngā ngutu, timo
beaker (plastic) ipurau kirihou
beam (light) haeata, hunu
beam (wood) kurupae, paepae
bean pīni, pīti, pītau
bean sprout pihi pīni
bear (*n.*) pea, tetipea
bear (*v.*) hari(-a), tari(-a), kawe(-a), mau(-ria)
beard paihau, pāhau
bearer kaikawe, karere kawe
beast kararehe
beat, musical taki, pātotō
beat, policeman's haerenga pirihimana
beat (strike) patu(-a), pao(-a), tā(-ngia), taupatupatu
beat about the bush hahani haere
beat, heart - mokowhiti
beaten pīti, mate, hinga, piro
beautiful ātaahua, hūmarie, kura, waiwaiā, rerehua
beauty ātaahua
became riro kē
because ināhoki, nā/nō te mea, tātemea, hoki (after word qualified)
beckon pōwhiri, tāwhiri, tungatunga

become riro hei, whaka + *noun* (e.g. whakamanu = become a bird)
bed (garden) mahinga kai, tāhuna
bed (river) riu, whaiawa
bed (sleep) moenga, pēti
bedraggled taretare, māhora
bedroom ruma moe, taiwhanga moe
bee pī
beech, silver - tawai
beef mītikau
beehive whare miere, heke pī
beekeeper kairaupī
beeline poka tata, mārō, haere hāngai, hāngai pū, ara pūkake
been kua + *verb*
beer pia
beet pīti
beet, silver- korare
beetle pītara, mūmū, pāpapa, huhu tataka
beetroot tāmore whero, kōkura, pīti, whero, rengakura
before i mua
befriend whakahoa(-tia)
beg īnoi(-a), pīnono, pati moni, pītoto
beggar rawakore pati moni, pīnono, pōhara
begin tīmata(-tia)
beginner tauhou
beginning tīmatatanga, orokohanga
behalf, on - of i runga i te tono, mō te āhua ki a
behave noho pai, whano
behaviour āhua o te noho, whanonga, hanga
behind kei/i muri, kei tua
being mea ora
being, alien - tipua
belch kūpa, tokopūhā, tokomauri, tokopuhake
belfry pourewa pere
belief whakapono
believe whakapono(-hia)
bell pere, pahū
bellbird korimako, titimoko, makomako
belly puku, kōpū, hōpara
belong nō, nā
belongings taonga
beloved tau pūmau, whaiāipo, hokoi, tau
below i raro i, ki/kei/i/ko raro, tō raro
belt whītiki, tātua
bench (seat) tūruroa, nohoanga
bench, work - papa mahi, tēpu mahi, tūpapa mahi
bend (curve) piko, kokonga, koki, huringa
bend knees whati ngā turi, hūpeke, hūpekepeke
bend over tūpou, tāpapa, tūohutanga
benediction whakapainga, manaakitanga
beneficial whaihua, whakapai, waimarie, manako
beneficiary tangata whai pānga, kaiwhiwhi takuhe, kāwai, uri
benefit takuhe, āwhina, painga, huanga
benevolent hūmārire, aroha
bent hake, hakoko, wheoro, koromeke
bent knees turipēpeke
benzine penehīni
bequeath tuku(-a) iho, mahue iho

bereaved pani, whānau pani
berry kākano, hua, pata
berth wāhi moe, wāhi herenga poti
beside (next to) i te taha, kei te taha, ki te taha
beside the point hape
besides hāunga, tua atu
besiege karapoti(-a), awhi(-tia), whakapae(-a), kopani(-a)
best pai rawa, te tino pai
best man hoa takatāpui, taituarā, hoa pono
bet peti
beta particle matūriki peta
betray tuku(-a), kaikaiwaiū, whakamoho(-a)
better than pai atu i, pai ake i
beware (. . . lest) kia tūpato kei + *verb*
bewildered pōhēhē, pororaru, pōrearea, pōauau
bewitch mākutu(-ria), whaiwhaiā, kōtē(-tia, -hia), whiti(-a)
beyond kei kōatu, kei tua
bi-cultural tikanga-ā-rua, kākano rua
bias tītaha, whakawā wawe
bib, netball - pare tūnga, pare tākaro
Bible Paipera
biceps uarua, io peke
bicycle paihikara
bid tono(-a)
bidibid (biddy-biddy) piripiri, hutiwai, piriwhetau
big nui, rahi, kaitā, pīki (before its noun)
big toe tonui, rongomatua
bigot upoko mārō, tuanui noa
bikini pikīni, kahukaukau paku nei
bilge riu
bilingual reorua
bill (invoice/account) kaute, pire, nama
bill of rights tūtohinga o te mana tangata
billboard pourewa pānui
billet wā noho o te hōia, nohoanga
billiards piriota
billion piriona
billycan pīkini, kēna
billygoat koati toa, pirikoti
bind paihere(-a), tui(-a), kōtui
binding (of book) tuarā pukapuka, paihere anga
bingo wharewhare
binoculars karu torotoro, karurua whakatata
biochemistry matūora
biodegradable ka taea te pīrau, pōpopo
biography tuhinga koiora, pukapuka mō te tangata, haurongo
biologist kaikoiora, kaimātai koiora
biology mātauranga koiora
birch tree petura
bird manu
bird, preserved - huahua
bird nest kōhanga, kōpae, kōanga
birdcage māhanga manu
birth whānautanga
birth control ārai hapū
birthday rā huritau, rāwhānau
birthmark ira, namu
birthrate kaute whānautanga, whānaunau

birthright mātāmuatanga
biscuit pihikete
bisect weherua, hāwhe(-tia), tapahi(-a)
bisexual taera rua
bishop pīhopa
bit (for horse) kumewaha
bit (piece) maramara, pita
bitch kurī uwha
bite (insect) wero(-hia)
bite ngau(-a), kakati, ū(-ria)
bitter kawa, pūkawa
bittern, little - kaoriki
bitumen korotā, pakakē
black pango, mangu
blackberry parakipere
blackmail tāwai(-tia)-ā-reta
blacksmith parakimete, ringa pīau
bladder tongāmimi, pokomimi
blade koinga, mata, rau
blade, razor - mataheu
blame whakawā(-kia), whakapae
blank ātea, mahea
blanket paraikete, papanārua
blaspheme kangakanga, kohukohu
blast wāwāhi(-a), uruhanga
blaze mura, toro
bleach whakahātea, whakatōki
bleached hātea
bleary harare
bleed toto
blemish tonga, tongakiri, nawe
blend whakaranu
blender kīnakinaki, whakahanumi
bless whakapai(-ngia), whakatapu(-a)
blessing whakatapunga, manaakitanga
blight paraiti
blind matapō, kāpō, kerepō
blind, window - ārai
blindfold kōpare(-a), ārai kanohi
blindness kāpōtanga, matapōtanga
blink kimo, kemo, kikimo, kimokimo
blinker paewhatu
blister hoipū, namunamu
blister, large - tetere, whēwhē
blistered pakō, kōpūpū, memeke
blizzard āwhā kino, huka pūkeri
bloat puru hipi, pupuhi
block (flats) whare tininohoanga
block (land) pīhi, poraka, whaitua
block (offices) whare tinitari
block of wood poro rākau, poraka, tumu
block up (obstruct) puru(-a), pā(-ia), ārai(-a), āpuru(-a)
blockade pā
blockage purupuru
blockhouse pā, whare pā
blonde kakaho, kōrito, kōrako, urukehu
blood toto
blood bank pūtea toto
blood clot katinga toto, katitoto
blood group tūmomo toto
blood pressure rere o te ia toto, taukapa o te toto
blood pressure, high - taikaha
blood pressure, low - kōteretere
blood transfusion whāngai toto
blood vessel ia toto
bloodshed ngā toto kua heke kē, parekura
bloodshot wherowhero

bloodstock hōiho kāwai
bloodstream ia toto
bloody pūtoto, purari
bloom pua, rea, hua
blossom puāwai
blotch ukupara
blotting paper pepa mautere
blouse humeuma, hikurere, hāketi
blow (snort) whengu
blow (strike) pao(-a), kuru(-a), patu(-a)
blow (wind) pupuhi (pūhia)
blow instrument whakatangi(-hia)
blow up pahū
blowfly ngaro, rango
blowhole (whale) tāpihapiha, pihapiha
blowlamp rama whakawera
blown away pūrere
blowpipe paipa pū roa
blubber (cry) tangi(-hia), tangiweto
blue black (indigo) tūtū, poropango
blue (colour) purū, kikorangi, kahurangi, ōrangi
blue cod rāwaru, pākirikiri, pātutuki
blue heron kākatai, matuku
blue penguin kororā
blue wattled crow kōkako
blueprint whakatakotoranga kaupapa
bluff (deceive) tinihanga, māmingatanga
blunder pōhēhē
blunderbuss pū wahanui
blunt pūhuki, more, nguture, pūnuku, pūnuki
blur rehu, whēkite, makaro
blush whero ngā pāpāringa, whakamā, pāhanahana
bluster tūpererū
blustering tupehu
boar tāriana, tame poaka
board (committee) poari, rūnanga whakahaere
board (wood) papa rākau
board of trustees poari whakahaere
boarding (lodging) nohoanga
boast whakapehapeha, whakaparanga
boastful pākiwaha, wahahuka
boat poti, waka
bobbin pōkai miro
bobby-calf tame kāwhe
bodily ā-tinana, ā-kiko
body tinana, kiko
body of people rōpū, ngare
bodyguard kaitiaki tinana
boffin kairangahau
bog repo
boggy repo, mawharu, pōharuharu
bogus rupahu
boil (ulcer) whēwhē, tāpoa
boil (water) koropupū, pāera(-tia), korohuhū, hū
boiler kōhua, kōhue, paere
boiling spring ngāwhāriki, ngāwhā
boisterous tarakaka, tūperepere, turituri
bold māia
boldly mārakerake
bolt (lock) raka, whaowiri, koro pā, whakarawa(-tia)
bolt (run) huke atu, oma atu
bomb pahū, pōma, popohū

bomb (nuclear) pahū karihi, poma nukiria
bombardment pahūtanga, taiparatanga, pāhūhū
bombshell pohūtanga
bond here
bone wheua, poroiwi, iwi
bone (debone) kokoti(-a)
bonito matiri
bonus hua
bony tūwai, tūai, whīroki
book pukapuka
book (reserve) tono(-a), kirimana(-hia)
book-keeper kaikaute
bookcase pū pukapuka
bookshelf papa pukapuka, whata pukapuka
bookstand tūnga pukapuka
boom (noise) hū, pakū, hāparangi
boost whakanui(-a), tautoko, hiki(-tia)
boot pūtu, kuhuwai
bootlace rēhi
border (boundary) rohe, taitapa
border (hem) remu, pakitaha
bore (drill) wiri, wero, kōwiri(-tia), poka(-ina)
bore (tire out) whakahōhā, takeo, maroke
bored (dull) hōhā, hāpeta
borer-eaten pōporo
born whānau, puta ki waho, whānaunau
borough rohe o te tāone
borrowed mea tono, mea tuku mai
Borstal whare herehere tamariki, whare tiaki tamariki
bosom uma, poho
boss pāhi, rangatira, pōhi
botany mātauranga huaota, ako tipuranga
both rāua tahi, tautokorua
bother whakatāuteute, raruraru, pēhi
bottle pātara, pounamu, kōkihi
bottle-opener huaki pātara
bottom raro, takere
bottom (base) take
bottom (person) kumu, nono, whero, tou
bough peka, manga
bought hokona
bounce tāwhana
bounce up and down tīrengirengi, pīringiringi
boundary rohe, pae aru, rohenga
boundary line tawhā
boundary marker pou rāhui, kotinga
bouquet (scent) kakara
bout (boxing) whawhai, tuawhainga
bow (arc) tāwhana, kōpere, koromahanga
bow (boat) ihu, tauihu, ngongohau, aupounamu
bow (weapon) kōpere, pewa, parori, piko
bow down koropiko, tuohu
bow-legged turihaka
bowels whēkau, aro, manawa, kumu, puku hamuti
bowels of the earth whatumanawa o te ao
bowl (ball) tuku, epa, pīrori, kuru
bowl (container) kumete, peihana, oko, kāhaka
bowled out hinga
bowler kaikuru, kaipīrori
bowling ball maita

box (carton) pouwaka, pouaka, pāka
boxing whawhai mekemeke, moto
boxing ring papa mekemeke
boxthorn pakitōne
boy tama, tamaiti tāne, poai
boycott whanakorekore, ārai(-a)
boyhood whanaketanga, taitamatanga
bra pari-uma, kopeū
brace tauteka, kaumahaki, whītiki, hōkai
bracelet kōmore, takore, taupua
braces perēhi
bracken rarauhe, rauaruhe, rahurahu
bracket (enclose words) aukatinga
braid tāniko, pare, whiri(-a)
brain roro, hinu, wairoro
brainwashing roro horoinga
brake whakatū, perēki
brake, hand- whakatū ringa
bramble tātaramoa, tairo
bran waru wīti, pāpapa
branch out toro
branch (roadstream) pekanga
branch (turn off) peka(-tia) atu
brand waitohu, parani(-tia), momo
brandy parani
brass parāhi
brat tamaiti kino
bravado whakapehapeha
brave māia, mārohirohi, toa
brave warrior manu tīoriori
bravery toa, toanga, māiatanga, hautoa
brawl whawhai, manioro
bray hīhō, ngengehe
breach of contract kore mau ki te tikanga
bread parāoa, rohi, taro
breadfruit poroporo, taro
breadline pōharatanga
breadth whānui
break (smash) whati(-a), pākaru(-tia), kokoti
break, day- haeata, maruata, tākiri
break down (decompose) whakapopo
break in (burgle) uru poka
break in (tame) whakarata
break (split) wāhi(-a)
break through pākaru(-tia)
break up ngawhere(-a)
break wind (fart) whātero, pātero, tē, putihi
breakdown (collapse) pakarutanga
breakdown (emotional) hūhē, hē rawa atu, tata pōrangi
breakfast kai o te ata, parakuihi
breakthrough kitenga hou
breakwater paetai, parepare tai
breast uma, poho
breastbone kōuma, whaturei
breastfeed whāngote
breaststroke tāhoe uma
breath manawa, hau, hā, ngā
breath, out of - hē te manawa
breath, take a - mapu, tā te manawa, ngāehe
breathalyser pū rongowaipiro
breathe whakangā, whakatā, whakahā, whakaeaea
breathe with difficulty hāhea, hēmanawa
breathing, rescue - hā whakaora
breeze angiangi, matangi, hauhau, hauangi

brethren tuākana, tēina
brevity poto
brew māhī, ī
briar tairo, tātaramoa
bribe tāwai(-a), utu whakapati
brick pereki, ukuahi
bricklayer tiri perēki, kaimahi perēki
bride wahine mārena hou
bridegroom tāne mārena hou
bridesmaid takatāpui, kōtiro puhi, taituarā
bridge piriti, arawhata, arahanga, arāwai
bridge of nose kaka o te ihu
bridle paraire
brief (legal) ripoata rōia
brief (short) poto
briefcase kopa, hō, kopamārō
brier (*see* briar) tūmatakuru, tātaramoa, tairo
brigade, fire - umanga kāpura
bright kanapu, ao, purata, kanapa, tiaho
brighten whakamārama
brilliant kanapu, koea, tino kakama, tahutahu
brine waitai, wai tote
bring kawe(-a), tiki(-na), mau(-ria), hari(-a)
bring up (care for) whāngai
brisk tere, whitawhita, tarahati
bristle tūtū huruhuru, taratara, wana, hīkaka
brittle mōhaki, maroke, waipawa
broad whānui, whārahi, paraha, raunununui
broadcast pānui, reo irirangi, pāho
broadminded whānui
broadside on huapae, kōpae, hīpae
brochure puka
broil tunu(-a)
broke pau ngā moni
broken off motu, whati, pororere
bronchitis mate ngōrahi, mare wharowharo
bronze kiripaka, parāhi
brood (progeny) kāhui, punipuni, whānau
brook (stream) manga wai
broom (tool) purūma, taitai, tahitahi
brothel whare pūremu, whare kairau
brother of girl tungāne
brother, young - (of male) teina, taina
brother, older - (of male) tuakana
brother-in-law of man taokete
brother-in-law of woman autāne
brotherhood nohotahi a te teina a te tuakana
brothers senior tuākana
brothers young tēina, tāina
brought mau mai
brow of head rae
brow of hill taumata
brown parāone, pākākā, pākā, hāura, parauri
browse honi(-a), āta kai, whakarapa(-tia), āta titiro, tirotiro
bruise kōparu, marū
bruised marū, hautū
brush paraihe, taitai, toroi
brush past pāheke, konihi
brushwood tāwhao, heuheu, puaka, huru
Brussels sprouts parete, ao nanī
brutal whakawiriwiri
brute kararehe kino, mohoao
bubble (*n.*) koropupū, mirumiru, haupuke

bubble (*v.*) koropupū, hīhī, hū, mirumiru
buck (jump) tūpoupou, kiorere, tanapu, maka(-ia), porotēteke
buck, to pass the - whakarare
bucket pēre, pākete, ipu heri
buckle tīmau, kati, whati
buckteeth niho tapiki
bud ao, matikao, toroihi, wana
budge pānekeneke
budget tātari pūtea moni, aronga o te whakapau moni, tahua
buffet paripari(-a), koheri
bug kiriwai, kēkererū, ngārara
bugger paka
bugle piukara
build hanga(-a, -ia)
builder kaihanga, kaimahi whare
bulb (light) pūraiti, pūrama
bulb (plant) pū tipu, tōpuku
bulge pupuhi, matakoma, kūtere, koropuku
bulk nuinga, mōmona
bull pūru
bull kelp rimurapa
bull roarer pūrerehua, wheorooro, huhū
bull's eye pūtahi
bulldozer koko mīhini, whakapana, mīhini ketu oneone
bullet matā, pokepoke
bulletin reta pānui
bullock ōkiha
bully whakawhiu(-a), whakatoi, kaiwhakaweti
bulrush raupō
bum nono, whero
bumble-bee pī rorohū
bump tūtuki (tukia), rutu(-a)
bumper rēra tūtuki, rōau tuki, pākaituki
bunch pū, tautau, pūtoi, kaui
bundle pūhanga, paihere(-a), aupatu, kākati, pōkai
bung puru, pangu, kāremu
bungy jumping peke waehere
bungle hē, whakapōhēhē
bunk moenga whaiti
bunker (golf) pōrea kiri
buoy kārewa, pāho
buoy up whakatere(-tia)
burden pikaunga, utanga, wahanga, kawenga
burglar kaitāhae, kaiwhenako, kaiā
burglary tāhaetanga, whānako, whēnako
burgle kaiā(-ngia)
burial tanumanga, nehunga, tāpuketanga
burly pūioio
burn (blaze) kā(-ngia), toro, ngiha
burn (ignite) tahu(-na), wera(-ina)
burnt wera ki te ahi
burnt dry pakapaka
burr piripiri
burrow (*n.*) rua, unu rāpeti, ana
burrow (*v.*) apu, tūrua
bursar kaitiaki pūtea moni
bursary karahipi takuhe, pūtea tauira tāpiri
burst papā(-ngia), pahū, haruru, puhake
burst into laughter pakiri te kata
bury nehu(-a), tanu(-mia), tāpuke(-tia)
bus pahi
bus stop tūnga pahi
bush (shrub) rake, pūihi
bush hawk kārearea, kāeaea
bushy pōruru, pōhuruhuru, mātotoru

B

business pakihi, mahi, ūmanga, kaipakihi, wāhi
busybody ihi pakiki, hakinohi
but otirā, heoianō, hoianō
but (after negative) engari, ērangi
butcher (*n.*) piha, pūtia, kaioka
butcher (*v.*) tapatapahi
butler tuari, pātara
butt (ram) tuki(-a), tūtuki (tukia)
butt of joke tāwai
butter pata
buttercup kawariki
butterfly pēpepe, pūrerehua, pepe
butterfly stroke kau aihe
butterfly, yellow admiral - kahukōwhai
buttocks papāihore, kōtore, whero, tou, papa
button pātene
buttonhole puare pātene, ō patene
buy hoko(-na)
buyer kaihoko mai, kaitango
buzz (feeling) pārekareka
buzz (noise) hohō, tamumu(-tia), rorohū, wheo
by (after passive verb) e (people), ki (things)
by (agent) i, mā (future), nā (past)
by and by taihoa
by way of mā, rā
by-election pōti motuhake
by-law ture o te wā, ture ā-rohe
by-product hua kē
bye (sport draw) hipa, whakanā
bypass taha, whakataha
bystander kaimātakitaki

C

cab tākihi
cabbage kāpeti
cabbage tree tī kōuka, tī whanake
cabin kōpuha, māhauhau, kapine
cable taura marohi, taura rino, taura maitai
cable car waka tautō, waka taura
cable drum pūwaea, pōkai waea
cactus tātā-tiotio
cadet āpiha tauira
caesarean section whānau hāparangi, motu whakawhānau
cafe whare kāwhi
cafeteria wāhikai, kāmuri
cage māhanga, karapotinga
cake keke
calcium konupūmā
calculate whārite, whakaōrite, tātai
calculator ōrite tātai, tātaitai
calendar maramataka
calf (animal) kāwhe
calf of leg tapuhau, takapū, ateate
calf-skin kiri kāwhe, hiako kāwhe
calibre (rifle) puare, kūpara
calico kāreko
call (name) tapa(-ia), tūā(-ina), hua(-ina)
call (shout) karanga(-tia), tīwaha, pararē, umere
call off whakakore(-hia)
callous ngākau raupā
calloused raupā, ūtonga, pātio
calm (*n. and adj.*) marino, āio, punuku
calm (*v.*) whakamarie(-tia)
calorie pūngoi
Calvary Kāwari
camel kāmera
camera kāmera, pūrere whakaahua
cameraman/person kaiwhakaahua
camp puni, kēpa, taupahī, pahī
camp fire ahi kōpae
campaign, political - pakanga tōrangapū, whakahau
campervan wakanoho, waka moe
campus (university) marae whare wānanga
can (able) āhei, taea e . . ., mōhio
can (tin) kēna, kēne, pīkini, tīni
Canadian Kanehiana
canal (water) waikeri, wai tawaka
cancel whakakore, whakakāhore
cancer mate pukupuku
cancer, cervical - mate pukupuku o te waha taiawa
Cancer, Tropic of - Kōpae Raro
candidate kaitono, kaiwhakauru
candle kānara
cane (supplejack) pirita, karewao, tokotoko
cane sugar tātā huka, tōtō
canine tooth niho rei
cannabis kanapihi, rauhea, whakamāngina
cannon pū repo
cannot ekore e taea
canoe waka
canoeing hoehoe tāwhai

canon (clergyman) kēnana
canopy uhi teitei, hīpoki
canteen wharekai hōia, pouaka mārau koripi
canvas kānaweaha, tāporena, kanaweti
cap pōtae, pōtaetae, kēpe
capability kaha, takatū, pakari
capable kakama, mōhio, māia
capacity te kī, raukaha, whānuitanga, kahapūpuri
cape (cloak) pueru
cape (headland) kūrae, matarae
capital (money) pūtea, tahua hautonga, haupū rawa
capital city tāone matua, tāone nui
capital gains moni hua
capitalise whakawhiti ki te moni
capitulate whakakauraro
capsicum kapikāna
capsize huripoki, tūpoki
capsule wāhi pūkoro rongoā
captain kāpene, kaitaki, kaiurungi
captive herehere, pononga
captivity whakarau, herenga
capture prisoner hopu(-kia, -kina), whakarau(-a)
car motokā
car boot raurawa
car manual pukapuka tiaki waka
car park papa waka
car racing whakataetae motokā
caravan waka noho, whare tāwhai, tōanga whare
carbon waro, konga
carbon dioxide hauhū
carbon monoxide haukino
carburettor hāhira
carcass tinana kararehe
card kāri, puka
cardboard pepa mārō, puka mārō, kāri ngātatahi
cardiac nō te manawa
cardiac arrest manawatū, manawahē
care tūpato, mahara, tiaki
care for manaaki(-tia), whāngai(-a), atawhai(-tia)
career umanga, tino mahi, momo mahi
careful tūpato
carefully āta (before verb)
careless pōrahurahu, ware, whakaaro-kore
caress haumiri, takamiri, mirimiri
caretaker kaitiaki
cargo utanga
carnation kāneihana
carol waiata Kirihimete
carp (fish) morihana
carpenter kāmura
carpet whāriki, takapau
carrier kaikawe, kaiamo
carrier bag kete
carrot kāroti
carry hari(-a), tari(-a), kawe(-a), mau(-ria)
carry in arms hiki(-tia), okooko(-tia)
carry it out mahia te mahi
carry off kahaki(-na)
carry on back pīkau(-ngia), waha(-ngia)
carry on shoulders amo(-hia)
cart kāta
carton pākete, kātene
cartoon waituhi whakakata, paki waituhi
cartridge kariri, kāreti
carve (artistic) whakairo(-tia)

case kēhi
case, in that - pēnā
cash moni, monitau, ukauka
cash-register hake ukauka, ōrite moni
cashflow te whiwhinga me te whakapaunga moni
cashier kaitātai moni
casing kēhi, pouaka
cask kāho
casket kāwhena, waka *(huia)*
casserole dish tīhake, kumete
cassette, audio - rīpene reo
cassette, video - rīpene ataata
cast maka(-ia)
cast ashore pae(-a)
cast away whakarere(-tia, -a)
cast, plaster - kōuku
castaway paeārau, rurenga
castoff kākahu whakarere, kākahu taretare
castor oil kātaroera
castrate poka(-ina)
casual labour mahi waimori
casualty aituā, hunga whara
cat tori, ngeru, poti, pūihi
catalogue (*n.*) rārangi ingoa, putu mōhio
catalogue (*v.*) whakawhāiti(-tia), whakarārangi(-tia)
catamaran katamarani, waka taurua
catapult kōpere
catarrh hupe, kuanu, taewa
catastrophe aituā nui, pāwera, parekura
catch (snag) māminga
catch breath hāhā, whakamau manawā
catch hopu(-kia, -kina), hao(-a), here(-a)
catcher (sport) kaihopu
catechism katekihama
catechist katekita
category momo, wāhanga, kāwai
cater takakai, whāngai
caterer (marae) ringa wera
caterpillar makorori, mūhara, hāwato
catfish ika pāhau
Catholic Katorika, whānui
cattle kau
Caucasian Kiritea nō Rūhia
caucus uepū, rōpū taki
caught mau
cauliflower kareparāoa, pūputi
cause take, pūtake
cause of death (legal) take o te hemonga, take o te matenga
caution whakatūpato
caution (warning) kupu tūpato
cautious tūpato, āta + *verb*, korita, matawhāiti
cave ana, rua
CD (compact disc) kōpae kiato, kōpaepae pūoro
CD-ROM kōpae rorohiko
cease mutu, kāti, whakamutu
cedar hīta, kawaka, kohekohe, pāhautea
cede momotu, tuku(-a, -na), tautuku
ceiling tuanui
celebrate whakanui(-a), hākari
celebrity whetū, tangata rongonui, tangata hau
celery hārere, herewī
celibacy noho takakau
cell (science) pūtau
cell, prison - ruma herehere, heremanga

C

cellar papararo
cello hero, whiranui
cement raima, apaapa
cement mixer numi-raima
cemetery urupā, wāhi tapu, parikarauna
censor kaiwhakamātau, kaiwhakawā
censure whakahē(-ngia), wenerau
census tataunga iwi
cent hēneti
centenary rau tau
centigrade henekeriti
centimetre hēnimeta
centipede wakapīhau, weri, peketua, waerau
central waenganui pū, poutokomanawa
centralisation whakakotahitanga
centre waenganui, pokapū, pūtahi
centre line paewehe
centre (maths) pūtahi, pū
centre (netball) puku
centre of gravity pokapū tō-ā-papa, pū kume-ā-papa
centre of rotation pū huringa, whatu o te hurihuri
century rautau
cereal pū kākano, huapata
cerebral palsy mate whakatīmohea
ceremonial ritenga, whakaritenga
ceremony kawa, tikanga
certain tino mōhio, mōhio tūturu
certain, a - tētahi, tētehi
certainly āna koia, tonu, kāore e hapa
certificate tiwhikete, pōkaitahi
certify whakapūmau, kī pono
cervical cancer mate pukupuku taiawa
cervical smear okoi waha whare tangata
cervix taiawa, waha whare tangata
chafe pākanikani, hikahika, mōhani
chaff pāpapa, tiāwhe
chain mekameka, tīni, herenga
chainsaw kani mihini, tātaretare
chair tūru
chairperson heamana, tiamana
chalk tioka, pākeho
challenge wero(-hia), taki(-na)
challenger kaiwero, kaitaki, kaituki
champagne waina piari
champion toa, whakaihuwaka
chance mea tūpono noa, pokanoa, heipūtanga
chancellor tumuaki
change rerekē, huri kē, puta kē, whiti kē, paheko
change clothes unu(-hia), tīni(-ngia)
change direction peka atu, taka kē
change, make - whakarerekē(-tia), kawe kē
changeable taurangi
changed, be - puta kē
channel roma, awakeri, hāwai
channel (television) hongere pouaka, wāhanga pouaka whakaata
chant waiata(-tia), karakia(-tia)
chap korokē, autaia, tāhae
chapel ruma karakia, whare o te Ariki
chaplain tiaparani, minita
chapter upoko, wāhanga
characteristic āhuatanga

charcoal waro, konga
charge (attack) huaki(-na), kōkiri
charge nurse nāhi matua, tapuhi matua
chariot hariata
charisma mana, karihima
charity āwhina rawakore, aroha
charm (allure) hūmārietanga, whakahoahoa
charm (magic spell) karakia, peha, ihi
charmed turipū
chart mapi, mahere, tūtohi
chart, wall - tauira whakamārama
chase aru(-mia), whai(-a), whaiwhai(-tia)
chasm pakohu, poka torere
chassis tinana
chastise whiu(-a)
chastity noho takakau
chat kōrerorero, muna
chatter (gossip) whawhe, kōrerorero, haunene, kapetau
chatter (teeth) kekekeke, ngakeke, ketekete, tiotio, tetēā
cheap iti te utu, ngāwari
cheat tinihanga, purei tāhae
check (inspect) āta titiro(tirohia), takina mai
check (slowdown) aukati, pupuri (puritia)
cheek (impertinence) tāwai, tutū, whakatoi, whakatete
cheek of face pāpāringa
cheer hāmama, umere, manahau
cheerful ngākau hari, manahau, ngahau, koa, manamanahau
cheese tīhi, tīwhiu
chemical matū, ranu
chemical reaction tauhohenga matū
chemist kēmihi, kaihoko rongoā, kairarau matū
chemistry mātauranga matū
cheque haki, tieke
cheque account pūtea haki
cherry hēre, tiere
chess whaikīngi, whakarau kīngi
chest uma, poho, rei, tarauma
chestnut colour pākākā
chew ngaungau(-a, -tia), ngonge, honihoni
chewing gum pia ngaungau, kauri, kōnani, kāpia
chicken pī, pīpī heihei
chief rangatira, amokapua
chieftainess kahurangi, tapairu
chilblain mangiongio
child tamaiti
childhood tamarikitanga, whanaketanga, ohinga
childless huatea, urikore
children tamariki
chill, catch a - maremare, rewharewha
chilly mātao, māeke, makariri
chimney tumera, timera, puta auahi
chin kauae
Chinese Hainamana
chip, potato - rīwai parai, maramara rīwai, tipi taewa
chip (wood etc.) maramara, kongakonga, haurewa, mōtete
chipboard papa maramara
chipped hawa
chiropractor kaikōwhakiwhaki, kaiwhakanao tuarā
chirp pī, pekī, ketekete, waiari, tei
chisel whao, mataora, purupuru
chocolate tiakerete

C

choice mea whiriwhiri, kōwhiritanga
choice! tapatapahi ana!
choir koaea
choke (strangle) rawa(-tia), raoa(-tia), nati(-a), tārona(-tia)
choked tanea, rāoa
cholera korara
cholesterol ngakototo
choose whiriwhiri(-a), kōwhiri
chop (meat) rara
chop poro(-a), topetope (topea), tapahi(-a)
choppy karekare
chorus huihuinga reo, ngaringari
Christian Karaitiana
Christmas Rā Whānau o te Kaiwhakaora, Kirihimete
chromium konupūmura
chronic mau tonu
chrysalis tūngoungou, kopi
chuckle kata puku
church (denomination) hāhi
church building whare karakia
Church of England Mihingare
church service whakamoemiti, karakia
chute hūrere
cicada kihikihi, tātarakihi, tarakihi, kiki whenua
cigar hikā
cigarette hikareti
cigarette lighter pūahi
cinders ngārehu, pungarehu, kūkā
cinema whare pikitia
cinnamon hinamona
circle around āmio haere, huri haere
circle (*n.*) porohita, āwhio, kōpae, ringi
circle (*v.*) huri potaka, āwhio haere
circuit ara iahiko, rarawe, āwhiotanga
circuitous āwhio, taiāwhio
circular porowhita
circulate porotītiti, hurihuri haere
circumference pae, āwhiotanga
circumstance āhuatanga, tū
citizen tangata whenua, kirirarau
city tāone nui
civil war kai-ā-kiri, riri tarā whare
civilise whakarata
civilization nohanga iwi mōhio
claim kerēme, tono, taunaha
claimant kaitono
clamp (*n.*) puritanga, purimau
clamp (*v.*) rawhi(-a), pupuri (puritia), kuku(-a)
clap pakipaki (pakia)
clap, thunder - papa whatitiri, wheorotanga
clappers tokere, pākōkō
clarify whakamārama
clarity māramatanga, pūrata
clash pā, papā
clasp tightly rarawe, whakakopa, taupiri
class karaehe, rōpū, hapori akoranga
clause, independent - aho tō
clause, main - aho kaha
claustrophobia mataku apiapi
claw (grab at) rapi(-hia)
claw (talon) maikuku, matihao
clay ūkui, paru, oneuku
clay land pangahu
clean mā
clean sweep haupapa hāro
cleaning tahitahi

cleanse horoi(-a)
cleansing ritual horohoronga
clear away whakawātea(-tia), waerea
clear ground ngaki(-a) taru, huti(-a) taru
clear nose tā te ihu
clear throat wharo
clear view mārama, ātea, tea, pūrotu, pūata
clear weather matatea, mahea
clearing waerenga, wāhi mārakerake
cleats matihao
clenched fist kamu, kumu(-a), kuku(-a)
clenched teeth kakati, kuku(-a)
clergy hunga minita, minita hāhi
clerk hekeretari, kaimahi tari
clever mōhio, kakama, ihumanea
click ngetengete, ngotongoto
client kaiutu, kaitono
cliff pari, tūpari
climate āhua o te rangi
climax whakaharaharatanga, teiteitanga
climb tūpiki, piki, kake(-a)
cling piri, pipiri, nanapi
clinic whare haumanu, whare hauora
clip tapahi(-a)
clip, paper - rawhi pepa
clock karaka
clog up taipuru(-a), kuka, kuta
clogged purutiti, puru
close (near) tata
close (shut) kati(-a), kapi(-a), whakakopi(-a)
close to the heart ngākaunui
close (with lid) taupoki(-na), kōpani
close together pātata, piri mai, tata
closed up kapi, pā, kati, hūhi
closing date rā e kati ai
closure whakakapinga, kotinga
clot (*n.*) tepe, puketoto
clot (*v.*) uka
cloth hākaru, papanga
clothe (dress) whakakākahu(-ria), whakamau kākahu
clothes kākahu, pūweru, pūeru, mai
cloud kapua, ao, rangiao, arorangi
cloudless ātea
cloudy kōngū, tāmaru, ehu
clover koroa, korouwa, koroua
clown kaiwhakakata, kaihangareka
club (any weapon) rākau, kuru
club (cards) karapu
clue tohu
clump of trees pū rākau, uru rākau, rake
clumsy hauwarea, pakihawa
cluster kāhui, tautau, rāpoi, mui, āpuru
clutch (engine) kānuku, whakatangatanga
clutch (grab) mamau, rarapi, aurara
coach (trainer) kaitohutohu, kaiwhakaako, kōti
coal waro
coalition kotahitanga
coarse taratara, kaitara
coast tahatai, ākau, tātahi
coat koti
coax whakapatipati(-ngia)
cobbler kaimahi hū
cobweb māwhaiwhai, wharepungāwerewere

C

cocaine rehukeka
cock (rooster) pīkaokao, tame heihei
cockabully uruao, hāwai, kōkopara, toitoi
cockle pipi, ahitua, tuangi, hūwai
cockroach kokoroihe, papata, kēkerengū
cocoa koukou
coconut kokonati
cod, blue - pākirikiri
cod, red - matuawhāpuku, rarai
cod, rock - rāwaru
code (computer) tohu pūmanawa
code, secret - uhingaro
coffee kāwhi
coffin kāwhena
cog hāupa, tara
cog wheel wira pokapū, hāupa, kōpaetara
cohesion piringatahi
cohort hoa tōpū, aropā
coil niko, whiri, koroi, kowiri
coincide tāpiri, orua, āhukahuka
coincidence tāpiritanga, oruatanga
colander kōputaputa, tātari
cold makariri, kōpeke, mātao, kōeke
cold-hearted tūkino, whakawiriwiri
coleslaw roi huamata
colic haku, kuku, pohopiri
collaborate mahi ngatahi
collar kara, kakī o te hāte
collarbone wheua o te kakī, paewai, paemanu
collate whakahiato
collateral taituarā, punga
colleague hoamahi
collect (*v. tr.*) kohi(-a), whakaemi (-hia), whakamine(-hia)
collect (*v. intr.*) whakapiri, huihui
collector kaikohikohi
college kāreti, kura teitei
college of education whare takiura
collide paoro(-tia), tūtuki (tukia)
collision tūtukitanga, paoro
colloquialism kīwaha
colon (intestine) whēkau, piro
colonel kānara
colour (*n.*) kara, ātanga, tae, kano
colour (*v.*) kauruku
column pou, poutahi, rārangi
coma, in a - kei te hemo, e hemo ana, mauri ngaro
comb (*n.*) heru, koma
comb (*v.*) heru(-a), wani(-a)
combat riri(-a), whawhai, tū atu
combat, single - kākari
combatant kairiri
combine whakakotahi(-tia), hono(-a)
combustion pahūnga, tahunga, ngingiha
comedian tangata hātekēhi, pukuhohe
comet unahiroa, upokoroa
comfort whakamārie(-tia), oranga ngākau
comfortable pai, āhuru, mahana, hāneanea, penapena
comforter kaiwhakamārie
comic cartoon pakiwaituhi
comic periodical kōmeke
comical hātekēhi, rawe, whakakakata
comma pika, pīroi
command whakahau(-a), tono(-a)

commander āpiha rangatira
commandment ture
commando whakatoke, tohu taua kōkiri
commemorate whakamahara
commend whakamihi
commercial fisherman kaihī ika hoko
commission komihana, whakaae, hua hoko
commit (pledge to) whakarato, here(-a)
commit crime mahi hē, hara, takahi i te ture
commit resources āta whakarite pūtea
commitment kaingākau, noho here
committed to ū ki, tino ū ki, here ana ki
committee komiti
commodity taputapu, taonga hoko, rawa
commodore āpiha hēramana
common (normal) māori, noa iho
common sense whakaaro mahara, āta whakaaro
commotion raruraru, āheihei
communal nō te iwi
communicate whakawhiti whakaaro, whakamōhio(-tia)
communiqué kupu whai mana
communism tōpūtanga-ā-iwi, noho ki tā Karl Marx
community nohonga whānau, hapori, iwi kāinga
community centre whare tapere
community group rōpū-ā-iwi, iwi whānui
community service whakatau āwhina i te iwi, ratonga ki te iwi
compact (tight) whāiti, pororehu, paerehu
compact disc kōpaepae pūoru, kōpae kiato
companion hoa, takahoa
companionship piringatahi, hoanga
company (business) kamupene, umanga
company (group) rangapū, rōpū, kāhui, hono
compare whakarite(-a), whakataurite(-a), ōrite
compartment wehenga, wāhanga
compass (directional) kāpehu, pūmahi tohu ara, taonga kimi huarahi
compassion arohanui, āroharoha
compatible rite, whakaritenga, hototahi
compel akiaki (ākina), ā(-ia), whakahau(-a)
compensate whakaea, utu(-a), paremata
compensation kapeneihana, kamupeneheihana, utunga
compete tauwhāinga, whakataetae, taupatupatu
competent kaiaka, ngaio, mātau, māia
competition whakataetae, tauwhāinga
competitor kaiwhakataetae, māia
complacent kiriora
complain amuamu(-tia), mūmū, haku
complaint whakapae, nawe
complete whakaoti, whakatepe, whakatutuki(-tia)

C

completed rite, mutu, oti, pau
completely katoa, *verb* + rawa
completion whakaotinga, tutukitanga, whakatutukitanga
complex matatini, whīwhiwhi
complicated tāwhiwhi, pakeke
complications pōauautanga
compliment mihi, whakamihi
comply hāngai, tautuku
compose tito(-a), hanga, tito
composer kaitito waiata, kaihanga waiata
composition hanga
compost pū wairākau, tongi, rongoā pōkoro
compound (science) pūhui, whakaranu
comprehension māramatanga, mōhiotanga
comprehensive whānui
compress whakawhāiti(-tia), kotē
compression pēhanga nui, pīnekeneke, kōpeketanga
compulsory whakature, here
compute tātai
computer rorohiko
computer screen whakaata rorohiko, mata rorohiko
computer terminal kāpeka rorohiko
comrade hoa pūmau
concave pakonga, kohu, kōpapa
conceal huna(-ia), whakapeke(-tia), kuhu(-a)
conceive (child) tō, whakaira(-tia)
conceived hapū, tō
concentration (substance) whakaerotanga, tepe, totoka
concentration (mental) hihiritanga, hiringa
concept whakaaro, arowā, hiringa mahara, ariā
conception whakatō tamariki
concern (worry) āwangawanga, matapopore
concerning ki, mō, e pā ana ki
concession tukunga noatanga
conciliate hohou rongo, tāpore
concise poto
conclude (finish) whakaoti
concluded oti, mutu
conclusion wāhanga whakamutunga, whakatau mutunga
conclusion, come to - tutuki rawa ake
conclusion, in - hei whakamutunga
concrete raima
concupiscence hiahia pūremu
concur whakaae(-tia)
concussion pōro, whitinga roro
condemn whakahē(-ngia), whakatau te mate
condensation tōhau, hāuaua, tōtā
condense whakawhāiti, whakapoto, whakatōtā
condition (state) āhuatanga
conditional āhuaranga, tāupeupe, herenga
conditions ture ka ūhia ki runga, āhuatanga mahi
condolence aroha pūmau, mamae tahi
condom pūkoro ure, uhi ure
conduct (actions) whanonga
conduct (direct) whakahaere(-tia), arataki(-na)
conduct (transmit) kawe(-a), pāho
conductor, electrical - pūkawe iahiko, kaikawe iahiko

conductor, bus - kaitiaki (pahi)
conductor (orchestral) kaiwhakahaere
conductor (physics) kaipāho
cone shaped koeko porowhita, kōrere
conference hui
confess whāki(-na)
confidence māiatanga, manawanui, tapu
confident māia, mātau, ngākau titikaha
confidential tapu, muna, matatapu
confine whakahere, roherohe(-a), whakatiki(-na)
confirmed tūturu
confiscate muru(-a)
conform whakaae(-tia), whai(-a)
confront anga ki, ahu atu
confronting ki mua i, whakaanga atu ki
confuse whakapōhēhē(-tia), whakararu(-a), pōkaikaha
confusion pōnānātanga, pōauautanga, pōhēhētanga
congeal tepe, totoka, kōpā, kukū
congenital mai i te whānautanga
conger eel ngōiro, kōiro
congratulate mihi(-a), whakamihi atu
congregate huihui, whakamine
congregation whakaminenga
conjunction i te taha o, kupuhono, pūtahitanga, tūhono
connect hono(-a), pā, āpiti, kapiti(-tia), hono
connect to server hono ki te tūmau
connection hononga, pānga, āpititanga
conquer tae(-a), whakahinga(-ia), raupatu(-tia)
conquered hinga
conscience hinengaro, ngākau whakawā, mōhio ki te tika me te hē
conscientious ngākau pono, ihupuku, ngākau tohu
conscious mōhio, mahara, oho, mauriora
consecrate whakatapu(-a)
consecutive e aru ana, e whai ana, rārangi
consensus tā te katoa e whakatau mai ai, whakatau a te katoa
consent whakaae(-tia)
consequence (importance) whai mana, hira
consequence (result) mea i puta, tukunga iho
consequently nō reira, hoi, heoi, heoi anō
conservation tiaki i te aoturoa, tiaki taonga a Papatūānuku
conservative tūpato
conserve tiaki(-na), tohu(-ngia), rokiroki, penapena(-tia)
consider whakaaro(-tia), whakarau kakai
considerate manawa popore, ngākau mahara
consideration whakaarohanga, ngākau maharatanga
consign tuku(-a, -na)
consignment tukunga
consist i roto
consistent with uru(-a) mai, rite ki
consolation tupoho
console whakamārie(-tia), wawao

consolidate whakaū, whakatōpū
conspicuous tiori, kōhure, mārama
conspiracy tinihanga, whakangārahu
conspirator kaikakai
conspire whakarau kakai
constable kātipa, pirihimana
constant pūmau, tau pūmau, taimau
constantly tonu
constellation tira whetū, tātai whetū, kāhui whetū
constipated tina te kōpū
constipation kōroke
constitution kaupapa-ā-ture
construct hanga, whakatū, waihanga
consul kairauhī, māngai kāwanatanga
consult akoako, uiui(-a)
consultant kaiakoako, kaitohutohu
consultation rūnanga, whakawhiti whakaaro
consumed pau, mōti, horomia
consumed totally orotā
consumer kaihokohoko, kaiwhakapau
contact whakaatu atu, whakapā, hoapā
contact lens arotahi
contact points pānga
contagious mauhoro, kapo
contain mau ki roto, pupuri (puritia)
container, closed - tokanga
container, open - paepae, pōha, ipu, kūmete
contaminate paru(-a), whakakino(-tia)
contemporary nō taua wā tonu, takiwā
contempt whakahāwea, whakamanioro
contend for tauwhāinga, tautohetohe, taukumekume
contented tatū, nā, toka te manawa
contest tautohenga, pakanga
contestant kaiwhakataetae, tauwhawhai
continent whenua rawhaki, whenua paparahi
continual turoa, tonu, whāroa noa, mau tonu
continuation roanga atu
continue (join) honohono(-a), haere tonu
continuous motukore, rōnaki, tāhuhu, āmiomio, mutukore
contraceptive ārai hapū
contract (agreement) pukapuka kirimana, kanataraka
contract (shrink) noti, komeme, tiango, kukuti (kūtia)
contractor kaitono, kaikānataraki, kaikirimana
contradict whakahē(-ngia), totohe, tātā(-ngia)
contradiction rerekētanga, whakaatu whakahē
contradictions ōna kino ōna pai
contrary ātete
contrast rerekētanga, pūrata
contribute whai wāhi ki, hoatu koha
contribution tākoha, koha
contributor kaikoha, kaihoatu
control (*n.*) mana whakahaere, mana
control (*v.*) whakarite, whakaū, whakahaere take

controller kaiarataki, tumuaki
controversial tautohe, wenerau
controversy whawhai, tautohenga, wenerautanga
convalescent tūmahu, mātūtū, okioki
convene karanga mai, whakamene mai
convenient haratau, ātaahua
converging lens mōwhiti ūngutu
converging rays hihi ūngutu
conversation kōrerorero, kōrero, takakī
conversion hurihanga, tahuritanga, tahuringa
conversion (rugby) whana whakaū, whana turuki
convex koropuku, tiriwhana
convey kawe(-a)
convict (*n.*) mauhere, herehere
convict (*v.*) whakahara(-ina), whakawā(-kia)
convoy taua poti
convulsion hukihuki, hūkeke
cook (*n.*) kuki, ringa wera, tūmau
cook (*v.*) tao(-na), tahu(-na), kōhue
cooked maoa, maoka, ngoungou
cooker tō
cookhouse whare umu, kāuta
cool hauangi, mātaotao, whakamātaratara
cooperate mahi tahi, mahi ngātahi
cooperative ohu, ngākau āwhina
coordinate (*n.*) tau tūranga, tau whakarite nohoanga
coordinate (*v.*) whakarite, whakahiato, tuitui, taururuku
copier mīhini whakaahua
copious nanaea, maringi, humi
copper kapa, konukura
copulate ai, onioni, mahimahi
copy whai(-a), whakatāuira, tārua(-tia), tauira(-tia)
copyright manatārua, manatū
coral wheo, kutakuta, kāoa, roke kanae
cord taura, au
cord, electric - taura hiko, uaua hiko
cordial (drink) waireka, wainene
core uho, whatu, kiko
cork puru, kāka, pangu
corkscrew wiri, takawiri, huripuru, wairori
cormorant kawau, kāruhiruhi
corn, fermented - kānga pirau, kānga kōpiro, kānga kopuai
corn (food) kānga, kānga waru
corn (on foot) tona, tonatona
corner kokonga, koki, ngao, poti, koko
cornflakes kāngarere, kāngawaru
coronary mate manawa
coronation koroneihana, karaunatanga
coroner kaiwhakawā o te kōti mō ngā tūpāpaku, kaititiro matewhawhati
corporal kāpara
corporation kaporeihana
corpse tūpāpaku, manu pirau a Tiki
corpulent mōmona
correct (*v.*) whakatika(-hia), pītika
correct (*adj.*) tōtika
correspond (equal) ōrite
corridor kauhanga roa
corroborate whakatūturu
corrugated iron haeana ngarungaru, rino ngarungaru

C

corrugation ngaru, kōawaawa, kōwakawaka
corrupt pirau, hē, kino, hāmate
corruption piraunga, hanehane, huhu
cosmonaut kairere whaitua
cost utu
cosy whakaawhiawhi
cot moenga pēpi, pouraka
cot death mate pouraka
cotton thread miro
couch nohoanga roa, hōpa
cough maremare, hāmaremare, wharo
council rūnanga, kaunihera
councillor mema o te kaunihera
counsel waha kōrero, rōia
counsel (advise) tohutohu(-a)
counsellor kaitohutohu, tumu kōrero
count tatau(-ria), kaute(-tia)
counter tūpapa
counter claim pānui tautohe, tāwari
counterfeit tāhae
counterpart ritenga
countless tataukore, ekore nei e taea te tatau
country whenua, motu, rohe
countryside tuawhenua
couple tōpū, taurua, punarua, takirua
coupon tīkiti
courage toa, māia, tara
courageous māia, manawanui, whakatara
courier kaiwaewae, karere
court (games) papa tākaro
court (woo) whai(-a), whakawhaiāipo, tākunekune
court of law kōti
courteous ngāwari, whakaaro rangatira, hūmārika
courtesy whakaaro atawhai
courtyard marae, tahua
cousin (*see* brother, sister) kaihana, teina, tuakana
cover (lid) taupoki, pōtae
cover over hīpoki(-na), uhi(-a), taupoki(-na), whakakapi(-a)
covered kapi
cow kau
coward hauwarea, tāwiri, whiore humi
cowardice tāwiri, kopī, kopīpipi
cowboy kaupoai
cower piri, tuohu, whakaririka
cowshed wharekau
coyote koiota
C.P.R. (Cardio Pulmonary Resuscitation) whakaora manawa
crab pāpaka, waerau
crack (break) pao(-a), wāhi(-a), kōara(-tia)
crack (in skin) tāpā
crack (landslip) ngātata
crack (sound) kekē, patō(-hia), pakō
crackle ngatete, pāhūhū
cradle ōhanga, moenga pēpi, poipoi, pouraka
craft (art) mahi toi, tohungatanga
craftsman tohunga, haratau
crafty nanakia
craggy taratara
cram opuru(-a)
cramp huhuti, uhu, uauawhiti, hakoko, parerori
cramp, leg - kaurapa
cramped matangerengere

crane (machine) tokorangi, hāpai, wakaranga, whakahiki
crash paoro(-tia), tūtuki, wheoro
crash (helmet) pōtae mārō, pōtae whara
crate kereiti
crawl ngaoki, ngōki
crayfish kōura, kīkēwai, kēwai
crazy pōrangi
creak ngakeke, pākēkē
cream kirīmi
cream colour kahotea
cream jug hāka kirīmi, tiaka kirīmi
cream, whipped - kirīmi pāhukahuka
crease whakakopa
create hanga(-a, -ia), whakatū, waihanga
creation hanga, orokohanga
creative wairua auaha
creator kaihanga
creature kirihe, kararehe, mea hanga, kaiora
creche wāhi tiaki pēpi
credentials pukapuka tautoko
credit moni tika kia utu
credit card puka nama, kāri nama
creditor kaituku nama
creek awawhāiti
creep ngaoki, konihi, kūpapa, ngoingoi
cremate tahu ki te ahi
cremation tahu tūpāpaku
crescent pewa, piko, kape
cress, water - wātakirihi
crest piki, hurutihi
crevice matata, kapiti, matatātanga
crew ngā hēramana, te waka
cricket (game) kirikiti
cricket (insect) pihareinga, kikipounamu, rirerire
crime hara, takahi i te ture
criminal tangata hara
crimson pākurakura, pūwhero
cringe whakamaoko, hūiki
crinkle mingo
cripple kōpiri, kopa, kohapa
crisis wā tino raruraru, wā mōrearea
crisp pakapaka, mato
criterion kaupapa, paearu, tikanga
critical error hapa nui
critical (fault finding) amuamu, kōrero hē
critical (important) tino whai tikanga, taumaha
critical factor wāhi hōhonu
criticism amuamu, whakahēnga, whakaparahako
criticise whakapae(-tia), whakahē(-ngia)
croak kakū, pakakū, whakarāoa
crock pot kārakaraka, tāpīpī
crockery uku, okouku
crocodile karakatara mokoweri, moko ngārara
crooked hapehape, tītaha, kohapa, hapa
crop (harvest) ngāhuru, kotinga (wīti), hua (whenua/rākau)
cross (*n.*) rīpeka
cross (*v.*) whiti, whakawhiti(-tia)
cross reference whakaaturanga whiti
cross-examine uiui
cross-eyed kanohi rewha
crossbar kaho, rōau
crossroads rīpekanga, pekanga, pūtahitanga

crouch whakapeke, tuohu, kūpapa
crow kōkako, ōngā, pakara
crowd (*n.*) huihuinga, whakaminenga, mātinitini
crowd (*v.*) inaki(-tia), popoke, poke, pūruru
crowd together apū, opeti, apuru(-a), karapoti
crowded kōpipiri, whāiti, apiapi, kikī
crown (*v.*) karauna(-tia)
crown (of head) tipuaki, tumuaki
crucial whai tikanga, hira, riwha, matawaenga
crucible rīhi whakawera, puoto whakawera
crucifix rīpeka
crucify rīpeka(-tia)
crude hauwarea, koropū, paruparu, karihika
crude oil hinu kōhatu, hinu nuku
cruel kino rawa, whakawehi, whakawiri
cruise āta haere
crumb kongakonga
crumble ngakongako
crumble by hand kōnatunatu(-hia)
crumble down horo(-a), ngahoro, ngawhere(-a), tanuku
crumbled to fragments kongakonga, ngakongako
crush kōhari, whakakopenu(-tia), kurutē
crushed kongakonga, kōharihari, kopenu
crusher whakapē
crust kiri mārō, kiripaka, kiriparāoa
crutch (support) tokowae, turupou
cry tangi(-hia), auē, wē
cry (bird) tio, tangi, koekoe(-a)
crystal atamaha, kōhatu piata
cub punua, kūao
cube whangaono rite, mataono rite
cuckoo, shining - pīpīwharauroa, nakonako
cucumber kamokamo, kūkamo, kūkama
cuddle tapapahu
cue (hint) tohu
cuff, shirt - whatīanga, hūmene
culmination pūāwaitanga, mutunga
culprit tangata nāna te hē
cultivate whakatō(-kia), ngaki(-a)
cultivation mahinga kai, māra, ngakinga
cultural ahurea
cultural difference āhua rerekē, mauri o ia iwi
culture, Māori - Māoritanga
culvert waikeri
cunning kakama, māminga, kanene, mūrere
cup kapu, ipu
cupboard kāpata
curate pirihi kaiāwhina, pirihi whakamahiri
curator kaitiaki
curb pupuri (puritia), nati(-a)
cure (heal) whakaora(-ngia), rongoā
cured (healed) ora
curious (strange) rerekē
curl up hūmene, takawiri, riporipo
curly hair mingimingi, karamengemenge
currency moni

current, electric - iahiko
current view tirohanga o nāianei
current (water) tāheke, ia, auhoki, roma, riporipo
currently o nāianei
curry kai kakati, kare
curse kangakanga, kohukohu
cursory tūao
curt (abrupt) kōrero wani, kōrero pōngaru
curtain ārai(-a)
curve tīwhana, piko, niko, ānau, kono
curved tāwhana, tīwhana, kōpiko tiriwhana
cushion pera, aupuru, urunga, kuihana, paretua
custard wai tōhua, kahetete, kātete
custodian kaitiaki
custody (child) whakatau tiaki tamariki, mana pupuri
custom ritenga, tikanga, ūmanga
customer kaiutu, kaihoko, kiritaki
cut haehae(-a), tapahi(-tia), kokoti (kotia)
cut off haukoti(-a)
cut open ripiripi, poka
cut up poro(-a), motu(-hia), haehae(-a)
cut with scissors kutikuti
cutter (instrument) kotikoti
cuttlefish wheke, ngū
cutty grass rautahi
cycle (phase) huri, huringa
cycle (ride) eke paihikara, hautu paihikara
cyclist kaieke pahikara
cyclone āwhiowhio, huripari
cylinder porotakaroa, puoto, rango
cynic pōkaikaha
cynical whakahāwea, whakahī, pūhohe
cyst whēwhē

D

dab muku(-a), hārau
dabchick weweia
dad pāpā, matua
daffodil tirara
dagger oka
daily ia rā ia rā, ia rā
daily limit tepe ia rā
dairy toa hoko miraka
dais atamira, tūāpapa
daisy parani
dam (river) matatara, pāpuni, pā
damage pakarutanga, tūkino, whara, potanga
damaged pakaru, kino
damages (expenses) utunga, utu paremata
Dame (title) Kahurangi, wahine rangatira
damn whakataua te mate, pei(-a) ki te iweri
damp mākūkū, haukū
dance kanikani
dandruff inaho, pakitea
danger tata mate, mōrearea, tātā tuma
dangle tawheta, iri, toutou
dare māia, kaha, tautapatapa, wero
dark (colour) āhua pango, parauri, pangopango
dark/darkness pōuri, pōuri kerekere, pō(-ngia)
darling tau, muna, whaiāipo, kahurangi
dart (weapon) pere, teka, neti
dash (punctuation) puta, pīwhai
dash (rush) kōkiri, rere haere, omaki
dashboard papa tirohanga, papatohu
data raraunga, whakaaturanga, hōtuku, tohutohu
database putunga kōrero, raraunga
date (day) rā
date (fruit) kano nīkau, kaihuia, teiti
date due rā whakahoki
date stamp pourā
date, make a - whakarite(-a) wā
daughter tamāhine
daughter-in-law hunaonga
dawdle karioi, āta haere, whakaroaroa
dawn ata hāpara
dawn, full - haeata, atatū, atapūao
day rā, rangi
day (next) aoake, āwake
day after tomorrow ātahirā
day and night i te ao i te pō
day off rangi whakatā
daybreak putanga o te rā
daydream wawata(-tia)
daylight awatea, whaiao
daytime awatea
dazed ānewanewa, wairangi, pōroa
dazzled whēkite, kōreko
deacon rīkona

deactivate whakanoa, taupāhohe, whakakaurapa
dead mate, hemo
deadline rā kati, paunga o te tāima
deadlock komutu(-a)
deadly whakamate
deaf turi, taringa noaiho, turikere
deafen whakaturi
deal cards toha(-ina), whiuwhiu(-a)
dealer kaihoko, kaihokohoko
dealings mahinga
dealt with poto, pai, ukupapa, ea
dean manutaki, tumuaki, kaiako whakahaere
dear (costly) utu nui
dearth mōmōhanga
death hemonga, matenga rawa
debar aukati(-a)
debase whakaiti(-tia), whakakino
debatable matawaenga
debate whakawhitiwhiti whakaaro, tautohetohe
debris kongakonga, porohanga, otaota
debt nama
debt, bad - nama kāore i utua
debtor kaitango nama, tangata noho nama
debut putanga tuatahi, kōkuhu tuatahi
decade ngahurutanga, tekau tau
decay pirau, pōpopo
decayed tooth niho tunga
decaying memeha
deceased mate rawa, kua hemo, tūpāpaku, hunga mate
deceit tinihanga, tāhae, teka, parau
deceive tinihanga(-tia), rūpahu
deceiver tangata māminga, kaimahi tinihanga
deceleration whakapūhoitanga, pāitiiti
decent tika, whanonga tika, ngākau pai
decentralise wehewehe(-ngia), wāwāhi (wāhia), tapatapa
deception hīanga, whakatūpapa
deceptive rauhanga, whakararuraru, nukarau
decide whakatau(-ria), whakarite(-a)
decided kua tau, kua rite, tutuki, tērā ka tau
decimal number tau-ā-ira, tongitekau, tau ngahuru
decimetre tēhimete, mita-tekau
decision whakataunga
decision, make a - hanga kaupapa, whakatakoto whakaaro
decisive niwha, whakahau tahi
deck raho, paparaho, rahoraho
deck of cards putu kāri, pūranga kāri
declaration whakapuakitanga
declare whakaatu(-ria), kī tūturu
decline (go down) heke iho, tītaha, tauheke
decline (refuse) whakakore, kāhore e whakaae
decompose pirau, kurupopo, pōpopo
decontamination purenga, whakanoa
decorate whakapaipai(-tia), rākai, whakaataahua
decorator kaiwhakapaipai, kairākai
decoy maimoa, ongaonga, manutaupunga

D

decrease iti haere, heke iho, whakaero, whakaiti(-tia)
decree pānui whai mana, whakahau a te rangatira
deduct tango
deed mahi
deed (legal) tiiti
deep hōhonu, matomato
deep-freeze pā hukapapa, pā tio
deer tia
default hapa, hapanga, tautuku, taunoa
defeated hinga, mate, piro, pīti
defect ngoikoretanga, hē, tōrōkiri
defector tangata tahuti
defence whakamarumaru, waonga, pukumaire, ārai hoariri
defenceless āraikore
defend wawao, whawhai atu, whakangungu
defendant mauherehere, tangata e whakapaetia ana
defender (sports) tuarā, kaiārai, kaiwawao
defensible taea te wawao, whakaaro whai tikanga
defensive papare
defer hiki(-tia) te wā
defiance whakatuma, ātetetanga, whakaioio
defiant whakatumatuma, whakaioio, whakatōrea, māia
deficiency pāharatanga, hohoretanga
deficient wharepā
deficit nama, tarepa, tūwhene
define whakatau(-ria), tautuhi(-tia), whakatūturu
defined whakarāpopoto(-tia)
definite tūturu(-tia)
definitely tika ana hoki, tino tika
definition tikanga, tautuhinga, kupu whakamārama
definitive whakatūturu, pūkapo, pūmau
deflate whakahūhū, heke(-a)
deflation hekenga wāriu
deflect karo(-hia), whakakotiti
deformity hakanga
defraud tāhae(-tia)
defuse situation whakamārie, hohou rongo
defy whakatumatuma(-tia), whakatōrea
degenerate heke iho, tipuheke
degrade whakakino(-ngia), whakaiti(-tia)
degrading hakirara, parangetungetu
degree (angle) wehenga kōpae, putu
dehydrate whakamaroke, whakatareho
dehydrator whakatauraki, pūrerewhāparo
deity Io-matuakore, kaihanga, runga rawa
dejected pōuri, auhi te ngākau, auwhi, tapou
delay whakaroa(-tia), takaware, roanga, taruna
delayed rangitaro
delegate (*n.*) māngai, rīwhi, reo kāwana, karere
delegate (*v.*) tono(-a), tautapa, kaitautapa
delegation rōpū tono, apatono
delete whakakāhore(-tia), whakakore, tapahi, muku(-a)
deliberately āta (before verb), mārika

deliberation whiriwhiringa, whakangārahutanga
delicate marore, pārore, ngoikore, tūwai
delicious reka rawa, kakato
delight hakahari, whakawaireka, rekareka
delighted manawarū, wehe, tino koa, āhuareka
delightful āhumehume
delirious pōrangi, kutukutuahi, tīhāhā
delirium ngutungutuahi, pūrori, kutukutuahi
deliver tuku(-a), rato, hoatu, mau(-ria)
deliver letters harihari reta
deliverance whakawāteatanga
delivery tukunga, hīkawekawe
delivery (birth) whakawhānau
deluded pōhēhē(-tia), pāhewahewa
delusion whakaaro horihori, pōhēhētanga
demand tono(-a), whakahau(-ria)
demand, on - inā whakahaua
demeanour tū, āhua
demobilise whakamarara
democracy kāwanatanga hōrite, manapori
democrat kaituku mana ki te iwi
demolish whakahoro, turaki(-a)
demon hātana, nanakia, atua ngau
demonic tipua
demonstration whakaaturanga
demonstrator kaiwhakatūtū
demoralize manene, whakakino
demote whakaheke mana, whakaheke
den rua, ana raiona, kahunga
denial whakakore
denomination momo hāhi, momo moni
denominator, common - tauraro pātahi
denote tohu(-a)
denounce whakapae, whakahorihori
dense mātotoru, ururua, ngaruru, apiapi
density mātotorutanga, ukanga, pururua
dent poka(-ina), komeme
dental tiaki niho, ā-niho
dentist pouniho, kaitiaki niho, rata niho
denture niho whakanoho, niho kēhua
denunciation ātetetanga
deny whakakāhore(-tia), whakateka, whakatito(-ngia)
deny access kaiponu(-hia)
deodorant kakara, rautangi, patu piro
depart haere atu, wehe atu, riro
departed from makere mai/atu
department tari, wāhanga, manatū
departmental ā tari
departure rironga, wehenga, haerenga
dependable pono, pou whirinaki
dependent piri, whakawhirinaki, whakamauru
deplete pau
deplorable weriweri, kiriwetiweti
deport nuku(-a) atu, terepu(-tia)
deportation pana(-ia) i te whenua
deposit whakatakoto
deposit (money) moni whakatau, moni tāpui (down payment)
depot kōpapa, taupuni
depraved hīkaka

depreciate iti haere te wāriu, whakahekenga
depreciation hekenga wāriu, whakapāhi(-tia), pēhi, hekenga uara
depress whakapēhi(-a), whakangoikore
depressed hākerekere, pōuri
depressing whakapāhi
depression (despair) ngākau hawarea, mate pāpōuri
deprive wetewete, tupe(-a)
depth te hōhonu, putu
deputation teputeihana, rōpū whaikōrero
deputise rīwhi, whakakapi
deputy tēputi, kairīwhi, kaitiriwā, piki
derelict mahue, hāhū, tūhea, paea
derisive pūhohe
derive puta mai, pū mai, pūhua
descend heke, makere ki raro
descendant uri, mokopuna, whakahekenga, aitanga
descent heketanga, hekenga
descent (lineage) whakapapa, tātai, ure pūkaka (male)
describe toi i te āhua, whakaatu i te āhua, whakaahua(-tia)
description whakaahuatanga, whakaaturanga
desecrate whakanoa(-tia), takahi(-a) mana, hāparu(-tia)
desert (leave) whakarere(-tia), mahue
desert (wilderness) koraha, mārakerake, hāhā
desertion whakarerenga
deserve tika ana mō, whai wāhi
design tauira, hoahoa
design (building) hoahoa, hanga
designate tohutohu(-ngia), whakaingoa(-tia)
designation ingoa
designer kaitātai, kaihoahoa
designer jeans tāngari motuhake
desirable minaminatia, hiahiatia, rawe
desire (crave) hiahia(-tia), pirangi(-tia)
desires (general) awhero
desk tēpu tuhi, tēpu ako, tēpu mahi
desolate whenua hāhā, pūreirei, mokemoke
desolation mokemoke, hakoretanga, hāhātanga
despair mate te ngākau, ngākau kore
desperate ngākau kore, āwherokore, mōrearea
despise whakaiti(-tia), whakakāhore(-tia), whakahāwea(-tia)
despite ahakoa, takarure
despot rangatira tūkino
dessert kai reka, kīnaki, purini
destination tauranga haere ai, ūnga, piringa e haere ai
destined tohua, whakaritea, ahu ana
destiny oranga ake, mutunga iho, whakaritenga
destitute rawakore, pōhara
destitution rawakore
destroy whakangaro(-mia), whakahoro(-a)
destroy (smash) wāwāhi
destruction ngaromanga, urupatu, orotā, nunumi
destructive orotā
detach wehe(-a), wete(-kina)

detachment wehenga kētanga, rōpū hōia motuhake
detail wāhanga iti, mokamoka, āmiki, taipitopito
detain pupuri (puritia), tautāwhi(-na)
detect rongo(-hia), kite(-a), hopu(-kina), mau, rapu
detection rapu hara, hopukanga, haurapa
detective kaihopu tangata hara, kairapu hara
deter pupuri (puritia), ārai atu, nati, whakaupa
detergent hōpi akuaku
deteriorate tāmi(-a), tupuheke
determination manawanui, hiringa
determine whakatau, whakaoti, whakatakoto, hua(-ina)
determined māia, ngana, mārō, tino pūkeke
deterrent whakaita, aukati, taupare
detest whakakino, whakahouhou
detour kōtiti, ara tīpoki, ara autaki, ākau roa
detract ngautuarā, kōrero kino, whakaiti
detrimental kino, whakawhara
devaluation mimiti haere te wāriu
devastate urupatu, urupoki, anea(-tia), ātete
devastation meinga hei ururua, aneatanga
develop whakatūtuki(-tia), whakaneke(-hia)
developer kaiwhakaahu, kaiwhakawhanake
development tupu, tipu, tū rangatira, pakari haere
deviate whakahipa, peka atu, kotiti
device pūrere, nuka
devil rēwera, tupua, hātana, atua kikokiko, taipō
devious nanakia, huna
devise hanga(-a, -ia), waiho(-tia), hakangārahu
devotion arohanui, whakaū, whakangākau
devour horomi(-a), apuapu(-tia), whāō(-na)
devout whakaaro ki te atua, kaha ki te īnoi, whakapono
dew tōmairangi, haukū, haurutu
dexterity harataunga
diabetes mate huka
diabolical mahi a hātana, puku hātana
diagnose rapu(-a) mate, tātari, whakatau(-a), whiriwhiri
diagonal hōkai, hauroki
diagram hoahoa, whakaahua, huahuatanga, mahere
dial (face) mataine, tohu kā, waea
dial (*v.*) rīngi, waea ki
dialect reo-ā-takiwā, reo-ā-iwi
dialogue whakawhiti whakaaro
diameter tārua, tawhā, ngawhā, rangiwhiti
diamond taimana
diaphragm (anatomy) pātūrei, pātūpoto
diaphragm (contraceptive) pā wai tātea, pātātea
diarrhoea rererere, tikotiko, torohī, kōrere
diary pukapuka rātaka
dice maka rota, mataono tạu
dice food tapatapahi(-a)
dictate pānui-ā-waha, whakahauhau(-a)

dictator rangatira tonotono, rangatira tūtahi
dictionary pukapuka rārangi kupu, tikinare, papakupu
die (expire) hemo, mate, hinga, mōnehu, makere
diet nohopuku, whakatinanga ki te kai
differ puta kē, rerekē
difference rerekētanga, kāore i rite
different rerekē, puta kē
differentiate wehewehe(-a), tītore(-a), whakarerekē(-tia)
difficult pakeke, uaua
difficulties, in - raruraru ana
diffident ahaaha
diffuse tohatoha, tūrererere, marara, roha
dig keri(-a), kari(-a), ketu(-a), kō(-ia)
dig up hahu(-a), huke(-a), tuakanga
digger kaikeri, mīhini keri
digit mati, whika
dignified amaru, āhua rangatira
dignitary rangatira
dignity tū rangatira, āhua rangatira
dignity and worth ihi me te wehi
digress kotiti te kōrero, kāweka, tīweka
dilapidated taretare, pūwhāwhā
dilate whakanui, roha
dilemma rangirua, matawaenga, ngākau kōnatunatu
dilute waimeha, pokepoke
dim light hina, kākarauri, kaurehu(-tia)
dimension āhuatanga, ine, korahi, ahu, ahe
diminish whakaruhi(-a), whakaiti(-tia), whakaero
dimple ngongo
din turituri, hoihoi, tararau
dine kai tina
dinghy waka pīhau, poti paku
dingy pōkē
dingy, inflatable - waka pīhau pūangi
dining room ruma kai, whare kai
dinner kai, tina
dinosaur mokoweri, mokotuauri
diocese pīhopatanga, tiohehi, rohe pīhopa
dip tou(-a), toutou, utu(-a), ruku
diploma tiwhikete, pūkairua, tītohu
diplomat takawaenga kāwanatanga
diplomatic maioha
direct (*adj., adv.*) tauaro, tika, tautika, hāngai pū
direct (manage) whakahaere
direction huarahi, aronga, aronui, ahu
directions tohutohu
directly tauaro
directly, look - titiro hāngai
directly (personally) a ia tonu, tika
directly affect hāngai pū
director mana hautū, kaiwhakahaere, tumuaki
directory rārangi kōpaki, whaiaronga, whaiara
directory (telephone) rārangi nama waea, rārangi tau waea
dirge apakura, keka
dirt paru
dirty paru, poke, mōrikarika, paruheti

disabled hauā
disadvantage ngoikoretanga, whakahōhā, pāharatanga
disadvantaged rawakore(-tia), whakatiki
disagreement taupatupatu, whakahē
disappear hanumi, whatungarongaro, ngaro haere
disappointed rarua
disappointment matekiri, pāpouri
disapproval whakahē, ātetetanga, whaiere
disapprove whakahē, ātete(-tia)
disarm by persuasion tupe(-a)
disarm tango rākau
disarray pōraruraru, poauau, kaumingomingo
disaster aituā, parekura
disastrous kiriwetiweti, maikiroa
disband whakamarara(-tia), whakakore(-ngia)
disbelieve whakateka, whakahori, whakaparau
disc porotiti, kīwhi, kōpae
discard whakarere(-tia), pare(-a), tūraki
discernable mārama hinengaro kakama
discharge (eyes) pīkaru
discharge (release) tuku(-a) kia haere, putanga mai
disciple akonga
disciplinary action whiu, hāmene
discipline arahi tika, raupapa, whakaako tikanga
disclaim kape(-a), whakakāhore(-tia)
disco paeoru
discoloured ehu, koehu, poapoa, wairau
discomfort hūhi, mamae, auhi
disconcerted pohēhē, pororaruraru, paraparau
disconnect wete(-a), momotu
disconsolate pōuri, mokemoke, rohai, pēhia ki raro
discontent riri, amuamu, pāhunu, nanu
discontented matangurunguru, tūreikura
discontinue whakamutu
discount whakaiti te utu, hekenga utu
discourage whakapāhunu, whakatūoi
discourteous takahi mana, āhuaatua
discover kite(-a), hura(-ina), tūhura
discoverer kaikimi, kaitorotoro
discovery kitenga, whakahuranga
discredit whakahāwea, whakanano
discreet marire, matawhāiti
discreetly hakune
discretion whakaaro nui, tūpato
discriminate tauwehewehe(-a), whiriwhiri
discriminate (show bias) whakahāwea, ngautuarā
discriminatory whakahāwea, whakaparahako
discus poroāwhio, kīwhi
discuss whakawhiti whakaaro, whiriwhiri
discussion kōrerorero, whakawhitinga whakaaro
disdain whakahihi, hīkaka(-tia), whakatoatoa
disease mate, tahumaero
disease, skin - hakihaki

disease, venereal - tokatoka, paipai
disentangle wewete (wetea), ui(-a)
disfavour mauāhara, kino, hae
disfigure haehae
disgorge whakaruaki
disgrace whakamā, hane, tāwai
disgruntled pukuriri, whakaahu
disguise whakaahua kē, whakaatu kē
disgust whakarihariha, weriweri, anuanu, matakawa
dish rīhi, paepae
dish (type of food) momokai
dishcloth ūkui horoi, weru, muku
dishearten whakapāwera, whakapāhunu
dishevelled tīwanawana, hūtoki, pūaweawe
dishonest hianga, tinihanga, kēā
dishonour takahi mana, whakaiti(-tia), numinumi
dishonourable māteatea
dishwasher mihini horoi rīhi, pūrere horoi maitai
disillusion matekiri
disillusionment matatewha ngā kanohi, matekiritanga
disinclined kōroiroi, iwingohe, ngākaukore
disinfectant patu huakita, patu whakapirau
disintegrate horo, kongakonga, pakaru rawa
disinterment hahunga tūpāpaku
disjointed nakunaku
dislike whakakino(-ngia), kāhore e pai ki, matakawa
dislodge wete(-a), tara(-a), whakanuku(-hia)
dismantle wetewete(-kina), whakamatara(-tia)
dismay pōuri, pōraru, pōtatutatu
dismount heke, tuku, makere, tatū
disobedience korewhakarongo, whakahoihoi
disobedient taringa turi, kore whakarongo, whakatuturi
disobey takahi(-a), takatakahī(-a)
disorganise pororaru, whakakūwawa
disorganised takoto hukihuki, kūwawa
disown mahue, whakahoe(-a), ākiri(-tia), whakarei(-a)
disparage whakakino(-ngia), ngautuarā, hahani
dispatch tuku, tono, kupu
dispensation whakawāteatanga, tukunga
disperse tītaritari, tohatoha, korara, rui(-a), tāhoro, tiri, horahora
dispersed kōtiwhatiwha, marara
displace hiki(-tia), pana(-ia), katote
display (*n.*) whakaaturanga, whakakitenga, whakaaritanga
display (*v.*) whakaatu(-ria), whakakite(-a), hora(-hia), kohura(-tia)
dispose of ruke (-a), porowhiu, pana(-ia)
disposition āhuatanga, tuakiri
disproportionate pāhikahika, tuwhena
disprove whakakore(-a), whakaparau
dispute tautohe, wenewene
disqualify (debar) whakakore(-ngia), whakatupe(-a), tātāki

disregard piki(-a), whakahāwea(-tia)
disrepair pakaru, whakahapanga
disreputable hanga whakahāwea, rongo kino, whakanano
disrespect tīkai, takahi mana, tōtōa
disrupt whakapōrearea, whakakino(-ngia), whakawhati(-tia)
dissatisfy whakaahu, wenewene
dissect tuaki, poka(-ina), mutumutu(-a), tapahi
dissected motu
dissection tuakitanga
dissent whakakāhore(-tia), whakahēnga
dissertation whakamāori kaupapa, kauwhau hōhonu
dissipate whakapau, whakaeto
dissolve memeha, whakaeto, whakarewa
dissuade whakapāhunu, whakapeau(-tia)
distance tawhiti, mamao, nuku o te whenua, roa
distant tawhiti, mamao
distil māturuturu, mahi māturu, iheuheu
distinct (clear) mārama
distinction rerekētanga, ritenga wehewehe, rongonui
distinguish between wehewehe, waitohu
distort whakapeka, whakapiko
distortion piari, hahaka, whakapekatanga
distracted kōnatunatu, pororaru, manawarū
distress ahotea, auhi, mamate, pāmamae
distressed ngākau pōuri, mamate, pōkeka
distribute tohatoha, hora(-hia), rui(-a), whakarato, tiritiri
distribution ratonga, tītaritanga, whakaratonga, tuaritanga
distributor kaitohatoha, tīrari, pūtoha *(hiko)*
district takiwā, tōpito, rohe, tiriwā
district court kōti-ā-rohe
district office tari takiwā
distrust whakahori, whakateka, matakana
disturb whakakorikori, whakararuraru(-tia)
disturbance pororaru, tutū te puehu
disuse mahue
ditch waikeri, awakeri, awarua
dither rikarika, pāremoremo, utiuti
ditto kia pērā anō
dive down (swoop) rere kōkiri, tūpou
dive for ruku(-hia), tō ki roto ki te wai
diverge haere weherua, kōtiti, tangongi
divert pātari, whakakōtiti, whakatītaha, kaupare
divide whakawehe, weherua, motu(-kia), tītore
divided motumotu, ritua, rangirua, wāhi(-a)
dividend (profit) moni i hua, tauwehe, tau mō te wehenga
diving board pae kōkiri, papa kōkiri
diving pool hōpua kōkiri, hāpua ruku
divinity atuatanga

division wāhanga, wehenga
division (army) mātua, whare
divorce (*n.*) wehenga mārena, wehe tūturu
divorce (*v.*) toko(-na), rau(-tia), tino whakarērea
dizziness ānini, āmai, rorohuri
dizzy aniroro, āmai, pōānini
DNA molecule pītauira
do mea(-tia), mahi(-a)
docker kaiuta (poti)
docket puka whakamana utu, puka rārangi taputapu, rihīti
dockyard papa hanga kaipuke, papa whakahou kaipuke
doctor rata, tākuta
doctorate tākutatanga, tohu wānanga tuatoru, tohu kairangi
doctrine whakaakoranga, whakaakotanga, whakapono
document pepa whai tikanga, tuhinga
documentary pakipūmeka
dodecagon tapa tekau mā rua
dodge a blow karo(-hia), wheta
dodge about hikohiko, kōtiti
dog kurī, kīrehe
dogmatic whakatuanui
doing e mahi ana
dole utu koremahi, penihana
doll tāre, karetao
dollar tāra
dollar sign pīwaka, tohu tāra
dolphin aihe
domain rangatiratanga, rohe, huinga pū
domestic nō te kāinga, tara-ā-whare
Domestic Purposes Benefit DPB Takuhe Matua Takitahi
dominance tū rangatira
dominant whai mana
domineering whakahīhī, whaka-topatopa
dominion rangatiratanga, tominiana
donation koha, takoha, aroha
done (finished) oti, taea, pau
done, what can be -? kia ahatia?, me pēhea?
donkey kaihe, hīhō
donor kaihomai, kaihoatu
don't kaua e . . ., aua e . . ., kei
doom aituā whakaweti, turakitanga, mate
door kūwaha, tatau, whatitoka
doormat waiku, waikawa
doorsill paepae poto
doorway kūwaha, kūaha
dormant e moe ana, taharangi
dormitory whare puni, whare moe
Dory, John - kuparu, pukeru
dosage inenga
dot tongi, ira, irakati
dotted iraira
double tāpara, taurua, kikorua, tōpū
double back hoki whakamuri
double cross tuku(-a), tinihanga(-tia)
double up (body) koropeke
doubled aparua
doubles takirua tokowhā
doubt, in - rangirua, āwangawanga
doubter ihupuku
doubtful pōkaikaha, weherua, kārangirangi, rangirua
doubtless kāhore ekore
douse fire tinei(-a)
dove kūkū, kūkupa

dowel titi, whao rākau
down payment moni tāpui, utu tuatahi
Down's syndrome mate pūira kehe
downgrade whakaiti wāriu
downpour ua tātā
downstairs pā raro
downward whakararo
downwards iho, ki raro
dowry koha mārena, hākari mārena
doze wāhi moe, kānewha
dozen tekau mā rua
draft (outline) takawhakaaro, tauira, kape tuatahi
drag tō(-ia), kume(-a), kukume
drag net kaharoa
dragon tarakona
dragonfly kapowai, tarakona, kakapōhai
drain (*n.*) awakeri, waikeri
drain (*v.*) rere atu
drain pipe waiputa
drainboard papa rerewai
drama (play) mahi a Māui, toi whakaari
draughts (game) porotaka, mū, mūwhiti, teraku
draw (game) ōrite, rite
draw (selection) whiriwhiringa
draw (sketch) tuhi, whakaahua, tā(-ia)
drawer (furniture) toroa, hautō
drawing whakaahua, tātuhi
drawing board papa tuhi
dreadful wehi, wetiweti, maruwehi
dream moemoeā, moehewa, maruāpō
dreamy pohewa, hākirikiri
dreary mōrearea
dredge koko, kārau, rou(-a)
dregs ota, nganga, waipara
drench (rain) kōpiro, kueo, whekuwheku
dress (*n.*) kākahu, pūeru, weru, mai
dress (*v.*) kākahu(-ria), whakakākahu
dressing gown kāhana
dribble (drool) turuturu
dribble (soccer) tiripara
dressing (wound) takai
dried maroke, mimiti, paku
drift tere, pae, maanu
drift net kaharoa
driftwood tāwhaowhao, pakatai moana
drill (tool) wiri, haorete, tirira
drill bit wirikoi, tūwiri
drink inu(-mia), unu
drinker (alcoholic) kairama, kaipia, porohaurangi
drip patapata, turuturu
drive animals whiu(-a), ā(-ia)
drive car taraiwa, whakahaere
drive forward kōkiri
driver taraiwa, kaitoko waka
driving force ānga, uruhi
drizzle hāuaua, pūnehu
drone (buzz) rōria
drool over whakawaiwai, hāware, whakanewa
droop tārewa
drop (*v. intr.*) marere, taka, horo, ngahoro, mauru (te hau)
drop (*v. tr.*) whakamakere(-tia), whakaheke(-a)
drop in peka
drop kick whanataka
drop of liquid turu, pata, kōpata
drop out makere i te (kura)

dropsy kōpū tetere, puku kōwhao
drought kore wai, tauraki, maroke
drowsy hiamoe, matemoe, hāmoemoe, nenewha
drowsy, make - rehu(-a)
drugs (medicinal) rongoā
drugs (psychotic) tarukino, rongoā whakananu
drugs habit mate warawara
drum taramu, pahū, pākiri, patatō
drunk haurangi
drunkard porohaurangi
dry (*v.*) whakamaroke, tauera(-tia), tauraki(-tia)
dry (*adj.*) maroke
dual takirua, paparua, tōrua
dubious pōkaikaha, rangirua
duck, tame - rakiraki
duck, wild - pārera, korowhiowhio
duck under rumaki
due nama
duet waiata punarua, waiata tōrua
dugout canoe waka tiwai, tīkohu
dull (blunt) pūhuki
dull (sky) pōrukuruku, pārūrū
duly rite
dumb wahangū
dummy, baby's - whakarata, ngote
dung tūtae, hamuti, haumuti
dungarees tāngari
dunk tou(-a)
duplicate tāruarua
duration roa, roanga
dusk ahiahi pō, kākarauri, kaunenehu, porehu
dust (*n.*) puehu
dust (*v.*) tahitahi(-a), muku(-a)
dustbin ipupara
dustpan tai puehu
Dutch Tatimana
duty (tax) tiuti, tāke
duvet papangarua hune
dux tauira tino mōhio o te kura
DVD kōpaepae whakaahua, ataata iamati wewete tohu
dwarf tauwhena, whena, roiroi whene
dwindle iti haere, mimiti
dye wairākau, tā
dying whakahemo
dynamic whakakorikori, akiaki
dynamite pohū, tainamaiti, taipohū, ahi pakū
dysentery tikotiko toto
dyslexia mate moraru kupu, tīpaopao kupu

E

each ia . . ., ia . . ., tēnā . . . tēnā, tētahi
each day ia rā ia rā
eager kaikā, hihiri, ārita, ngākaunui
eagerly māhorahora, āritarita
eagle ēkara, kārearea, kērangi
ear taringa
earlobe hoi, pokopoko, toke
ear pendant mau-taringa, whakakai, kapeu, koko-tangiwai
earl eara, ēra
early moata, wawe, tōmua
earn whiwhi moni, utunga
earnest whiwhita
earth (soil) oneone, paru
earth (world) ao
earth mother Papatūānuku
earth oven hāngi, umu, hapī
earthquake rūwhenua
earthworm toke, noke
ease whakangāwari(-tia), whakaeaea
easily ngāwari, māmā noaiho
east tai rāwhiti, taha marangai, tai tamawahine
Easter Aranga, Pākate
easterly hau rāwhiti, pieke, hau waho
easy māmā, ngāwari, mārū
easygoing ngāwari, hanga noa
eat kai(-nga)
eat greedily kaihoro
ebb-tide tai timu, tai heke
ebony eponi, rākau mangu
eccentric autaia, tupua, hārakiraki, korokē
echo paoro, kō, oro, kowaro, reo kō
eclipse (moon) pounga o te marama
ecology rangahau taiao
economical tūpato ki te whakapau moni
economics ohaoha, ōhanga
economise whakamoamoa
ecstasy manawarū, takaahuareka
eczema kiri pāpaka, hikako tongako
eddy (water) ripo, auhoki, riporipo, okiri, okori
eddy (wind) hauripo
edge taha, taitapa
edgy āmaimai, āwangawanga, kārangi
edifice whare teitei, whare rangatira, karuhi
edit whakatikatika(-hia), whakatika
edition tānga pukapuka, putanga
editor takatā, kaiwhakatika, kaiwhakatika tānga
educate whakaako(-na)
educated mōhio, whakaakona
education akoranga, whai mātauranga
eel tuna
eel pot hīnaki, punga
eerie kēhua

effect hua, tukunga iho, ariā
effeminate tāne mate tāne
efficiency kakama
effluent wai para
effort kaha
egg hua manu, hēki
egg cup ipu huamanu, ipu hēki
egg shell pāpapa
egg white whakakahu, kahu
egg yolk tōhua
egret matuku-moana, kōtuku
Egyptian Ihipiana
eiderdown papanārua
eight waru
eighteen tekau mā waru
eighth tuawaru
eighty waru tekau
either . . . or rānei . . . rānei, rainei, ahakoa pēhea, ia
eject pana(-ia), pei ki waho, tuha(-ina)
elaborate whakaranea, āta whakamārama
elastic (flexible) tāwariwari, roroha
elastic (rubber) inarapa, kumewhītiki, rāhiteka, ngoi tāwari
elasticity ngohenga, kōpētanga
elbow tuke, tuketuke, whatīanga
elder brother/sister tuakana, hāmua
elder child muanga
elderly people mātāpuputu, kaumātua
eldest child mātāmua
elect whiriwhiri, whakatū(-ria)
election pōtitanga
electorate rohe pōti
electric current ia hiko
electric kettle tīkera hiko
electric shock whiti hiko
electrical energy pūngao hiko
electrician kaihiko, kaimahi hiko, mataara hiko
electricity hiko
electrify whakahiko(-tia), whakaoho(-tia)
electrocardiogram hikonga huahuaki, whakaahua hoki manawa
electrocute mate whitihiko
electromagnet autō-ā-hiko, aukume-ā-hiko
electron irahiko
electronic mail karere rorohiko, īmera
electronics tāhiko
element, chemical - pūmotu, horomatanga, urutapunga
element, electric - whakapōkākā
elephant arewhana
elevated platform pourewa
elevator ararewa, arakawe
eleven tekau mā tahi
eleventh te tekau mā tahi
eligible arotau, tika, māraurau
eliminate whakakore(-ngia)
elocution whakahua kupu
elope paheke
eloquence korokoro tūī
else, someone - tētahi atu
elsewhere ki wāhi kē, tētahi atu wāhi, ki hea rānei
email īmera
embalm whakapakoko
embankment maioro
embark eke(-a, -ngia)
embarrass whakamā, whakapārahu
embarrassed whakamā
embarrassment pōrahurahu

embassy kāinga rua o te kāwanatanga, māngai o te kāwanatanga
embed mau(-a), tāmau
embers ngārehu, ngaerehu, pungarehu
embitter whakapūkawa, whakariri, takarita
emblem tohu
embody whakatinana(-tia)
embolism puru o te ia toto
embrace awhi(-tia), rarawhi, pā ana ki, piri tahi
embracing topetū
embroider tuitui(-a), whakapaipai
embryo kākano, kune, kukune
emend whakatika(-hia)
emerge puta mai
emergence putanga (ki waho)
emergency mate whawhati tata, ohorere, ohotata
emergency service ratonga ohorere, ratonga mate whawhati tata
emigrant manene atu
emigrate heke(-a) atu, maunu(-hia) atu
eminent rangatira, ikeike
emission tuku, whakaputanga
emit pahupahu, whakahā(-ngia), whakataka(-ina)
emotion hinengaro, tokomauri, manawa
emphasise whakapūmau, whakatauākī
employ people tuku mahi, whakawhiwhi mahi
employee kaimahi, hunga mahi
employer kaituku mahi, kaiwhakawhiwhi mahi
employment tūranga mahi, mahi
empower whakamana(-hia)
emptiness tahangatanga, tīareare, piako, hematanga
empty (vacant) takoto kau ana, piako, piango, kau, putua
empty out whakapiako, maringi
enable whakamana(-hia), āhei(-tia), whakahohe
enamel, tooth - reu, pakiri
encase whakawhāiti, kōpani
enchant manawareka, rehia, ātahu
encircle taiāwhio(-tia), hao(-a), awhe(-a)
encircle with rope niko(-a), natinati
enclose taiapa(-tia), rāihe, pākorokoro, rau(-a)
enclosure (animal) rāihe
encompass awhi(-tia), rawhi(-tia)
encourage akiaki(-tia), tautoko(-tia), whakamanawa
encroachment auraratanga
encrusted kiri taratara
end (completion) otinga, tukunga iho
end (extremity) pito, tōpito, moka
end (finish) mutunga, whakamutunga
end user kaiwhakamahi mutunga
endanger tuku ki te mate, whakamōrea(-tia)
endeavour whakapau kaha, tohe(-a), whakauaua, whāinga
ended mutu, oti, pahi
endless mutunga kore, pūmau tonu
endorse tautoko(-tia), whakaae(-tia), whakamana(-tia)
endowed with whakawhiwhi(-a)
endowment moni tuku iho, putea moni matua

E

endurance tohe
endure matatū, tohetohe
enema werowero whakatiko, kuhitou
enemy hoariri, wheiwheinga
energetic pukumahi, whakauaua, hihiri, kaha, nakawhiti
energise whakakaha(-ngia), whakahohe(-tia)
energy pūkaha, ngoi, kaha, pūngao, hiringa, konga
energy output hiringa pūngao
energy (nuclear) hiko karihi
enforce āki i te mana, uruhi(-na), whakaū
engaged (betrothed) taumau
engender hanga, whakaari, whakaatu
engine mīhini, pūkaha, initia, pūrere
engine room puku mahi
engineer enetinia, kaipūkaha
engineering pūkahatanga
England Ingarangi
English Ingarihi, Reo Pākehā
engrave whakairo(-tia, -hia)
engraver kaiwhakairo
engulf hanumi, roromi (romia), momi(-a), poki(-a)
enhance whakakaha ake, whakarei(-a)
enigma panga, muna, paki
enjoy koa(-a), hari, hākinakina
enjoy rights whiwhi painga
enjoyable pārekareka, rekareka
enlarge whakanui(-a), whakarahi(-tia), whakaita(-tia)
enlargement whakarahinga
enlighten whakamārama(-tia)
enlist whakauru(-a), haina(-tia), taunaki(-tia)
enmesh tāwhiwhi, tāweka, tākeke
enmity mauāhara
ennoble whakarangatira
enormous nui whakaharahara, tino kaitā, tuangea
enough nuinga, ka nui, rawa ake, ake (after adj.), rawaka
enough! kāti, heoi anō, ka nui
enquire pātai(-ngia), ui(-a)
enquiry urupounamu
enrol whakauru(-a) te ingoa, rēhita(-tia)
ensign haki
ensilage karaehe toroi
enslave whakahere(-a)
ensure whakapūmau
entangle tākeke(-tia)
enter (register) whakauru
enter tomo(-kia), kuhu(-a), uru, hou ki roto, ō
entertain (host) manaaki, atawhai, whakamanuhiri
entertainment mahi whakangahau, rīhia
entertainment house whare tapere, whare rōpā
enthusiasm kaikā, ngākaunui, ngākau whakapuke
entire katoa
entirely huri noa huri noa
entitle whai kerēme, whai wāhi
entrails whēkau, ngākau, puku
entrance tomokanga, kūwaha, ngutupā
entrance, marae - ngutu o te marae
entrust hoatu hei tautīaki
envelop kōpaki(-na)
envious pūhaehae, harawene, mahira, hae
environment ao tūroa, ao taiāwhio, taiao

envy hae
ephemeral rangitahi
epilepsy mate hūkiki, mate ruriruri
epilogue kōrero tāpiri
episode wāhanga
epitaph kupu whakamaumahara
equal rite, ōrite, hōrite
equal, approximately - pātata te rite
equalise whakaōrite, whakarite(-a), inea
equality ririte
equate ōrite
equation taurite, whārite, ōritetanga
equator kōpae waenganui o te ao
equestrian kaieke hōiho
equip utauta(-ina), whakarawe(-a)
equipment utauta, taputapu
equipped whai mea ana, kei a ia te mea
equivalent te rite, hau rite, ōrite, taurite, rite tonu
era tau whai tikanga
eradicate whakakāhore(-tia), haepapa(-tia)
erase muku(-a), horoi(-a), ūkui(-a)
erect (*n.*) tū ana, tutū, tū tika, tū torotika
erect (*v.*) whakatū(-ria), whakaara
erection whakatū, hanga, tore
erode ngaungau(-a), whakahoro(-a)
erosion horo whenua, whakahoro (-a)
erotic karihika, hiahia onioni, taera, hawene
err kōtiti haere, taka ki te hē
erratic kōtītiti, horehore
error hē, hara, pōhēhē, hapa
error, margin of - pae hapa
erupt hū, pahūtanga, pakarutanga
escalate nui haere, whakakaha
escalator arakawe, aranekeneke, ara maiangi
escape (get away) oma, puta, wehe atu
escaped pahika
escaper kaioma, kairere
escort haere tahi, taupaepae
especially mārika, tino (before adj.), ake anō
espresso kāwhe kūtētē
essence uho, waiwai, hā, ngako
essential tino pūtake
essentially tino
establish pou(-a), whakaū(-kia), whakapūmau(-tia)
established ū, pūmau, tūāki, taketake
estate agent takawaenga hoko whenua
estimate āta tatau, whakatau tata, whakaaro(-tia, -hia)
estimation whakataunga tata, mahinga tau pātata
ethical take mana tangata, matatika
ethnic tikanga-ā-iwi, matatika
etiquette tikanga, kawa
eucalyptus purukamu
eucharist Miha, ūkaritia, Hapa Whakamutunga, ūkarie tapu
euthanasia whakamate mamaekore
evacuate hōnea, ngaro atu, whakatahi(-a)
evaluate whakamātautau, tātai, āta wānanga
evaporate mimiti, eto

evaporate, make - whakaeto, whakangaro wai
evasive karo, parori
even (equal) tautika, taurite, ōrite, rite tonu, riterite
evening ahiahi
event tauwhāinga, pāpono, takahanga
eventual i roto i te wā
eventually rawa atu (after verb), roa rawa, mutunga iho
ever mō ake tonu atu, tonu
evergreen māota, māotaota
everlasting mutungakore, ora tonu
every (all) katoa
every (each) ia
every day ia rā ia rā
everyone ia tangata, puketī puketā
evict pana(-ia), pei ki waho
eviction peinga, pananga
evidence taunakitanga, kōrero a te kaititiro, whakaaturanga
evident mārama
evil omen aituā, tohu kino
evil kino, whiro
evolution tupunga, mārohatanga, whanaketanga
evolve tupu ake, puta mai
ewe hipi uwha, io
exact tino tika, tika pū, hāngai tonu
exactly mārika
exaggerate whakarahi, whakanui, hangarau
exalt whakahōnore, whakanui
examination whakamātautau
example tauira
example, for - hei tauira noa
exasperate whakahōhā
excavate huke(-a), keri(-a), whakakōrua(-tia)
excellence pai, hiranga, kairangi
Excellency (title) Tou Whakaritenga
excellent rawe, kairangatira, hiranga, mounga
except hāunga, awere, ahakoa
exception rerekētanga, okotahi
exceptional rawe
excess hau, tāwere, nui rawa, inati
exchange hoko(-na), whakawhiti(-tia)
excise (tax) moni tāke
excitable whakaongaonga
excite nanawe, hawene
excited nanawe, hūrere, huamo, ohorere te ngākau
excited (angry) manawa wera
exciting whakaihiihi, wana, nanawe, hiamo
exclaim karanga, peha, whakapāha
exclamation karanga, umere, tīwaha
exclamation mark tohu hauhā, pīoho, tohuhā
exclude mahue
excluding hāunga, āunga
exclusive tapu, tāporo, motuhake, aukati
excrement tiko, haumuti, paru, tūtae
excuse (defend) whakatikatika, takunga, ari, takunga
execute command kawe(-a)
execute (kill) whakamate(-a)
executive officer kaiwhakahaere
executive powers mana whakahaere
exemplary rangatira, pai, tauira, hiringa
exempt whakawātea(-tia)

exercise (physical) korikori tinana, whakaataata
exercise (practise) hei mahi, mahinga
exert whakauaua, whāwhai, whakatīeke, āki(-na)
exhale whakahā, hengihengi, pupuhi, hānene
exhaust, car - pāipa auahi, puta auahi
exhibit whakaari(-a), whakaataata(-ria)
exhibition whakakitenga
exhibitor kaiwhakaatu
exhort whakakīkī, akiaki, āki(-na)
exhortation whakangahau, whakamanawa
exhume hahu(-a) tūpāpaku, ehu(-na)
exile manene, noho manene
exist noho, ora, puta, tīari
existence oranga
existing system āhuatanga kua takoto kē
exit putanga, puta, waiho
expand whakawhānui, whakarea (maths), whakaroha
expansion whakawhānuitanga, whakareatanga
expect tūmanako, tatari
expedition ope, haerenga, pahī, hiku
expeditiously tere, horo
expel pana ki waho, tūwhiti, pei(-a)
expendable mea noa iho, meamea, iti, wenewene
expense moni whakapau, utu
expensive nui te utu
experienced waia, taunga, tautōhito, momōhio
experiment kaupapa whakamātau, whakamāhunga
expert (specialist) pouwhiro, tohunga, matatau ki, pū
expertise tohungatanga, mākohakoha
explain whakamārama(-tia), whakamōhio(-tia)
explanatory whakamārama
explicit mārama, pū
explode pahū, pakū, papā(-ngia)
explore āta tirotiro, rangahau(-a), torotoro haere
explorer kaipōkai whenua, kaitorotoro, whakahura
explosion pahū, hū, pakūtanga
export hoko ki tāwāhi, hoko ki tai, kaweake
expose (dig up) huke(-a), keri(-a)
exposed mārakerake
expulsion peinga, pananga
extend whakawhānui, toro, whakaroa(-tia)
extended mārō, umaraha, hōrapa
extension roanga, nukuhanga, whakawhānuitanga
extent nui, roanga, whānui, kōrahi
exterior ā-waho
extinct pau, mōtītī, ngaro, weto
extinguish fire patu ahi
extinguished pirau, poko, weto
extort apo(-hia), tango moni
extra hara, āpiti, tua
extra (cricket) hemi
extraordinary autaia, mīharo, whakaharahara, korokē
extravagant (wasteful) maumau, tōtōā, whakapau moni
extremely tino
exude mapi, patī, pātītī

exult whakamanamana, whakahākoakoa, umere
eye kanohi, karu, whatu, mata
eye shadow panikamo
eye socket kape
eyeball kamo, karu
eyeball to eyeball whakarau
eyebrow tukemata, pewa, peru, kape
eyelash kamonga, kemokemo, kamukamu
eyelid kamo, rewha, paerunga, paeraro
eyewitness kaititiro

F

fable pakiwaitara
facade roro o te whare, āhuatanga
face (*n.*) kanohi, mata
face (*v.*) anga ki, ahu atu/mai, aro atu/mai, whakaangaanga
face value (maths) uara mata, wāriu mata
facial eczema karukaru hipi
facilitate kimi huarahi
fact he mea pūmau, mea e mōhiotia ana, meka, pono
factory wheketere, aupoke, tohitū whakanao
fade memeha, iti haere, hātea, maroke huakore
faeces hamuti
fahrenheit, degree - waeine mahana F, tohutua
fail hinga, ngaro, hē, makere
failure takanga, hinga, wetonga, matenga
faint (*adj.*) māwhe, iti haere, hātea
faint (swoon) hemo, hauaitu
fair (just) tika, pai, i runga i te pai, pono
fair skin kiritea, kiri mā
fair weather paki
fairly (rather) āhua + *adjective*
fairy heketoro, patupaiarehe, tahurangi
fairytale kōrero paki, pakiwaitara, pakiwaituhi
faith healer tohunga whakaora-ā-wairua
faith whakapono
faithful pono, tūturu
fake rūpahu, teka, meho
fall (drop) taka, tāheke, tanuku, rutu
fall apart pakaru
fall asleep warea
fall out (disagree) kōhetehete
fallacy hē, pōhēhē
falling star kōkiri, tūnui-ā-rangi, tūnui-ā-te-ika
fallout, nuclear para iratuki
false hē, horihori, tito, parau
false start hapa, timata hori, hēhē
falter (hesitate) whakaroa, tawhitawhi, tapatu, tapepa
fame rongonui
familiar waia, taunga, rata
family whānau
family support takuhe whānau
family tree whakapapa, tātai, kāwaitanga
famine wā matekai, wā tūpuhi, pakaroa, tau kūī
famous rongonui, ingoa nui, ingoa hau
fan (admirer) kaiwhaiwhai
fan (for wafting) pakihau
fan (*v.*) kōwhiuwhiu, pōwaiwai, tāwhiri
fan out wherawhera(-hia)
fanatic kiriweti, tūkaha, pōrangi whiwhita
fantail pīwaiwaka, pīwakawaka

fantastic! ka mau te wehi!, pārekareka, tupua
farewell! (off you go) haere rā!
farewell! (remain) e noho rā!, hei kōnei!
farewell, to - poroporoaki, poroaki
farm (*n.*) pāmu, whāma
farm (*v.*) ahuwhenua, mahi whenua
farmyard papanga pāmu
farther on kō atu
fascinate manawarū
fashion momo kākahu o te wā, tikanga o te wā
fast (quick) horo, tere, hohoro, kama
fast (starve) nohopuku, whakatiki
fasten whakaū, whakamau(-a)
fat (grease) hinu, ngako
fat (obese) mōmona
fatal whakamate
fate (end) tukunga iho
fate (nemesis) aitu, aituā
father-in-law hungawai, hunarei
father pāpā, matua tāne
fatherhood matuatanga
fatherless matuakore
fatigue mate ngenge, ngoikore
fatten whakamōmona
fatty hinuhinu
fault hē, hapa
fault-finding whakahē, wani, ngautuarā, tāpiapia
favour (*v.*) aronui(-tia), aro(-ngia), hānga mai/atu
favourable arotau, atawhai
favourite makau, mariu, puiake, taonga arohatia nuitia, matareka
fear mataku, wehi, hopo te ngākau
fearless mātātoa, wehikore
feast hākari, haukai
feat whakatutuki mīharo, mahi nanakia
feather piki, hou, huruhuru
feather, red - kuraraukura
feature āhuatanga, tirohanga
federation whetereihana
fee utu
feeble ngoikore, iwikore
feebleness ngoikoretanga
feed whāngai(-a), kainga, kame
feedback paoro whakahoki
feel (sense) rongo(rangona), whīra, ariā
feelers, crayfish - hihi, weri, kawekawe
feelers, insect - pūtihi, pihi, pūhihi
feelings hinengaro, whakaaro
feijoa pītoa
feint māminga, wheta, whakahopo
feline tā te tori, tā te ngeru
fell (chop down) tua(-ina), tope(-a), turaki(-na)
felt pen pene whītau
female (womanly) wahine
feminism tohe mana wahine, kōkiri mana wahine
fence (enclosure) taiepa, taiapa, taepa, tūwatawata
fence with sword matātuhi hoari
fend off ārai atu, pārai, whakangungu(-a)
ferment toroī, moī
fermented kōpiro, mara
fern tawatawa, pikopiko, kiwakiwa, makawe o Raukatauri
fern-root aruhe, roi, renga
fern, black tree - mamaku

fern, bracken - rārahu, rarauhe, mahuika, manehu
fern frond, coiled - koru
fern frond, young - miha
fern, gully - pūnui
ferocious autaia, whakamataku, māhinahina
ferry (*n.*) poti whakawhiti, waka kōpikopiko, perepoti
ferry (*v.*) whakawhiti(-tia)
fertile land whenua mōmona
fertile whai hua, haumako
fertilisation whakatō kākano
fetch tiki(-na), kawe(-a)
fetish mauri, māwe, manea
feud wheinga, toheriri
fever kirikā, pīwa, eku
feverish kauanu
few torutoru, ruarua, itiiti, ouou, kōtahitahi
fiancé taumau, whaiāipo, tahu
fibre muka, akaaka, kaka, weu
fibreglass papamuka
fickle taurangi, matuarua, kihirua
fiction pakiwaitara, kōrero paki
fictitious teka, rūpahu, horihori
fiddle (violin) whira
fidelity pono
fidget oreore, manawarū, maikutu
field whīra, taiepa, pātiki, raorao
field, sports - papa tākaro, topa
field, to - ball hopu(-kia), mau, hopukuru
fielder (sports) tārake, kaihopu, kaitopa
fiend hātana, whiro, rewera
fierce āritarita, nanakia, muha
fiery pūkākā, pukuriri
fifteen tekau mā rima
fifteenth te tekau mā rima
fifty rima tekau
fig piki, whauwhau
fight whawhai(-tia), riri(-a)
fight back rautupu, tū atu, whawhai atu
fighter toa, hōia, kikopuku
figure (body) tinana, ropi, hanga
figure (shape) āhua, whakaahua, hoahoa
figurehead tauihu, tētē, tekoteko, pītau
file (office) kōnae, pūkohi, kōnae kōrero, pūāhari
file (rasp) whairu, tiwani, waru
file reference tohu kōnae kōrero
fill whakakī(-a)
fill with liquid utu(-hia)
filled kī, kī pai, kapi(-a)
film (movie) pikitia
film producer kaitukuata, kaitaki
film projector pūrere tukuata
filmstrip rīpene whakaahua, kiriata
filter tātari
filter, to - tātari(-tia)
filthy pirau, piro, hawa
fin of fish tira
final (championship) tuku mātātahi, whiringa toa
final (last) whakamutunga
finalise whakaoti
finally rawa (after verb)
finance moni āwhina, pūtea, punga, tahua
financial year tau pūtea
financier kaitohatoha pūtea
find kite(-a), kimi(-hia), rapu(-a)
find fault whakahē(-ngia), eke(-a)
finder kaitoro, kaikite
finding otinga
fine (good) pārekareka, rawe

F

fine (penalty) whaina
fine weather paki
finger matihao, matimati
finger, little - kōiti
finger, ring - mānawa
fingerboard papa piana, papa pātuhi
fingernail maikuku, matikuku, kotikara
fingerprint tapumati, tapukara
finish (complete) oti, whakaoti(-a)
finish (stop) mutu, whakamutu(-a)
finished (used up) pau
fire ahi, kāpura
fire (weapon) pupuhi (puhia)
fire alarm whakatūpato ahi, pere whakaoho kāpura
fire escape tipa kāpura, rerenga ahi
fire extinguisher whakaweto ahi, poko ahi
fire service ratonga ahi, rōpū tinei ahi
firebreak whakarake kāpura
fireguard ārai ahi, takuahi
fireplace pākai-ahi, takuahi
fireproof werakore
firewood wahie
firm (*adj.*) ū, mau mārō, uka
first tuatahi, wawe, mātua
first born mātāmua, pekepoho
first-born female tapairu
first light tākiritanga o te ata, ata hāpai, ata pūao, ata tū
first officer āpiha mātua
fish (*n.*) ika, ngohi
fish slice hīpae ika, kauhuri ika
fish with line hī ika
fish with net hao(-a)
fish-hook matau, pīhuka
fisheries ahumoana, tauranga ika
fisherman kaihī
fishing charm kaha
fishing ground taunga ika
fishing industry ahumoana
fishing line aho hī
fishing net kupenga, haohaonga
fishing rod matira, tautara
fist ringa meke, ringa whakapuku, ringakuti
fit (clothing, etc.) ō
fit (convulsion) ruriruri, hūkiki, hukeke
fit (healthy) ora, kaha, whiti, hauora
fit into ō, whiti ki roto, uru pai ki roto
fitness taha oranga, nakawhiti
fitting (try out) whakamātau
five rima
fix whakamau, whakatau, whakatina, whakaū
fix, in a - kei te raruraru
fixed ū, mau, pūmau, tina
fixed asset hua pūmau
fixture, sports - whakarite(-a) kēmu
flabbergasted tumeke
flabby wairuhi, ngohungohu
flag haki, kara
flagpole pou haki, pou kara, pou pīwari
flagrant māia, hema, hākune
flair (talent) pūmanawa
flake rau, whā
flame mura, hana
flange ngutu paipa
flank taha, kaokao
flanker poutaha
flannel ūkui, tauera iti
flap (*n.*) paki, tāreparepa

flap (*v.*) kapakapa, takarure(-tia)
flap (*v. intr.*) tīrepa
flap wings takarure
flapjack parāoa parai, parāoa takakau, taringa kurī
flare mumura, papahū
flare up mura, toro, papā
flash hikohiko, rapa, uira, muramura, kohiko
flask takawai, kotimutu
flat papa, haupapa, papatū
flat (lodging) kāinga noho, whare rīhi
flat surface papatahi, paparahi, paraha, papaku
flattened takapapā, parehe, papatahi
flatter whakapatipati, eneene, mirimiri
flattery patipati
flavour hā, reka, tāwara, kakara
flaw ngoikoretanga
flaw in timber tōrōkiri
flax harakeke, korari, paritaniwha
flax, dressed - muka
flea puruhi, keha, tuiau
fledgling pipi, kōhungahunga, pīrere
flee omaoma, whati, turere, rere
fleet of canoes kaupapa, tāruru waka
flesh kikokiko
flic-flac tupana rapa
flick tākiri(-tia), pere, kōpere
flicker kopura, pūrēhua
flickering pūrehua
flier paerata, kaiwhakarere
flight of stairs arapiki, pikinga
flimsy rahirahi
flinch kōemi, kōrapa
fling whiu(-a), maka(-ia), panga(-a), ākiri(-tia)
flint matā, kiripaka
flintlock ngutu parera, kauamo
flip (*n.*) pore
flip (*v. intr.*) takapore, porotēteke
float (*n.*) pōito, kārewa, kautere
float (*v.*) mānu, māunu, tere, rewa, whakatere(-tia)
flock of birds pōkai, kāhui
flog wepu(-a), whiu(-a)
flood waipuke(-tia), parawhenua, roma
floor papa, raho, whorōa
floor, first - papatahi, papa tuatahi
floor, ground - papatū, papa whenua
floor plan hoahoa papa
floor (storey) kaupapa, rewanga
flop (failure) koretake, hinga
floppy disc kōpae pīngore
florist kaihoko putiputi
flounder (fish) pātiki
flounder about kowheta
flour parāoa pūrere
floury mangaro
flow (run) tārere, tere, rere
flow (tide) pari
flow (together) kūtere
flower (blossom) putiputi, puāwai
flowering pūāwaitanga, whai pua
fluctuate rere atu rere mai, ripo atu ripo mai
flue tīmere
fluff kerehunga, perehunga, tāhuna
fluffy tāhunahuna
fluid huatau, kūtere, taurangi
fluke (worm) toke

F

fluorescent kōrekoreko, mataaho
fluoride pū kōwhai
flurry (squall) apū
flush (cards) whare kotahi
flushed (angry) uraura, hēmanawa
flute kōauau, pūtorino
flutter kapakapa, pepe
fly (insect) ngaro, rango
fly (soar) tere, rere, whakatopa
fly headlong rere whakateka
flyblown popo, iroiro
flying fox taura rere
flying tackle rutu rere, whakateka
flying visit peka ohorere
flyover ara runga
flyswat papaki rango
flywheel tōhito
foal kūao, punua hoiho
foam hukahuka, pūhuka, kare, pua
focus (*n.*) hāngai, arotahi
focus (*v.*) whakangahu(-a)
focusing arotahi
fodder mauti, kai kararehe, hei pakakau, kokinga waru
foe hoariri, wheiwheinga
foetus kahu, kōngahungahu, kukune
fog kohu, pūkohu, tūkōrehu
foil, aluminium - pepa hiriwa, pepa konumohe
fold (*n.*) pōkaitanga, whētui
fold (*v.*) whakakopi(-a), pōkai, tākai, kopa
folded aparua, whētui
folder kōpaki
foliage raurau
folio whārangi
folk-song mōteatea
follow whai(-a), aru(-mia), turuki(-na)
follow up whāinga i muri mai, whāia ake
follower kaiwhai, akonga
following whāinga, e whai ake nei
following wind hau whainga
fond of rekareka, matareka, mateoha
fondle mirimiri (miria), haumiri(-a), takamori(-tia)
food kai
food chain mekameka kai, kaitīni
food supplies ō
fool hākawa, hukehuke
foolish kūware, heahea, wairangi, pōauau
foot waewae, take, pū
foot (twelve inches) pūtu
football whutupaoro, whana poikiri
footer (footnote) hiku, kupu tāpiri
foothills take maunga, take puke
foothold wāhi tū
footnote kupu tāpiri, hiku, kīwae
footpath ara hīkoi
footprint whārua, tapuwae, paparahi
footrest kaupeka
footstep tapuwae, takahi
for mō, mā, hei, hai
for (because) ina hoki (after predicate)
forbid whakakāhore(-tia)
forbidding paraheahea
force, come into - mana te ture
force (compel) āki(-na), taikaha
force open kōara(-tia)
forcefully taumaha
forcibly remove kāhaki(-na), kāwhaki(-na)

ford whakawhitinga awa, kauanga wai
forearm tāhau o te ringa, kikowhiti
foregone conclusion whakatau noa
forehead rae
foreigner tangata rāwaho, tauiwi, tipua
foreman pāhi
foresee matakite, waitohu(-a)
forest ngahere, Waonui-a-Tāne
forethought whai whakaaro
forever āke, āke, āke tonu atu; mau tonu
forfeit whaina, whakahapa
forge (counterfeit) mahi tāhae
forgive muru(-a), hohou te rongo
forgotten wareware
fork paoka, mārau, whāka
fork, garden - tihoka māra
forked stick mārau
forklift waka uta
form (paper) puka
form (shape) āhua, kāhua
formal contract whakarite mana
formalise whakamana, whakatika
format whakatakoto, whakahōputu
formation hanga, whakariterite, ako, whakatū
formative whakaahua
formative years whanaketanga
formerly i mua
formulate policy whakatakoto kaupapa, whakahiato
forthcoming e ahu mai nei, e haere mai nei
fortieth te whā tekau
fortification pā, parepare, maioro
fortnightly ia rua wiki
fortunately waimārie, i pai ai, mokori anō
fortune raki, waimārie, taonga nui rawa
forty whā tekau
forum wānanga
forward direction whakamua, kokimua
foster child whāngai, tamaiti atawhai
foster parent matua whāngai
foster (tend) whāngai(-a), tautoko(-tia), whakatairangi
foul (sport) hapa, hara
foul throw (sport) maka hē, maka hara
found kitea
foundation tūtake, tūranga, taketake, kaupapa
foundation institute tūāpapa, karuhi
founder papahoro, kaiwhakaū
fount puna
fountain punawai taratītī
fountain pen pene puna, pene pāhihi
four whā
four at a time takiwhā
four sided porowhā
fourscore waru tekau
fourteen tekau mā whā
fourth in order tuawhā
fourth toe/finger mānawa
fowl heihei, tīkaokao
fox pokiha
foyer roro, hōro tomokanga, paepae
fraction hau, wāhi, hautau, hautanga, wāhanga
fracture (snap) whati
fragile rahirahi
fragment ngato, kongakonga

frail ngoikore, tūwai, memeha, kopī
framework pou tarāwaho, kaupapa, anga, kautawa
fraternity rōpū atawhai
fraud tinihanga(-tia)
fray(-ed) taretare, tāwekoweko
freak tupua
freckle ira, iraira
free wātea, ātea, māhorahora
free (gratis) marere, kāhore he utu
free (liberate) tuku kia haere, whakawātea(-tia), wete(-kia)
free from tapu whakanoa(-tia), taumahi
freeze whakahaupapa, haupapa(-ngia), whakatio
freezer pākatio, papakeo, pātaka hukapapa
freezing works whare patumīti
freight utanga, kawekawe
freighter poti utanga
French Wīwī
frenzied pōrangi, wairangi, hōkeka
frequently tonu, tini ngā tāima, putuputu
fresh (food) kaimata, hou, mata
fresh (growth) ururua, rea, hou
fresh air pūangi, hauhau, hauangi
fresh water wai māori, wai hou
friction hika, orooro, waniwani, ūkuitanga, waku
Friday Paraire, Rāmere
fridge pouaka hukapapa, pātaka mātao
friend hoa
friendless mokemoke, korehoa
fright pāwerawera, mataku, tumeke
frighten whakamataku(-ria)
frigid makariri, anuanu, hōtoke, kōpeke
fringe kawekawe, kurupatu, paenga
frivolous hangahanga noa iho, aweke, mahi tamariki
frock poraka
frog pēpeke, poroka
from i atu i, mai rā, nō, nā, mai i
front mua
front of house whatitoka, roro
front of person aroaro
frontiers rohe whakatakoto
frost(y) huka, haupapa, hukapapa, hukahuka
frostbite mate hukapuri
froth hukahuka(-ina), pāhuka
frown koromingo te rae, tiro kau, puku te rae
frozen haupapangia, tio, pātiotio, tonga (poetic)
fruit hua rākau, haemata
fruit salad purini huarākau
fruit stone anga
fruitful whai hua, makuru
frustrate taupare atu
fry parai
frying pan parai, raupane
fuel konga, waro, hinu, kai mō te ahi, kora
fulfil tutuki, whakatutuki(-tia), whakatau
fulfilled rite, ea
full kī, renga, puhapuha, kīpuha
full moon rākaunui, tōhua
full of holes putaputa, koroputaputa
full stop irakati, pītū, kopi
fullback whurupēke, pou muri, hiku
fumble hūrapa

fume (feel mad) whakatakariri
fumes au paitini, haupiro
fun hākinakina, hari, koa
functional whai taka
fund (money) tahua moni, pūtea moni
fundraising mahi moni
fundamental pū o te taketake, te orokohanga mai
funeral nehunga
funeral director kaiwhakarite uhunga
fungus harore, tūtae kēhua, anuhe
funnel kōrere, tīmere
funny hangarau, whakakatakata
fur huruhuru
furious tino riri, wairangi
furnace oumu rino
furniture taonga ā whare
furrow ripa, awaawa
further kōatu, tua atu
fury riri, pōrangi
fuse wiki
fuse together hono(-a)
fussy mārehe(-rehe)
futile koretake, maumau
future a muri ake nei, wā e heke mai nei
fuzz kerehunga, pūtete

G

gable of house maihi
gadget taputapu
gain whiwhi, painga, whakawhiwhi, hua
gala rā hākari nui, rā taurima, rā hokohoko
gale āwhā, tūpuhi
gall bladder kouawai, au
gallon kārani
gallop tūpeke, hārapa, toioma
gamble petipeti, purei moni, tūpono
gambler kaipeti
game tākaro, rēhia, purei, whakangahau
game (of set) kaupeka, kaikape
gang rōpū kaioraora, kēnga
gangrene kikohunga
gangway araheke
gaol (jail) whare herehere
gap āputa, wāhiruatanga, kōhao, mokoā
gape matata(-tia), kowhera
garage whare motokā, karāti
garden māra, mahinga kai, kāri
garland tīpare
gargle whakararā
garlic kāriki, kanekane
garlic crusher whakapē kāriki
garment kākahu, pūeru, weru
garnish whakapaipai, whakarei, kīnaki, whakarākai
garotte nanati te kakī
garrison puni hōia
garter kume tōkena, kāta
gas hau, korohū, kāhi, kēhi
gas cooker toā kapuni, umu kapuni
gas cylinder puoto haumāori, puoto kapuni
gash āhiwahiwa, ripi(-a), haratua
gasp for breath kūpā, kiha, tāre, pupuha, ngāngā
gate kuhunga, kēti, ngutu pā, putanga
gatecrash whakaete, pokonoa te uru
gatepost pou kēti
gateway kū(w)aha, tomokanga, waharoa
gather (collect) kohi(-a), whakakao(-tia), whakaemi(-hia), taiope(-tia)
gather (convene) whakamine, mene, mine, huihui
gauge ine, ōrite (penehīni), mēhua
gay (happy) hari, koa, manahau, manamanahau
gay (homosexual) tāne mate tāne, takatāpui
gaze titiro matatau, mōtoi, mātakitaki
gear (mechanical) panoni, niho, kia, nihowhiti
gear (kit) tueke
gear lever tokonuku
gearbox pouaka nohiwhiti, waka niho, pouaka kia
gelignite whakapohū, kāpohū, piapahū

gender iratāne, irawahine, huanga, ira tangata
genealogy whakapapa, kāwai, tātai
general (army) tianara
general election poti kāwanatanga, poti whānui
general knowledge mātauranga whānui
general public hunga tūmatanui
generate whakatō(-ngia), puāwai, hanga, waihanga
generate electricity huri hiko, pukuhiko
generation whakatupuranga, ahunga, whakapaparanga, reanga
generous atawhai, rangatira, marae, marere, wahawaha, pūkoro takere
genitals raho, tawhito
genius tohunga mīharo, tipua
genocide kōhuru iwi, whakangaro iwi
gentile tauiwi
gentle atawhai, mārire, humārika, mārū
gently (before verb) āta
genuine houtapu, tino tika, tupu, motuhenga, matatika
geography mātauranga papa whenua, mātai mata whenua
germ ngarara moroiti, iroriki, mero mate
German Tiamana
gesture tohu, rotarota, tāwhiri, korikori ringa
get (obtain) whiwhi ki, riro i + *subject*, tae
get off (climb down) heke mai/iho
get out of the way! pōuri ake, puta atu
get the feeling puta mai te rongo
get up ara
geyser puia, waiariki
ghost kēhua, kīhau, pakepakehā, ngū, kekokeko
giant tangata roroa, maero nui rawa, tipua, kaitā
giant petrel omakura, pāngurunguru
giant strides (swing) moari, mōrere
gibberish hīwawā, kohe, reo kihi
gib-board kahupapa
giddy āmai, āmiomio, ānini, takarangi
gift koha, mea homai noa, hākari
gifted (talented) pūmanawa ki
gigantic hautupua, tuangea, nui whakaharahara
giggle tīhohe, pākirikiri, kata(-ina), hohe
gills pihapiha, piha, parepare, hawa
gin tīni
giraffe hirāwhe, tīrapa
girdle whītiki
girl kōtiro, hine, kōhine
girl! e kō!, e hine!
give away whiu(-a), hoatu
give back whakahoki
give in (yield) hinga
give out (distribute) horahora, whakarato
give up tuku(-a), whakamutu
give way tautuku, tukukoa, whakangāwari
give/n hōmai, hōatu
giver ringa māhorahora, kaihoatu

glacier awa kōpaka, awakeo, huka pō
gladden whakaharihari
gladness hari, tūranga hākoa
glamour ātaahua, waiwaiā
glance māwhiti, titiro kōhura
gland repe
glare (scowl) whetē
glare of fire kōnakonako
glass karaehe, karāhe, kōata
glasses (specs) karu mōwhiti
glassy mōhinuhinu
glaucoma papahewa
glaze whakapīata, mōhinuhinu, kiri mohinu
gleam kanapa, uira, pīata, kōhara, hahae
glib māngai maeneene, ngāwari
glide tauhōkai, tipi, reti
glider waka rerehau
glimmer kōpura, whēriko, kātoretore
glint hikohiko, kōhā
glisten iraira, kapukapu, kawata, whakaira
globe ao kōpio, ao māhere
gloomy pōuriuri, matapōuri, hākerekere
glorify whakakorōria
glory korōria, hākinakina
gloss piatatanga
glossy mōhinuhinu, whakahinuhinu
glove karapu, kahu ringa, komo ringa
glow-worm pūrātoke, titiwai
glucose waitī
glue kāpia, waipia, tāpia, wai whakapiri
glut apu(-hia), tūwhena
glutton kaihoro, pukunui
gnash tetēā, whakatetēā, pakiri, tautau
gnat waeroa
gnaw ngau(-a), kakati
go haere(-atu), makara, hanatu, whano
go! e oma!, haere, pōuri ake
go after whai(-a), aru(-mia)
go around āwhio, umiki, huri haere, takataka
go aside peka
go away hanatu, haere atu, riro, hanake
go back hoki whakamuri
go by hipa, taha haere
go down (sun) tō te rā
go on! hoatu!, whoatu!
go on one side whakataha
go out (light) poko, weto, pirau
go out (tide) timu
go over (examine) hihira(-tia), āta titiro, whakawhiti
go to and fro kōpikopiko
go with haere tahi
go wrong tupono hē
go-between takawaenga
go-slow whakapōturi
goal (ambition) whāinga, kōrā, ū, tohenga
goal line pae ū, rārangi tae, rārangi whai, pae paneke
goat, billy - koati toa
goat, nanny - koati uwha, nanekoti, nanenane
god Atua, Io-Te-Matuakore, Io Matua, Runga Rawa
goddess mareikura
godparent matua wairua
godwit kūaka
goitre tenga
gold kōura

goldfish morihana
goldmine rua kōura
gold miner kaikari kōura
goldsmith kaimahi kōura
golf korōwha, hau paoro
golf club patu haupaoro
gone (left) riro, ngaro
gone (used up) pau
gone by hori, hapa
gone for good oti atu
gong pahū, parāihe turituri, pakū
gonorrhoea mate paipai
good pai (*pl.* papai), tika
good for nothing koretake noa iho
Good Friday Paraire Tapu
good humour ngahau, hūmārika
good job! e koe!, kaitoa!
goodbye (to one going) haere rā
goodbye (to one staying) hei konei rā, e noho rā
goodness te pai, painga, whakapainga
goods rawa, hanga, taonga
goods-train tereina utanga
goose kuihi
gooseberry kuihipere
gospel rongo pai
gossip pakiwaitara, paki, whawhe
gouge out tāwhārua(-tia)
gourd hue, tahā
gout koute, porohau, puhipuhi
govern whakahaere tikanga
governing rangatiratanga
government kāwanatanga
governor kāwana
governor general kāwana tianara
grab kōrapurapu, mau, mamau, rutu(-a)
grace (theological) keratia, atawhai a Ihowa
grace ātaahua, aroha noa
graceful ātaahua, tau, huatau
gracious ngākau aroha
grade (*n.*) āhuatanga, koeke, tohu taumata
grade (*v.*) tārati (tāria)
gradient pikinga, rōnaki
gradual āta
graduate (*n.*) tauira, tāura, paetahi
graduate (*v.*) puta hei
graduation whiwhi tohu mātauranga
graffiti tuhituhi anuanu
grain pata kānga
gram karama, koma
grammar wetereo, papa wetereo, tūturutanga reo
granary whata wīti
grand whakahirahira
grandchild mokopuna
grandfather tipuna tāne, tupuna (*pl.* tūpuna), karani pāpā
grandmother tipuna wahine, tupuna (*pl.* tūpuna), karani māmā
grandstand nohoanga matai, nohoanga nui, karapitipiti
granite kawikawi
grant (*n.*) toha moni, takuhe, takoha, koha
grant (*v.*) tuku(-a), whakaae(-tia)
grant permission tuku mana
grants (money) whakawhiwhinga pūtea
grape karēpe, aka waina
grapefruit kerēpi-whurutu, hua hīmoemoe
grapevine aka waina
graph kauwhata, inetohu, tōpū hōtuku, huahuatanga
grasp tango(-hia), rarau, mamau

G

grasping hold huirapa
grass karaihe, otaota, mauti, tarutaru
grasshopper kōwhitiwhiti, māwhitiwhiti, koeke
grasslands tahora
grassroots nō te iwi tonu
grate (*n.*) rī
grate (*v.*) pakepakē, pākēkē(-tia), waru(-hia), kauoro, harakuku
grateful whakawhetai, whakamoemiti, hari te ngākau
grater kūoro, waru
grating tītara
gratuitous homai noa, hoatu noa, mahanoa
gratuity takuhe
grave (burial) poka, rua
grave (solemn) hōhonu, taumaha
gravel kirikiri
gravity toā-ā-papa, akinga tō, kukume o te ao, kume-ā-Papa
gravy wairenga, wairanu, whāranu
graze (eat) kai karaihe
graze (touch) miri(-a), hohoni, tahitahi, pāhore
grease (*n.*) hinuhinu
grease (*v.*) whakahinuhinu
greaseproof pepa ārai hinu, pepa mau hinu
great nui (*pl.* nunui), rahi, kaitā, hira
greatly tino
greed apo, touapo, matekai
green colour kākāriki, kirīni, karera, kāriki
green vegetables korare
green, bowling - papa maita
greenfly weo
greengrocer kaihoko huawhenua
greens hua whenua, korare
greenstone pounamu, kawakawa, inanga
Greenwich Mean Time (GMT) pae tāima o te ao
greet mihi(-a), kupu oha, aumihi
grenade pohū ringa
grey hina, kiwi, pūmā, pūhina, pūmangu, mōhinahina
grey warbler riroriro, koriroriro, pītongatonga, korire
grid mātiti, tukutuku, rī
grief stricken pāmamae, pūkatokato
grievance pōrahurahu, aureretanga, pōuritanga
grieve mamae te ngākau, māpura, pōuri, kōingo
grill (*v.*) tahu(-na), tunutunu, ngunu
grim whakawiri, muha, mōkinokino
grimace pūkana, whāitaita, menemene kino, weru, whakapī
grime paru, para, pakānoni
grin menemene pai, pakiri
grind kauoro(-hia), huri (-hia), kūoro, kōmiri(-a)
grindstone hōanga
grip pupuri (puritia), kākati(-a), rou, puringa
gristle pakaua, uaua kiko
grit (in eye) pura
grit one's teeth kākati
gritty kirikiri, māngēngenge, māngūngungu
groan auē, aurere, ngunguru puku
grocer kaihoko huawhenua
grog rama
groggy rorirori

groin tapatapa, tapa o te kūhā
groom animal taitai (hōiho), paraehe
groom tāne mārena
groomsman hoa takatāpui, tama tautoko
groove awaawa, haehae
grooved kōawaawa
groper hāpuka, whāpuku
gross (total) rauemi katoa, peke
ground (land) whenua
ground rules kaupapa
groundbait tāruru
grounding waiwai, whakaakoranga
groundless koretake, papakore, kaupapakore
groundsheet whāriki inarapa, tāporena, papahīti, tīanga
groundwork (preparation) whakatake, whakariterite, mahi tumu
group whakahuihui, rōpū
grovel koropiko
grow kunenga, whakatupu, rea, tipu, ohi
growl ngengere, ngunguru
growth tupu, tipu, kunenga, turuki
grub (insect) huhu, kutukutu, mokoroa, tunga rākau
grubby paruparu
grudge amuamu, kaiponu
grumble amuamu, hakuhaku
grumpy takarure, pukuriri, kutukutuahi
grunt nguru, ngohia
guarantee (ensure) whakaū
guard (sentry) kaitiaki, tūtei
guard (sport) kaiārai
guard (*v.*) tiaki(-na), rauhī
guarded matatū, tūpato
guardian kaitiaki, matapopore
guess hua, ohianoa, raparapa(-ina)
guest manuhiri, tūwaewae
guide (*n.*) kaiārahi, tauira
guide (*v.*) ārahi(-na), hautū
guided missile rākate ārahi
guideline kaupapa arataki, ara tohu
guillotine poro māhunga, pororere
guilt hara, hē, kino, whai hara
guilty mau tūturu, mau tangetange
guitar kitā, kutā
gulf whanga nui
gull (godwit) kuaka, kūaka
gullet korokoro
gulp food whaupa, horopukutanga
gum (glue) pia whakapiri
gumboot kamupūtu
gumption mōhio
gums (mouth) pūniho, tako, ngangore
gun pū
gun powder paura
gunwale niao, rauawa
gurgle kokō, tatangi
gurnard kumukumu, kumikumi
gush hīrere
guts whēkau
gutter awakeri, rere tuanui, kōrere
gym mats whāriki takahuri
gymnasium whare takahuri, whare taka porepore
gymnast kaipītaka
gynaecology mātauranga kōpū wahine

H

habit āhuatanga, ritenga, tikanga, waranga
habitable pai hei nohoanga
hack hahau(-a), ripi(-a), poroporo(-a)
hacksaw kani maitai, kanini, kani haehae
haemorrhage ikura, tahe toto
haemorrhoid tero puta
hagfish tuere
haggle tautohe(-a) te utu
hailstones ua nganga, ua whatu, waitara
hair huruhuru(nga), makawe(nga)
hairy pāhuruhuru
half hāwhe
half-caste hāwhe-kaihe
half-moon ōhua
half-past hāwhe pāhi, hāpāhi
half time wā haurua
half-witted kūare, pōauau
half, centre - (soccer) kaunuku
halfback poutoko, hāwhe, takuahi
halftime hauruatanga, wā haurua, whakamatuatanga
halfway waenganui, wehenga ruatanga
halfway line paewehe
hall urumanga, hōro, whare nui
hallucination moemoeā
hallucinatory whakarangirua
halt tū, whakatū
halve hāwhe, tapahi(-a), whakahaurua
ham poaka totea, poaka tauraki
hamburger hamipēka, pākī
hammer hama(-ia), pao(-a), kuru, pākuru
hamper (hinder) ārai, whakawarea, whakakōroiroi
hamper (basket) tokanga nui
hand ringa(ringa)
hand down tuku iho
hand to mouth pōhara, korekore noa
hand-pick āta whiriwhiri(-a), taupuhi(-tia)
handbag pāhi, kete, pēke-ā-ringa
handcuffs rinoringa, mekameka, ringamau
handful kapunga, kamunga, kutanga
handicap hape, whakararu
handicap (golf) tohurehe
handicrafts mahi-ā-ringa
handkerchief aikiha
handle (*n.*) kakau, puritanga
handle (*v.*) whāwhā(-tia), popoi(-a)
handle (manage) whakahaere, tae(-a)
handover tuku
handover (league) tukupoi
handrail kahokaho, puringa ringa, rōau
handshake rūrū, harirū, ringaringa
handsome ātaahua, pūrotu, ranginamu
handspring tūpana

handstand porotēteke
handwriting tuhituhi, tuhi-ā-ringa, tuhiringa
handy ngāwari, māmā, pātata, whai painga
hang (dangle) iri, tare, tārewa
hang by neck tārona(-tia), tārore(-tia)
hang gliding rereangi
hang in clusters tautau, rāpoi
hang on (grasp) kia mau, pupuri, tīrou
hang (wait) taihoa, āta whakarongo
hang out tāmuimui, nohanga
hang up (suspend) whakairi, whakanoi(-a)
hanger, coat - irikaka, tare kākahu
haphazard whakaaro kore, pōrahurahu, kotiti, kōpeka
happen riro, puta, tūpono
happiness hari, koa
happy hari, koa, tūpai, hākoakoa
harangue whakahau, āki(-na)
harass whakatīwheta, inati
harass, sexually - whakatīwheta hemahema
harbour wahapū, whanga
harbour development whakatina wahapū
hard (difficult) uaua
hard (firm) pakeke, mārō, pakiri, ūtonga
hard copy tānga
hard core porno pūremu whakarihariha
hard covering anga, ūtonga
hard disc kōpae matua, kōpae mārō
hard drug rehunanu
hard headed ūpoko mārō, pōturi, taringa pākura
hard hearted taringa turi, whakahoe(-a), ngākau pakeke, ngākau whakawiri
hard nosed atawhai kore
hard up pōhara
hard wearing pūioio
hard-case (funny) hāte-kēhi
hard-pressed pēhia, pōraruraru
hard-working pukumahi, mamahi, ahuwhenua
hardback (book) anga mārō
hardboard papa mārō
hardly whakauaua
hardness mārō
hardship mamae, uauatanga, whakawiritanga
hardware (computer) kōpae rorohiko, taputapu rorohiko
hardy pakari, mārohirohi, ūtonga
hare hea
harelip ngutu riwha
harem whare wahine maha
hark back maumahara
harlot kairau
harm kino, whara, whakamamae
harmful whakakino, takakino
harmless waimarie, hūmārie
harmonica pūtangitangi
harmonious tangi reka, whakaaro tahi
harmony noho rangimārie, ōrua
harness hānihi, whītiki
harp hāpa, haapa
harping on kutukutu ahi
harpoon haeana rāti
harrier hawk kāhu
harrow karawhaea, rakaraka
harrowing rakuraku
harrowing (worry) āwangawanga

H

harsh kawa, matangerengere, matanui, kaitara
harvest-time ngahuru, hauhakenga
harvest, to - hauhake, kotinga
hassle pōraruraru, whakatīwheta
hasten tuoma, hohoro, rere
hat pōtae
hat-stand iringa pōtae, whata pōtae
hatch pao, puta
hatchet pātītī, toki, piharoa, pānekeneke
hate mauāhara, whakakino
haul tō(-ia), kume(-a), huhuti (hūtia)
haunt kuku(-a), poke(-a)
haunted kukua
have kei a (*see Brief Grammar*)
have a say whai wāhi
have not kāhore + *possessive*, kāhore ōku mea
have time whai wā, whai tāima
hawk kāhu, kārewarewa
hay hei
haystack tākehei
haze kohu, rehu, whēkite, kōkōuri
hazy kōrehurehu, māhinahina
he ia
head mātenga, upoko, toihau, māhunga, rito (poetic)
head a ball pā upoko, tuki(-a) paoro
head (of fish) pero
head (of grain) puku
head (of river) hikuawa
head off haukoti(-a)
headache ānini, ngāruru, mōngurunguru
headband tīpare
headboard papa peru, papa hamo
headdress tīpare, tia, kōtaha, tikitiki
headfirst dive rere tūpou
heading upoko, whakaupoko, panekōrero
headland matarae, rae, kūrae, more
headlight rāitimua, rama mua
headline upoko, taitara
headlong tūpou
headmaster tumuaki
headmistress tumuaki
headphones taringa kawe rongo
headquarters marae, whare matua, tari takuahi
headstone kōhatu whakamaharatanga
headwind hau tūmū, hau pāuma
heal whakaora(-ngia), whakamahu(-ngia)
healed ora
healer kaiwhakaora
health hauora, oranga, waiora
health (best of) ora matomato
health clinic whare paia
health facility ratonga hauora
health protection ārai māuiui
healthy toiora, pakari, hauora
heap (pile) pū, pūkai, tahua, taupū, pūkei
heap up ahuahu(-ngia), pūkai, pūranga
heap, lie in a - putu, pū, tāwheta, ahu, kauika
hear rongo(-hia), whakarongo
hear hear! koia ra!
heard pā te reo, hau, rangona
hearing (enquiry) whakauiuinga, whakawā
hearing (sense) rongonga, rongo
hearse waka tūpāpaku

heart ngākau, manawa, whatumanawa, uho
heart attack manawatū, mate manawa, manawahē
heart murmur kōkihi manawa, manawa wawaro
heartbeat mokowhiti, pātuki, kapakapa manawa
heartburn rei, pohongawhā, tokopā
heartland tuawhenua
heartless ngākau pakeke
hearts (cards) hāte
heartwood kāpara, kōhiwi, taikākā
heat mahana, wera
heat (race) whiringa
heater whakamahana, okeoke
heathen tauiwi, mohoao
heatwave hīrangi, pakapaka
heaven rangi
heavy taimaha, taumaha
heavy duty pakari, kaha
hebe (shrub) koromiko, kōkōmuka
Hebrew Hiperu
heckle taunu(-tia)
hectare hekitā
hectic pōrangi, pōhauhau haere, manahau
hedge hēti, maruhau, pātūtū, pāhuki
hedgehog tuatete, hetiheti
heel rekereke
heel over tītaha
hefty pakari, pūioio, kōpaka
heifer kūao kau, hewha
height ikeike, roa, hauroa, tōroa, tiketike, teitei
heinous whakawiriwiri
heirloom manatunga, kura
helicopter herikopeta, pōwaiwai, reretopa
hell (ancient) rarohenga, pō
hell (modern) iweri
hello (good wish) kia ora
helmet pōtae mārō, pōtae tuapaka
help āwhina(-tia)
helpless pārera maunu, paraheahea, ngoikore
hem remu
hemmed in pākakatia, karapotia
hemp kōaka
hen heihei, tīkaokao
hence nō reira
henceforth a muri ake nei
hepatitis mate kōwhai, mate ate kakā
her (*possessive*) tōna (*pl.* ōna), tāna (*pl.* āna)
her(-self) ia
herald kaipānui, karere
herb rau kakara, amiami
herbivore kaitipu, kaitarutaru, kaiota
herd (mob) kāhui, māpu
herd (muster) atiati(-a), ā(-ia), tāwhiu(-a)
here konei, kei konei
hereditary tuku iho, he momo
heritage taha tuku iho, taonga tuku iho
hernia whaturama
hero toa, māia, tuatangata
heroin rehunanu, taimiri
heroine wahine toa
heron, blue - kākatai, matuku moana
heron, white - kōtuku
herring aua, kātaha
hers nāna, nōna, āna, ōna

herself ia tonu, nāna tonu, nāna ake
hesitate tawhitawhi
hibernate aumoe hōtoke
hiccough tokomauri, tokopuhake
hidden ngaro, hunahuna
hide (conceal) huna, kuhu, hīpoki, whakangaro
hide oneself whakapeke, piri, peke
hideous whakarihariha, hautupua, weriweri
hiding place piringa, hunanga, whakapupuni, wāhi whakapeke
high teitei, tiketike, ikeike, roa
high commissioner māngai kāwanatanga
High Court Kōti Matua
high blood pressure taikaha o te ia toto
high rank tūranga teitei
high school haikura, kura tuarua
high tide pari, tumu
highway huanui, huarahi
hike haere mā raro, hīkoi, waeraka
hill puke, rangaranga
hilltop taumata, tuatara, kehokeho
hillside kaokao o te maunga, tahamaunga, harapaki
hilly pukepuke
him ia
hind (deer) tia uwha
hind quarters takamuri, papa
hinder ārai(-a), tinaku, whakakōiroiro
hinge kaurori, īnihi, whatīanga, kokopi
hip hope, humu, himu, pōrori
hip-bone papa toiake, humu, hope
hippopotamus hipohipo
hire rīhi, utu mō te wā, tango mō te wā
his tāna, tōna, āna, ōna, tana, nōna, nāna
hiss hū, huhū, hihī
historic onamata, o ngā tau ki muri
history mahi a ngā tūpuna, hītori
hit patu(-a), hau(-a), moto(-a), kuru(-a)
hit song waiata rorotu, waiata pao
hit, be - pā, whara
hitch huti(-a), tākiri
hitch-hike pati ekenga, haere pakituri
hoard pūtea, whakaputu
hoarse whango
hoax māminga, tinihanga
hobble (fetter) waehauā, herenga waewae
hobble (limp) totitoti
hockey hōki, haupoi, hake
hoe (*n.*) tipitipi, karaone, hetiheti, timaroa
hoe (*v.*) kari whenua
hogget punua hipi, hōkete
hoist huti(-a) ake
hold pupuri (puritia)
hold back pupuri (puritia), whakatōmuri
hold down pupuri iho, pēhi(-a) ki raro
hold of ship riu
hold out tohe roa
hold still āta noho
holder (container) pouaka
hole poka, rua, kōwhao, puare
holes (full of) putaputa
holiday hararei, wā kore mahi

holistic medicine rongoā whānui
hollow gourd piako, puango
hollow in ground whārua, pokorua, pokoruarua
holy tapu
home (base) papa kāinga
homecoming hokinga mai
home, feel at - āhuru, ngaio
home kāinga, toi whenua
homebrew paikaka, tou korere
homeland kāinga tupu
homeless kāinga kore, manene pōhara
homosexual man tāne moe tāne, tāne takāpui
homosexual woman wahine moe wahine, wahine takāpui
honest tika
honesty mahi tika, mahi pono
honey honi, miere
honeycomb honikoma, aremiere, pīhangaiti
honeymoon hanimunu, wā rekanga kanohi
honeysuckle rewarewa
honour (*n.*) hōnore
honourable tino tika
hood pōtae monaki, uhi mātenga
hoof maikuku hōiho, pāua
hook kape(-a), weku(-a), matau, pīhuka, hūka
hook and eye pikopewa
hooker (rugby) waekape, kaikape
hooligan korokē pōrangi
hoop whiti, mōwhiti, pīrori, tāwhiti
hoot of owl koukou, peho, tangi
hop hītoko, hītoki, hīteki
hope tūmanako(-tia), āwhero, manawa ora
hopeful awhero, hiahia
hopeless koretake, hauwarea
hops hāpī
horizon pae, mātāhauariki, taharangi, tahatū, huapae
horizontal pae, whakapae
hormone wai ira, pūora repe, taiaki
horn (cattle) maire, pīhi, haona
horn (musical) pū, pūtara, pūtoto, pūtangi
horrible mōrikarika, weriweri, whakamataku
horrify poutuki, whakamataku
horror whakawehi, whakamataku, tūwiri
hors d'oeuvre fork mārau iti
horse hōiho
horse racing purei hōiho, whakaomaoma hōiho
horticulturalist ihu oneone
hose pāipa, ngongo wai
hose down mapu(-a)
hospital hōhipera, hōhipere
hospitality manaaki, taurima
host tangata whenua, kaimanaaki
hostage mauhere hei taumau
hostel kāinga taiohi, kāinga taupua
hostile kairiri, pukuriri, whakaara
hostilities pakanga, whawhai
hot wera, pāwera
hot spring waiariki, ngāwhā
hot tempered kiriweti
hotel hōtēra, pāparakauta
hour hāora
hourglass tārihāora
hourly ā hāora
house whare
house (lodge) (*v.*) whakanoho(-ia)
house trained rata ki te noho whare

H

household whānau, whāmere
housemaid hāwini
hovel wharau, hēti
hover whakatopa, whakaparo, ārohirohi, topaki
hovercraft waka mania hau, waka topaki
how? pēhea?, pēwhea?
how many? e hia?
how much? e hia?, he aha te utu?
however heoi, hoianō, kia ahatia
howl ngawē, auē, whakaparoro, whakapū
hub pokapū
hubcap taupoki wira
huddle torohū
hug awhi, kēkeke
huge nui whakaharahara
hum tāmanu, hāmumu(-tia), whewheo (wheotia), tāwara
human tā te tangata
human rights mana tangata
humane manaaki, ngākau atawhai
humankind uri tangata, ira tangata
humble māhaki, whakaiti, hūmārire, whakamōwai
humbug hamupaka
humdrum hōhā
humid takawai, pīpīwai
humidity haumākū, pīpīwai
humiliate whakaiti(-tia), whakamōraro
humility ngākau pāpaku, māhaki
humour wairua nēnene, whakakata, pukukata
hump hiwi
hunchback tuarā tuapuku
hundred rau
hundredweight hānarete, hanaweiti
hunger/hungry hiakai, hemokai, matekai
hunt whaiwhai(-a), kimi, rapu
hurdle taiapa, tāepa, taiepa
hurdler kaipeka taiapa
hurdles, 100 m - taiapa rau mita
hurricane tūpuhi, huripari, taupoki, hau āwhiowhio
hurry tere haere, auraki, whakahoro, wakewake
hurt, be - whara, tū, ngaua, pāmamae
hurtle parahutihuti
husband tāne, hoa tāne
hush! turituri!, hoihoi!, kāti!
husky voice whango
hustle ā(-ia), tute(-a)
hut wharau, wāhi whare, mahau
hydrant maero ngutu, tukuwai, kōmanawa, waipēhi
hydro-electric hurihiko
hydrocarbon pūwaro
hydrogen hauwai, waiwaro
hyena haiana
hygiene horoinga kia mā, tikanga akuaku
hymn hīmene
hyphen pīhono, tohuhono, tohu wehe
hypnosis rorotu, whakamoe(-a)
hypocrite ngutu kau
hypothesis whakaaringa whakaaro, whakapae
hypothesise whakapae
hysterical wairangi, keka

I

I ahau, au, awau
ice haupapa, hukapapa, tio
ice cream aihikirīmi
ice skater kairere hukapapa
iceberg motuhuka
icicle tiotau, ngira hukapapa
icy haupapa, mātaratara, mākinakina
idea whakaaro, mōhio, titiro, kaupapa, ariā
ideal whakaaro rangatira, tauira pai
identical taurite
identify tohu(-ngia), whakaatu(-ria), whakamōhio
identity ingoa, tuakiri
idiom kupu taukī, kōrero taukī, kīrehu
idiomatic speech mita o te reo, kīwaha, rerenga kupu, pepeha
idiot pōrangi, kīkiki, pouāwai, ākonga tā
idol whakapakoko, pakoko
idolize whakahōnore, whakamihi, ngākaunui
if me, mehemea, ki te (mea), ā pā anō
if not ki te kore
if only mehemea noa
ignite whakakā
ignition pātīmata, tungi
ignorant kūware, kūare
ignore waiho ki te taha, whakaiti(-tia), whakanoa(-tia)
ill pāngia e te mate, mate ana, tūroro, māuiui
ill health matemate, hangamate
ill-treat tūkino(-tia), whakawiri(-tia)
illegal pokanoa, kore ture, kore mana, hē-ā-ture
illegality kore mana
illegitimate pōriro, meamea
illiterate kūare ki te tuhi me te pānui
illogical pōrewarewa, huakore
illumination whakamāramatanga
illusion moemoeā, hewahewa
illustrate whakaatu(-ria), tohutohu, whakaahua
illustrator kaiwhakaahua, kaitā
image āhua, pakoko
imaginary mea whakakitea mai, pohewa
imagine whakaaro noa, matakite
imagine, wrongly - pōhēhē
imitate whai(-a), whakatau(-ria), tāwhai, pakoira
imitation whakatauanga
immediate i nāianei tonu, tere tonu, mea kau
immense nui whakaharahara, whakatikotiko
immigrant manene ki tēnei whenua
immigrate heke mai ki tēnei whenua
imminent tata tonu mai, āianei puta

immobile ekore e taea te korikori, tū tonu
immoral karihika, kino, paru, makihuhunu
immortal ekore e mate, ora tonu ake ake, mutunga kore
immune rauhītia, whakamarumaru
immunise whakatō kano, ārai mate
immunity wātea i te mate, ārainga i te mate
impact pā, tukinga, papātanga, panga
impatient pōnānā, pukuriri, tākare, kiriweti
impatiently pōtatutatu
impede haukoti(-a), ārai(-a), taupare
impediment kati, aukati, tauārai
impediment, speech - hauātanga kōrero
imperfect pokapoka, riwha, takarepa
impertinent haututū, toroihi, āhuaatua
impervious pītongatonga
impetuous kaikā, āritarita, manawarere, kowheta
impetus pana, tute
implement (tool) taputapu mahi
implement (*v.*) whakatutuki(-tia)
implement policy whakatinana kaupapa
implementation tukitanga, whakaū, whakakaupapa
implicate hīrau(-tia), whakatuaki
implicit kei roto tonu, piri tahi
imply whakaatu(-ria), tohu(-ngia), whakapae
import hoko mai i tāwāhi, whakauru mai
importance mana, mananui, hiranga, huapai
important whai tikanga, hōhonu, hira
impose whakahau(-a), pou(-a), uta(-ina)
impossible ekore e taea
impotent tūpaku, kōpīpī
impracticable uaua te whakaoti
impregnable whakawhenua, tū tonu, ekore e horo
impregnate whakatō(-kia)
impress on whakamōhio mai
impression āhuatanga
impressive hōhonu, whakamīharo
imprison mauhere(-tia), whakarau(-tia)
imprisonment whakaraunga, noho herehere
improbable rangirua, whakamāpuna, kārangirangi
improve (*v. intr*) pai haere, pūāwai, piki
improve (*v. tr.*) whakapai atu, whakaohooho(-ngia) ake
improvise hangahanga
imprudent kūware
impudent tutū, whakatoi, whakatenetene
impulse pana, pirangi, rere
impulsive tūkaha, rere tōtōā
impure paru, para
impute whakatau, whakairi, whakapae
in kei roto i, i roto i, ki, rō
in, will be - hei, hai, hei roto
inability kahakore, ngoikore
inaccurate hē, kotiti
inactive noho hū, māngere

inarticulate tapepe, pakoki, nanu
inattentive muhukai, pohepohe, morimori
inaudible hīrea, hakiri
inbuilt whakaurua
incapable koretake, kahakore, ngoikore
incapacitate whakaruhi(-a), ngoikore
incarnate ā-tinana
incautious hīkaka, manawarere
incentive whakangahau, toitoi, manawarū
incest kaiwhiore, ngauwhiore, irawaru, raweke
inch inihi
incident takanga, tūponotanga, mea
incinerate tahu(-na) ki te ahi
incite ueue(-a)
inclination āronui
incline (*n.*) heketanga
incline (*v.*) tītaha
include tāpiri mai, take(-a) mai, āpiti mai/atu
inclusive tāpiti, urutomo, āpiti, peke katoa
income utu, hua, rauemi, moni whiwhi
incompetent kūare, koretake, hakorea
incomplete hukihuki, taurangi, tarepa
inconsiderate ngākau kaiapo, kaiponu, pakirara, pōrahu
inconsistent hārakiraki, kōtītiti, maiorooro
incontinent mate tōngāmimi, hīkaka
inconvenience whakapōrearea
incorporated manatōpū
incorporation kaporeihana
incorrect hē, kei te hē
incorrigible pakeke te ngākau
incorruptible ekore e pirau, tika tonu
increase neke atu, whakapiki, nui haere, pikinga ake
incredible tino mīharo, teka mārika
incur riro mai
incurable whakamate, manako kore
indecision āwangawanga, rangirua
indeed hoki, mārika, anō, koinā
indefinable rehua
indefinite noa
indefiniteness noatanga
indelible pūmau, mau tonu
independence mana motuhake
independent motuhake
indescribable ekore e taea te whakahua
indestructible mau tonu, kore rawa e ngaro, toitū, matatū
index (*n.*) whakaaturanga tere, rārangi ingoa
index (*v.*) tohu-ā-kupu
Indians, American - kiriwhero, tangata whenua o Amerika
indicate whakaatu(-ria), tohu, tautuhi
indication tohu whakamārama, āhuatanga
indicator whakaatu, kaitohu, rāiti tohu, tūtohu
indict whakapae, tāpae tuhinga
indifference whakaaro kore, whakahoe

I

indigenous toi tupu, taketake, nō te tangata whenua
indigestion tokopā, tokopaha, kunāwhea
indignant riri, whakatakariri
indignity whakaheke tupu, whakaiti
indirect tītaha, kōtiti
indiscipline mohowao, tāwēwē noa
indiscreet mākūware, manawarere
indisputable mārama, hua
indissoluble mau tonu
indistinct mōnehunehu, pūrehurehu, kurehe
individual takitahi
individuality tuakiri, tangata ake
indivisible wehekore
indoor roto whare
induce whakawai(-a), mōunu(-tia)
induction arataki
indulge whakawaireka, tuku(-na), popore
industry (manufacture) ahumai, mahi
ineffective kore hua, hauwarea, koretake
inefficient hauwarea
ineligible ekore e tau, kore e āhei
inequality ritekore
inert mate, whakaroau, nohopuku
inertia tūpuku, ukauka, ngoikore
inevitable kore e taea te karo, heipū tonu
inexact noa
inexhaustible kaha tonu
inexperienced ihupuku, kūare
infancy kōhungatanga, tamarikitanga
infant kōhungahunga, pēpi, pēpe
infantry hōia hīkoi
infatuation whakawairangi, kanehe
infect ngau(-a), whakapoke
infected pāngia, whakapokea
infection mate
inferior iti iho te wāriu, iti iho te uara, i raro i
infernal nō te iweri, nō rarohenga
inferno pūkūkā, iweri, kāpura
infertile (human) rautahi, pukupā
infertile (land) pākihi
infertility pākoko
infest mui(-a), poki(-a), ohu(-a)
infestation pokipoki
infinite mutunga kore
infinity paenga kore, mutunga kore
infirm tūroro, tōrutu
inflame whakakā(-ngia), whakaoho(-ngia)
inflamed toretore, kakā
inflammatory whakakakā
inflate puhapuha, pupuhi (puhia), whakamakoha
inflation hekenga o te wāriu, hekenga uara moni
inflict whakapā, whakawhiu(-a)
influence (affect) kawe mana, hāngai mai/atu, whakaako(-ngia)
influence (aura) mana, āhuatanga hei arataki, mana whakahaere
influence (bad) kukuti (kūtia)
influential whai mana
influenza rewharewha, whurū
influx mui(-a), whakamui, hounga, tomonga
inform whakaatu(-ria), mea atu, whakamōhio

informal noa, kōkau
informed mārama
informer kaituku, kaiwhāki
infrared pōkākā
infringe takahi
infuriate whakariri, whakanguha(-tia), whakaririhau
infusion tāpiri
ingenious pūmanawa, tene
ingratiating popore
ingratitude mihi kore, whakaaro kore
ingredients whāranu
ingredients, add - kīnaki(-hia), whakaranu(-a)
inhabitant tangata whenua, iwi kāinga, kainoho
inhale ngā, whakangā, whakataka manawa
inherent pūmau
inherit whiwhi(-a), whakatau(-a), tango mai
inheritance oha, manatunga, mea tuku iho
inhospitable kiripiro, whenua hāhā, manaaki kore
inhuman ngau kino, kāhore e tika mō te tangata
inimitable ekore e taea te whakarite, tōtahi
initial tuatahi, mātua
initiate tīmata(-ngia), take(-a)
initiation tīmatanga, tomo
initiative kōkiri, kakama, kaupapa
inject wero(-hia) ki te ngira
injunction aukati, whakahau, whakahōtaetae
injure takakino(-tia), tūkino(-tia)
injured whara, tū
injury aituā, whara, mate
injustice hara, takahi mana, tūkino
ink ingiki, waituhi
inland roto, uta, tuawhenua, whakaroto
inlet awa, whanga, kokoru
inlet stroke horohau
inn hōtēra
innate nō te whānautanga, mauhere
innocent harakore, kore mōhio
innovative wairua hihiko, wana, auaha
innumerable manomano, e hia mano, mano tini
inopportune kāhore e tika te wā, poka noa
inorganic mea hanga
input uru atu, kōkuhu, tautoko, tāuru
inquest uiui mō te tūpāpaku, uiui mate whawhati tata
inquire pātai(-ngia), ui(-a), pākiki
inquiry patapatai, tomo, uiuinga
inquisitive pakiki, mahira
insane pōrangi
insanitary āhua mate, poke
inscription whakairo, tuhinga
insect ngārara, pēpeke, mū
insecticide patu ngārara
insecure pāhekeheke, pānekeneke, tītengi
insecurity noho āwangawanga
insensitive ūpoko mārō, ngākau pakeke
inseparable tāpui, piri tonu
insert, to - whakauru(-a), puru(-a), kuhu(-ngia)
insertion whakatōnga, kuhunga
inshore ki uta
inside i/ki/kei/ko roto i, ki rō

I

insidious nanakia
insight matakite, mōhio
insignificant hauarea
insincere rūpahu, kōrero teka
insipid waimeha, mākihakiha
insist tohe(-a), uaua
insolent whakatoi, pīnanauhea
insomnia mate koheko, tūrama tonu
inspect mātakitaki, mātai, āta titiro
inspection āta tirotiro, mātaki
inspector kaitirotiro
inspire whakaara, whakahiwa
instability pāhekeheke
install hanga, whakatika, whakanoho, tāuta
instance (example) tauira
instantaneous i taua wā tonu, i namata
instead tētahi atu, mahue kē, mea anō, whakakapi
instinct rongo, aro
instruct tohutohu, whakaako
instruction tohutohu, whakaakoranga
instructive whai tohu
instructor kaitohutohu, kaiwhakamātau, kaiwhakaako
insubordinate tutū, haututū, whakawhana
insufficient kōpaka, pahara, takarepa, hohore
insulate ārai
insulation ārainga
insulator ārai, kaupare
insult kanga, whakahāwea, whakatoi, muhani
insurance rīanga, inihua
insurrection whana, ātete, mahi tutū
intact paruhi katoa, mau tonu
intake tango mai
intake of food horomi kai
intake of people urunga mai
intangible memeha
integrate kōmitimiti, whakakotahi(-tia), whakauru(-a)
intellect hinengaro
intellectually handicapped hunga hauā hinengaro
intelligence mōhiotanga
intelligent mōhio
intense hōhonu, kakati
intensity kaha, nui, pakari
intensive tōtōpū, ngaio, uhupoho
intent on mau tonu ki, whakatau ki
intention whakaaro
intentional mauritau
intently whakatau, matatau, kakati
interaction whakawhitiwhiti, taunekeneke, whakaaro tahi
intercede īnoi(-a)
intercept haukoti(-a), kotipū, rohehape
interchange whakawhiti
intercom whōunu takawaenga, tuku kōrero
intercourse (sexual) onioni, ai(-tia), moe(-a), mahimahi
intercourse (social) tūtakitanga
interest (profit) hua moni, itarete
interest, to - aro(-ngia), hiahia(-tia), pīrangi(-tia)
interesting pai ki te whakarongo
interface hononga tahi, atanga
interfere hūrau, hārau, rahurahu
interior roto, tō roto
interior (of land) ki uta, tuawhenua

intermarry moe tauiwi, moe whakawhiti
intermediary takawaenga
intermission (lull) pārīrā
intermittent tāmutumutu, kōhikohiko
internal whakaroto, raroto, puku
international nō te ao nui, huri noa te ao, ā taiao
Interpol Rōpū Pirihimana o te Ao
interpret whakamāori(-tia), whakapākehā(-tia)
interpreter kaiwhakamāori, kaiwhakapākehā, etc.
interracial waenganui i ngā iwi, ā iwi
interrogate uiui(-a), patapatai(-hia)
interrupt haukoti, aruaru, inake
interruption pōrearea, whatinga, kaiwaenga, kokoti
interval takiwā, wā, ā puta
intervene hohou rongo, wawao, whakatau
interview uiuinga
intestine whēkau, puku, kōpiro
intimidate whakamataku, whakahakahaka
into ki roto ki
intoxicant waipiro, rama
intoxicate whakahaurangi
intransigent pakeke, upoko mārō
intricate whakairoiro, pikopiko
intrigue whakangārahu
introduce person whakamōhio
introduce thing whakauru(-a), kuhu
introduction whakataki, whakamōhio, tīmatatanga
intrusion (social) whakararu-ā-noho, urutomo
intuition matakite, pūmanawa
invade whakaeke(-a), urutomo(-kia), uru(-a)
invader kaiwhakaeke, hoariri whakaeke
invalid (sick) tūroro, matengia ana, maki
invalid (worthless) koretake, muhu
invariable pūmau, tūturu
invasion urutomo, whakaekenga
invent (make up) tito(-a)
inventor kaihanga, kaitito, kaitene
inventory rārangi taonga
inverse kōaro, taupoki
invertebrate kirihe whaituara, hātaretare
investigate (inquire) kimi(-hia), āta titiro, āta uiui
investigate (search) hōpara, kimikimi (kimihia)
investigation hōparatanga
investigator kaitirotiro, kaihōpara, whakatewhatewha
investment pūtea penapena, moni pūtea, moni whakatakoto
investor kaiwhakarato moni
invigorate whakahohe, whakakaha
invincible ekore e whakaekea, tū tonu, ukauka
invisible kāhore nei e kitea, aringaro, huna
invitation reo karanga, pōwhiri, tono
invite tono(-a), pōwhiri(-tia)
invoice puka nama
involuntary kāhuki, oho, pōkerehū
involve whai pānga, whakauru
inward whakaroto

Irish Airihi
irk whakatakariri
irksome hōhā, hīrawerawe
iron (*n.*) haeana, rino, maitai
iron (*v.*) haeana(-tia)
irony kupu hākiki
irradiate whakapīata, patu ā-iraruke
irregular whakahipahipa, kūhikohiko, hikuwaru
irreligious whakapono kore
irreparable tūkino
irresolute āwangawanga
irresponsible wairangi, tōtōā
irreverent takahi mana, tōtōā
irrigate uwhiuwhi ki te wai, hāwaiwai
irritable pukuriri, kārangi
irritate ongaonga, mangeo, namunamu
is/are show by word position (*see Brief Grammar*)
island motu, moutere
isolate whakawehe(-a), mawehe
isolated wehea rawatia, taratahi
issue, to - whakaputa(-ina), tuku(-a)
it tērā, ia (repeat noun)
italic momotuhi tītaha
italics tītaha
Italy Itari
itch mangeo, rekareka, hakihaki, waihakihaki, ngāokooko
itinerant kaipaoe, kaipāwe, tipiwhenua
itinerary tikanga haere
its tōna, tāna, ōna, āna
ivory rei, ipori

J

jab wero(-hia), poka(-ina), pātuki
jack, lifting - hiki waka, tieki, whakarewa
jacket koti poto, tiakete, hākete
jackknife naihi piko
jackpot pūtaonga
jade pounamu, waipounamu
jagged taratara, mākini, koikoi
jail whare herehere
jam (food) tiamu, hāmu
jamb pou, whakawai, tuturu
James Hēmi
jammed tāmi
jandal hūrekereke
Japanese Hapanihi, Tiapani
jar (container) pounamu
jarring sound pāorooro, wheoro
javelin tao, tete
jaw kauae, kauwae
jawbone paewai
jealous haehae, harawene, pukā, kiriweti
jealousy pūhaehae, pūngaengae
jeans tarau tāngari
jeer tāwai, taunu, whakahīhī
jell ete, eke
jelly kai kori, purini, hēri, tiere, wai petipeti korikori, ware tatakī
jerk korowhiti, tuke, rutu, nape
jersey poraka, kānahi
jest hangareka, kārikarika, hangarau, whakanene
Jesus Christ Hēhu Karaiti, Īhu Karaiti
jet pūkaha-hū
jet of gas pūtororē
jet plane rererangi pūkaha-hū
jetlag ngenge rererangi
jetsam tītītai, punipuni, kōkīkī
jetty wāpu, tauranga poti
Jew Hūrai
jewel rei, kahurangi
jib (balk) whakahē
jiggle whakakorikori, whakaoreore, tīemiemi
jigsaw puzzle panga hono, tāpaepae
jilt whakarere(-a), paheke
jingle tatangi
jitters āmaimai, ihiihi
job (work) mahi
job description kaupapa-ā-mahi
jock strap tātua raho
jockey tiōki, kaieke hōiho
jog tuoma, toitoi
John Dory kuparu, pukeru, ika a Mohi
join (enter) uru ki roto, hui mai, hui atu, kuhu
join battle whakapiri(-a), harapaki
join material hiki, hono, haumi
join together apiti(-ria), hono(-a), whakauru(-a), tūhono (-a)
joiner kāmura
joinery taitapa
joint (articulated) pona, monamona, punga, momonga
joint (connection) hononga, taihonotanga

jointly ngātahi
joist kurupae
joke (jest) whakakata, tinihanga, kōrero kata, hīanga
jot tuhituhi, iota
journal rātaka, hautaka, tuhitaka
journalist kaituhi kōrero, kairīpoata
journey haerenga, rerenga
jowl kauwae raro
joy hari, koa, hākoakoa, oranga ngākau
joyful harikoa
jubilee tiuperi, hākari
judge (adjudicate) whiriwhiri(-a), whakawā(-kia)
judge (justice) tiati, kaiwhakawā
judge (selector) kaiwhiriwhiri
judgement whakawākanga
judicial nō te kōti, ā ture
judo hūto, ruturutu, nonoke
judoka kairutu
jug hāka, tiaka, ipu, takawai
juggle whiuwhiu
juice ranu, wai, wairaraua, tarawai
jumper (jersey) paraka, poraka
junction hononga, tūtaki
junction-box ūngutu, kōhaohao
jungle mātotorutanga ngahere, wao nui
jungle gym pikipiki, tīrewa
junior teina, taina
junk otaota
junk, Chinese - waka hainamana
junk food kai paraurehe
junket waiū korikori, miraka korikori, waiū pupuru
junkie kaiwarawara tarukino
jurisdiction mana whakahaere, mana ture
juror kaiwhakawā manaiti
jury hūri, tekau mā rua, rōpū whakawā, hunga whakawā
jury trial whakawā-ā-hūri
just (fair) tika, tōtika
just (only) noa, kātahi, heipū, oroko
just then inā tonu
justice mahi tika, mahi tōkeke, ōrite, haepapa
justifiable tōtika
justified tika
justify whakapai(-tia), whakatika, whakamana
justly i runga i te tika
jut out tauwhare, kou(-a)
jute fibre hipora
juvenile nō te rangatahi, taitamariki, pūhouhou
juxtapose tāpiri, āpiti

K

kangaroo kangaru
karate karāti
kauri gum kāpia
keel takere, tangere
keen (eager) kaikaha, matangareka, ngākaunui
keep tiaki(-na), pupuri (puritia), mau ki, penapena
keep close to whakapiri(-a), rūnā
keep in place whakamau, taumau, pupuri (puritia)
keeper kaitiaki
keg kāho
kelp rimurapa, pakake
kennel whare kurī
kerb pae-ara
kernel iho, whatu, kākano, karihi
kerosene karahīni
ketchup wairanu tōmato
kettle tīkera
key kī, uakī
key, tab - pātuhi ripa
keyboard, computer - papa pātuhi, papapātuhi
keyhole puare kī
kick whana(-a), kiki(-a)
kicker kaiwhana, waewhana
kickoff tīmata
kid (goat) punua koati, tamaiti
kidnap kāhaki(-na)
kidney tākihi, whatukuhu, whatikuhu, whatumanawa
kill patu(-a) kia mate, whakamate
killed hinga, mate
killer kaipatu
killing patunga
kiln umu perēki
kilo kiro, mano
kilogram kirokarama, komamano
kilometre kiromēta, manomita
kilt rāpaki, piupiu Kōtimana, panekoti Kōtimana
kind (helpful) atawhai, ngāwari, manaaki, ngākau aroha
kindergarten kura kōhungahunga, kura pūhou
kindle tahu(-na), hika(-ia), tou(-a), tūngi(-a)
kindling tungitungi, kōetoeto, whakakā
kindness atawhai, manaaki
king kīngi
kingdom rangatiratanga, kīngitanga
kingfish warehenga, haku
kingfisher kōtare
kink koromeke
kiss kihi(-a), ūngutu
kit kete
kitbag tueke
kitchen kīhini, kāuta
kite manu aute, pākau, manu aute
kitten punua ngeru, kuao pūihi
kiwifruit huakiwi
kleptomania mate ringarau, ringarau
knapsack tueke
knead pokepoke (pokea)
knee turi, pona

kneecap popoki
kneel tūturi, koropiko
knees bent turipēpeke
knickers maromaro
knife naihi, māripi, pokapoka, oka piha
knit (*v.*) tuitui wūru, whatu wūru, niti(-a)
knitting needle patui whatu
knob, door - puritanga, pātene, reke
knock pātōtō, pātukituki
knock over rutu(-a), pātuki(-a)
knot pona, kono, pūtiki, tapona, nota
knotty timber pūioio
know mōhio(-tia), mātau (-ria), matatau, kite (-a)
knowledge mātauranga, mōhiotanga, toi
knuckle pona, monamona
knucklebones kōruru, kaimakamaka, kohikohi, huripapa
Koran Korāna
koru sign pikopiko rarauhe
kūmara kūmara, kōreherehe, kura a Māui, kōrae
kūmara, dried - kao, kōmaemae

L

label pepa-ingoa, tapanga, tohu piri
laboratory taiwhanga pūtaiao
laborious uaua, papatoiake, hihiri
labour mahi-ā-ringa, hunga mahi
Labour Day Rā Whakatā o Reipa
lace (fabric) hikuhiku, rēhi, pawero
lacebark tree hoihere, wheuwhi, houhi
lack kore, mate, kōpaka, hapa
lactic nō te waiū
ladder arawhata, arahanga, arohata
ladle kōutuutu, koko
lady kahurangi, tapairu
ladybird mumutawa, ngoikura, kui
lag behind takamuri, tonanawe, akutō
lager beer pia kāho
lagging (wrapping) kōpaki paipa
lagoon whanga moana, hāpua, muriwai, pūroto
laid out (stretched) whārōrō, mārōrō, ngāhora
lake roto, moana
lamb reme
lame hauā, hapehape, ngongengonge, kopa
lament (*n.*) mōteatea, tukeke, apakura, auraki
lament (*v.*) tangi, uhunga, auē
laminate whakapaparanga
lamp rāiti, rama, rātana
lamprey piharau, puhikoro, korokoro
lampshade maru rāiti
lance tao, huata, rāti
lance corporal kāpara iti
land (*n.*) whenua, oneone, taiwhenua
land (*v.*) tatū, whakaū, tau, whakatau(-ria)
land agent kaituhi whenua, kaihoko whenua
Land Transport New Zealand Ikiiki Whenua Aotearoa
landing place tauranga, ūnga waka
landless whenua kore, iwi konene
landlord/lady kaireti whare
landowner kaipupuri whenua
landscape kāinga kanohi
landslip horo(-a), horowhenua
landwards ki uta, whakauta
lane (track) ara kuiti
language reo
language, sign - reo-ā-ringa, reo rotarota
lanky tokoroa, kawekawe
lantern rātana
lap (lick) miti, pakipaki
lap of track huringa
lap-dog mōkai kurī
lapel whētui
lapse kaewa, taka
lapse in karakia karakia tapepe
lard hinu poaka
larder pātaka

large nui, rahi, kaitā, whakahara, morahi
lark (bird) whāioio, pīhoihoi
larva uhu, huhu
laryngitis mate korokoro
larynx korokoro, pouaka reo
laser taiaho
laser beam hihi taiaho, haeata puaho, reihā
lash together whakamau, aukaha, ruruku(-tia)
lasso taura hopu kau, kono here hōiho, whāpiko
last (final) whakamutunga, mātāmuri, toenga
last night inapō, nōnapō
last resort tino hēmanawatanga
last week wiki ka taha ake nei, te wiki kua pahure
last year tērā tau
last, at - nāwai rā, kātahi anō
lasting mau tonu, ukiuki, taketake, ukauka
latch rawa, whakarawa, whakamau
late tūreiti, tōmuri, takaroa, takaware
late (deceased) kua mate
lately ināianei, inānoanei, ināia tata nei, i muri nei
latent e moe ana, torohū, āhua huna
later ā taihoa, ā muri ake nei
latex wai inarapa, tawau
lath (batten) kaho
latrine whare paku, heketua
latter tōmuri
laugh kata(-ina), katakata
launch (*v.*) whakarewa(-tia), whakamānu(-tia)
launching pad papa tuku
laundrette toa horoi kākahu
laundry basket pūtea, pūtē
lava rangitoto, tahe puia
lavatory whare paku, whare mimi
law ture
law-abiding tūtika
law, according to - e ai ki te ture
lawful tika, whaimana
lawless turekore
lawn pangakuti, whenua otaota
lawyer rōia, poutoko ture
laxative whakatiko, rongoā whakatiko
lay (place) whakatakoto(-ria), waiho(-ngia), tāpae(-tia)
lay down policy whakatakoto kaupapa
lay open wāwāhi (wāhia)
lay out tahora(-tia), whakatau(-a)
layer kaupapa, papanga, paparanga
layout (plan) hoahoa, whakatakotoranga
lazy māngere, rare
lead (*v.*) ārahi(-na), arataki (-na), taki(-na), ahu
lead (metal) matā, konumata
lead astray whakakotiti(-tia), whakapōhēhē(-tia), whakakonuka
leader kaiārahi, amokapua, kaihautū, amorangi
leaf (page) whārangi
leaf (plant) rau, whā
leaflet puka
leakage turuturu, urukōwhao, rere kōhao
leaky turuturu, wairere
lean (skinny) tūpuhi, tūwai

lean against wharara ki, whakawhirinaki
lean meat pūioio
lean-to wharau, manutahi
leap mahiti, tarapeke, tūpeke, whiti
learner ākonga
lease rīhi
least te iti rawa, tino iti
leather rera, kiri kararehe, kirikau
leathery kiriuka, pakaua
leave (depart) haere atu, wehe atu, riro, maunu(-hia)
leave behind waiho(-ngia), whakarere(-a)
leaven rēwena
lecture kauhau
lecturer pūkenga
ledge kārupe, whata
ledger pukapuka kaute
leek rīki, ririki, rikiroa
left behind mahue, toe, waiho
left handed ringa mauī, hemārehe
leftover toenga, para, toenga kai
leg waewae
legacy taonga tuku iho, ōhākī mō āpōpō
legal ā-ture, nō te ture, whai mana
legal decision whakatau whai mana
legal system tikanga ture
legalise tuku-ā-ture
legend kōrero pūrākau, pakiwaitara, pakiwaituhi
legible tuhituhi mārama
legislate hanga ture
legislation ture paremata, tirohanga i te ture
legislative i raro i te ture
legislator kaihanga ture
legitimate tika, tā te ture
legitimise whakamana(-ia)
leisure noho noa iho, hararei, wā whakatā
lemon rēmana
lemon sole pātiki tōtara
lemon squash waipē rēmana
lemonade wai rēmana, waireka
lemonfish pioke, mangō
lend tuku(-a) mō te wā, hoatu tārewa
length roa, te roa, hauroa
lengthen whakaroa(-tia), katete(-tia)
lenient ngāwari, mārire
lens whatu, mōwhiti pūata, taukamo
Lent Rēneti, wā whakatiki
leopard rēpata
leotards kahupiri
leprosy tūwhenua, tūhawaiki, mate ngerengere
lesbian wahine moe wahine, wahine takāpui
less iti iho
less than (sign) iti iho
lessee kaitango rīhi
lesser iti iho
lesson akoranga
lessor kaituku rīhi
lest kei, koi
let (lease) rēti, rīhi
let down tuku iho, whakaheke
lethal whakamate
lethargic momoe, tūrūruhi, ngoikore
letter (missive) reta
letter of credit reta moni kia utua
lettuce rētuhi, arata
level (academic) taurangi, taumata, āhua, kōeke

level (flat) paparite, tautika, taumata
level (tool) rēwara
lever hua
liability taunaha, pīkaunga, nama
liable herea ki te kaupapa, āhei ki te utu
liaise kōrero tahi, noho tahi, takawaenga(-tia)
liaison takawaenga, whakapiringa
liaison officer kaitakawaenga, takawaenga
liar kaikōrero teka, rūpahu, kaitito
libel ngautuarā, pānui hē, tuhinga (whakakino)
liberal whānui te whakaaro, atawhai
liberate whakawātea(-tia), wewete (wetea), wetekina
liberator kaiwhakaora, kaiwhakawete
liberty wātea i ngā tikanga here, wāteatanga
librarian kaitiaki pukapuka, kaimahi whare pukapuka
licence raihana
lick mitimiti(-tia)
lid taupoki, kōmutu
lie (untruth) teka, tito, rūpahu, horihori
lie across pae, paeroa, kurupae, kaupae
lie down takoto(-ria), tāhinga
lie in heap putu, kauika, pūkai, pūhāngaiti
lie scattered horahora
lieutenant rūtene, tēneta
life ora, oranga, manawa, wairua ora
life insurance inihua ora
lifeless mate, hemo, tūpāpaku
lifelong ā-mate-noa, pūmau
lift (elevator) hiki tāngata, ararewa
lift in arms hiki(-tia), hikihiki(-tia), hāpai(-tia)
lifted up mōrunga, maranga, hāpaitia
ligament nape, uaua
light (weight) māmā, pūhau
light bulb rāiti, rama
light fire tahu(-na)
lighten (brighten) whakamārama
lighten weight whakamāmā
lighter flame whakakā
lighthouse whare rāiti hei tohu, tīramaroa, whare tūrama
lightning uira
lightning rod tira uira
like (be fond of) pai ki, hiahia(-tia)
like (similar) taurite, ōrite, rite
like that pēnā, pēraka(-tia), pērā, whērā
like this pēnei, whēnei
likely tērā pea, āhua nei
likeness ōritetanga, ritenga, āhuatanga
likewise hoki, waihoki
liking hiahia, mataareka, pai
lily riria, rengarenga
limb peke, kaupeka
lime raima
limestone pākeho, ngako
limit whakawhaiti(-tia), rohe(-a), kotinga, raina, tepe, here
limitation whakawhāititanga, tawhā
limited whāiti noa
limited funding pūtea paku nei, pūtea iti nei
limitless rohekore

limp (slack) parure
limp along totitoti, toti haere
limpet ngākihi, piritoka, ngāpaki
linear rārangi
liniment hinu mirimiri, rongoā whakamahana
linen rīnena, papamuka
liner (ship) kaipuke
linesman's flag haki kairota
ling hoka, hokarari
linger whakaroa, āta haere, karioi, whakananawe
lingerie āhumehume
lining pairi, whakapaparanga
link hononga, taura here, here o te mekameka, hoto, hono(-a)
linkage hononga
linoleum kahupeka, whāriki takitahi
lintel pari, kārupe, kōrupe
lion raiona
lip ngutu
lip service āwhina-ā-ngutu
lipstick pani ngutu
liquefy rewa
liquid wai, teretere, inu, wē
liquidate whakaea nama, whakakore(-a)
liquor rama
liquor, strong - wai whakahaurangi
liquorice rikiriki
lisp ārero tehe
list (*n.*) rārangi
listen whakarongo, taringa whakarongo
listener kaiwhakarongo
listening post tumu whakarongo
listless anuhea, hāngenge, ngoikore, korou kore, iwingohe
listless, grow - tārure
literal ā-kupu
literate mōhio ki te pānui pukapuka
literature āhua momo tuhituhi, tuhituhinga whānui
lithe kamakama, ngohe, ngāwari, moruki, tirimāka
litre rita
litter (rubbish) otaota, parahanga
little iti, nohinohi (*pl.* nonohi), pakupaku
little person roiroi whene
liturgy tikanga karakia
live (dwell) noho
live happily āta noho
livelihood mahi whakakiko, umanga
lively hauora, ngahau
liver ate, ate whanewhane
livestock kararehe pāmu
living room rūma noho
lizard moko, ngārara
lizard, green - mokomoko kākāriki
load (*n.*) wahanga, pīkaunga, kawenga
load (*v.*) uta(-ina)
load equipment utauta
load gun whāngai pū
loaf rohi parāoa
loam one matua, whenua taepu
loan moni āwhina, pūtea taurewa
loathe mauāhara, whakaetieti(-tia)
loathsome whakahouhou, whakarihariha, weriweri
lob (*v. and n.*) panga teitei, tīkoke
lobby tomokanga, roro (o te whare)
lobe of ear hoi, pokopoko, toke taringa

L

local ā-rohe, paetata, o te papakāinga
local anaesthetic rongoā whakakēkerewai
local authority mana-ā-rohe
local body kaunihera
local government kāwanatanga-ā-rohe
local people tangata whenua
locality rohe, wāhi
locally i te takiwā
lock (of door) raka, kati
lock, rugby - kaiwhītiki
lock of hair pū makawe, io makawe
locker wāhi kāpata
locksmith kaimahi kī
lockup wharau kati, whare herehere
locomotive tereina
locust kihikihi, kikihitara, tātarakihi, pihareinga
lodge (room) kāinga, whare
lodgings kāinga noho
log (timber) poro rākau, rākau, tūporo
logic whakaaro arorau, whakaaro mārama, whakaarotahi
logo moko, waitohu
loiter whakaroa, whakatinaku, tatari
lolly rare
lone mokemoke, mōrearea
loneliness mokemoketanga
lonely mokemoke, mehameha
long roa, tāroaroa
long ago nonamata, i neherā
long for hihiri(-tia), hiahia(-tia)
long jump kairērere
long past nehe, o nehe rā
long standing tūroa
long suffering manawanui
long term mō te wā roa, mauki
longevity mauriroa
longing warawara, kōingo, manako, matenui, turou
longitude rārangi tū, aho pou
look titiro (tirohia), mātakitaki
look after tiaki
look at (inspect) whakawā(-ngia), tirotiro
look down (despise) whakahāwea, whakamania
look for rapu(-a), kimi(-hia), ārohi(-a), haha(-ria)
look on mātakitaki, whakaata(-ria)
look out! kia tūpato
look up (improve) whakapai ake, pai haere
look up to whakamihi, whakamīharo
looking glass whakaata
loop koru, koromeke
loose (free) taka, maunu
loose (not tight) tangatanga, korokoro
loose (of a post) tungāngā
loosen wetewete (wetekina), mawheto, korokoro
loot pārau, parakete
lop poroporo
lopsided tītaha
lord ariki
lore tikanga-ā-iwi
lorry taraka
lose ngaro
loss hapanga, rarunga, hinga
loss of status whakaheke tupu, hēanga
lost ngaro, makere, kore
lot (many) tini, maha, nui
lottery rota

Lotto Rōtō
loud tangi nui, hū, pehū
loudspeaker whakanui reo, tukuoro
lounge rūma noho
louse kutu
love aroha(-ina), kaingākau
love charm/spell ātahu
love child pōriro
love-struck wewehe
lovely hūmārie, ātaahua
lover tahu, makau, tau, whaiāipo
loving aroha, atawhai
low-born ware, tūtūā
low (shallow) pāpaku, i raro, hakahaka
low tide timu, tai mimiti, timutanga, pakeke
lower (*v.*) tuku ki raro, whakaheke
lowly mahaki, hūmārire, ware
loyal piri pono
loyalty pūmautanga, ngākau pono
lubricant whakamaene, hinu
lubricate whakahinuhinu(-tia)
lucid mārama
luck waimarie
luckily waimarie, māringanui
lucky waimarie, momoho, māringanui
lucrative whai hua
ludicrous katakata, manuware
luggage kawenga, mauranga
lull whakanā, aupaki
lullaby oriori, pōpō, taiapo
lunacy pōrangi
lunatic pōrangi
lunch tina
lunge rere, whātoro, rāti
lungs pukapuka, ate wharowharo, pūkahukahu
lure poapoa, pātari
lurk kurupae, whakapupuni
lush growth pāhautea, matomato
lust ngākau pūremu, tīweka
luxuriant hira, huhua, māpua, ngahoro
luxury houkura, hāneanea, whai rawa

L

M

macaroni makaroni, tīkohu parāoa
machete oka, toki māripi
machine mīhini, pūrere
machine-gun pū mīhini, tiripapa
mackerel tawatawa
mackintosh meketoiho
macron tohu tō, pīmakarona
mad pōrangi
madam whaea
made mahia, hanga
magazine makahīni, maheni, puka maheni
maggot iroiro, kutukutu, iro, kete
magic mākutu, māui, tūmatarau
magistrate mahitareta, kaiwhakawā manaiti
magnesium konuhina, konupura
magnet autō, haeana kumemau, rino kume
magnetism maneatanga
magnificent whakahirahira, rawe, ahurei
magnify whakanui(-a)
magnifying glass puata whakanui, mōhiti whārahi, karu whakarahi
magnitude rahi, nui, kaitā, rarahi
magpie kōkako, makipai
maid kōtiro tūmau, takakau, hāwini
mail mēra, kōpaki
main tino, matua
mainland tuawhenua, mokoroa
mainstream auraki, tino rerenga, riuroa, rīroa
maintain whakaū(-ria)
maintenance tiakitanga
maize kānga
majestic rangatira
majesty mananui, tū rangatira
major-general meiha-tianara
majority nuinga
make hanga(-ia), whaihanga(-tia)
make known whakaputa(-ina), pānui(-tia)
make out (discern) kite(-a)
make up (atone) hohou rongo, whakahoa, hakahāngai(-tia)
make up (cosmetics) pani kanohi, kanohi whakapaipai
make up mind tau te whakaaro
make-believe māminga, whakatakune
make-do whakamōmori
maker kaihanga, kaimahi
malaria eku
male (animal) toa, tame, pūru, tāne
male gender ira tāne
malevolent whiro, ngākau kino
malformed hauā, hakoko, manau
malfunction pakaru, mahi hē
malignant kino, whakamate
mallet kuru, tā
malnutrition whakatiki, kore kai, kai kino
mammal kararehe ngote ū, kararehe whāngote

man tāne, tangata, ira tangata
man-of-war manuao
manage (direct) whakahaere
manager tumu whakahaere, kaitiaki, kaiwhakahaere
mange waihakihaki
manger takotoranga kai
mangle takakino, kōnatunatu
mangle (wringer) mīhini perēhi kākahu
mangrove mānawa, paetai, waikure
mangrove fish parore, parakoka, kopīpiro
mangy waihakihaki
manhandle pupuri-ā-ringa, rarahu
mania mate pōrangi
maniac pōrangi
manifestation whakakitenga
manifesto pānui kaupapa
manipulate whawhe, whakanao(-a), whakarere, waihanga(-tia)
manliness tūtangata
manner āhua
mannish whakatāne
manoeuvre nekeneke, whakaoreore
manslaughter whakamate tangata
manta fish whai
mantelpiece kārupe
mantis rō
manual (by hand) ā-ringa
manufacture hanga
manufacturer kaihanga
manure maniua, tongi
manuscript tuhituhinga
many huhua noa, nui, maha, tini, pio, ngero
Māori perspective wairua Māori, tirohanga Māori, tā te Māori titiro
map mapi, mahere whenua
marathon omaoma a Tōhē, waetea taumano
marble hītimi, māpere, māpara
marblefish kehe, kawikawi, koeae
march hīkoi, rangatū
mare hōiho ūha, kātua
margin rohe, taha, paenga, tawhē
marijuana rauhea, whakamāngina
marina tauranga poti, herenga waka
marinate pūkarakara, whakapūkara-ā-wai, whakamara
marine nō te moana
marine reserve tāpui taimoana, āpure moana
maritime nō te rere moana
mark tohutohu(-ngia), whakatohu(-ngia)
mark up whakapiki utu
marked waitohu, iraira
market mākete
market garden mahinga huawhenua
marlin takeketonga
marmite īhipani
maroon colour ura
maroon (strand) pae(-a)
marquee mākī, atorua
marriage mārena, moe(-a), mārenatanga
marriage, de facto - moe māori, moe puku
marrow (vegetable) kamokamo
marrow, bone - wai mongamonga
marry moe wahine, moe tāne, hono mārena

Mars Matawhero, Tūmatauenga
marsh repo
marvel (*n.*) mea mīharo
marvel (*v.*) whakamīharo, whakamihi
marvellous tino pai rawa, mīharo, whakaharahara, ka rawe hoki
mascara taekamo
mascot mōkai
masculine tautāne
mash penupenu, whakapē
masher penu
mask pae kanohi, karu mowhiti, hīpoki
mason kaimahi perēki
Mass (service) Miha
mass, solid - papatipu
massacre parekura, tārukenga, whārona awatea
massage romiromi, mirimiri
massive nui whakaharahara
mast māhi, rewa
mastectomy pokanga ū
master rangatira, māhita, matua
Master of Ceremonies (MC) kaiwhakahaere
master's degree tohu wānanga tuarua, tohu paerua
masterly tohunga
masterpiece taonga whakahirahira
mastitis mate titikau
masturbate tītoi, pīkoikoi, hika kikokiko
mat whāriki, takapau
match (game) kēmu, whakataetae
match (light) māti, kaunati
match up taupatu, taurite, ōrite, whakarite(-a)
matchplay tauwhāinga
mate hoa takatāpui
material (fabric) papanga, kākahu, ārai
maternity kōkōtanga
maternity home whare kōhanga, whare omahu
mathematics ngā mahi whika, pāngarau
matrimony mārena
matron kaiwhakahaere tapuhi, kuia, whaea
matron, hospital - nāhi tumuaki, kaiwhakahaere hōhipera
matted rapa, rīrapa
matter (science) matū, huinga korakora
matter, it doesn't - hei ahakoa
matting whāriki
mattock pākururoa, mārau, mātiki
mattress matarehi, moenga, whāriki moenga
mature pakari, maoa, kōkā
maturity pakeketanga, tuā pakari, maoa
maul, rugby - kōkiri tā, kaunuku
maximum te tino nui, te nui rawa, kīnga, mōrahi
maximum security aukati pākaha, whare herehere whakatiki
maybe pea, tēnā pea
mayfly piriwai
mayhem tukitukinga, tīrangorango
mayor meia, mēa, koromatua, kahika
me ahau, au, awau, wau
meadow pākihi, raorao
meal kai, hapa
mealy māngaro
mean (denote) tikanga
mean (stingy) kaiponu, matapiko, apo

meaning tikanga, ritenga, e mea ana
meaningful whai tikanga, whai take
means ara, huruhuru
meantime i taua wā, mea ake nei
measles karawaka, mītera
measure ine, mēiha(-tia), mēhua, tīeke(-tia), ine(-tia)
measurement mēhua, mēiha, ine(-a), inenga
measuring tape taura ine, rīpene mēhua, taura tīeke
meat mīti, kikokiko
mechanic kaiwhakatika pūkaha, tohunga mīhini
medal mētara, tohu toa
meddle tutu, raweke, haukeke
media huarahi rongo kōrero, hunga pāpāho
mediate takawaenga
medical facilities whare hauora
medical research rangahau mahinga rongoā
medicine rongoā, wai rākau
medium waenganui, weheruatanga
Medusa (jellyfish) pūkahukahu
meek waimarie, māhaki
meet tūtaki(-na), huihui(-a), whakataki
meet (of roads) pūtahi
meeting hui, tūtakitanga
megaphone whakanui reo
melancholy pōuriuri, mānatunatu, matapōuri
melanoma kiritona pukupuku, tonapuka
Melbourne Poipiripi, Merepana
mellow maoa
melodious rōreka, tangireka
melody rangi waiata
melon merengi, mērana
melt (*v.intr.*) rewa, koero
melt (*v. tr.*) whakakoero
member mema, tangata o tua whare
membership mematanga
membrane kiriuhi, tewe
membrane, eye - harare
membrane, foetal - kahu
memento manatunga, maharatanga
memorable whakamau mahara
memorandum whakaaturanga, manatu, pānui
memorize maumahara, pupuri
menace whakamataku, whakaweti
mend tapi(-a), whakatika(-hia)
menstruation werawera ā-toto, tahe, mate wahine
mental handicap hauā hinengaro
mental health oranga hinengaro
mental illness mate hinengaro
mentality hinengaro
mention kī, kōrero, mea, whakahua
merchandise taonga hokohoko
merchant kaihoko taonga
merciful atawhai, ngāwari
mercury konuoi
mercy aroha(-ina), tohu(-ngia), atawhai
mere noa
merit pai
merry koa, harakoa
mesh mata, papa, tākekenga
message kupu, kōrero, karere
messenger karere, kaiwaewae
metal konganuku, rino, maitai, mētara

meteorology mātauranga huarere
meter mehua, ōrite, purere ine
methane pūwaro tahi, mewaro
method tikanga, āhuatanga mahi, kaupapa
methodical whakatepe, whakariterite
Methodist Wēteriana, Metoriti
meticulous mahi utiuti, mārehe
metre mita, tuke
metric system pūnaha rau, pūnaha tuke, pūnaha ngahuru
mezzanine atamira, papa waenga, huarewa
microbe ngārara moroiti, mororiki
microbiology mātauranga koiora moroiti
microdot tongi meroiti
microfilm tukuata meroiti, kiriata mōkito
microphone taonga whakanui reo, uruoro, hopuoro, hopu reo
microscope whatu whakanui, tiro mārama, karu whakarahi
microwave oven umu ngaru iti
midday poupoutanga o te rā
middle waenganui, waenga
midge naonao
midget itiiti, whena
midnight weherua pō, tūrotowaenga
midsummer raumati
might (power) kaha, ihi, mana
mighty whakahira, mārohirohi
migraine ānini
migrate heke(-a)
migration, bird - pīrere
migratory hekeheke
mild ngāwari, māhaki, marino
mildew hekaheka, hauku, puruheka
mile maero
milk miraka, waiū
milker kaiwhakatētē kau
milking miraka, whakatētētanga
milkshake mīraka whakaranu
Milky Way Ika-o-te-Rangi, Mangōroa
mill mira
millet miriti
millimetre mirimita, mitamano. tuke haumano
million miriona
millstone kōhatu mira, kōhatu hanga
mimic pakoire, whakahuahua(-tia)
mince meat mīti kōnatunatu
mind (intellect) hinengaro
mind, never - hei aha!
mind, to make up - whakamau whakaaro
mine, coal - rua waro, poka
mine (bomb) pohū whenua, pohū moana
mine (my) nāku, nōku, āku, ōku
miner kaikeri (waro)
minimise whakaiti(-tia), whakamōkito
minimum iti rawa, mōkito
minister minita
ministry (caring) mahi atawhai
Ministry (political) Manatū
minnow kāeaea
minor (underage) tamariki
minority itinga, torutoru, tokoiti
mint flavour hīoi
minus tango(-hia)
minuscule matariki
minute (time) meneti

minute (tiny) iti rawa, meroiti
miracle merekara
mirror whakaata, mira, karāhe
misadventure aituā
misapprehension pōhēhētanga
misappropriate tāhae, whēnako
misbehave mahi tutū
miscalculate tātai hē
miscarriage materoto, whakatahe
miscellaneous tūāhua katoa, huhua
mischief hīanga, mahi hīanga, hanariki
mischievous tutu, hanariki
misconduct (sport) reho, hē
miser matapiko, makitaunu
miserable auwhi, pōuri, matapōuri
misery pōuritanga
misfit autaia
misfortune aituā
misgiving āwangawanga, enga
misguided pahewa, wawau
mishandle haukeke, whāwhā hē, nanao hē
mishap aitu, aituā
misjudge horihori
mislead whakakotiti(-tia), whakatakē
misprint tā hē
mispronounce kōwiriwiri kupu
misrepresent kōrero tito, kōrero teka
miss whakataha, pahemo, taha
Miss (form of address) e whae!, e kō!
miss out hapa, kāore i te whiwhi
miss target tohipa, hauare
misshapen haka, hake, pīari
missile matārere, pere
missing ngaro
missionary karere o te Rongo Pai, mihinare, mihingare
misspell tuhi hē
misspent moumou
mist kohu, pūnehu, kōrehu, pūrehu
mistake heā, pōauau, pōhēhē, pīhē, hapa
mistake in chant kōrapa
mistress (lover) hoa wahine, whaiāipo
mistrust hokirua, matakana, hoto
misunderstand pōhēhē
mite moroiti
mitigate whakangāwari
mitten karapu kope, pūāhuru ringa
mix substances ranu, whakawhenumi, whakaranu
mix with water pokepoke, korori, kaurori
mix-up (muddle) raruraru, pōhēhē, pōrahurahu
mixture whakaranunga, ranunga, raranu
mixture of solids pokepoke
mob mano tīneinei, mano tīwekaweka, māpu
mobile (ornament) tautau
mock whakatoi(-a), tītoi, tāwai
model (*n.*) tauira, momo
model (*v.*) whakatauira, whakakite kākahu, whakaatu
modem whakarerekē ngaru, pouwhanga
moderate waimarie, ngāwari
moderately tūā-. . . (as prefix)
modern hou, o nāianei
modernize whakahou(-ngia)
modest hūmārie, whakaiti

modification whakarerekētanga
modify whakarerekē(-tia), whakahou, whakakē
modulate whakangāwari, whakatikatika
module (education) kōwae ako
moist mākūkū
moisten whakamākū
moisture mākū, haukū
molar niho pū, niho kauoro
mole (animal) mora
mole on skin ira
molecule rāpoi ngota
molest raweke(-tia), whakakino
moment hēkene, wā poto, takitaro
momentary puta whakarere
momentous whai tikanga rawa
momentum neke rāhaki, āinga, torohaki
monarch butterfly kahuku
money moni, herengi
money-lender kaitaupua moni
mongrel mangarū
monitor (computer) pane, kaupane, aro turuki
monitor (*n.*) kaiāwhina akonga
monitor (*v.*) āta whakamātautau, aroturuki, tirotiro-ā-wā
monitoring rarangi me te tātari
monk monaki
monkey maki, hako
mono-cultural tikanga tōtahi
monogram moko
monopoly mana tokitoki, whakatopatopa, apunga kaipakihi
monotony hōhā
monster parangēki, ngārara nui
monstrosity mōrikarika
monstrous tipua, weriweri
month marama, kaupeka
monument tohu whakamaharatanga, kōhatu whakamaharatanga
monumental nui rawa atu
mood wairua
moon marama
moon, full - tōhua
moon, new - hina marama
moonbeam ·atarau
moonlight atarau, ata marama, ata māhina
moor (tie up) here(-a) poti
mooring tauranga
moorland whenua akeake
mop ūkui
moppet tāre, wāhi kōtiro
moral tika, matatika, take whanonga
morale wairua kaha, wairua whakakake
moralise whakakaupapa mō te noho tika
morbid āhua mate, pōuri, aewa, tiwhatiwha
more nui atu i, ētahi atu
moreover ka mutu, heoi anō, kātahi
morepork ruru
morgue whare tūpāpaku
Mormon Mōmona, Te Hunga Tapu o Muri Nei
morphine rehunanu (rongoā)
mortal pīrau, matemate
mortality mea matemate
mortar (cement) raima, whāpiri
mortar (gun) pū mōtā
mortgage mōkete(-tia)
mosquito waeroa, ngaeroa, naenae
moss pūkahukahu, kohukohu, pūkohukohu

most te nuinga
motel mōtēra
moth pūrerehua, pēpepe, pepe
motheaten taretare, pōpopo
mother whaea, matua wahine, māmā, ūkaipō
mother earth Papatūānuku
mother tongue reo tupu
mother-in-law hungawai, hungarei
motherland toi whenua
motion nekenga, oreore, haere
motion (legal) mōtini
motivate whakaara, whakapakepake, toitoi Manawa
motive pūtake, kaupapa
motor pūrere, mīhini
motor-car motokā
motorbike motopāika
motorway ara nui, huarahi aranui
motto whakataukī, pepeha
mould (fungus) heka, pirau
mould (shape) whakaahua(-tia), waihanga ritenga, tauira inarapa
mouldy waitau, puruhekaheka
mouli kūoro
moult kounu, turuki
mound ahu, haupū, puke
mount (*n.*) hōiho
mount (*v.*) eke(-a), piki
mountain maunga
mountain peak taumata
mountain range paemaunga
mountaineer piki maunga
mourn tangi, uhunga, taukiri
mournful pōuri, taukiri, tīkapakapa
mourning tangihanga, uhunga, pōuritanga
mouse kiore iti
moustache hurungutu, pāhau, whenguwhengu
mouth māngai, waha
mouth, open - whakahāmama(-tia)
mouth, river - ngutuawa, wahapū
mouthguard ārai waha
mouthwatering whakamākūkū, mōwaiwai
movable taea te nekeneke
movable property rawa neke
move (*v.intr.*) nuku, neke, korikori, whanake, hanake
move (*v. tr.*) neke(-hia), whakaoreore, whakanekeneke
move in game mū
move motion mōtini
move towards ahu
movie pikitia
mow tapahi karaehe
mower panga kuti, moua
much nui
much better pai kē atu
mucus hupe, kea
mud paru
muddle whakahēhē, pōraruraru
muddy paruparu, ehu, powharu
mudguard paeparu
muesli mūrihi, patahua
muffle tāpeka, whakakopa, whakakōmau
muffle oneself up whakangenengene
muffler, vehicle - puta auahi
mug maka, panikena
mug (beat up) rure(-a), patu(-a)
muggy weather pūmāhu, takawai, haitutu
mulch apu(-ria) raurau, hora(-hia) maniua
mule muera
mull over whakaaroaro

M

mullet kanae, aua, hauhauaitu, kopuwai rerekē
multi-media rongorau
multi-racial iwi maha
multinational nō te ao whānui
multiple taurea
multiplication whakareatanga, whakarautanga
multiply (maths) whakarau, whakarea
mum whaea, wahangū
mumble kowhete, hāmeme, pararāwha
mumps mate kōpuku korokoro, mate pupuhi repe
munch kamu
murder kōhuru
murky pōuriuri
murmur kōhumuhumu, ngunguru
muscle uaua, iaia, maihara, ioio
museum muheama, papa tongarewa, whare pupuri taonga
mushroom harore
mushy kōpē
music rangi waiata, pūoru, whakatangitangi
music scale raupapa tohu tangi
musical instrument taonga pūoru, mea whakatangitangi
musical note tohu tangi
musician kaiwhakatangi
musket (double-barrel) tūpara
mussel kuku, kūtai
mussel, black - hānea, tukuperu
mussel, freshwater - kākahi, kāeo
mussel, horse - waharoa, hururoa
must (as command) me + *verb*, kia + *verb*
must (ought) kua takoto te tikanga
muster whiu(-a), tāwhiu(-a)
musty puruhekaheka, hōpuru
mutate whakarerekē, irakē, nonoi
mute (*v.*) wahangū, whakangū
mutilate mutumutu, takarepa
mutiny whakakeke, tutū ki te ture, whana(-ia)
mutton mātene, mīti hipi
muttonbird tītī, oi
mutual mahi tahi, whakaaro tahi
muzzle (animal) mōkā, whakamōkā(-tia), pōnini
muzzle (gun) ngongo
my tāku, āku, tōku, ōku, taku, aku
myopia kahurua
myself ahau anō
mysterious tupua, māminga
mystery kaupapa huna, pirikoko, mea ngaro
myth pūrākau, pakiwaitara
mythical purākau
mythology kōrero o neherā, pūrākau

N

nag kōwhetewhete, amuamu, ungaunga
nail (*n.*) nēra, whao
nail (*v.*) titi(-a), whakamau(-a)
nail (hand/foot) kotikara, maikuku, matikuku
naive heahea, ngākau tamariki
naked kirikau, tahanga, pakiwhara, takahore
name (*n.*) ingoa
name-plate papa ingoa
nameless ingoakore
namely arā
nanny whaea, kuia, kaitiaki
nanny-goat nanekoti
nap (of cloth) kerehunga, tawhe
nappy (baby) kope, kōre, nāpū
narcotic rehunanu, whakapōauau
narrate pānui(-tia), kōrero(-tia)
narrator kaikōrero, wahapū
narrow whāiti, kuiti, kawiti, mānihi, angiangi
narrow escape ora iti
narrow-minded whakahīhī, mōhio
nasal nō te ihu, whango
nasopharynx pū ihu, awa ihu
nasty kino, weriweri, piro
nation iwi, motu katoa
national ā-iwi, nō te motu katoa
national affairs take whānui o te motu
national anthem ngaringari o te motu
national debt nama o te motu
national guidelines arataki o te motu
national park rohe mō te iwi whānui
National Party Nahinara
National Superannuation Penihana Kaumātua
nationalism wawao whenua
nationality momo iwi
native tangata whenua, māori, toi
natives tāngata whenua, toi
natural nō te tangata, tūturu, māhorahora, māori
natural death mate tarāwhare
natural gas hau māori, hau manawa
natural resource hau-ā-papa, rawa whenua, rawa taiao
natural selection whiringa taiao, whiringa māori
naturalised tangata whenuatia
nature (character) āhua, momo, uho
nature personified Haumiatiketike
naughty tutū, ka kino!, kino, mākoi, hanariki, hīanga
nausea whakapai ruaki, paipai ruaki
nautical nō te moana, nō te waka
naval tauamoana, nō te heramana
naval ship waka taua
navel pito, ihonga
navigable taea te whakatere

navigate whakatere (moana), urungi
navigator kaumoana, amotawa, kaiwhakatere
neap tide tai ririki, tai kōwāwā, tai torepuku
near pātata, pūnui tahi, kei te taha, marutata
near, draw - tata(-ngia), whakatata
nearby pātata, kainamu
nearly tata pū, tatangia
neat (elegant) tau, kua tau kē!
neat (tidy) tika, pūhangaiti
necessary tino pūtake, mea nui, hiahiatia, me + *verb*
necessity hiahia, uaratanga
neck kakī, porokakī, tākakī, ua
neck pendant hei, mau kakī
necklace hei tiki, tāhei
nectarine neketana
née ingoa whānau
need(s) uaratanga, ingoingo, hiahia, huene
needle ngira, mātuhi, patui
needlework tuituinga
needy pōhara, mahue
negative kāhore, kore-tōhito, kāhoretanga, korehanga, tōraro
negative (neutral wire) pito iho
negative charge hihi iho, tāhiko
neglect, to - whakarere(-a), whakahapa, tīkape
neglected mahue
negligent wareware, kore whakaaro
negligible iti noaiho
negotiate whakawhiti whakaaro, whiriwhiri, kōrero hei māngai
negotiation whakaritenga
negro kiri mangu, mangumangu
neigh tupererū, whengu
neighbour hoa tata, hoa noho tata, whakaritenga, kiritata
neighbourhood takiwā, tiriwā
neon hauhō, haukura
nephew irāmutu, tama, tamaiti
Neptune Tangaroa
nerve io, uaua, ioio
nervous matangurunguru, āmaimai, taiatea
nest kōhanga, ōwhanga
nestle whakaahuru
net (*n.*) hao, kupenga, koko kahawai
net (*v.*) hao(-a)
net (sports) mātiratira
net, crayfish - pouraka, tukutuku
net, games - mātiratira
net, shrimp - whakapuru
netball netipaoro, poi tūkohu, poi tarawhiti
nettle ongaonga, taraonga, pūnitanita
network (*n.*) tūhonohonotanga, whātuinga, kōtui
network (*v.*) whātuitui, kōtuitui
network, join - hono(-a) ki te kupenga
neurosis mate āwangawanga
neurotic pōrārā tonu, mānuka rau, pōhewahewa
neutral (not taking sides) kūpapa
neutralise whakaruhi, whakakūpapa, whakapāhare
neutron iramoe
never kore rawa, kei
never mind! hei aha!, aua atu!
nevertheless otirā, ahakoa, hei aha koa
new hou, hōu
New Testament Kawenata Hou

new year tau hou
New Zealand Aotearoa, Aotearoa me Te Waipounamu, Niu Tireni
newcomer waewae tapu, tangata tauhou
news kawenga kōrero, rongo kōrero o te wā, kupu rongo, karere
news, according to the - e ai ki ngā kōrero
newspaper niupepa, nūpepa
newsreader kaipāho, kaipānui
next (coming) e heke iho ana, tētahi atu, panuku
next day aonga ake
next of kin whanaunga tata
next to kei te taha
nib, pen - timopene, kīra
nibble tītongi, kōhonihoni, timotimo, hārau, kinikini
nice reka, pai, rawe, ka tau
nick (mark) panihi, tongari, pakini
nickel konumāuka
nickname ingoa kārangaranga, ingoa tāpiri
nicotine nikotīni, paratūpeka
niece tamāhine, irāmutu, tamaiti whakaangi
niggle whakatara(-tia), nanamu
night pō
night watchman kaimataara o te pō
night-dress kākahu moe
night-work tūāpō
night, last - inapō
nightfall pōnga, ahiahi
nightly ia pō ia pō
nightmare kuku, moepapa, moehewa
nil kāhore, horekau, kore
nimble kakama
nine iwa
ninth tuaiwa
nip kukuti (kūtia), kākati, kuku(-a)
nipple kōmata, ū
nit riha
nitrogen hauota
no kāo!, kāhore, ehē, tē
no good koretake
nobility kāwai rangatira
noble rangatira, whatukura, rangatira motuhenga
noble lady mareikura, tapairu, kahurangi
nobody horekau tangata, ware, kora
nocturnal ohopō, moerā, moeao, aohuna
nod tūngou, tūohu
nodule tonatona
noise turituri, hoihoi
noiseless whakahū
noisy hoihoi, turituri, tawetawē
nomad iwi haerere, manene, taurangi
nominal ā-ingoa, ririki
nominate whakaingoa(-tia), tautapa(-tia), tapa(-ina)
nominee tautapa
non-existence korenga, horekau
non-fiction (book) pukapuka take tūturu
non-stick pirikore
non-stop tahi tonu, haere tonu
non-threatening tumakore
nondescript hanga noa
none horekau, korekore
nonetheless ahakoa
nonsense pōhauhau, kutukutu-ahi, koretake

N

nook kona, kokonga
noon poupoutanga o te rā
noose koro (o te rore), tāwhiti, koromāhanga, rore
nor kāhore rānei
normal tā te tikanga, tō te ritenga, māori, pūnoa
north raki, raro, tai tokerau, muriwhenua
northeast pā whakarua, karapu
northwest māuru, tapatiu, uru mā raki, tapatapa atiu
northerly ki te tokerau
northern nō raro, nō te tai tokerau, nō te raki
northward ki raro, ki te raki, whakararo
nose ihu
nose flute kōau pongaihu
nosedive tūpou
nosey pākiki
nostalgia murimuri aroha, kaimomotu
nostril pūtāihu, pongāihu, pongaponga
not ehara i te + *noun,* kāhore + *verb,* kīhai, tē
not, do - kaua e + *verb,* aua e + *verb,* kauaka hei + *verb*
not knowing aua
not only hāunga
not yet kāhore anō, kīanō
notable whai tikanga, rangatira
notation tuhi whika, reo tohu
notch kāniwha, kakari, pakini
note (money) moni pepa
note (musical) tohu waiata, orotahi
note, written - whakaaturanga, tuhinga, kupu ako, tuhipoa
notebook puka-tuhi
notepaper whārangi-tuhi, pepa-tuhi
nothing kore
nothingness te kore
notice (advert) pānui, pānuitanga, whakaaturanga
notice, to - kite(-a), āro(-ngia)
noticeboard papa pānui
notification whakaaturanga
notion whakaaro, ariā
notorious rongo mōiriiri, ingoa kino
notornis takahē
nought hore, kāhore, kore
noun tūingoa, kupu ingoa, kupu ingoa uku
nourish whāngai(-tia), whakatipu(-ria)
novel (*adj.*) hōu, rerekē
novel (story) kōrero pūrākau, tuhinga pūrākau, pakiwaitara
novice tauhou
now i nāianei, āianei
now (first time) kātahi anō
now then! tēnā!, nā
now, from – on ā muri ake nei
nowadays i ēnei rā
nozzle ihu, waha
nuclear karihi, matū piere
nuclear armed rākau karihi
nuclear bomb pōma nukiria, pahū karihi
nuclear energy kaha karihi, pūngao karihi
nuclear physics akoranga karihi
nuclear powered hiko karihi, pūngao karihi
Nuclear-Free New Zealand Aotearoa Karihi-Kau
nucleus whatu, karihi ngota, tūrito

nude kirikau, tahanga
nudge tute, tuketuke
nuisance hōhā, taitāhae, haututū, pōrearea
nullify whakanoa, whakakore
numb matarekereke, uhu, kōpā, matangerengere
number nama, tau, whika, tātai, tātakitanga
number, decimal - tau-ā-ira
number, even - taurua
numberless tātaikore, miriona, manomano tini
numeral tātai, whika, tohu tau
numerous huhua, maha, manotini
nun whaea tapu, none, tuahine tapu, ngoi atua
nuptials mārenatanga
nurse (*n.*) nāhi, nēhi, kumanu, maimoa
nurse (*v.*) tiaki(-na), whakatapuhi
nurse baby piripoho, hiki(-tia)
nurse, charge - tapuhi matua
nursery kōhanga, wāhi tiaki kōhungahunga, whare pārekereke
nursing home kāinga tiaki tūroro
nut (fruit) nati, whatu hua rākau, kārihi hua rākau
nut (metallic) peru
nutcracker huaki nati
nutshell anga, nganga
nuzzle whakaahuru
nylon nairona, ngaiaku

O

o'clock karaka
oak tree oke
oar hoe
oarsman/woman kaihoe
oath (curse) kangakanga, kohu
oath (formal) oati(-tia), kupu taurangi
oatmeal ōtimira
oats ōti
obedience whakarongo
obedient ngāwari, whakarongo
obese mōmona
obey āta whakarongo, rongo
obliterate whakangaro(-mia), wawāhi(-a), whakakore(-ngia)
oblivion wareatanga, te kore, te pō
oblivious wareware
oblong tapawhā
obnoxious whakarihariha
obscene karihika, mōtekoteko
obscure kaurehu, māhina, rehu, whakapōrearea
observant hiwa, kakama, korita, matakana
observation (comment) whakaaro, whakataki
observation (watching) mātakitaki
observe (watch) mātakitaki(-tia), tirotiro (tirohia)
observer kaimātakitaki, kaitirotiro
obsessive pokepoke, kuku
obsidian matā tūhua
obsolete tino tawhito, nonehe, ruha
obstacle ārai, pā, taupare
obstinate taringa rākau, hoi, taringa kōhatu, pakeke, ūpoko mārō
obstruct ārai(-a), pā(-ngia), taupā, whakahōtaetae
obstruction haukoti, kati, taupare, hōtaetae
obtain(-ed) riro i, whiwhi ki
obvious mārama, marake, mārakerake
occasion wā, takunetanga
occasional ia wā ia wā
occult mea huna, wānanga, tipua
occupancy nōhanga
occupant kainoho, tangata e noho nei
occupation (job) mahi, umanga, whakatāuteute, kaipakihi
occupy kapi(-a), noho(-ia)
occur taka
ocean moana nui
ochre karamea, kōkōwai
octagon tapawaru (rite)
octane pūwaro waru, wāwaro
octopus wheke
ocular nō te kanohi
oculist kaitiaki kanohi
odd (function) panga hangarite kore
odds (betting) tautaunga, tūponotanga
odour haunga, piro, hā, kehakeha

of o, a, nō, nā
off (to side) tahaki
off and on taratahi
off-key rongo kawa, porokawa
offcut poronga
offence (wrong) hara, hē, mahi hē
offend hara
offended pāpōuri
offender tangata hara, kaimahi hē
offensive weriweri, mōrihariha, whakapiro
offer hoatu, tuku(-a), tāpae(-tia), whakatotoro
offering whakamakanga, whakaherenga, koha, tahua
office tari
Office, Race Relations - Tari Whakawhanaunga-ā-Iwi
officer āpiha, kiriārahi
officer, traffic - āpiha tiaki huarahi
official (*adj.*) nō te ture, atoato
officiate whakahaere tikanga
offset print tā whakaahua
offshoot wene, rerenga, peka
offsider kaitautoko, hoa mahi
offspring uri, tamariki, punua, punuka
often rite tonu (*verb* + ai), tini taima
oil hinu
oil (perfume) rautangi
oil-rig papahinu
oilfield rohe papahinu, whira poka hinu
oilstone hōanga hinu
oily hinuhinu
ointment pūreke, rongoā pani, hinu whakaora
old tawhito, pakeke
old fashioned nā mua, onamata, o neherā
old man kaumātua, koeke, koroheke
Old Testament Kawenata Tawhito
old woman kuia, rūruhi, ruahine, nehe
olive ōriwa, karikihaura
Olympic Games Taumāhekeheke o te Ao, Whakataetae Orimipia
ombudsman kaiwawao, kaitiaki mana tangata, poungaio
omelette omareta, hēki kōrori
omen aituā, tohu mate, takiari
omen, bad - koara, inati, kōtua, pūhore
ominous kaiora, kōara, tāmaki
omission whakarere(-a)
omit kape(-a), tīpoka(-ria), whakarere(-a), waiho
omitted mahue, awere
omnipotent kaha rawa, tino nui
on i/kei runga
on demand inā whakahaua
on ramp pekauru
on the other hand engari
once wā kotahi
once (formerly) i mua
one tahi, kotahi, tētahi
one another tētahi tētahi
one-sided whakaaro tītaha
one-way aratahi, ahutahi
onerous taumaha
ongoing haere tonu ana, mo ake tonu atu, hei kaupapa
onion aniana, riki
onlooker kaititiro, kaimātakitaki
only noa, anake, nahenahe, kau, ka mutu anō ki
onrush of water upoko wai

onslaught huakitanga
onward whakamua
ooze pipī, patī, pātītī, kūtere
opaque paroro, tāpōuri, hīnakipōuri, māhinahina
open (*adj.*) puare, tuwhera(-tia), mārakerake, māhorahora
open country tahora, pākihi
open out tūhāngai, wherawhera, manahua
open question kāhore anō kia tatū, kāhore anō kia mārama
open up huaki(-na), puaki(-na), whakatuwhera(-tia), whakapuare(-ngia)
open waters au o te moana, moana tūraha
open wide tūwhera, kōwhera
open-minded whānui
opener huaki
opening tūwheratanga, whakapuakitanga
opening ceremony kawanga, whakapuaretanga, whakahuakitanga
operate (surgery) tapahi(-a), poka(-ina)
operate whakahaere(-tia), whakamahi(-a)
operate policy whakatutuki kaupapa
operation (maths) paheko
operation, come into - wana mai (te ture)
operator kaiwhakamahi
opinion whakaaro, kaupapa whakaaro, titiro, huatau
opium rehunanu
opossum paihamu
opponent hoariri, hunga kāhore i whakaae, hoa tauwhāinga
opportunity wā kia puta, wā tika, huarahi kua wātea mai, angitū
opportunity, give - tuku(-a, -na), whakatakoto tikanga
opportunity, have - whai wāhi ki
oppose whawhai atu, ārai, tautohe, ātete
opposite hāngai, āronga kē, anganui, anga, tauaro
opposite position kōaro
opposition hoariri, whawhainga, mautohe
oppress pēhi(-a), tāmi(-a) iho, aupēhi(-a), whakawhiu(-a)
oppressor kaiwhakawhiu, kaiwhakawiri
opt for whiriwhiri(-a), whakatau(-ria)
opt out puta
optic whatu
optician kaimātai whatu, kaimōwhiti
optimism mariu, whakaaro pai
optimist kirimariu
optimum tika rawa, pai rawa, nui rawa
option ara, huarahi, kōwhiri, ara hei whāinga, whiringa
opulence tino hāneanea, whai rawa
opulent whai rawa, utu nui
or rānei (after word qualified), rainei
oracle matakite
oral ā-waha
orange (fruit) ārani
orange coloured pārakaraka, karaka
oration whaikōrero
orator pūkōrero, manu kōrero
orbit āwhio, huarahi āwhio, āmionga

orchard uru rākau hua
orchestra ōkerehā, pēne pūoruoru, tira pōuru
orchid paratawhiti, hutukiwi
ordain whakatapu(-a), whakarite(-a), momotu(-hia)
ordeal mōrearea, mamaetanga
order (command) ōta, whakahau, tono(-a)
order (sequence) raupapa
ordinary noa iho
organ, bodily - whēkau, wāhanga tinana
organ (musical) ōkena, ōkana, pūkeru
organisation (institution) whakahaere
organiser kaiwhakarite
organist kaiwhakatangi ōkena
orientation whakawaia, whakataunga, takotoranga
origin pūtake, ūkaipoā, pū, toi
original toi, kaupapa, taketake
originate tīmata, take(-a), whakatakune
ornament whakapaipai, rei, rākai, whakakai
ornament of greenstone kuru pounamu
ornamental whakapaipai
ornate whakarākei, nekoneko
orphan tamaiti pani, whāngai
orphanage whare tiaki pani
orthodox haratau, tika
ostentatious whakahīhī, rangiwhata, hahaki
osteopath kaiwhakaora wheua
other tērā, ērā, tētahi, wāhikē, tētahi atu
other day i tērā rā, inākuarā
other hand engari, ērangi
other people iwi kē
other side rāwāhi
otherwise pēnei kē, rerekē, ki te kore
ought me + *verb*
ounce aunihi
our tā/tō mātou, tā/tō tātou, ā/ō mātou, ā/ō tātou
ourselves mātou ake, tāua, tātou
out (absent) kei waho, kua haere kē
out (extinguished) piro, pirau, poko
out of breath hēmanawa, pau te hau, tūngāngā
out of date tawhito, hapa
out of one's mind pōrangi
out of order (broken) pakaru
out of reach āritarita noa, kaiawe
out of work kore mahi
out-tray paepae reta atu
outback tuawhenua
outbreak urutā
outbuilding wharau tāpiri
outburst pahūtanga
outcast whati, whakahoe, peinga
outcome tukunga iho, whakatutuki, hua o te mahi
outcry auētanga
outdoor o waho
outer space ātea tawhiti
outfit kākahu
outflow whakatetere, whakaputa
outgoings utunga
outgrow tipu ake, kōwaowao
outing haereere
outlaw pihareinga, whakapakonga
outlay moni whakatakoto
outlet putanga, puahatanga, paipa, tāwaha
outline (*n.*) paetuhi, hua, hoahoa

outline (*v.*) whakatakoto(-ria), whakarārangi(-tia)
outlook tirohanga
outnumber tini ake, hipa, rahi atu
outpatient tūroro torotoro, tūroro noho kāinga
outpost porewa tautiaki, taupuni tawhiti
output hua, whakaputa, pūtea, huaputa
outrageous whakarihariha, mōrihariha
outrigger ama, amatiatia, kōrewa
outright oti rawa, hāngai atu
outside a/i/ki/kei waho
outspoken waha kōrero, whakaputa whakaaro
outstanding tino rawe, hīranga
outstanding debt nama tonu
outstretched totoro, tāwhangawhanga, whera
outward mōwaho, whakawaho
outweigh hira ake
outwit nukarau, tinihanga, rorerau
outworn ruha, pū nguru
oval porohita tītaha, matahua, porotītaha
ovary whare kano, kōhanga hēki
ovation mihi nui, umere
oven umu, oumu, hapī, omu
over ki runga ki, mā runga
over (finished) mutu, oti, ora mai anō
over and above tua atu
overalls tangari, tarau waho
overbalanced titoki, taka
overboard roto wai
overburden taumaha rawa
overcast whakapōrearea, kēkēao kōpiupiu, tukupū
overcharge utu tāhae
overcoat kotinui
overcome (*v. intr.*) mate, weto, taea, hinga
overcome (*v. tr.*) whakahinga, whiu(-a)
overcrowd apiapi, kikī, opurua
overdose (O.D.) inati te kai tarukino, areare whakapuhake, tuhene rawa
overdraft moni nama, moni tuhene, pau rawa
overdue takaroa, tūreiti, hapa
overeat mōrikarika, puku kai
overestimate tatau horihori
overflow waipuke, pūrena, huri(-hia), puhake
overflowing waipuke(-tia)
overgrown ururua, wheu, heuheu, kōwaowao
overhang tauwhare, matahao
overhaul whakatika(-hia), pahemo
overhead ki runga
overhead projector (O.H.P.) rauata
overhead resources rauemi rauata
overheads (expense) utu, raruraru
overland mā tuawhenua
overlap inaki(-tia), tāpiki
overlook mahue, tīpoka
overnight mō te pō, ia pō
overpower turaki(-na), whakaruhi, tāmi(-a)
overrated tairangaranga, tahuperatia
overreach (defraud) tāhae
overrun pōpoki, poka
overseas tāwāhi, tāwauwau

oversee tirotiro (tirohia)
overshadow marumaru
oversize tino nui
oversleep moeroa
overstayer noho roa, noho tūwhene
overtake paneke, rokohanga, mau
overthrow tahuri(-tia), kuru hipa, turaki(-na), taupoki(-na)
overtime mahiroa, haora tūwhene
overturn tahuri(-tia), turaki, hurihanga, huripoki
overwhelm apuru(-a), huri(-hia)
owe nama
own (personal) ake (e.g. tōku ake, tōna ake)
own (possess) whai + *noun*, whiwhi, āna
own up (confess) whāki(-na)
owner kaipupuru
owner of tangata nōna te
ownership rangatiratanga
ox ōkiha
oxygen hā ora
oyster, pacific - tio
oyster, rock - karauria, ngākihi
ozone hāora-toru, hau ārai
ozone layer papa hāora-toru

P

pace (step) hīkoi, toihā
pacemaker (heart) whakatika manawā
Pacific Islanders Hunga o ngā Moutere
pacify hohou rongo, whakarata(-hia), whakamārie(-tia)
pack (load) pīkaunga, kawenga, peketua
package pāhi, mokihi, pūhera, mōkī
packaging pōkaitanga, takai
packet pākete, takai
packhorse hōiho tarapēke
packing case pouaka whakamātā
pact whakaritenga, maunga rongo, whakaaetanga
pad (cloth) pākākano
pad, writing - puka tuhituhi
padding (sport) parepare, whakapuru
paddle hoe(-a)
paddle, steering - hoe urungi
paddling pool papawai pōhutuhutu
paddock taiepa, whira, pātiki
padre tiaparani, minita hāhi
page whārangi
paid for ea, rite, utu(-a)
pain mamae, kikini, kakati
painkiller rongoā whakamāuru
painless mamae kore
painstaking hihiri, tūpato, mārehe
paint peita(-tia), pani(-a), tā, waituhi
painter (artist) tohunga pēita
painting (art) waituhi, kōwhaiwhai
pair pea, pūrua
pairs, in - takirua
Pākehā kiri mā, kiritea, iwi kē
palatable reka
palate (taste) korokoro, piki-arero
pale (complexion) mā, tuatea, kōmā
pallet kauamo
palm nīkau, kaihuia
palm of hand kapu, paro
palpable taea te whāwhā
palpitate papaki, pātukituki
palsy pararutiki
pampas grass toetoe
pamper morimori
pamphlet pānui whakamārama
pan parai, ipu tahu, kōhua
pane (glass) karaehe wini, pihanga
panel (people) rōpū whiriwhiri, nohoanga tiati, paepae
panel (wall) tūparu, tukutuku
panelbeater kaiwhakapapa, takapapa
panic mataku, hopohopo
pannier kete kōpae
pant whakaeaea, hotuhotu, mapu
panties maromaro
pants (trousers) tarau
pantyhose marowae, pirikiri
papaya pōpō

paper pepa, pukapuka, niupepa
par (golf) uhau, eke pai, tā te kāri i tohu ai
parachute heketau, kapohau, hekerangi
parade porohehio, whakatūtū
paradise paratiho, pararaiha
paragraph whiti, kōwae, pourangi
parakeet kākāriki
parallel lines whakarara
parallel parking tau whakarara
paralyse pararaiha(-tia), pōrewarewa
paralysed pararutiki, kōpā
paralysis mate iotanga, io kerewai
paralytic pararutiki
paramount tino teitei rawa
parapet pātatara
paraphrase whakapuaki kē, whakamārama anō
parasite werau, pirinoa, parakūkā
parcel kōpaki, pūhera
parched maroke rawa, pakupaku, pakoa
pardon muru hara, tohungia
parent matua
parish pāriha, pārihe
parking warden kātipa papa waka, kātipa tūranga waka
parliament pāremata, whare miere
parlour rūma noho
parole tukuihere, kupu pono, tuku whakamātau
parrot kākā, kea, pōrete
parry a blow karo(-hia), whakangungu
parsley pāhiri
parsnip pāhinipi, uhitea
parson minita
part (piece of) wāhi, wāhanga
part-time work mahi hangere, harangotengote
participant tangata whai pānga, kaiuru, kaiwhakauru
participate uru mai ki, uru whānui, whai wāhi ki
participation whai wāhitanga, urunga
particular ake, hakune
particular, in - te mea nui
particulars (data) whakaaturanga
parting wehenga
partition wāwāhi, roherohe, pakitara wehewehi
partly āhua
partner hoa, hunga mahi ngātahi
party (feast) hākari, ngahau
party (group) ope, pahī, tira, rōpū
party politics tohe mō te rōpū
paschal feast Pākate, Aranga
paspalum tuhui
pass (authorisation) tikiti hipa, whakawātea
pass (throw) kuru, whiu
pass away memeha, mate, hemo, pahemo
pass behind nunumi
pass by pahure, hipa, pahemo, whakarere, pana(-ia)
pass down tuku iho, heke iho
pass exam pāhi, riro i a ia, puta i te whakamātautau
pass out (faint) takarangi, tāporepore, tīrehe
pass sentence whakataua(-a)
pass through puta(-ina)
passage putanga, ara, haerenga
passed over hapa
passenger pāhihi
passerby tangata haereere, taha noa

passing tahanga, hīpanga
passing lane arahipa
passion (ardour) tokomauri, aurere, kohara
passionfruit kōhia, riritoki, rīpeka
passionate tūkaha, remurere
passive ngoikore, ngāwari, kūpapa
passport pukapuka uruwhenua
password kupu waitohu, kupuhipa
past wā o mua, wā o nehe
past (the hour) pāhi
pasta parāoa rimurapa
paste pia whakapiri, kuku, whakapiri
pastor minita, hepara, pirihi
pastry tāparaha, pōhā
pasture pātiki karaihe, tarutaru
pat paki(-a), taupaki(-tia), popo
patch (in cloth) pāpaki, pāti
patchwork kōpurepure, kānihinihi
patent (licence) raihana
pathway huanui
pathetic hinapōuri, aroha, koretake
pathfinder kaiārahi
patience manawanui
patient (sick) tūroro
patient care service ratonga atawhai tūroro
patiently mārie, i runga i te rangimārie
patio tūāpapa, rueke
patrol ope tirotiro, tautiaki, tira
patrol car waka rauhī
patronage tautoko
patronise (condescend) whakaparahako
patronise (support) tautoko(-na)
pause okioki, tatari
pavement paeara
pavilion mahau
paw (foot) waewae, matihao
pawpaw (fruit) pōpō
pay utu(-a)
pay attention aro ake
pay heed aro atu
pay visit toro, peka atu
paymaster kaitātari moni
payment utu, utunga
payroll pūtea moni utu kaimahi, rārangi utu
pea huapī, pī
peace rangimārie, āiotanga, maungārongo
peace, make - mau rongo, hohou i te rongo, tahi i te tahua, whakaāio(-hia)
peace keeping pupuri i te rongo
peace offering puruwaha, koha hohou rongo
peaceable āta noho
peacemaker whakaāio whenua
peach pītiti
peacock pīkao
peak tihi, tara, keo
peal tangi pere, tatangi
peanut pīnati
pear pea
pearl peara
pebble kirikiri, kōhatu
peck tongi, timotimo
peculiar (special) motuhake
peculiar (strange) autaia, motuhake
peculiarity rerekētanga
pedal (push) takahi(-a)
pedestrian kaiwaewae, haere raro
pedestrian crossing ara kaiwae, ara hīkoi

pedigree kāwai rangatira, whakapapa
pedlar tangata oruoru, kaihokohoko
pee mimi
peek mātaki, whakataretare
peel (*n.*) kiri
peel (*v.*) waru(-hia), tīhore(-a), pīhore(-hia)
peeler māripi waru, naihi waru
peep tiro, pekī
peer group hunga ōrite
peer through piātaata
peg (*n.*) titi, poupou, tīrau, rawhi
peg (*v.*) titi(-a)
pelican perikana
pellet (shot) pokepoke, hāmoamoa
pelt (throw) epa(-ina), whakaruke(-a), kurukuru
pelvis papatoiake
pen, animal - rāihe, taiapa
pen, writing - pene
penalise whiu(-a)
penalty whiu, hara tautuku
penance mahi ripenetā
pencil pene rākau
pencil sharpener whakakoi pene
pendant hei tiki, hei taringa, koko, tautau
pending taihoa ake nei, tārewa
penetrate uru(-a), wero(-hia), titi(-a), tomo(-kia)
penetrating werowero, poka, uruhanga
penguin pokotiwha, tawhaki, kororā, hōiho
penicillin rongoā paturope
peninsula kūrae, matarae, raenga kuiti
penis ure, tara, tehe, ngarengare, korio
penny kapa
pension penihana
pensioner whai penihana
pensive whai whakaaro, kainatu
pent up kaupēhia
people tangata, iwi, hunga
pep-talk whakahau, whakakorikori
pep-up (animate) whakakaha, kinaki
pepper pepa
peppers (veg.) kikini
per mā, i
per annum ia tau
per capita ia tangata
percent paihēneti, ōrau
perception tirohanga, kitenga
perceptive mōhio, kakama
perch (fish) matuawhāpuku, pohuiakaroa
perch (land on) tau
perch (twig) pae
percolator whakamama kāwhi
percussion taramutanga
perfect pai rawa atu, tika pū
perfection painga rawa atu
perforate whao(-na), wero(-hia)
perforated tūwatawata, ngangengange
perform mahi
performance mahi whakakite (konohete), mahinga
performer kaitutū
perfume (*n.*) rautangi, kakara, taramea
perfume (*v.*) whakakakara
perhaps pea, ekene, akene, puano
peril whakapawera, tata mate
perilous whakamataku, mōrearea

perimeter āwhiotanga, paenga, ripa
period wā, takiwā, tau, wāhanga
period (menstrual) tahe
periodic ia wā ia wā, pokapoka
periscope poutiro
perishable ka pirau
periwinkle pūpū, karahu, tītiko, ngaeti
perjury oati teka
perk painga
perk-up whakaoho, whakakaha
permanent tūturu, pūmau, mō ake tonu atu
permissive whakaae tonu, ngoikore, whakaae ngāwari
permit (*n.*) puka tuku
permit (*v.*) tuku(-a), tuku mana
perpendicular hāngai, rārangi tū, tū tika, poupou tonu
perpetual mutunga kore, pūmau
perpetuate whakapūmau
perpetuity ake tonu atu
perplexed rararu, raru, raupeka
perplexity whakaaro pōaru
persecute whakawhiu(-a), tūkino(-tia), pēi(-a)
persevere tohe(-a)
persevering pāuaua, ngana, urupū, pūnoke
persist tohetohe, tū tonu, nana, whakakeke
persistent taikaha, tū, pūtohe
person tangata, tuakiri, tinana
person, notable - ihorei, rangatira pū, ahurangi
personal taha tangata, whaiaro, matawhaiaro, ā-tangata
personal name tūmoko
personality whaiaro, mauri, tuakiri
personnel officer kaitiaki kaimahi
perspective, from the Māori - ki tā te Māori titiro, ki tā te wairua Māori
perspiration werawera
perspire werawera
persuade whakapati, whakawhere
pest (bug) riha, kīrearea
pest (nuisance) nanakia, hōhā
pester whakahōhā, pākiki, whakatoi
pesticide paihana, patukīrea, patu riha
pet mōkai, mokamōkai
petal raupua
petition īnoinga, petihana
petitioner kaiīnoi, kaipetihana
petrel titi, ōi, korure, kūaka, takahikare
petrify whakakōhatu(-tia)
petrol penehīni, kōhinu
petrol gauge ōrite kōhinu, ine kōhinu
petrol station pā penehīni, pā kōhinu
petticoat panekoti, hītau, āhumehume
phantom kēhua, kīhau, pō mariko
pharmacist kēmihi, kaitaka rongoā, kaiwhakaranu rongoā
phase wā
phase in āta whakauru
phase out whakakore haere
pheasant peihana
phenomenal nui noa atu, tino rerekē, taniwha
phenomenon putanga mīharo, tītohunga

phial ipuipu
philosopher pūkenga
philosophical taumauri
philosophy whakamātau, rapu hinengaro, mātauranga whakaaro
phobia mate wehi, mae
phone whounu, waea kōrero
phoney horihori, whakatau, hāwatewate
phosphorus pūtūtae-whetū
photocopier pūrere whakaahua, mihini tauira whakaahua
photocopy kape whakaahua
photograph (*n.*) whakaahua
photograph (*v.*) tango(-hia) whakaahua
photographer kaitango whakaahua, kaiwhakaahua
phrase kīwaha, kīanga
physical ā-tinana, mataora
physical abuse tūkino ā-tinana
physical contact pā tinana
physical exercise kori tinana
physically handicapped whara
physics ahupūngao
physiotherapy whakaora mirimiri, whāwhā wheua
physique tipu o te tinana
piano piana
piccolo pikoro, pōrutu itiiti
pick (*v.*) whiriwhiri(-a), tīpako
pick at timotimo
pick out (glean) tīpao, tīpakopako
pick out dimly kite rehu
pickaxe keriwhenua, pika
pickle pīkara
picnic pikiniki, pōkeka
picture whakaahua
picture frame kōpari
pictures (cinema) pikitia, whare pikitia
picturesque ātaahua
pie pae
piece wāhi, maramara
piece of string moka taura
piece together raupapa(-tia)
piece, broken off - porohanga
pier aratai
pierce wero(-hia), poka(-ina), hoka(-ina), tioka(-tia)
piercing tīhaehae
piercing noise tioro
piety noho tapu, whakaaro tika, wairua karakia
pig poaka, puaka
pig-dog kurī whakangau
pigeon kūkupa, kererū, kūkū
pigment tae, wai ngārahu, kano
pigskin kiri poaka
pikelet panekeke, paraha, paekete, pōwaitengi
pilchard mohimohi
pile (heap) tahua, pūkai, pūkei, pōkai, putu, putunga
pile (carpet nap) kahupapa
piles (haemorrhoids) tero puta
pilgrim manene
pill pire
pillage kaiā, muru, huhunu
pillar pou
pillow pera, urunga, kōpaki
pillow case pera kēhi
pilot, air - paerata, kaiwhakarere
pilot light pū whakamura, hana
pilot (marine) kaiurungi, paerata, kaiwhakahaere
pilot whale paraki pihi, upokohue
pimple huahua, kiritona, mariao, mokamoka

pin pine(-a), tāpine
pin up pine(-a), whakaahua kōtiro ātaahua
pincers pīnohi, kuku, timo, matihao
pinch kikini(-tia), nonoti (notia), kukuti (kūtia)
pinchbar hua maitai, whiti
pine tree paina, mataī, miro, rimu, kahikatea, kahika
pineapple paināporo, āporopaina
pingpong tēpu tēnehi
pink māwhero
pinnacle tihi, taumata
pinpoint pūwāhi, tongi, tautuhi
pioneer manane, pōkai whenua, tuatahi
pious tapu, kaha ki te karakia
pip kākano, pata, karihi, hira
pipe paipa, kōrere
pipe, musical - pū
piper kaitioro paipa
piper fish hangenge, ihe, kareha, takeke
pirate, sea - paerete, kaiā moana
pistol pītara, pū hurihuri
piston pātuki, kōkeke
piston ring tawhe pātuki, tarawhiti
pit rua, poka, mārua, kōrua
pita bread pāpita, pāpaki
pitch dark pōtangotango, pōuriuri
pitch (field) papatākaro
pitch (throw) epa, kuru, whiu(-a)
pitch of roof hoahoa
pitcher (softball) kaiepa
pith iho
pitiless kino nanakia
pity aroha, āhitu
piupiu flax paritaniwha
pivot takahuri, kaurori
pivotal uptake
pizza parehe
placard pānuitanga
place name tūtakiwā
place (*n.*) wāhi, tūranga, tūnga
place (*v.*) waiho(-ngia), whakatakoto(-ria), maka(-ia)
placeholder puriwāhi
placement whakanoho
placenta ewe, whenua
placid mārire, tū, māhuruhuru
plague urutā
plaice mohoao
plain (clear) mārama
plain (grassland) mānia, raorao
plain (ordinary) noa iho, māori, tōkau, hauarea
plaintiff kaiwhakapae, kaiwhakapā hē
plaintive tīkape
plait whiri(-a), raranga (rangaa)
plan (arrange) whakatakoto tikanga, whakakaupapa(-tia)
plan (scheme) tikanga, kaupapa
plane (tool) waru
planet ao ātea, ruanuku, aorangi
plank papa rākau
planning hanga tikanga, whakatau, whakatakoto kaupapa
plant (cultivate) whakatō(-ngia), ono(-kia)
plant (herb) otaota, tipu, taru
plant (industrial) rawa ahumahi, rawa whakanao(-a)
plantation māra, kāri, tinaku
plaque tohu moko, tuhinga pānui
plaster (*n.*) raima piri
plaster (*v.*) whakapiri, whakapuru, pē
plastic kirihou, paratiki
plastic surgery whakarapa kirihou, whakamōhou kiri

plate pereti
plateau mānia, paepapa
platform pūhara, atamira, tūāpapa, poutaka
play tākaro, kori, purei, hīanga
play (theatrical) mahi whakaari, whakatautau
play dough kerepeti, poikere
play instrument whakatangi(-hia)
play sport hākinakina
play the ball ū ki te poi
playback whakahoki
player kaitākaro
playful hīanga, manahau
playground papa tākaro
playoff whiringa toa
playtime wā tākaro
plead īnoi(-a), tohe(-a)
pleasant āhuareka, reka, pūrotu, hūmārie
please (*v.*) whakawaireka(-tia)
please (as request) me + kupu mahi
pleased pai, manawareka
pleasure hari, koa, mea whakahari
pleat numi(-a), kōnumi, rererua
pledge oati(-tia), takoha, kī taurangi
Pleiades Matariki
plentiful tini, maha, huhua, hira
plenty huhua, maha, tini, hāwere, rahi, nui, makuru
pliable ngāwari, ngohe, kōpē
pliers kūmau
plod takahi
plot (cultivation) ngakinga
plot (*n.*) kaikaiwaiū, kōrero kōhuru, kara
plot (*v.*) kakai(-tia), whakatakoto kara
plotter kaikaiwaiū
plough parau
plover turiwhatu, tuturuata, kohutapu
plover, wry-billed - parore
pluck whawhaki
plug puru, kāremu, purunga
plum paramu
plumb line tēwēwē, whakahāngai
plumber parama, kaiwhakatika ngongo, mataaro kōrere
plump kukune, kunekune, mōmona
plunder muru(-a), pārure
plunge pou(-a), tūpou
plural takitini, kikorua
plus tuku atu, me, tāpiri, āpiti
ply (thickness) paparua, kanoi wūru
plywood rākau kahupapa, rākau kōpē, papatāpatu
pneumonia niumōnia, pūkahu kakā
poach (cook) kōhua, koropupū
pock marked koroputaputa
pocket pākete, pēke, pūkoro
pod pākano
pod of whales kauika
poem (chanted) waiata, pātere, pao, tangi
poem (teaching) oriori, mōteatea
poem (verse) whiti
poet toikupu
point blank tata pū
point, decimal - ira tekau, ira
point, on - of tatangia, tata tonu
point (score) whiwhinga, māka
point, sharp - koi, tara, tongi, matamata
point, what's the - ! hei aha!
pointer tokotoko tohu, ngira, atatohu

pointless koretake, wairangi, heahea, kikokore
poise tū rangatira
poison paitini, paihana, tāoke
poke wero(-hia), koko
poker machine pūrere hao
poker, game of - hipikāri, poka
polar bear pea poara
pole-vault tūtoko
Police, N.Z. - Ngā Pirihimana o Aotearoa, Ope Pirihimana, Ratonga Pirihimana
police station teihana pirihimana
policeman pirihimana
policy take whakahaere, kaupapahere, mahere
polio mate iotuarā, whakamemeke
polish whakapiata(-tia)
polite manaaki, ngāwari, huatau
political whakaara ture, tōrangapū, whakahaere-ā-tangata
political party rōpū tōrangapū
politician kaitōrangapū, mema pāremata
politics tōrangapū
poll tatau pōti
pollen hae, kōnehu
pollinate whakaaiai, haetanga, rui hae
pollutant para whakakino
pollute poke(-a), whakanoa(-tia)
pollution parahanga, paru, tiko, pokenga, tūkinotanga
Polynesia Moutere o te Moana-nui-a-Kiwa
Polynesian Porinihia, nō ngā Moutere
polytechnic kuratini
pompous whakamanamana, whakahīhī, aweawe
pond punawai, hāroto
ponderous taumaha
pontoon kōrewa, poranga
pony kuao hōiho, poniponi
pool hōpua wai, kōpua
pool, swimming - terenga
pool, thermal - waiariki, puia
poor (mediocre) koretake, kei raro iho
poor (needy) rawakore, pōhara, tuakoka
poor land whenua pākeka
pop pakō, patō
pop group tira pūoru, pēne manako
pop in (visit) peka atumai
pop out puta ki waho
popcorn kānga pāhūhū
Pope Pāpā, Pōpa
poplar pāpara
popular kaingākau, pai ki te katoa, manakohia
popularity rongonui
populate nohonoho
porch roro, whakamahau
pork mīti poaka
porous pōareare, koropungapunga
porpoise pāpahu, aihe, tūpoupou
porridge pāreti
port (harbour) tauranga poti, taunga tima, tauranga
port, computer - kōhao tūhono
portable taea te hiki, whakanekeneke, hīkawe
porter kaiāwhina, kaiamo, kaihari, rōpā
pose tūranga, whakarārangi
position tūranga, takotoranga, tūnga
position, in a - to āhei

positive inetahi, tau ake, tōrunga, tōhiko
possess whiwhi, whai (mea)
possession taputapu, rawa, taonga
possessive weu tohu pānga
possibility tūponotanga, āheinga
possible tae(-a), āhei
possibly pea
possum paihamu
post (mail) mēra, pōhi
Post, N.Z. - Poutāpeta
post office poutāpeta
post mortem tirotiro tūpāpaku, uiuinga tūpāpaku
postage stamp pane kuini/kīngi
postal ā mēra
postcard pānuituku, kāri
postcode tātai poutāpeta, waehere poutāpeta
poster ikitia pānui, pānui whakaahua
posterity uri whakatupu, whakatupuranga
posthumous murimate
postie kaiamo mēra
postmaster poumāhita
posture tū
pot kōhua, pāta, pātara, tīhake
pot plant otaota ipu
pot-bellied pukutihe, pukuwheti, porohatete, torohū
potassium konurehu
potato rīwai, taewa, parareka, rua
potato masher pehu rīwai, penu taewa
potato peeler tahi rīwai, tahi taewa
potency kahanga, pakaritanga
potential pūmanawa moe
pothole kōhao
potted meat huahua
potter kaipokepoke, kerepeti
pottery pokepoke uku, tārai kōhua, matapaia, kerepeti
potty paepae pēpi
pouch pūkoro, kopa
poultry heihei
pound (beat) tuki(-a), pao(-a), kuru(-a), āki(-na)
pound (money/weight) pāuna
pour riringi (ringihia), maringi, tārutu, tāhoro
pour in popou
pouring rain ua tātā, pūpūwai
poverty mūhore
poverty stricken rawakore, tuakoka
powder nehu, paura
powder, gun - paura wāwāhi
power kaha, ngoi, mana whakahaere, ihi
power (maths) pū
power, electric - hiko
power line waea hiko
power point kohao hiko
power station pāhiko
powerful kaha rawa, ngoi
powerless ngoikore, hangenge, rōrā
practise akoako
practise (rehearse) whakatū, whakawai, whakaharatau
praise whakapai(-ngia), mihi, whakamoemiti(-tia), whakamihi(-a)
pram waka hari pēpi
prawn koura
pray īnoi(-a)
prayer īnoinga, karakia
pre- i mua i
pre-school education mātauranga kōhungahunga

P

preach kauwhau(-tia)
precaution whakatūpato
precious kahurangi
precipice tūpari, pari
precipitous paripari, hūkere
precise pū
precision tika pū
preconceived idea whiriwhiringa noa, whakawā noa
predecessor tōmua
predetermined whakatakotoria
predict matakite, tiro ki mua, waitohu, poropiti(-tia), matapae
prediction matakitenga, titiro whakamua, matapae
predisposition whakaaro tītaha
preface whakataki
prefect piriwheke, kaihono
prefer hiahia, pai kē, whiriwhiri
pregnant hapū
prehistoric onamata
prejudice whakawā wawe, whakatoihara
prejudicial whakatītaha
preliminary whakataki
preliminary round whiringa
premature waitau, mata
premier (leader) pirimia
premonition waimate
prepare whakatau(-ria), whakatika(-hia), whakarite
prepare food taka kai
prepayment utu tōmua mai
Presbyterian Perehipiteriana
preschool, Maori - kōhanga reo
prescribe whakaatu rongoā
prescription puka rongoā, rongoā i whakahaua, perehana
presence aroaro, mana
presence of mind taumauri, tauwhiro
present (*n.*) koha, whakaaro, mea homai, taonga hei tukunga
present (*v.*) tāpae(-tia), whakaatu(-ria)
presentation whakaaturanga, tukunga
presenter kaipānui
preserve tohu(-ngia), tiaki(-na)
preside whakahaere (komiti)
presidency tūnga perehitini
president perehitini, tumuaki
press conference hui pāpaho
press down pēpehi
press (journalism) perēhi, niupepa
press (squeeze) pēhanga, pēhi(-a), tāmi(-a), inaki(-tia)
press noses hongi
pressure pēhanga, tāmi
pressure cooker kōhua perēhi
prestige mana
presumptuous whakahīhī
pretence whakataunga, tinihanga, takunetanga
pretend māminga, hangarau, takune
pretext whakatakune
pretty ātaahua, pūrotu
prevailing pūmau
prevailing wind hau ukiuki
prevent ārai(-a), aukati(-a), whakahōtaetae
preview kite wawe, arokite
previous mātua (before verb), tōmua
prey ika, patunga, kai
price utu
priceless kāmehameha, kore e taea te utu
prick wero(-hia)
prickly taratara, koikoi, tiotio
pride whakahīhī, whakapehapeha

priest pirihi, tohunga, amokapua, amorangi
primary tuatahi, mātua, mātāmua
primary objective tino kaupapa
primary school kura tuatahi
prime tino pai rawa
prime minister pirimia
primeval nonamata, tua whakarere
primitive pūhungahunga, kōkau
prince piriniha
princess pirinitete
principal mātua
principal (head) tumuaki
principle kaupapa, tikanga, mātāpono, pono
print (publish) tā(-ia), perēhi(-tia)
print (script) tuhi mātoha
printer (machine) pūrere tā, purueretā
printer (person) kaitā
printing press pūrere tā, perehi
prior i mua
priorities, its/his - āna mahi nui
priority, high - tino take
prise open kōwhiti
prism tapatoru pīataata, pororua tapa
prison whare herehere
prisoner mauhere
private puku, tapu, tūmataiti
private bag pouaka motuhake
privilege hōnore, painga, rawa
privileged whakapaingia kē, whakarangatira
prize (*n.*) paraihe, kaingākau, kahurangi, parakete
prize (*v.*) kaingākau, matapōpore
prize-giving tukunga paraihe
prized possession iti kahurangi, hei māpuna
probability tūponotanga, heipū
probable pea
probably inā pea, tēnā pea
probate whakamau wira
probation tuku whakamātau, poropeihana, tuku matakana
probation officer pou-awhi
probationer tangatanga, tangata e whakamātauria ana
probe rangahau(-a), wero(-hia)
problem panga, rapanga, mate, raruraru
procedure huarahi, raupapa mahi, tikanga
proceed whānui haere, whano, haere atu anō, tahuri
proceeds moni hua
processing tukanga, mahi whakatika
procession kapa, porohēhio
proclaim pānui
proclamation pānuitanga
procreate ai(-tia), whakatō(-kia), whakawhānau(-tia)
produce (product) hua
producer kaiwhakaari
product hua, otinga
production whakanaonga, whanonga
profession umanga, mahi-ā-ngaio
professional ahorangi, ngaio, tohunga
professor ahorangi, pūkenga, tohunga toihau
proficiency tohu
proficient matatau, tohunga, kakama
profile kōtaha, anga whakaaturanga
profit hua (moni)

P

profitable whai hua
profitless kore hua
profound hōhonu
profuse maha, tini, huhua
progeny uri, aitanga
program (computer) papatono
programme (TV) whakaari, whakahaere
progress kauneke, anga whakamua, neke atu
project (scheme) kaupapa, kaupane
projection (bulge) kohuki
projectionist kaiwhiti pikitia
projector pūwhiti āhua
prologue tuwheratanga, kupu whakataki
prolong kumeroa
prominent nui, whakahira, whakarae, kōhure
promise oati(-tia), kī taurangi, whakaari(-a)
promote tautoko(-tia), whakatairanga(-tia), whakahauhau
promotion kakenga, hāpainga, whakawhānui, whakapakari
prompt (punctual) wawe, moata, horo, tere
prongs mārau, kōrapu
pronoun huanga kē, tūkapi
pronounce whakahua(-tia)
proof (evidence) tohu pono, whakaponotanga, hāponotanga
prop tautoko(-na), tokotoko, tauteka, poutoko
propel pei, pana, tītoko
propeller hurirere, pōwaiwai
proper tika, arotau
property (characteristic) āhuatanga
prophet poropiti, porohēte
prophetic matakite
proportion ōwehenga, hāngai rite
propose tono(-a), kī(-ia), whakatakoto, mōtini
propulsion āki, peinga, pananga
prosecute tuku ki te kōti
prosecutor kaiwhiu, kaiwhakapae
prospector kaihaurapa
prospects takahanga, huarahi, tūmanako
prosper tupu, whai hui
prosperity tōnuitanga
prosperous whai rawa, whai taonga
prostate repe tātea, repe ure
prostitute kairau, wahine pūremu
prostitution mahi kairau
prostrate tuku papa, tīraha, whakaparure
protect whakangungu(-a), whakaruruhau
protection pad aupuru
protective gear pānga ārai, parekiri
protein poroutīni, pūmua
protest amuamu, tautohe, tohetohe
Protestant Porotehana
protester kaitohe, hunga whakahē, waha tautohe
protocol kawa, tikanga i whakaaetia, kaupapa
proud whakahīhī, whakakake
proud of ngākaunui ki
prove hāpono(-tia), whakamātautau, whakapono(-hia)
proverb whakataukī, whakatauākī
provide service tuku ratonga

providence manaakitanga
provider kaihoatu, kaiwhāngai
province porowini
provisions kai, ō mō te huarahi
provisions, dried - paka
provocation whakatakariri, whakatenetene, mātoatoa
provocative kōrero taki, tuki, taunanawe
provoke whakataritari, whakariri, pātari
prowl whakamoka, ninihi
proxy rīwhi, māngai
prudent tūpato, whai whakaaro
prune (cut) kokoti (kotia), whakaiti(-tia), kaikawau
prune (fruit) kano nīkau maroke, paramu kūreherehe
psalm waiata, hāmi
pseudo whakatakune, whakakitoika
pseudonym ingoa tuhi, ingoa kē
psychiatrist rata mate pōrangi
psychic matakite
psychologist rata mate hinengaro, tohunga hinengaro
psychology mātai hinengaro, mātauranga hinengaro tangata
pub hōtēra, paparakaute
puberty pukehuruhuru, pakaritanga
public iwi whānui, ā-iwi, hunga tūmatanui
public, make - pānui(-tia), hora(-hia), whakapuare(-tia)
public service ratonga mahi ā-iwi, mahi a te kāwanatanga
public works mahi mō te katoa
publish pānui(-tia), perēhi(-tia), tauaki(-tia)
pudding purini
puddle tōhihi
puerile heahea, mahi tamariki
puff puhipuhi
puffball tūtae atua
pugnacious ririhau, puku ngangare
pull kukume (kumea), tō(-ia), kurari(-hia)
pull apart heu(-a), wehe(-a)
pull down turaki(-na)
pull faces pūkana, tārera, whāita
pull opposite taukumekume
pull up (hoist) huhuti (hūtia), kōhiti(-tia), nuku(-hia), hiki(-tia)
pull up (stop) tū
pullet pīpi heihei
pulley tauru, tuarā, wira whakanuku
pullover puraka
pulp puru, kōrapu, karukaru
pulpy kōpē
pulsate patupatu, kapakapa, pātuki
pulse hotu manawa, manawa o te ringa, mokohiti o te ia toto
pulverise tāpāpā, ngotangota, hungahunga
pumice pungapunga, koropungapunga, tahoata
pump mapu, papu, pana hau
pumpkin paukena
punch meke(-a), pangu(-a), kuru(-a), moto(-kia)
punch (tool) panihi
punctual ū, ki te taima, tae mua, ki te haora i whakaritea
punish whiu(-a)
pupil (eye) whatu
pupil (student) ākonga, tauira
puppet karetao, kararī, tare pekepeke

P

puppy kūao kurī, punua kurī, papī
purchase hoko(-na) mai
purchaser kaihokohoko
pure mā, urutapu, harakore, horomata
purge pure(-a), horoi(-a), muru(-a)
purged oti te pure
purify mea(-tia) kia mā, horoi(-a), whakapai(-ngia)
purity horomatanga
purple pāpura, pōkere
purpose, for what -? he aha ai?
purpose whāinga poto, tikanga
purr ngunguru
purse pāhi, pēke, pūkoro
pursue aru(-mia), whaiwhai(-a)
pursuit (chase) whāinga, arumanga
pus ero, pirau
push pana(-ia), pei(-a), akiaki(-na)
puss (cat) puihi
put waiho(-tia), maka(-ia), uta(-ina)
put down (deposit) tuku(-a) ki raro
put forward whakapuaki, neke whakamua
put into practice whakatinana(-tia)
put on (don) whakamau(-a), whakakākahu(-tia), kuhu(-a), unu(-hia)
put on weight whakamōmona
put out (quench) tinei(-a), poko
put out tongue whātero
put together apiti(-tia), huihui(-a), whakakaupapa
putrefy whakaero, pirau
putrid piro, pirapirau, kerakera
puzzle panga, kai
puzzled kūraruraru, whakapōauau
puzzling manganga, autaia
pygmy tauwhena
pyjamas kākahu moe
pylon pou hiko
pyramid piramiti, whanga tapatoru
python paihona, nākahi korōi

Q

quack kēkē, koaka
quadrangle tapawhā, wāhi tapawhā
quadriplegic pararutiki, hauā pekewhā
quagmire repo, pōwharu, mawharu, wharu
quail koreke, koitareka, tāreka, kōriki, kuera
quaint rerekē, autaia
quake wiriwiri
quake, earth - rūwhenua
qualifications tohu mātauranga, reta tautoko
qualified whai tohu mātauranga
quality pai, huanga, tikanga rangatira, kounga
quality of life oranga tinana, pai o te noho
quarantine wehenga ārai mate, pūrei kararehe
quarrel kowhete, ngarengare
quarrelsome tumatuma, totohe, whakatenetene
quarry, stone - takere, rua keri kōhatu, tākongakonga
quarter koata, hauwhā
quartet tokowhā kaiwaiata
quartz kiripaka, matā, takawai
quay tauranga poti
queasy whakapai ruaki
queen kuini
queer rerekē, tāne moe tāne
quench (fire) whakaweto, tinei(-a)
quench (thirst) mākona, ngata
query pātai, uiui(-a)
quest kimihanga, rapu ara
question pātai(-ngia), ui(-a), urupounamu
questionable pāhekeheke
questionaire rārangi pātai
queue rārangi tangata, tira, tūtira
quick hohoro, tere, kakama
quickly wawe
quicksands ōi, repo
quiet hū, wahangū, hāngū, waimarie, māhaki
quietly āta noho, mārie, mauru, haupepe
quicken whakahoro
quilt kuira, papanārua
quince kuinihi
quintet tokorima
quirk rerekētanga, tautahitanga
quit whakamutu, wehe atu, riro atu, wātea
quite mārika, tika pū, tika rere, āhua + *adjective*
quiver (flutter) kakapa, wiriwiri, oreore, korikori
quiver of arrows pūkoro pere
quiver the hands whākapakapa, aroarowhaki, wiriwiri
quiz kēmu patapatai, pākiki
quota wāhanga, whāinga hautonga
quotation kōrero, āna ake kupu, pepeha
quotation marks tohu kī, pikorua

R

rabbi rapi
rabbit rāpeti
rabble hunga ware, tūtūā
race (contest) tauwhāinga, tauomaoma, whakataetae, omanga
race (ethnic group) iwi, momo iwi
race course papa purei hoiho
race relations noho-ā-iwi
racial ā iwi
racism whakahāwea iwi, aukati iwi
rack, clothes - iri kākahu, mātiti
racquet rākete
radar hihiani, whakaata pāoro
radial pūmoka
radiance mataaho, pīataata, kōrekoreko
radiant kanapa, kanapu, mārama, tiaho, aho
radiate tiaho, wherawhera
radiation tokowhiti, parawhiti, pūhihi, ira rukeruke
radiation sickness mate iratuki
radiator retieta, whakapongi, whakamahana
radical wāwāhi tikanga, whakaaro hōhonu
radio reo irirangi
radio wave hihi irirangi
radioactive ira tukituki, ira rukeruke
radish rarihi, rātihi
radium konutuki, konuruke
radius pū moka, pūtoro, āpiti, kāpiti
raffle rāwhera(-tia)
raft mōki, mōkihi, kahupapa heke
rafter heke
rag ruha, karukaru, maramara
rage riri, nguha
ragged taretare
ragwort ranglora
raid whakatorotoro, huaki(-na)
raider kaipahua, ope huaki, marau
rail rēra, pouheni, rōau, puringaringa
railway rērewē
rain ua(-ina), marangai, kōuaua
rain, heavy - āwhā
rainforest ngāhere ua, waoku, Waotūnui-a-Tāne
rainbow kōpere, āniwaniwa, uenuku, atua piko, kahukura
raincoat meketoiho, tāporena, pākē, koti ua
raindrop patapata ua
raise hāpai(-tia), whakarewa(-tia), hiki(-na), whakatū(-ria)
raise (bring up) whakatupu
raise eyebrows rewha, pewa
raise money kohikohi moni, mahi moni
raise the flag tare te haki
raised morunga
rake rakaraka, rakuraku, hirou
rally hui
ram (*v.*) tuki(-a)

ram (male sheep) hipi toa, rāme
ramble haere noa iho, haerēre, ānau
ramification kōtititanga, rara, peka
ramp ara rōnaki
rancid pirau
rancour pukuriri, mauāhara
random noa, poka noa, mata pōkere, tupurangi
range (scope) whānuitanga, momo āhuatanga
range, mountain - pae maunga, tuarā maunga
range, statistical - ine whānui
ranged in order tūtira, tōtai
rank data whakaripa
rank (position) tūranga
ransack muru(-a), hunuhunu(-a)
ransom utu, utu tuku
rap (fast monologue) pātere, ngeri
rap (hit) patupatu, pātōtō
rape pawhera(-tia), pahera(-tia), raweke(-tia)
rapid horo, tere
rapids tāheke
rapier hoari matire
rapist kaipahera, kairaweke wahine
rare (uncommon) torutoru, puiaki, onge, rerengatahi
rash, skin - kōpukupuku, tongatonga uri, uiranui, harehare
rasp rāpare, rakuraku, wharo, ngakeke, harakuku
rasp (tool) tīwani, waru
raspberry rāhipere
rat kiore
ratchet hāupa
ratepayer kaiutu reiti
rates, property - tāke nohoanga, reiti
rather (instead of) otirā, engari (with negative)
ratify whakamana
ratio ōwehenga, taupāpātanga
ration wāhanga
rattle tatangi, tatetate(-a), patatō
rave tīhāhā, whakahāhā
ravenous warawara, hemokai
raw mata, ota, torouka
ray (type of fish) whai, whai keo, whai repo, mātā
ray of sunlight hihi, ihiihi
razor heu
razor blade mataheu
reach (arrive at) tae atu ki, tūpono, tutuki
reach land ū, tae ki uta
reach out totoro (toroa)
react tāwhana, tauaro, urupare, tautohe
read kōrero pukapuka, rīti, pānui(-tia)
reader kaipānui, kaikōrero pukapuka
readiness rite, takatū
readjust whakamau(-a) anō, whakatika anō
ready rite, reri, takatū
real tino
realise huatau, mōhio(-tia)
realistic tika, whai kiko ana
reality pono, ā tinana, tino pono
reap hauhake(-a), kokoti(-a)
reappear puta anō, ea anō
rear (stern) muri, hiku
rear-vision mirror whakaata muri
rearguard whakatautopenga, pūmanawa, muriope

reason (basis) take, pūtake, kaupapa, tikanga
reasonable whaitake, ngākau whai whakaaro
reassurance oranga ngākau
reassure tautoko(-tia), whakamāmā, whakaahuru
rebate whakahoki(-a) moni
rebel (*n.*) hunga tutū, hunga whakakeke
rebel (*v.*) mahi tutū, whakaeke whawhai
rebellious tutū, whakatoi, whana
rebound tāwhanawhana, turupā
rebuff ākiri(-tia), whakarere(-a), kape(-a)
rebuild hanga anō, hiki anō
rebuke kohete(-tia), whakatūpehupehu
recall (re-appoint) whakatū anō
recall (remember) mahara
recapture whakamau anō
recede hoki haere, timu
receipt puka whakamana utu, tohu atu, kāwhiwhi, rīhīti
receive tango(-hia) mai, whiwhi
receiver kaitango
recent hou, nō nā noa nei, inatatanei, ngātata tonu
recently inā tata nei, nō ko tonu ake nei, inakuarā
receptacle paepae, oko rāpihi
reception (party) hui pōwhiri, hākari
reception (radio) tangi mai, tangohanga
receptionist kaiwhakatau manuhiri, taupaepae, kiripaepae
recess (break) wā whakatā, hiki
recession wā kore mahi, whakahekenga wāriu, kairuaki
recidivist kairuaki
recipe tohu tao, tikanga tunu kai
recipient kaitango, kaiwhiwhi
reciprocal hokohoko, tāutuutu, tau taupoki
recite whakahua(-tia), takitaki, tataku, takutaku, whiti(-a)
reckless wairangi, pōrangi, nanakia
reclaim tono(-a) anō
reclamation whakaū whenua, tāmata whenua
recline tīpapa, tīraha, takoto
recluse mohowao, moke
recognise mōhio(-tia), hukahuka, āhukahuka
recoil tākiri, whana whakamuri, tupana
recollect mahara(-tia)
recommend tohutohu, whakahau, tautoko ā-kupu
recompense whakahoki(-a), muru(-a)
reconciled māha, tau te rangimārie
reconciliation maungarongo
recondition whakahou(-ngia), tapi(-a)
reconnoitre torotoro, hunuhunu
reconsider āta taute, whakaaro anō
reconstruct hanga hou(-tia), whakatū anō
record (disc) kōpae pūoro
recorder, tape - rekoata, mīhini hopu reo
records, written - pepa whai tikanga, mauhanga
recover whakaora
recreation whakangahau, hākinakina, mahi ngahau
recreational hākinakina

recrimination whakapae, whakawā
recruit (*n.*) hōia hou, kaimahi hou, ika tauhou
recruit (*v.*) taritari ope, kimi tangata, kimi kaimahi, haina
rectangle tapawhā tākonga, tapawhā hāngai
rectify whakatika(-hia)
rectum tero, tongatiko, tou
recumbent takoto ana
recur riro anō, hokihoki
recycle whakahou(-tia), huri (kēne/pepa)
red whero, kura
red admiral pūrerehua, kahukura, pūrehurehu, pēpepe mōrea
red blood cell toto pūwhero
red cod hoka
red feather kura
red glow pākura, umurangi
red ochre kōkōwai
red pine rimu
red-haired urukehu
redeem hoko(-na), utu(-a), whakaora
redeemer kaiwhakaora
redeployment tohatohanga
redevelop whakahou, whakapai anō, hanga(-ia) anō
red hot mumura
redistribute tītari anō, tohatoha anō, rato
redoubt pā tūwatawata, pā kaha, pā tūhāhā
redress whakamāhea, utu(-a)
reduce whakaiti(-tia), whakaheke
redundancy pay utu whakamutu mahi, utu hapanga
redundant kore mahi, hapa, tāwere
reduplication pūruatanga, whakahuahua
reed kākaho, kuta, tohetohe
reef toka pūkawa, tāhuna, ākau, pūkawa
refer the matter tuku(-a), tono(-a), whakamōhio
referee rewheri, kaiwawao
reference (apropos) whakapānga
reference, our - tohu mai
reference, your - tohu atu
referendum pōtitanga, whakataunga-ā-iwi, tāpaetanga pōti
refill whakakī anō
reflection whakaata, ataata, atārangi
reflex action tāwhana, whetau, kahuki
reflex angle koki mowaho, koki hāpūpū rawa
reform whakahou(-ngia)
reformation whakahounga, whakatikanga
reformer kaiwhakahou
refresh oneself whakangā, whakahauora, tāmata
refrigerator whiriti, pātaka mātao, whata mātao
refuge piringa, rerenga, kohanga, punanga
refugee rerenga, manene
refund whakahoki moni
refusal whakakorenga, kore whakaae, kapenga
refuse (deny) whakakāhore(-tia), tohe(-a), whakapeka, kape
regarding mō, mō te taha ki a
regardless matakūare, manawarere, hīkaka
regenerate tipu anō, whakaora

R

regeneration tupu hou
regime tikanga whakahaere
region rohe, wāhi, takiwā, whaitua, wā
regional ā-rohe
register rēhita, kaituhi
registration rēhitatanga, whakauru
regret aroha(-tia), pā pōuri, kōnohi, āwhitu
regretful pouri, manawapā
regular rite tonu, auau
regulation (govt.) ture tuku a te (kāwanatanga)
rehabilitation whakanohonoho, whakaaurakitanga
rehearse whakaharatau
reimburse whakahoki utu
reincarnation whānau hou
reinforce whakakaha(-ngia), tautoko(-tia), whakapakari(-tia)
reins paraire, reina, taura
reject ākiri(-tia), whakarere(-a)
rejoice hari, koa
relapse pārore, ngoikore haere, matahoki
relating to pā ana ki
relationship with people whakaipotanga, tūranga whānau
relative (kin) whanaunga, uri tata, karawa, huānga
relax whakatā, whakangā, tīraha whakamuri
relaxation okioki, whakatā
relaxed pārore, parohe, mākohakoha
release (free) tuku(-a) kia haere, puta(-ina), wetewete(-a)
relentless (nature) papahūeke
relentless (person) kaikiko
relevant hāngai pū ana, e pā ana ki, mōhio hāngai
reliable mau tonu, ū, taea te whakawhirinaki atu, pono, tika
relics taonga tuku iho, taonga tapu, ohaoha
relief (ease tension) rangimārie, whakangāwari, whakamāmā, oranga ngākau
religion whakapono, hāhi
relish kīnaki, whakarehu
reload whāngai anō
reluctant kōroiroi, koroukore, whakakumu
rely on whakawhirinaki(-tia)
remain (left over) toe
remain (stay) noho
remains toenga
remake mahi hou(-tia)
remand mau ki te whare herehere
remark (*n.*) kupu, kōrero
remark (*v.*) whai kupu
remarkable mīharo, hautupua
remember mahara(-tia) ki, maumahara(-tia)
remembrance whakamaharatanga, manatu
remind whakamahara(-tia)
reminisce kōrero whakamahara, whakahoki mahara
remit (cancel) muru(-a)
remittance moni tukua
remorse pāmamae, pōuritanga
remorseless kaikiko, whakaweriweri, autaia
remote kei tawhiti, mamao, pāmamao, tūhāha
remote control pūataata mamao
removal nekehanga, tangohanga
remove (take) tango(-hia)

rename tapa hou(-tia), whakarerekē te ingoa
rendezvous tūtakitanga, rauhītanga, taupunipuni
renegade kaituku, kaikaiwaiū
renew whakahou(-ngia)
renewal whakahoutanga
renounce whakarere(-a), papare(-a)
renovate whakahou(-ngia), hanga hou(-tia)
rent (hire) rīhi
reorientate whakahuri(-hia), anga
repair whakapai(-ngia), whakatika(-hia)
repay utu
repeal whakakore
repeat (recite) takitaki
repeated tāruarua, auau, toai
repel pana, ārai atu, whakahoe
repellant atiati
repent rīpenetā(-tia), pōuri(-tia)
repentance rīpenetatanga
repercussion rarā, paorotanga
repetition tukurua, tāruatanga
replace whakahoki(-a), whakakapi, whakahou(-tia)
replacement whakakapinga
replica kape, tukurua
reply whakahoki(-a), whakautu(-a)
report pūrongo, whakataunga, rīpoata, rongo kōrero
reporter kaituhi pūrongo, kairipoata
repossess taumanu taonga, tango, muru
representative māngai, kaihautū, repe
repress pēhi(-a), aupēhi(-a), tāmi, pei ki raro
reprieve tohu(-ngia)
reprisal ngaki utu, rautupu
reproduce whakahua tuarua(-tia), hanga hou(-tia)
reproduction aitanga, whānautanga, hanga(-a)
reptile ngārara, ngāngara
repudiate whakarere(-a), ākiri(-tia), whakaparahako
repugnant weriweri, kawa
repulse pana(-ia), ārai atu
repulsive wetiweti, wehiwehi, mōrikarika
reputation rongo, ingoa pai
request īnoi(-a), tono(-a)
require hiahia(-tia), whakatakoto(-ria)
require staff whai kaimahi, whai āpiha
requirement mea tonoa, whakaritenga
requisition tangohanga, taumaunga
rescue whakaora(-ngia)
rescue breathing hā whakaora
rescuer kaiwhakaora
research rangahau(-a), hurapa, rapuraputanga
researcher kairangahau, kairapurapu
resemblance ritenga
resemble rite ki, āhuahua
resent tūkino(-tia)
resentful mānatunatu
resentment mauāhara, hīkaka
reservation (booking) nohoanga
reservation (sanctuary) wāhi tapu, rāhui
reservoir kurawai nui, hikuwai
resign tuku(-a) te tūranga, rihaina(-tia)

resignation, feeling - ngākau māha
resilient ngāwari, tāwhana, ngohe, manahau
resin kāpia, māpara
resist whawhai atu, riri(-a), ārai(-a), papare
resistance parepare, tohenga, ātetehanga, pare ārai
resolution whakataunga, mōtini
resort, last - parepare whakamutunga
resound pāoro
resource puna taonga, whakaipurangi, pūtea
resources, natural - hua-ā-Papatuanuku, rawa taiao, rawa whenua
respect, treat with - whakanui(-a), manaaki(-tia), aroha atu
respectable noho tika
respected whakahōnoretia, rongonuitia
respond whakautu, urupare(-a), anga ki
response whakautu, urupare, whakahoki, tāoro
responsibility mana whakahaere, kawenga
rest (relax) okioki, whakangā, whakatā
rest (remainder) toenga
restful mārie, whakaaio
resting place okiokinga, tauranga, taumata
restitution whakaritenga, whakahoki taonga, utunga
restless okeoke, tūtehu, tourepa, tūrama
restore whakahoki(-a), whakaora, whakahou(-ngia)
restrain pupuri (puritia), here(-a), whakatina(-ia)
restrained ārikarika, whakatikia
restraint herenga, whakaita, tautāwhi, puritanga
restrict kukuti (kūtia), whakatiki(-a)
restriction aukatinga, tikanga whakatiki
restructure whakahou(-tia)
result tukunga iho, hua
resume tīmata anō, haere anō
resumé whakarāpopotonga, tauākirongo
resurface (pop up) whakaea anō
resurface (tar-seal) hīra hou, hīpoki anō
resurrect whakaara ake anō
resurrection aranga ake
resuscitation whakaora anō, whakahauora(-tia)
retain pupuri (puritia), mau
retaliate rapu utu, rautipu
retard whakatū, punga(-a)
retarded kāore i pūāwai
retarded (mentally) pōhauhau, rorirori, pungā
retention pupuri, mau, tango, rūnā
retentive maumahara, kakama
retire (withdraw) hoki whakamuri
retire from work wātea te tūranga
retrace hīkoi whakamuri
retract unu(-hia), kume(-a)
retreat (go back) hoki whakamuri, hokinga, taui
retreat (refuge) piringa, punanga
retrieve tiki(-na) atu, tīki(-na), whakahoki(-a)
retrograde kino iho
return (give back) whakahoki(-a)

return (go back) hoki, auraki
returns (profits) hua
reunion tūtakitanga hoa, huinga anō
reveal whakakite(-a)
revenge utu, rapu utu, ngaki mate
revenge, get - rapu utu, ea, whai takapau
revenged ea (te mate)
revengeful kaikiko
revenue whiwhinga tāke
revere hopohopo, whakahōnore
reverent tapu, whakakoha
reversal hokinga whakamuri, whakahokinga
reverse hoki whakamuri
revert hoki(-a)
review mātaki(-tia), tiro(-hia)
review, written - tātaritanga ā-puka
revile taunu(-tia), whakahāwea
revise whakapai ake
revision whakahounga
revitalize whakahou(-tia)
revival aranga anō, whakakorikori anō
revive whakaora(-ngia), whakahauora(-tia), whakahou(-tia)
revived paiake
revoke whakakāhore(-tia)
revolt tutū, whakarere, whana
revolting (horrid) whakarihariha
revolution (uprising) tutū, whananga, pāhoro
revolutionary kiriweti, whakawhana
revolve takahuri, huri(-hia)
revolver pūhuri
revue konohete
reward utu
rewind takai anō
rhetoric whai kōrero
rheumatism rūmātiki, kaikōiwi, uhumona
rhinoceros rinorino
rhubarb rūpapa
rhythm mita
rib kaokao, rara, tāiki
ribbon rīpene
ribbonwood hoihere, houhere
rice raihi
rich whai taonga, whai rawa, mōmona
rid whakawātea, maka(-ia)
riddance whakarerenga, makanga
riddle panga, makitaunu
riddled putaputa, pōkarakara
ride bareback kopi kau
rider (jockey) kaieke
ridge hiwi, pae maunga, tārawa, ripa
ridgepole tāhuhu
ridicule whakahāwea, whakarōrā
ridiculous rorirori, rōrā, wawau
rife mui(-a)
rifle raiwhara
rift whatinga
right (correct) tika, tōtika
right, individual - mana tangata, rangatiratanga, whai take
right, serves you - kaitoa
rights, human - tikanga tangata, mana tangata
rigid torotika, mārō
rigorous pakeke
rim ngutu, tapa
rind (peel) hiako, peha, kiri
ring, boxing - papa mekemeke
ring (circle) rīngi, porohita, mōwhiti
ring bell tangi, whakatangi(-hia)

ring-finger manawa
ringlet māwhatu
ringworm muna
rink (bowls) ara maita
rinse horoi(-a), opeope
riot whakatupu raruraru, whakatutū
rioter hunga kakai
riotous torere kino
rip pāwhara(-tia), tīhae(-a), tīhore(-tia), haehae
rip, tidal - kauere
ripe maoa, tāngōngō, māngaro
ripple kōriporipo, okori, okiri, kare, pōkarekare
rise (go upwards) eke, piki, rewa
rise and shine hī(-a)
rise from sleep ara, maranga
rise of emotions tokotū, pupū
rising ground pānaki, tuahiwi, pāhaki
risk tata mate, whakararu
rite karakia, tikanga tapu, pure
ritual karakia
rival hoa tauwhāinga, tāwhai
rivalry haetanga, tauwhāinga
river awa
riverbank parenga, tāhuna, paretai
riverbed whaiawa
riverside pārengarenga
rivet whao rino, rīwiti
road huarahi, ara, rori, huanui
road code tikanga huarahi
road-block aukati, ārai huarahi, whakatūtaki ara, tūtaki ara
roads, cross - pūtahi
roadside taharori, tohu haere ara
roam haerēre, āmio haere
roar rarā, haruru, pararē, horu tai
roast tunu(-a), parahunu
roast on spit hukihuki(-a)
rob tāhae(-tia), whenako(-tia), whānako(-tia)
robber tāhae, kaimuru
robe kākahu rangatira, pueru
robin pītoitoi, toutouwai
rock (lurch) whakapiopio
rock (stone) kāmaka, toka, kōhatu, kōwhatu
rock cod taumaka, rāwaru
rocket rākete, tākirirangi, karuru
rod katira, matire
roe, fish - hākari, hua, pewa ika
rogue tāhae, nanakia, nauhea
role tūranga
roll call karanga ingoa
roll (*v.*) pīrori(-a)
roll over hurihuri, porotiti, takahuri
roll up pōkai, takai
roll, voting - rōra, rārangi pōti
rolling pin rākau pokepoke, takapapa
Roman Catholic Katorika
romance whaiāipo, kōrero whaiāipo
roof tuanui, tuani
roof of mouth ngao
room (cf. space) taiwhanga, ruma, wāhi, wāteatanga
roost pae manu, nohonoho manu
rooster tame heihei, pīkaokao
root (source) take, puna
root (taproot) kōmore
root of tree pakiaka, pīakaaka, paiaka
rope taura, kaha, ropi
rose (plant) rōha, roiho, rōhi, pūārōhi
roster rārangi ingoa
rotor pōwaiwai

rot (putrefy) pirau, koero, hanehane
rotary hurihuri
rotate tītakataka, hurihuri, tītaka, huri(-hia)
rotation hurihanga
rotten pirau
rotten wood pūkorukoru, popo
rouge kōkōwai
rough taratara, tāpā, raupā, tiotio
round porotaka, porowhita, porotiti
round about āwhio, taiāwhio
round eyed tītoretore kanohi
round the point hahani haere, kōpiopio
round up sheep whiu(-a) hipi
roundabout, traffic - takaāwhio, ara kōpae
roundness porotīti
rouse whakaoho, whakaara
route ara, huarahi, ararere
routine tikanga mahi
row (fight) riri, kohete
row (line) tira
row boat hoe(-a)
royal roera, a te Karauna, tapairu
rub ūkui(-a), miri(-a), muku(-a)
rub off kōmuku(-a), ūkui(-a)
rub out kōmuru(-a)
rubber (eraser) inarapa, tahirapa
rubber stamp pourapa, moko inarapa
rubber tubing ngongo inarapa
rubbery ngorengore
rubbish (debris) otaota, parapara, rāpihi
rubbish bag pōtete para
rubbish bin paepae para, ipupara, rau kapurangi
rubble kapurangi, kongakonga
rubella kōpukupuku
ruby rupi
ruck (rugby) hōkeri, ketuketunga
rudder urungi, urunga
rude (impolite) whakatoi(-a)
rude (indecent) pohane, whakapohane
ruffian tainanakia
ruffle tara(-a), kuku(-a)
rug pōrera, paraikete, whāriki
rugby league rīki
rugby union hutupaoro
rugged toretore, pukepuke
ruin (spoil) takakino, ururua, patu, whakangaro
ruined pakaru, maroro, ngaro
rule tikanga, ritenga, ture
ruler, measuring - rūri, rākau ine, tauine, rauru
ruling whakatau
rum rama
rumble wawā, haruru, ngunguru
rumour wara, wawara, hū
run oma(-kia), omaoma, tūoma, rere
run away tahuti
run down whakahē, ngautuarā
run out (reel) hoka, rere
rung kaupae, takahanga
runner kaioma, waetea, kairere
runner-up tuarua
running omaoma
runny kūtere, waiwai, kōtere
runt pōtiki
runway aratau
rupture (hernia) whaturama
rural tuawhenua, taiwhenua
rural delivery karere tuawhenua
rush (attack) kōkiri, whakaeke, huaki

rush (dash) hīrere, rere, whāwhai, whana
rush (wind) pūkerikeri, kari
rush into rere patiko
rush of water hīrere, tūpou
rushes wīwī, kūwāwā, kuta
rushing wind hau keri
rust waikura
rustling noise ngaehe, wara, tihitihi
rusty waikura
rut kōawaawa
ruthless whakawiriwiri
rye grass karaehe rae

S

sabbath hāpati
sabbatical wā whakatā, wā hararei
sabotage tuki huna
sack potato/sugar pēke (rīwai/huka)
sack (dismiss) pana(-ia)
sacrament hākarameta, hākari tapu
sacred tapu
sacrifice patunga tapu, whakahere
sacrilege takahi tapu, whakanoatanga tapu
sad pōuri, hinapōuri, āroharoha
saddle tera, hea, nohoanga
saddleback (bird) tīeke
saddlecloth whakapuru tera
sadness hinapōuri, matapōrehu, ahotea
safe (okay) oraiti, haumaru, marutau
safe (strongbox) paemoni, pouaka tiaki taonga, kiato
safeguard maru
safety oranga, ora, whakaruru, marutau
safety belt tātua turu, whakatina
safety measures whakatūpatotanga
safety pin autui, pine mau
safety rail rōau whakatonu, rēra whakatonu
safety seat nohoanga hauora
sag pītawitawi, tapore, tāwharu, wheoro
sago hēko
sail (*n.*) hēra, rā, kōmaru
sail (*v.*) rere, tere
sail of windmill rapa
sailor hēremana, kaumoana
saint tangata tapu, hunga tapu
sake, for the - whakaaro ki
salad huamata
salary utu kaimahi, utu ā-wiki, utu ā-tau
sale hokohoko
sale of assets hokonga taputapu
saliva hūware, tūwhare, hāware, huare
salmon, Atlantic - hāmana
salmon, pink - para-karaka
salt tote(-a), kurutai
saltpetre totepita
saltwater waitai
salty mātaitai, totetote
salute mihi, pōwhiri, tohu-ā-ringa
salvage whakahou(-ngia), tohu(-ngia)
salvation whakaoranga
same rite, ōrite
sample tauira, tautauira, tīpakonga
sample (try out) whakamātau, tīpako(-a)
sanctify whakatapu(-a)
sanctions whakawhiu
sanctuary piringa, wāhi tapu, punanga
sand onepū, oneone kirikiri

sand-dune tāhuna, taipū, tāhuahua
sandal pārahirahi, pārairai, korehe
sandbank parehoru, one tāhua, matatāhuna
sandfly namu
sandhills tāhuahua, taipū oneone
sandpaper pepa hōanga
sandstone tunaeke, hōanga, keho
sandwich hanawiti, tapatorukai, hānewiti
sandy one, kirikiri
sane ngākau ora, mōhio, hinengaro hauora
sanitary parakore
sanitary inspector kaititiro o te ora
sanitary pad kope
sanitation hauora
sap pia, taitea
sapling māhuri, kōhuri
sapphire hāpira
sapwood taitea
sarcasm kupu whakahāwea
sarcastic kōrero kawa, whakahāwea
sardine aua, hārini
sash rāpaki, whītiki
Satan Hātana
satchel kopa, tākopa
satellite waka tawhio, ao tawhio, amiorangi
satin kākahu mōhinuhinu, papamōhinu
satire whakahāwea, whakarōrā, pūhohe
satisfaction tatūtanga, ngata, mānawa
satisfied rite te hiahia, nā, whiu, mākona
satisfy whakanā, whakawhiu
saturate tōpuni, waiwai
saturation pīpī ki te wai
Saturday Hātarei, Rāhoroi
Saturn Rongo, Parearau
sauce wairanu, whāranu, kīnaki
saucepan hōpane, hōhi, kōhua
saucer hoeha, hōhi
sausage hōtiti, notinoti, tōtiti
sausage roll tōraha tōtiti taparaha
savage kino, tūkino, mohoao
save (computer) tiaki, pupuri
savings pūtea moni, moni whakaputu
savings account pūtea penapena
saviour kaiwhakaora
saw (tool) kani, kani mīhini
sawdust kota, para rākau
sawmill mira
say kōrero(-tia), kī(-ia), mea(-tia), whakapuaki(-na)
saying whakataukī, pepeha, e meinga ana
scab paku, raupapa, pāpaka, mate huata
scabbard pūkoro
scabies hakihaki
scald wera ki te wai, kōhua
scale fish unahi(-a), inohi(-a)
scallop, queen - tipa, tupa
scalp kiri angaanga
scalp of enemy kawiu
scaly unahinahi, pāpākiri
scan āta titiro, titiro whakatau
scandalous rongo hanihani
scanner pūmatawai (roro), whakaata kimi
scantling papa rākau
scanty rahirahi, pakiwhara
scapula (bone) hakikoko, pākaukau

scar nawe, wenewene, kutiwera, riwha
scarce ongeonge, torutoru, pūhore, ruarua
scare (fright) mataku, wehi
scare (frighten) whakawehi, whakamataku, whakaataata
scarf kāmeta
scarifier karawhaea
scarlet hīwera, whero
scarlet fever kākura
scatter rui(-a), hora(-hia), tohatoha(-ina)
scatterbrain rorirori, heahea
scattered marara, hora, mahora
scavenger paraketu, hamuhamu
scene (stage set) wāhanga, kāpeka
scenic hei tirotiro, whakakitekite
scent kakara, tīere, hā, rautangi
schedule kupu āpiti, rārangi, hōtaka
scheme kaupapa, aronui
schizophrenia pōauau, wairua tuakoi
scholar ākonga, tauira, pia, ngore
scholars hunga wānanga
scholarship karahipi, tahua ngore
school kura, whare kura
school certificate kura tiwhikete
school leaver tamaiti mutu te kura
school of fish tara ika, tere ika
school teacher kaiako
schoolbag kopa-kura
science pūtaiao, taha taiao
sciences āhuatanga o te Ao
scientist kaipūtaiao, kaimātai putaiao
scissors kutikuti. kapekapetau
scoff taunu, tāwai
scold kōwhete(-tia)
scone kōno, takakau iti
scoop koko(-a), kowha, karo, ope(-hia)
scorch hunuhunu, rārā(-ngia), pakapaka
scorched tāwera
score a try kua whai piro
score (result) kaute, piro
score tae(-a), tapeka, piro, paneke
scoreboard (sport) papa tātai
scorer (marker) kaitatau, kaiāmiki
scores, old - take tārewa
scoria rangitoto, rahoto
scorn taunu(-tia), atamai
scornful taunu, pūhohe
scorpion ngārara timo, hiku timo, koropiona
scorpion fish matuawhāpuku, rai
Scotsman Kōtimana, Katimana
scoundrel taurekareka
scour (rub) ūkui(-a), rari, aka
scout tūtei, hunuhunu, torotoro, matataua
scrabble (game) ketu kupu
scramble oke, takaoraora, whāranu
scrap (piece) maramara, parakai, kuha
scrape waruwaru(-hia), hāro, raku(-hia), huke(-a)
scraper kota
scrapped (torn up) nakunaku, whakarere
scrappy rikiriki
scraps toenga, maramara, paka
scratch rapirapi, rakuraku(-hia), raraku, ketuketu(-tia)
scream auē, koekoe(-a), hāparangi, tiwē
screech tīoro, ngoengoe, kīrea
screen ārai(-a)

S

screen, cinema - rīanga
screen, computer - mata
screen, protective - kahupapa, takitaki, ārai(-a), whakaruru
screw wiri, kōwiri, whakawiri, whakahurihuri
screwdriver huriwiri
script (text) tuhi-ā-ringa, hōtuhi
Scripture Karaipiture, Tuhituhi Tapu
scroll (computer) hurinoa
scrotum pūkoro raho, pūraho
scrounge kaipaoke
scrub (bush) rarauhe, tūmatakuru, tāwhao, taekai
scrub (clean) horoi(-a), āka(-hia)
scrubber (cleaner) kaiwaru
scrum kakari, kirimiti, taupurupuru, nonoke
scruple āwangawanga, pohopā
scrupulous uhupoho
scrutineer kaitirotiro
scrutinize āta tirotiro
scuff waru(-hia) hū, pūnguru
scuffle āpiti tū
scull hoe urungi, ue(-a)
sculptor kaiwhakairo, tohunga tārai pakoko
sculpture whakairo
scum parawai
scurf inaho, pakitea
scurvy mate kāwei, mate hapa, kōpaka hauora
scythe haira
sea moana, tai
sea breeze muritai, hau moana
sea egg kina, toretore
sea lion kakerangi, kekeno
sea shell anga, kota
sea snail pūpūtai
sea urchin kina
sea wall paetai
sea water waitai
seabed papamoana
seafarer hēremana, kaumoana
seafood kaimātaitai
seagull karoro, katete, tarapunga, tara
seahorse manaia, kiore moana, kiore waitai
seal (animal) kekeno, pakaka
seal (stamp) hīra(-tia), kati(-a), moko-whakapiri
sealer kaipatu kēkeno
seam (cloth) tuinga, maurua
seamstress kaitui
seamy paru, taretare
seaplane wakarereretai
search rapu(-a), kimi(-hia), hāhā(-ria), rangahau(-a)
search warrant raihana kimi, tukunga kupu kimi
searchlight rāiti haurapa, rāiti kimi, rama rapa
seashore tahatai, tātahi, ākau, takutai
seasick rūaki moana, mate moana
seaside takutai
season (time) wā, wātau, peka o te tau, takiwā
seat nohoanga, tūru, nohonga kumi
seat, orator's - paepae, taumata
seaward ki tai, ki waho
seaweed rimurimu, rimurēhia, monauri
seaworthy whakapiri, pihi
secede wehe(-a), kounu
secession kounutanga
secluded mokemoke, punanga, puni
seclusion noho mōwai, wā wehe

second (of time) hēkena, hākona, kimonga
second (support) tautoko
second sight matakite
secondhand oruoru, tawhito, ruha
secret (mystery) mea ngaro, mea huna, ngaro, muna
secretary kaituhi, hēkeretari
secretive toropuku, huna
sect rōpū wehe, hāhi motuhake, wehenga hāhi
section (land) hua, tēkihana, tūāporo whenua
section (part of) wāhanga
sector wāhanga, taha
secure (fix) whakamau(-a), whakaū
secured tawhiwhi
security taituarā, punga
sedate (with drug) whakarokiroki
sediment para, parakiwai, parawai, parataiao
seditious takahi mana kāwanatanga
seduce poapoa, pātaritari, whakawai, whakapati(-tia)
see kite(-a)
see for oneself kite kōiwi, kite ā-kanohi
see out (last out) tautohe
see-saw tiemi, pīoi, pīoni, tīeke
seed pua, purapura, kākano, pata, hira
seed, go to - puarere
seedling parahia (kūmara), pihi, rea, wanatipu
seek kimi(-hia), rapu(-a), rangahau(-a)
seek revenge whai utu
seem te āhua
seer matakite, tohunga mata, tohunga matuhi
seethe ī, nganangana, koropupū
segment tapahanga, wāhanga, wāwāhi, paranga, wāhi
segregate wehewehe, mehameha, whakatāuke
seismic rū whenua
seize hopu(-kia), kapo(-hia), rarawhi(-tia), herepū(-tia)
seized mau
seizure hukihuki ohorere
seldom torutoru nei wā, uaua
select kōwhiri(-a), whiriwhiri(-a), kōhari, whakapena
selection, natural - whiringa taiao, whiringa māori
selection panel kaitātari
selector kaiwhiriwhiri, kaitīpako
self tinana, aroaro, ake, anō, whaiaro
self importance whakahīhī
self-assured pakari, māhaki
self-defence ārai mate whaiaro, wawao tinana, parahau whaiaro
self-explanatory mārama noa
self pity aroha-ā-kiri
self-reliant tū tangata
self-respect tū tika, kiri huarangi
self-righteous whakapehapeha
self-sacrifice oha noa, whakapau manawanui
self-satisfied kiri manawareka
self-sufficient tū motuhake
selfish kaiponu, mōhū, kaiapo, matatoua
sell hoko(-na) atu
seller kaihoko
sellotape tēpa whakapiri, hāpiapia
semen wai tātea

semi-colon irapiko, pīwehe, kopipiko
semi-skilled worker kaimahi hakorea, ihupuku
seminar rūnanga, wānanga
send tono(-a), tuku(-a, -na)
send for tono, tiki atu
send-off pana(-ia)
senior tuakana, tōmua, kaumātua, mātāmua
sense rongo(-hia), hārau, āronga, matatau
sense of humour āronga hātekēhi, āronga ngahau
sense of smell ihu
sense, common - whakaaro noa, atamai, mōhio noa
senseless kūare, pōrewarewa
sensible whai whakaaro
sensitive whakarongo, ngāwari, aro atu, aroha
sent tonoa
sentiment ngākau
sentry hēteri, kaimatire, tūtei
separate māwehe, whakawehe(-a), momotu (motukia)
separation wehenga, taratarangā
separation, legal - whakamana wehenga
separator hepareta, whakawehe
septic ero, pirau
septicaemia toto paihana
sequel roanga, huanga, wāhanga whai mai
sequence raupapa upane, takapiringa
serenade waiata whaiāipo
serenity noho mārire
sergeant haihana
sergeant-major haihana-meiha
serial raupapa, hātepe, tāuhu
series raupapa, rārangi, rangatū, tapeke raupapa
serious taumaha, nui whakaharahara, pono mārika
sermon kauwhau(-tia) kauhau
serrated edge mīkara, pūtaratara
servant hāwini, tūmau, pononga, wharerā
serve manaaki(-tia), aro atu ki
serve (games) tuku(-a), hau(-a)
serve food whiu(-a) kai, whakarato, hora(-hia) kai
server (tennis) kaituku
service, fire - umanga kāpura
service, medical - umanga whakaora
service provider - kaiwhakarato
service, religious - hui karakia
service station pā hinu, papa rato
serviceman (maintenance) kaimahi
servicemen, returned - rōpū pāraeroa
set (backdrop) tūrākai
set free tuku(-a) kia haere
set out (lay out) whakarārangi(-tia), tātai(-a)
set-square tapatoru tākonga
set (sun) tō, torengi, tōwene, tōene
settee hōpa, pae hānea
settle tatū, tau, noho tūturu, whakatau(-ria)
settlement (agreement) whakataunga
settlement (village) kāinga
settler hunga whai whenua, kaiwhakanoho whenua
seven whitu
seven-a-side kapa tokowhitu
severe uaua, taumaha, pākaha

sew tuitui(-a)
sewage system pūnaha parakaingaki
sewage treatment whakapai parakaingaki
sewer pininga parakaingaki
sewing tuituinga
sex tānetanga, wahinetanga
sex, have - ai(-tia), onioni, mahimahi
sexual abuse raweke, taitōkai
sexual desire taera
shabby taretare, karukaru, kanukanu, haratete
shack kuha kāinga, māhauhau, wharau
shade whakamarumaru, maru rāiti
shade eyes kaupare, tūpare
shaded maru, taumaru
shadow ata, atārangi, ariā, ataata
shag kawau, kawau paka, kāruhiruhi
shaggy pūhutihuti
shake (*v. tr.*) ueue(-a), rutu (-a), ngāruerue
shake (*v. intr.*) wiriwiri, korikori, rū, ngāueue, tāwiriwiri
shake hands rūrū, harirū
shake (liquid) whakakarekare
shallow pāpaku
sham tinihanga
shameful whakamā, āniu, mōkinokino
shampoo hopi makawe
shape āhua, whakaahua
share (food ration) tōtō kai
share (part of) wāhi, wāhanga, pānga wehewehenga
share dividend pānga
shareholder tangata whai pānga
shark mangō, pioke, mako, reremai
sharp koi, koikoi
sharpen whakakoi(-a)
shatter mongamonga, kongakonga, pakaru, tukituki(-a)
shave heu(-a), waru(-hia)
shavings warunga
shawl tarapouahi, katekate, hikurere
she ia
shear sheep kuti hipi
shearer kaikuti hipi, kaikatikati
sheath (holder) pūkoro
shed (shack) pākoro, wharau, wuruhēti, hēti, kōpuha
sheep hipi
sheepdog kurī hipi
sheepish tā te hipi āhua, whakakumu
sheer paritū, harapaki
sheet hīti
sheet of paper whārangi, pepa, puka rau, tāwhera pepa
shelf tarenga, kārupe, papa, whata
shell (armament) pohū nui
shell (nut) anga, papa
shell, remove - kōwhā(-tia)
shell, sea - kota, papa tio, anga
shellfire waipū
shellfish kaeo, pūpū, pipi, kaimoana
shelter (protect) whakamarumaru(-tia), tāwharau(-tia)
shelter (refuge) pātūtū, whakaruruhau, pārae, kurupae
shelter, take - ruru
shelve tukua ki te taha
shepherd hēpara

shield hira, pākai, puapua, whakangungu rākau
shift (budge) nuku(-hia), neke(-hia)
shift work wehenga mahi, mahi tiriwa, mahi tīpako
shifting pānekeneke
shimmer whakaira, korakora
shin tātā, tāhau
shin guard āraitā
shine (glow) mura, hahana
shine (polish up) whakatiaho, whakapīata
shine (sun) whiti, hana, ura
shingle (pebbles) kirikiri
shingle (roof) toetoe tuanui
shining tiaho, pīata, kohara
shiny pīataata, kānapanapa, ūiraira
ship poti, kaipuke, tima
shipwreck paenga kaipuke, paeārau
shirk pāuhu, paunu, anga kē, whakataha
shirt hāte
shit tiko, tūtae, hamuti
shiver wiriwiri, tūhāwiri, tūhauwiri, wanawana
shoal of fish rāngai ika, tere, rara, matatuhi
shoal (sandbank) tāhuna, tuahiwi
shock (surprise) oho, tumeke, whakaoho(-ngia), hotohoto
shock, electric - whiti hiko
shocking harehare, weriweri
shoe hū
shoelace kaui
shoot (growth) tupu, pihi, wene, toro
shoot (gun) pupuhi (pūhia)
shop (purchase) hoko(-na)
shop (store) toa
shopping centre toamaha, papa hokohoko
shore takutai, ākau, taha moana
shorn tīhore, tīmore
shorn of branches morimori, tūmoremore
short poto
short-circuit ia (hiko) whati, āwhiotanga whati
short cut poka pū
short-sightedness titiro tata, kahupō, kahurua, atarua
short stature hahaka
short-stop tuku poto, tū tata, kaitū tata
short tempered wetiweti, kiriweti
short-term deposit pūtea penapena huapoto
short-term wā poto
short third man (cricket) tuatoru tata
short time ago i mua tata ake nei
short-wave ngaru poto, aratuku poto
short winded hau poto
shortage hapa, kōpaka
shortcoming ngoikoretanga
shortcut pokatata
shorten whakapoto(-a)
shorthand tuhi tere
shortly takitaro ake, meake nei
shorts tarau poto
shot (ball) matā, hōta
shot (bang) pakūtanga
shot (pellets) kariri
shot (photo) whakaahua
shot putt panga matā
shotgun tūpara
shoulder pokohiwi, pakihiwi, peke

shoulder blade hakikoko, pākoukou
shout pararehe, karanga(-tia), tīwaha(-tia), hāmama
shove tute(-a), pei(-a), pana(-ia)
shovel hāpara, tākoko, koko(-a), hāwara
show (exhibit) whakamārama, whakaatu(-ria), whakakite(-a)
show (exhibition) whakakitenga
show off whakahīhī, whakaparana
showcase pouaka whakakitekite
shower of rain tūāua, ua tīhengi
showerbath kōrere turuturu, hīrere
shrapnel maramara pohū, matā korere
shred ngakungaku, haehae, hungahunga
shred (small bit) kara, para
shredded tītore, harotu, nguha, ngakungaku
shrewd mōhio, kakama, pūmahara
shriek tīoro, tarakeha
shrimp kōuraura, kōurarangi, uraura, koeke
shrine ahurewa, tūāhu
shrink kōmae, tīngongo, kūreherehe
shrivel whakatarehe, memenge
shrug hikihiki pakihiwi
shrunk kōmae, kawiu
shudder wiwini, ihiihi
shun whakahāwea
shut ko(-a), whakakopi(-a), tūtaki(-tia), kati(-a), pā(-ia)
shut in hautoki, haukoti
shutter papa kati
shy (*v.*) tumeke
shy (reserved) whakamā, pūihi
sick tūroro, mate ana, māuiui, pāngia e te mate
sickly memeha, hanga-mate, matemate, anuhē
sickness māuiuitanga, mate, aitu, kōero
sickness benefit takuhe tūroro
side taha
side by side āpiti
side, other - (of object) tua
side, other - (of sea) tāwāhi
side, to one - tahaki, autaha
side wall kōpai, kōpainga
sides, on all - taka noa
sidestep karo
sidetrack peka atu, ara taha, whakatītaha
sidewalk pae ara
sideways korotaha, tītaha
siding taha rērewē, pekanga tereina
siege whakapaenga, karapotinga
sieve (*n.*) hītari, kōputaputa
sieve (*v.*) tātari(-tia)
sift tātari(-tia)
sigh kiha, mapuhau, tangi te mapu
sight kite
sign on haina(-tia)
sign with hands rotarota, kapo
significance tikanga, tāpua
significant kaha nui, kaha hōhonu
signify waitohu(-ngia)
silence mūmū, nohopuku, wahangū
silk hiraka, papamāene
sill, of door paepae, pehipehi
silly heahea, rorirori
silo pākoro mauti, kōpapa

silt kenepuru, parakiwai, parahua
silver hiriwa, kākonu
silver beech tawhai
silver beet korare, ruruhau
silver-eye tauhou
silver fern ponga
silver paper pepa hiriwa
silverside mīti tote
silversmith kaipatu hiriwa
similar āhua ōrite, tauriterite, pēnei, ōrite
similarity āhuatanga tūriterite, ritenga
simile kupu whakarite
simmer korohuhū
simple māmā noa iho, ngāwari noa iho, mataiti
simplify whakamāmā, whakangāwari
simulate whakatau, whakarite(-a), waihanga
simultaneous tukutahi, i taua wā tonu, tautokorua, ngātahi
sin hara, hē
since (because) inā hoki, nō te mea, hoki (after predicate)
since then mai anō, i muri mai nei, mai i te
sincere tika, kōrero pono
sincerely yours nāku noa
sincerity ngākau pono
sinew iaia, uaua, ioio
sinewy pakaua
sinful hara
sing waiata(-tia), toiere
singe hunuhunu(-a)
singer kaiwaiata
single minded whakaaro tahi
single (one) tōtahi, tapatahi
single (unmarried) takakau, rōpā
singlet hingareti
singly takitahi
sinister kino, whakaweti
sink (kitchen) puoto, peihana kihini, kāraha
sink (submerge) totohu, uru
sinker kōhatu whakataimaha, māhē, maihea
sinking sun rāwhakawhenua
sinner tangata hara
sinuous āwhiowhio
sinus ngongo, pakohu
sinusitis purua te ihu, pakohu kakā
sip ngongo
siphon (*n.*) paipa ngongo
siphon (*v.*) ngongo(-a)
Sir Tā
sir! e koro, e pā, e rangi
sirloin kiko hope kau
sister of female, older - tuakana
sister of female, younger - teina
sister of male tuahine
sister-in-law of female taokete
sister-in-law of male auwahine
sister (religious) whaea tapu, āwhina (rātana)
sit noho(-ia)
sit exam whakauru
sit on heels tineinei
site tūnga, papanga, paenga
sitting nohoanga, nohanganui
sitting room nohomanga
situation tūāhua, āhuatanga, pūāhua
six ono
sixth tuaono
size nui, rahi, kaitā
sizzle pākēkē, parai, hihī
skate, ice - panunu tio, retireti hukapapa, mania haupapa
skateboard papa reti

skeleton tuahiwi, angaanga, kōiwi
sketch tuhi whakaahua, tuhi haehae, huahua
skewer kōhiku, pūrou
ski panuku hukarere, retireti hukarere, reti huka
ski-pole tokohuka
skid (sliding device) motumotu tōroa
skid (slip) mania
skier kairerehuka
skiing retihuka, retireti hukarere
skilful mātau, punenga, mōhio, tohunga
skill mōhio, tautōhito, pūkenga
skilled person pūkenga, pū, tohunga
skim surface tipi, riripi
skimmed milk miraka waiwai
skin (*n.*) kiri, hiako, peha
skin (*v.*) tīhore(-tia), hīhore
skin-tight pirikiri, marowai
skink mokomoko
skinny tūwai, tūpuhi, iwikau, paparewa
skip (hop) piu
skip (omit) kape(-a)
skipper kāpene
skipping rope piu, peke taura
skirmish kōkiri, haupatu
skirt panekoti, kenakena
skis papa retihuka
skit whakakata, whakatoi
skite kōrero whakahīhī, whakaparanga, wahanui
skittle (*n.*) pine rākau, poutuki
skittle (*v.*) pātuki
skua gull hākoakoa
skull anga, pōangaanga, pareho, pārihirihi
sky rangi, kikorangi
sky-blue kikorangi
skyscraper whare tino tiketike, rakuraku rangi, whare tīkoke
slab papa
slack (loose) tangatanga, kaewa
slacken tukutuku(-a), whakakaewa(-tia), whakangoru(-a)
slacks tarau, kahuwae
slander ngautuarā
slang kōrero noaiho, mātāhae, kōrero ā-takiwā, kupu ōpaki
slant tītaha, konana, whakatītaha(-tia)
slap papaki (pākia)
slash ripiripi, kōripi, tapahi
slasher hūka-tāwai
slat kārapi, taratara
slate pakohe, ōnewa maru, mākoha
slate (account) kaute
slater howaka
slaughter patu(-a), tārukenga
slave mōkai, apa, kahunga, tūmau
sledge kōneke
sleek maheni, mohimohi
sleep moe
sleep, put to - moe(-a), whakamoe(-a)
sleeper, railway - rōau rērewē, kurupae
sleeping pill pire whakamoe
sleepy hiamoe, mate moe
sleepyhead moeroa
sleet hukarere
sleeve ringa
slender tūpuhipuhi, pūhihi
slice (*n.*) tapahinga
slice (*v.*) tapahi(-a) kia rahirahi, kōripi(-a)
slide (slip) mania, paheke

slide (transparency) kōataata, kiriata
slide projector pūrere kōataata
slight tūwai, pūhihi
slim tūpuhipuhi
slime hāware
slimy hāwareware, hāwaniwani
sling (*v.*) piu(-a)
sling (support) takaiwhata
sling (weapon) kōtaha
slink toropuku, whakamoho, haere hū, konihi
slip (fall) paheke, mania, horo(-a)
slip (underwear) āhumehume, panekoti, hītau
slip off pahuhu
slip-rail kēti roau, kēti rēra
slipknot koromāhanga
slipper hiripa, panaena
slippery hāwaniwani, pāhekeheke, mania, māniania
slipway whakarewa
slit hahae(-tia), hōripi
slither about pārikoriko
slobber hārua, whakahāware
slogan whakataukī
slope, gentle - pānanaki, aupikinga, pīnakitanga, āu
slope, steep - harapaki, rāpaki
sloppy (wet) kōparu, waia, tāpiapia
slot pūaha, ahaaha, kāniwha
slouch pōrohe, parohea
slovenly taretare, hakirara
slow pōturi, pūhoi, āta, akitō, tīraha kau
sludge paruparu, kenepuru
slug ngata, putoko
sluggish turikore, takurutu, pūroto
sluice kēti pāpuni
slum kuha kāinga, whare hawa
slump hekenga iho, makeretanga
slurry oneone pokepokea
sly nukurau, māminga
smack papaki (pakia)
small iti, nohinohi, paku, wāhi (before noun), muimui
small minded harawene
smallpox mate koroputaputa
smart (clever) kakama, mataara
smart (sting) kakati
smell (*n.*) haunga
smell (*v.*) hongi(-a), rongo (rangona), hā
smelly haunga, piro
smile menemene
smog kohupara, kōtuhi
smoke (*n.*) paoa, auahi, kauruku, kauruki, ahuahi
smoke (*v.*) momi hikareti, kai tūpeka
smoke-free auahi kore, auahi-ātea
smoke tobacco kai paipa, momi hikareti
smoker kaipaipa, kaingongo tūpeka
smoky kaurukiruki, ponga
smooth mōhani, maheni, māeneene, moremore
smother hē manawa, tāmi(-a)
smoulder mohu, ponguru, muramura
smudge ukupara, penu
smug whakahīhī
smuggle mau huna, kawe toropuku
snag taitā, tāiki
snail ngata, kauri, pūpūrangi
snail, mud - whetiko, titiko
snake nākahi, neke, ngārara
snap motu, whatiwhati, kē, patō

snapper (fish) tāmure, karatī
snapshot whakaahua hopu noa, hopuāhua
snare tāwhiti, māhanga, tārore, ā-here, tāhere
snarl ngengere
snatch kapo(-hia), tākiri(-tia)
sneak (creep) haere toropuku, konihi, haere ninihi
sneaky tautauwhea
sneer tāwai, whakahīhī, whakareko
sneeze tihe, matihe, tīhewa, mātihetihe
sniff hongihongi
snigger tīhohe
snooker tauwhāinga ārai
snore ngongoro, peru te ihu
snorkel ngongohā
snort whangu, whawharo, horu
snot hūpē, paku
snout ihu
snow huka, hukarere
snowfield papahuka
snowman tānehukapapa
snowy pūmā
snub whakahāwea, whakatoatoa
so (in that way) pēnā, pērā
so (therefore) hoianō, heoi, heoi anō, nō reira
soak tuku ki te wai, kōpiro(-tia)
soak up miti, ngongo
soap hopi
soap-powder rehu horoi
soar aloft whakatopa, hokahoka ake
sob hotuhotu, anuhea, anohea, tangi puku
sober taumauri, tau, pūmahara, nguengue
soccer tiripara, poiwhana, poikiri
social (community) taha noho tangata, hapori, pāpori
social welfare toko i te ora
socialism mana hapori
socialist manawa hapori, kaikōkiri mana hapori
society noho-ā-iwi, porihanga, pāpori, hapori
sock tōkena
socket kōhao, tūranga
soda houra
sofa hōpa
soft (to touch) ngāwari, ngohengohe, kūteretere
soft sound āta tangi, māriri
soft-drink waireka
softball poiuka
soften whakangāwari
softly mārire
soggy kōparu, pī
soil oneone
solar eclipse rā kūtia, whenumi rā
solar system Ika Matua-a-Tangaroa, rerenga o Tama-nui-te-rā
solder (*n.*) piuta, konuhono, tūhoto
solder (*v.*) hono(-a)-ā-konu
soldier hōia
sole (alone) anahe, kotahi, mokemoke
sole of foot takahanga, tapuwae, kapukapu, raparapa
sole, lemon - pātiki
solemn nui, tapu, amaru, tū rangatira
solicit inoi(-a), pati
solicitor rōia
solid mārō, pakeke, ukauka, papatipu

solidarity kotahitanga, whakawhanaunga
solidify whakapapapatipu, whakaū(-ngia), kukū, whātoka, totaka
soliloquy whakaputa whakaaro
solitude noho mokemoke
soluble rewa
solution (answer) tau otinga
solution, liquid - wairewa
solve (*v.*) whakatika, whakarite, whakautu
solvent whakarewa
solvent-abuse hongi kāpia
some etahi, he, wetahi
somehow pēhea
someone tētahi, a wai rānei
somersault takahuri, pōtēteke
something tētahi mea
sometime ā te wā
somewhat hanga, āhua
somewhere hea
son tama tāne, tamaiti
son-in-law hunaonga
sonar paoro
song waiata, tau
sonic pāorooro
sonic boom papārangi
soon meākenei, āianei, ākuanei
soon as possible tere tonu, taro ake nei, āpōpō ake tonu nei
soot awe, kūkāwhare, kuka
soothe whakamārie, mirimiri, whakamaene(-tia)
soprano reo tōiri, teitei, reo kōtike
sore (painful) mamae
sorrowful pōuri, pāpōuri, aroaroā, aroha aha te āhua
sorry (my fault) nā tōku hē, nāku te hē
sort (type of) tū, momo, āhua
sorter kaiwhiriwhiri
sortie tuki, kōkiri
soul wairua
sound tangi, hau o te waiata
sound track ara pūoru
soundwaves parangēki
soup hupa, waihāro
sour kawa, kakati
source mātāpuna, matatiki, matamata, hukinga, whakaipurangi, takenga mai, puna, pūtake
south tonga, ki runga
southeast tongawhiti
Southern Cross Taki-o-Autahi, Pūtea-iti-a-Reti
Southern Lights Ngā Kurakura-o-Hinenuitepō
souvenir manatunga
sow (pig) poaka uwha
sow seed rui(-a)
sow-thistle pūhā, rauriki, pororua
spa puna waiōpapa, wai koropupū
space (area) ātea, wāhi, tiriwā, takiwā
space, outer ao takiwā, ātea, tūārangi
spacebar pātuhi mokowā, pātuhi wehe kupu, pae mokowā
spade (*n.*) kō, hō, kāheru, hoto
spade (*v.*) keri(-a), tūkari(-a)
spade (cards) pēti
spaghetti pāketi, noke parāoa, kihu parāoa
span of bridge tīpae
spanner tānakuru, mauhuri
spar (pole) rākau
spare (extra) motuhake
spark korakora ahi

spark off whakaongaonga, tahu(-na)
spark plug puru kora, puru konga
sparkle tīaho, whakaira
sparse tihetihe, tūrukiruki, takitahi
spasm waitākiri
spastic mate hukihuki
spatter uwhiuwhi, kōpatapata
spatula koko parai, rapa parai
spawn hua rākau, hua paru, toene, whānaunau
speak kōrero(-tia), mea (meinga), kī(-ia)
speaker (talker) kaikōrero
speaker's bench paepae, taumata
spear (*n.*) huata, tao, matarau, kōpeo
spear (*v.*) wero(-hia)
special motuhake, hirahira, rawe
special character mauri
specialised skill tautōhito whāiti
species momo
specimen (sample) whakaaturanga, tauira
speck tongi, kora
speckled kōtiwhatiwha, kōtingotingo
spectacle tirohanga
spectacles mōwhiti, karaehe
spectator kaimātakitaki, kaititiro
spectrum, wide - tūāwhiorangi
speculate peti, rapa noa, whakaaro noa
speech whai kōrero
speechless wahangū
speed te horo, te tere
speed up whakatere
speedometer ine tere
speedy hohoro, tere
spell (*v.*) tātaki kupu
spell, magic - mākutu, karakia, ātahu, ihi, kānewha
spellbound manarū
spell-check pūmanawā takikupu
spelling pūnga kupu, takikupu
spent pau, ruhi
sperm tao tātea, wai o te ure, wai tāne
spew ruaki
sphere kōpio, pororino, poi, tīraka
spice raukikini, namunamuā
spider pungāwerewere, pungaiwerewere, ngārara
spider, poisonous - katipō
spike taratara, koi
spill ringi(-hia)
spin thread miro(-a), whenu(-tia)
spin off whai hua anō
spin round tāhurihuri, āmiomio, tāwhiowhio(-tia)
spinach kōkihi, rengamutu
spinal cord ua, aho tauiwi
spine (backbone) tuarā, tuaitara, tuaiwi
spines of fish tara
spiny tūaitara, taratara
spiral āwhiowhio, takarangi, tōrino, makaurangi, rauru, pitau
spirit wairua, kēhua, manawa
spirit level rēwara
spirits, in good - hauora
spiritual nō te taha wairua
spit tuwha, tuha
spit, roasting - hukihuki
split (cleave) wāwāhi (wāhia), tīhore, hōrepe, ritua
split (crack) tapa, matatatanga
split (division) tūwhangawhanga
split off hautepe

S

split open kōwhā, raparapa, kōara(-tia)
spoil takakino, pāhua whakakino(-ngia)
spoke of wheel titi
spokesperson reo, māngai
sponge pūngoru, kōpūpūtai, hautai
spongy pukahu, pūkahukahu, kōpuka
sponsor tautoko
spontaneous noa
spool taka (miro), porotakaroa, pōkai
spoon pūnu, koko, pune
sport tākaro, hākinakina
sportswear kahu whakataetae
spot korotiwha, tongi, kōpure
spotless parakore
spotlight raiti tiaho, raiti tū tonu, ramataiaho, tīwhiri
spotty kōpurepure
spout kōrere
sprain one's back tanuku tuarā
sprained tanoi, takoki, taui
sprat kupae
sprawl takoto(-ria), tīraha, pukoni
spray of flowers rau pūāwai
spray, sea - rehutai
spread (distribute) tohatoha, haranui
spread (radiate) torotoro, ripo
spread of disease urutā
spread on ground whāriki(-tia)
sprig (twig) tākupu
sprightly tatara, kakama
spring (coiled) whana, tākiri(-tia), kōwiri
spring (*v.*) peke, tarapeke, kōwhiti, hūpeke
spring of water puna
spring season kōanga
spring tide tai nunui, huki
sprinkle uwhiuwhi(-a), ruirui(-a)
sprinter kaikōkiri, wae kōpere
sprocket nihomeka, tara
sprout tupu(-ria), pihi, tīnaku, toroihi
spur kipakipa
spy (scout) kaitūtai
squabble kōhetehete
squad uepū, rōpū
squalid pōpopo, anuanu, mōrihariha, weriweri
squalor whakarikarika, hawahawa
squander maumau
square tapawhā rite, porowhā rite
square, all - rite, ōrite
squash kōpē(-ngia), kōpiri, kōahi, kōpenu
squash drink waipē, kamokamo
squash game poipātū
squat (chunky) hakahaka
squat (crouch) noho hītengitengi
squeak pipi, wē, koekoe(-a), hītawe
squeaky koē, ngawī
squeal auē, ngawī
squeal (inform) whakamoho, tuku(-a)
squeeze romi(-a), kōpē(-ngia), whakatē, kōrapu, korotē(-hia)
squelch patihi, paratī, pasī (*sic*) pai
squint keko, rewha, karepa
squirm takaokeoke, oke
squirrel kirera
squirt tarapī, karepa
stab wero(-hia), oka(-ina)
stabilise whakamatua, māhoi, whakawhena

stable for animals tēpara
stable (firm) ū, mau
stack (*v.*) tāke(-tia), tāpae(-tia), whakapū, poutū, rokiroki
staff (personnel) kaimahi, rōpū mahi
stag tiatoa
stage (platform) whatarangi, atamira
stage, at what - āhea . . . ai
stagger hūrorirori, putuputu, tūrori, hōrorirori, kaurori
staggered start putuputu
stagnant pūroto
stain tae, pūriko, whātae, tawau, whākano (pūtau)
stained poke, poapoa
staircase arapiki
stake poupou, tumu, tokotoko
stalactite koeko iri
stalagmite koeko tū
stale pirau, pipirau, kōpuru, tawhito, kōwhau
stalk of plant kakau, tātā
stall for time taruna, whakaroa, kumeroa
stall wharau hoko, tēpu hoko
stallion tāriana
stammer kakakaka, kīkiki, nanunanu
stamp (impress) tohu, tā
stamp the foot takahi(-a)
stamp, postage - pane kuini
stampede rere marara
stance tū
stand by (wait) tatari (tāria)
stand in line tūtira
stand legs apart kūwhera(-tia)
stand-offish whakahīhī
stand over tactics tikanga kaioraora, mōkinokino
stand (place erect) whakatū(-ria)
stand (rack) tūranga, tūnga mātakitaki
stand to attention takitutu
standard (class) karaihe
standard, education - paerewa
standard of living tikanga whaiora
standing committee komiti whāiti, komiti tū
standing orders ture arahi, tikanga raupapa, ōta mau tonu
standing toe to toe apitutū
standpoint tūranga, tirohanga
staple (wire) mau, makatiti
staple diet kai matua
stapler whakamau, whakatēpara
star whetū
starch tāhi, māngaro
stare titiro pū, whetē, tiro mākutu, mātiro, whākana, manana
starfish pekapeka, pātangatanga, kōtoremoana
starling tāringi, whātete
starry kōpura
start (begin) tīmata(-ria)
start (jump) oho, ohotata
start up computer whakaoho
starter kaitīmata
startle whakaoho(-ngia), tūmeke
starvation hemokai
starve matekai, hemokai
starving hauhauaitu
state (condition) āhuatanga, auaha
state funded tautoko(-tia) e te kāwanatanga
state sector taha ki te kāwanatanga, tari kāwanatanga
statement pūrongo, pānui, kī
statesman kaiarahi o te iwi

static tū noa iho, pateko
station teihana, taupuni
station wagon teihana wākena
stationary tū tonu, whakapahoho
stationery pānga tuhituhi, toa pukapuka
statistic tatauranga, tataunga, tauanga, raraunga
statistics tatauranga, ngā tatau
statue whakapakoko, whakaahua
stature tipuranga, tū teitei
status mana tangata, tūnga whai tikanga, tūnga
staunch kaha, pāpuni, pūmau
stay (*v.*) noho(-ia)
steady tina, mārō, whakamauru(-tia)
steak kotinga mīti, tapahanga mīti, motū (*see* matū)
steal tāhae(-tia), whānako(-tia), whēnako(-tia)
steam mamaoa, korohū, piua, koroahu, koromaomao
steamer (cooker) tima
steamer (ship) tima
steamy pūmāhu
steel maitai, tīra
steep (vertical) tūpoupou, tūparipari, poupou
steep bank tahataha
steep in water kōpiro, waiwai, tou(-a)
steeplechase tauomaoma taiapa teitei
steer tia, urungi(-tia), rūnā(-a), whakahaere
stem kakau, tīwai, tātā
stems, from which takea
stencil whakaahua, whakatauira
step hīkoi, tapuwae, hōkai, kaupae
step ladder arawhata tūnoa
step parent matua whāngai
step (stair) pae
stepfather pāpā whakaangi
stepping stone tapuwae kōhatu, papa tiriwae
stereo pāho tangi huarua, tīwharawhara
stereotype tauira
sterile korekore, pāhoahoa
sterilize (disinfect) patuero, ārai popo, whakahoromata
stern (strict) whakaioio, uaua
sternpost taurapa
stew mīti paera, tiu(-a), tatao
steward tuari
stick (adhere) piri, whakapiri(-hia), rapa
stick-dance tī rākau
stick-figure tuhi tuahiwi
stick-insect rō, whē
stick in (poke) titi(-a), tia(-ina)
sticker pānui whakapiri
sticking plaster whakamahu, tāpi
sticky piripiri, ū, raparapa, hāpiapia
stiff mārō, pakeke, kōpā, mākiri
stifle nanati
stifling pongere
still (even now) tonu
stillborn materoto, ngūngū, whānau kahu
stilts poutoti, waewae, rākau
stimulant rongoā whakakori
stimulate whakaaraara, whakakorikori
sting (insect) wero(-hia), tū(-ngia), nanamu, timo
sting (pain) kakati
stingray whai, pūkaurua, tarawhai

stingy tūmatarau, kaiponu
stink piro, haunga
stir tīkapekape, kōrorirori, whakakaurori(-hia), whakatutu
stir-fry parai kōrori, parai kapekape
stirred up tutū(-tia)
stirrup terapu, tarapu, tōeke
stitch tui(-a), tuituinga
stock car wakapare, waka tukituki
stock (cattle) kātua, kararehe pāmu
stock (of gun) kaurapa
stockade pā, tūwatawata
stocking tōkena
stockpile tōhīanga, whakapuranga, putu
stocktaking kaute taonga
stocky tūpoto
stockyard taiepa, papanga kararehe
stolen whānakotia, tāhaengia
stomach puku
stone (rock) kōhatu, pōhatu, kāmaka
stone, fruit - whatu, karihi, nganga
stoned out of mind rehu i te tarukino
stony kirikiri
stool tūru
stoop tuohutanga, tūpou, tuohu, piko
stop (block) aukati
stop (halt) tū, whakamutu, hō
stop (prevent) ārai(-a), ārei(-a), pupuri (puritia)
stop cock puruwai, katiwai
stop up puru(-a), pā(-ia)
stopper (bung) puru
stopwork komutu mahi
storage rokiroki, whakaputu, pukeinga
store (shop) toa, whare hoko
storehouse pātaka, whata, pākoro, kōpapa
storey rewanga, papa, whakapaparanga
storm tūpuhi, āwhā, kaiaohia
stormy tūpuhi, paroro
story kōrero paki, pūrākau, kōrero pakiwaitara
storyteller kaipūrākau
stout mōmona, kaha, tetere
stove tō, oumu, umu
stow whakapuranga, whakaputu
straddle tirera
straggle tūtārere, tāngāngā, whakatakere
straight torotika, tōtika, heipū, hāngai
straight as a die tika rere
straight away i nāianei tonu
straight flush hātepe
straight on mārō tonu, tika
straighten whakatika(-hia), whakahāngai(-tia)
strain (effort) whakapau kaha, riaka
strain (fatigue) ngoikore, tanuku, pau te kaha
strainer, fence - whakamārōrō
strainer (kitchen) kōputaputa
straits, dire - pōharatanga, tata mate
strand (thread) kanoi
stranded pae, teo
strange autaia, rerekē, tipua
stranger tauhou, tautangata, manene, ruranga

strangle noti(-a), tārona(-tia), nanati(-tia), kōnati(-a)
stranglehold kōnati
strap tarapu, tātua, tōeke
strategy rautaki, nuka, kaupapa neke atu
straw kakau witi
straw, drinking - pū ngote, pū ngongo, ngongo waireka
stray (wander) haerēre, kōtititi, kaihanu, pakoke haere
streaky ropiropi
stream (brook) wai, awa iti, rerenga
streamline whakamaene
street tiriti
street kid tamaiti ihongaro
strength kaha, ngoi, pākahukahu, torokaha
strenuous uaua, tūkaha
stress pēhi, taumahatanga
stretch (lengthen) whārōrō, toro, whakaroa, whakamakoha
stretch forward tautoro
stretch legs hōkarikari(-tia), whakatīhaha
stretch tight whakamārō(-kia), kume(-a)
stretcher (litter) whata amo, kauamo, takotoranga tūroro
strict pakeke, pākaha, nohoture
stride out whakaraka, tāwhai(-tia), whārona
strife riri, tōtohe, pakanga
strike patu(-a), hahau (haua), hauhau(-tia), pātukituki
strike (collide) tūtuki
strike down turaki(-na)
strike home ū
strike out for au atu ki
strike (game) haukae, poitika
strike (punch) moto(-kia), kuru(-a), meke(-a)
strike sparks pātōtō ahi
strike together papaki
striking ātaahua, tau, mīharo
string aho, toina, tuaina, tiringi, tau
string game whai, hūhi
strip off kōmuku(-a), unu(-hia), pāhu(-tia)
striped whakahekeheke, ropiropi, kotikoti
strive whakapau kaha, tohe(-a)
stroke (caress) mirimiri (miria), haumiri(-a), hokomirimiri
stroke (medical) ikura roro
stroke, on the - of i te tangi o te karaka
stroke play (golf) tapeke hahau
stroke (swimming) tāhoe
stroll about hāereere
strong kaha, pakari, pāuaua
stronghold pā kaha, pā tūwatawata
struck pā, whara, tū, taotū
structure anga, hanga, wāhanga, whakaritenga
struggle momou, arawheta, nōnoke (nōkea)
strut about whārona, whakatāmaramara
stubble tātākau, paihau poto
stubborn whakatete, pake, upoko māro, taringa pōturi
stuck fast ita, whakapiria
stud (pile support) pou
stud, ear - titi taringa, mako kōura
student ākonga, tauira, pia
studio rūma whakatauria, taupuni mahi, papa mahi
study whai mātauranga, mātai, ako(-na)

study room tari, rūma ako, mātaitanga
stuff (fill) puru(-a)
stuff (rubbish) parahanga, rāpihi
stuff mouth apu(-a)
stuffed puru, apuapu
stuffy hau piro, hēmanawa
stumble tūtuki, tapepe, tārutu
stump of limb mutumutu
stump of tree tumutumu, take
stunned pōro, warea
stunted pūkiki, hūtoitoi
stupefy pōrewarewa
stupendous nui whakaharahara
stupid rorirori, kūare, heahea, moho
stupor pāhoahoa, pōro
stutter nanunanu, kīkiki, kakakaka
sty, pig - rāihe poaka
style āhua, ritenga, momo, tikanga, kāhua
sub-committee komiti raro
subconscious rehu moemoeā, mauri pōtere
subdivided wehewehea, wawae(-a)
subdivision wāhanga
subdued rata
subject (topic) take, kaupapa, matapaki, akoranga, marau
subjected to taurekarekatia, meinga hei pononga
subjective view whakaaro tuakiri
sublime teitei rawa, tino rawe, rekanga kanohi
submachine gun pū aunoa māmā, taiparapara
submarine (boat) kaipuke ruku wai, waka ruku, waka whakatakere
submerge ruku(-hia), ngaro(-mia), toremi
submission (proposal) tono, tāpaetanga, tukunga mai
submissive whakarongo, iro
submit (give in) tuku(-a, -na)
submit proposal whakatakoto, tāpae kaupapa
subscribe whakaae(-tia), uru ki roto, ohauru
subscription koha, utu noa
subsequent whai ake ana, o muri mai, mea whai mai
subside heke(-a), mimiti wai, mauru, tuku
subsided māwhe
subsidence hū whenua, horowhenua, tanuku
subsidise tāpiri(-tia), pūtea
subsidy pūtea tāpiri, moni tāpiri
subsistence oranga noatanga
substance matū, hanga, mea whai kiko, tino tikanga
substantial tino whai tikanga, whai kiko, whai take
substitute whakakapi(-a), whakawhiti(-tia), kakapi
substitute (sport) tāpui, piki, whakahirihiri
subtract tango(-hia)
suburb pūwaho, moka tāone
subversive turaki, manini kē
subway ara raro
succeed tutuki pai
successful whai hua, mōmohu
succession whai atu ana, tauatanga
successor kairīwhi, rīwhi, piki tūranga, uri
succulent tuawhiti, reka rawa, ngaore

S

suck in ngongo, ngote, momi
sucker (plant) hihi, hekerua
suckle whakangote(-a)
suckling piripoho, punua
suction ngote, momi
sudden whakarere, tata, rere, whawhati tata
suds hōpi huka, hōpi huhuka
sue whakapae-ā-kōti, whakapahuhu
suede kirinane, perehunga
suet ngako, aro
suffer mamae, pā te mamae
sufficient nui noa atu, ka nui, kāti, nanea, ranea
suffix arohere matau, kūmuri, hiku
suffocate noti(-a), hēmanawa
sugar huka
sugar-cane tātā huka
suggest whakahua(-tia), huatau
suggestion tohutohu, whakaaro, huatau
suicide tarona, whakamate i a ia anō
suit (clothes) hūtu, pūeru
suit (harmonize) tau
suit of cards whare
suitable tau, rawe, tōtika, arotau
suitcase pāhi kākahu
suitor tahu, whaiāipo
sulk tupere ngutu, whakakeke, whakapāeko
sullen haumaruru, whakamoroki
sulphur whānariki, pūngāwhā, pāpapa puia, pungatara
sulphuric acid hāmoemoe ngāwha
sum total pupūtanga, tapeke
summarise whakarāpopoto, tīpoka
summary whakarāpopotonga
summary offence hara whakapae
summer raumati
summit tihi, toi, teitei, taumata
summons (legal) hāmene(-tia)
sump rua
sun rā
sunbathe pāinaina, rārara i te rā, pāeneene
sunbather kopāina
sunbeam hihi o te rā
sunblock ārai hihirā, pare tīkākā
sunburn tīkākā (i te rā), wera i te rā
Sunday Rātapu
sunglasses mōwhiti whakamaru
sunk totohu
sunlight mārama o te rā, hihi o te rā
sunray hihi
sunrise whitinga o te rā, putanga o te rā
sunset torengitanga o te rā, tōnga o te rā
sunshade marumaru
sunshine rāhana, rāura, rāmaru, rāwhiti
sunstroke rangiroro i te rā
suntan kiri painaina, kiri rauwhero
superannuation penihana koroua
superb mīharo
superficial kirimoko
superfluous mahuetanga
superhuman atua
superintendant kaiwhakahaere, kaitiaki
superior tumuaki
superiority hīranga ake
superlative inetoru, kupu tawhiti
supermarket toa hokomaha

supernatural o te ao wairua, mahi atua
supernatural power mana atua
superstition mataku atua, wehi mea ngaro, ohiti
superstitious whakataputapu, manawa hopo
supervise whakahaere, tiaki
supervision tohutohu
supervisor kaiwhakahaere mahi, rangatira mahi
supper hapa, kai o te ahiahi, tina pō
supple ngāwari, pīwari
supplejack pirita
supplement mea āpiti, tāpiri(-tia)
supplier kaiwhakarato, kaihomai
supplies taonga, putunga
supply tuku(-a), hoko(-na), hoatu, homai
support (uphold) hāpai(-tia), tautoko(-na), taunaki(-tia), whirinaki
support services ratonga mahi
supporter kaitautoko, tatao, apataki
suppose whakaaro(-tia)
suppository pire tou, kuhi tou
suppress pēhi(-a), tāmi(-a)
supreme kaha rawa
Supreme Court Kōti Matua
suprise (wonder) mīharo
sure (certain) tino mōhio(-tia), ka pono rā, engari tonu
sure enough ehara!, tika tonu, āna
surely kāore ekore
surety punga
surf (breakers) karekare, hukahuka, auheke
surf-ride whakaheke ngaru, paheke ngaru, moki
surface mata, kiri, papa
surface (water) kārewa, karetai
surfboard papa retingaru, kōpapa, paparetirā
surge whakapuku, pōrutu, āmai
surly pukuriri
surname ingoa whānau
surpass hipa
surplus toenga, koha, tarepa
surprising whakamīharo
surround karapoti(-a), pae(-a), whākau(-tia), hao(-a)
surroundings wāhi tata
surveillance titiro
survey rūri(-tia), wea, tiro whānui, patapātai, tirohanga
surveyor kaiwea, kaituhi whenua, kairūri
survive noho ora, puta, orapito
survivor mōrehu, makorea tangata
suspect (*v.*) tūpato, whakaaro(-tia), whakapae
suspend tārewa(-tia), whakatare(-a), whakairi(-tia)
suspense māharahara, pohopā, āwangawanga
suspicious whakatūpato, tūpato, manaka
sustain tautoko, ukauka
swagger haere whakapehapeha
swallow horomi(-a)
swallow (bird) warou
swallow whole horopū, horopuku
swamp repo, hūhi, mātātā, nowaiwai
swamp hen pūkeko, pākura
swampy pīpī, kūkūwai, tihau, tokakawa
swan wani, kakīānau

S

swap hoko mai hoko atu
swarm around mui(-a), pōī, karamuimui
swarm of bees kāhui pī, rāpoi pī, mui
swastika rīpeka piko
swat papaki (pakia)
sway rutu, tīoioi, koiri, whakapioioi
swear (curse) kanga, kupu tiotio, kohukohu
swear (oath) ōati(-tia)
sweat werawera, kakawa, tihau, tokakawa
sweater poraka
sweaty werawera
sweep ā(-ia), tahitahi(-a), purūma(-tia)
sweepstake peti tahua
sweet reka, rōreka
sweet corn kānga
sweet potato kūmara
sweeten whakareka
sweetheart taupūmau, whaiāipo, kaihou
sweetness rekareka
sweets rare
swell puku, pupuhi, tetere, kukune
swell (sea) āmai
swelled head whakahīhī
swelling pūpuhitanga, kotere, tetere, uruhua, kōpuku
swelling (sore) kikohunga, kikokā, hore
swerve parori, tataha, tītaha
swill, pig - kokinga waru
swim kaukau, kauhoe
swimmer kaikaukau
swimming pool kaukauranga, hōpua
swimming togs kākahu kaukau, kahukau
swindle tinihanga
swine poaka
swing open kauhuri
swing the hands karawhiu(-a), piupiu
swing, child's - moari noho, tārere tamariki
swing poipoi, tārere, whakapiu(-a)
switch (*n.*) pana whakakā, pana raiti
switch (*v.*) pana(-a), whakakā, whakaweto
switchboard papahiko, papa waea
swoop down rere kōkiri, whakatopa
sword hoari
swordfish haku, paea
sworn whakaoatitia
syllable wāhanga kupu, kūoro
syllabus marautanga, ngā marau
symbiosis taupuhipuhi
symbol tohu
symmetry hangarite, auaha
sympathise aroha atu
sympathy pūaroha, aroha
symptom, illness - tohu mate
synagogue hinakoha
synchronised tukutahi
synchronise whakaōrite, tukutahi
syndicate rōpū
synod hīnota
synonym kupu ōrite, kupu taurite
synonymous rite tonu
synopsis whakarāpopotonga, pānui poto

synthesis whakarāpopotonga, kōtuitanga
synthetic kōtui, hori, waihanga, kēhua
syphilis pākewakewa
system pūnaha, whakahaere, ara
systematic nahanaha, tātai

T

T-shirt tī hāte
table tēpu, ripanga
table of data ripanga hōtuku
table-tennis tēpu tēnehi, poi kōpiko
tablecloth uhi tēpu, papakai, takapapa
tablespoon koko toha
tablet (medicine) parehe, pire
tabulation whakaripanga
tacit haumūmū, nohopuku, huna
tack (sailing) waihape, whakaripi
tackle (grab) rutu, ruturutu(-a)
tacky piripiri
tact arero reka, kupu matareka, whai whakaaro
tactful manawa pai
tactic(s) taupaepae, tātai, rauhanga
tadpole papane, puna poroka
tag waitohu, pinerua
tag (game) wi, tauwhai, whai
tag (touch) pā(-ngia)
tail (bird) remu, kotore, tou
tail (fish/sperm) hiku, tāwiriwiri
tail-bone iwi timu
tailor kaitui
tailwind hauhiku
taint piro, whakakino(-ngia), poke
take tango(-hia), hari(-a), tari(-a), mau(-ria)
take by force kōhaki(-na), kōwhaki(-na)
take care of tiaki(-na), maimoa(-tia)
take-home pay utu ki te ringa
take in dress whakawhāiti
take into account whai whakaaro
take off (doff) unu(-hia), tango(-hia), makere
take place tū(-ria), puta
take pleasure hari, koa, pārekareka
take that! anā!, anā tō kai!, e koe e koe!
take time āta haere
takeaways maukai, ō rangaranga
taken riro, taea
talcum powder nehu, paura, papaurangi
talk kōrero(-tia), kī(-ia), mea (meinga), whaikōrero(-tia)
talkative hautete, ngutu pī, waha rera
tall roa, teitei, tāroaroa
tally (*n.*) te maha
tally (*v.*) ōrite
tally up kaute, tatau, tare
tame rata, whakarata
tame pet mokamōkai
tampon puru taiawa
tan (brown) parauri i te rā, pākākā
tangelo āraniriki
tangible papatupu
tangle pōwhiwhi, rīrapa, tāweka, tārore
tank (military) mihini maitai, waka taua, taika
tank (water etc.) kurapuri, kurahinu, kurawai

tanker wakahari (penehīni), wakahari hinu
tantamount rite tonu ki
tantrum hukihuki, taruke, manawawera
tap dance kanikani pātōtō
tap (faucet) kōrere, katiwai
tap (knock) pātōtō, patopato, pā(-ngia)
tap root kōmore, more, tāmore, toi
tape (record) hopu(-kia) *reo*, tēpa(-tia)
tape (ribbon) rīpene, tēpa
tape, adhesive - rīpene piri
tape measure mēhua, tīeke
tape recorder pūrere hoputangi, pouaka kapo reo
tape, recording - rīpene hopu reo
tapered kāwitiwiti, kōekoeko
tapestry tāniko, tuituinga, whenu
tapu, free from - whakanoa(-tia), whakahoro(-ngia)
tar mīmiha, kauri tawhiti, tā, tahewaro
target keo, pārure, ūnga
target, on - hei pū
tarnish poke(-a)
tarpaulin tāpōrena
tart tāta
taste (*n.*) kai, hā, rongo, tāwhara
taste (*v.*) rongo (rangona)
tasteless ware
tasty reka, mākarakara, matū
tattoo (*n.*) moko
tattoo (*v.*) tā moko
taunt whakatete, tāwai(-a)
taunting chant kaioraora
taut tānekaha, whena
tax tāke, takoha, whai takunga ki
taxi tākihi, waka tono
tea tī
tea bags kori tīraurau, pēke tī
tea leaves tīraurau
teach ako(-na), whakaako (-na), whakamōhio(-tia)
teacher kaiako, kaiwhakaako, māhita, pūkenga
teaching tohutohu, whakaako-ranga
teal pāpango, pāteke
team tīma, kapa
teapot tīpāta
teardrop roimata
tearful matawaia
tease whakatoi, tāwai(-a), hangatītī
teaspoon pūnu tī, pūnu korikori, kokoiti
teat titi, ū
teatree mānuka, kahikātoa
technical toi, hangarau
technology pūtaiao taha tangata, hangarau
teddy bear teti pea
tedious hōhā, takeo
teenager taitamariki, rangatahi, mātātahi
teething tupunga niho
teething ring ngaungau
telecast pāho whakaahua
telegram karere waea, kupu-ā-waea
telephone waea, whounu, rīngi, waea kōrero
telescope karu whakatata
teletext pānui whakaata
televise whakaata(-tia), tīwī(-tia)
television tīwī, pouaka whakaata, terewīhana
telex waea whakaata, waea tuhi
tell whakaatu(-ria), mea(-tia), whāki(-na)

T

tell off kohete, kohukohu
tell-tale ngautuarā, kawekawe kōrero teka
teller kaikaute, kaitatau
temper, bad riri(-a), taikaha
temperament āhuatanga
temperamental taurangi, tukoki
temperature te mahana, te wera, ine mahana
tempered, even - whakaaio, hūmārie
temple (building) temepara
temple (of the head) rahirahinga
temporary mō te wā, rangitahi
temporary place taupua
tempt whakawai(-a)
temptation whakawainga
tempter kaiwhakawai
ten tekau, ngahuru
tenacious piri tonu
tenancy nohonga
tenant kainoho, kairēti
tend towards anga ki, peka ki, poro + *noun*
tendency whakawhirinakitanga, āronui
tender-hearted atawhai, whakangākau
tender (soft) ngāwari, tāngohengohe
tenderize whakangāwari, whakangohengohe
tendon io here
tendon, Achilles - io peke, io punga
tenement whare tini wāhanga
tennis tēnehi
tennis court papatēnehi
tenor (voice) reo iere, reo tāne teitei, reo tāmāori
tense (edgy) rika, whakaririka
tension (anxiety) tūtakarerewa, manawapā, manawa popore, maniore
tension (tightness) mārō, renarena
tent tēneti, whāpuni
term, school - wāhanga o te tau
terminal (ending) pito, moka
terminal illness māuiui whakamate, mate tuamatangi
terminate whakamutu, poro(-a), whakaoti
terminus mutunga, tauranga pahi
terms of reference ture whakahaere
terms, in - of te āhua nei
tern taranui, taraiti
terrace tūāpapa, parehua
terrestrial nō te whenua, nō Papatūānuku
terrible wehi, whakaihi, whakamataku
terrier kurī kerikeri
terrific tū te wanawana
terrified ihiihi, pāwerawera, mataku
terrify whakamataku(-hia), whakawehi(-ngia)
terrifying whakamataku
territorial waters rohe moana
terror winiwini, wanawana, pāwerawera, wehi
terror-stricken pāwera
terrorism mahi kōhuru, whakatumatuma
terrorist kaikōhuru
test whakamātautau(-ria), tēhi, whakamātau
test-tube ipuipu
test-tube rack mātiti ipuipu
testicles raho
testify kī pono, whakaatu pono

testimonial kupu tautoko, taunaki pūmanawa
testimony kupu pono, whakaaturanga pono
testing whakamātauranga
text tuhituhi, tuhinga, kupu
textbook pukapuka matua, pukapuka ako, pukapuka kaupapa
than i
thank mihi, whakapai(-ngia), whakamoemiti(-tia)
thank you kia ora (rawa atu), e tika hoki, taikiu
thanksgiving whakamoemiti, whakawhetai
that tērā, koirā, tēnā
that is koia rā, arā, tērā
that near you tēnā, koinā
thatch rauwhare, tāpatu(-tia)
thaw rewa, koero
the te (singular), ngā (plural)
the other tētahi, tērā
theatre whare tapere, tiata
theft tāhae, whēnako, whānako
their (plural) ō rāua, ā rāua, ō rātou, ā rātou
their (singular) tō rāua, tā rāua, tō rātou, tā rātou
them rāua (2), rātou (3+)
theme kaupapa
theme song waiata maioha
themselves rāua ake, rātou ake
then kātahi, kāhi, ianā
theoretical ā-roro, ki tā te whakaaro
theory ariā, kaupapa
therapeutic whakaora, haumanu
therapy whakaoranga, haumanu
there kōnā, kōrā, reira, raka
thereafter ā/i muri ake nei
therefore nō/nā reira
thermal wai ariki, puia
thermometer ine mahana, inewera
thermostat whakaū wera, whakaū mahana
thesaurus punakupu taurite
these ēnei, wēnei
thesis take kōrero, whakatakotoranga kaupapa
they rāua (2), rātou (3+)
thick mātotoru, kuku
thicken sauce kukū, ete, takaete
thief tāhae, whānako, kaiā, tōhē
thigh kūhā, kūwhā, heke
thimble temani, temara, pōtae mati, huhi mate
thin (lean) tūai, whiroki, tūpuhi, rahirahi, angiangi, pīrahirahi
thin (watery) waimeha
thin with water pokepoke
thing mea, hanga, taru, taputapu
think whakaaro(-tia), mahara(-tia), hua(-ina), mea(-tia)
think mistakenly pōhēhē(-tia), pēnei tonu, pohewa
think, one would hua atu
think over whakaaroaro, kohuki(-a)
think seriously āta whakaaro
third tuatoru
thirst matewai, hiainu, wheinu
thirteen tekau mā toru
thirty toru tekau
thirty love toru tekau ki te kore
this tēnei, tēneki
this place kōnei
thistle pūnitanita
thistledown puarere
thong here kirikau, pātui
thorn koikoi, tātaramoa, tara

thoroughbred momo rangatira, horomata
thoroughfare huarahi
thoroughly āta, mārire
those ēnā, ērā, wērā, ēraka
though ahakoa
thought mahara, whakaaro
thoughtful whai whakaaro, pūmahara
thoughtless(ly) pokerenoa, wareware
thousand mano
thrash kari(-a), patu(-a), whiu(-a), karawhiu(-a)
thrash about okeoke
thrashing whiunga, patunga
thread (fibre) miro, tarete, io
thread (screw) wiwiri, takawiri
thread (*v.*) tui(-a)
threat tuma
threaten whakaweti, kaioraora, whakawehi
three toru
three of a kind tokotoru
three-ply toru papanga
threefold tōtoru
threshold paepae
thrift penapena, tiaki moni, kaiponu
thrill wanawana
thrive tupu tonu, tupu matomato
throat korokoro, kakī
throb kapakapa, panapana, hotu
thrombosis ikura roro
throne torōna
throttle (choke) noti i te kakī, nonoti
throttle (engine) kātere, katihinu
through (via) mā, mā roto i/ki
throughout puta noa, whānui
throw away pana(-ia), ākiri(-tia), ruke(-a), maka(-ia)
throw (cast) panga(-a), epa(-ina), porowhiu(-a), maka(-a)
thrush (bird) tiutiu, korohea, koropio, piopio
thrush (disease) waihakihaki
thrust forward kōkiri(-tia), wero(-hia), tīhoka(-tia)
thud ngahoa, haruru
thug kaikōhuru
thumb koromatua, tōnui, kōnui, tokonui, koni
thump kuru, tākurukuru
thunder whatitiri, whaitiri
thunderbolt epa
thunderstorm pāroro
thunderstruck pōro, mae noa, poutukia
Thursday Tāite, Rāwhā, Rāpare
thus pēnei
thwart (block) taupare
thwart of boat taumanu, kiato, ama, paemanu
thyme tāima
tic hukihuki, pana, tākiri
tick (parasite) kutu
ticket tīkiti
tickle whakakoekoe, ngāokooko
tidal paria e te tai
tidal wave ngaru taitoko
tidal zone paetai, ara o Hinekirikiri
tide tai
tidemark upoko o te tai
tidings rongo kōrero
tidy (*n.*) tau, nahanaha
tidy (*v.*) whakatika, whakatau, whakawhāiti
tie (bind) here(-a), whītiki(-ria), hōtiki(-na)

tie (drawn game) taurite, haupārua
tie in bundle paihere(-tia)
tie, neck - neketai, tai, kāmeta
tie together here(-a), ruru, pūtiki, herepū(-tia)
tier tānga
tiger taika
tighten whakakikī
tightrope taura kikī
tights pirikiri, tarau kirimau
tile taera, papa
till (until) kia . . . rawa
till soil kari(-a), keri(-a), tāmata, ngaki(-a)
till, cash - tiriwā
tiller hoe urungi
timber rākau, papa rākau
timbre pūoro
time wā, tāima
time consuming whakapau tāima
time-honoured nō namata, nō ngā tūpuna
time, keep in hautū
time sheet puka wāmahi, puka haora mahi
timekeeper kaimātai wā, kaituki
timer tohu wā
time, at - i ētahi wā, i roto i te wā
times, how many -? kia hia?
timetable wātaka, wā haere, wā mahi
timid wehi, mohoao
timing whakauru haere
tin (container) kēna, puoto
tin (metal) tini
tin opener tīwara
tinfoil pepa konumohe
tingle tīoro, whaoro, wheo(-tia)
tinker with rāwekeweke
tinkle tatangi
tinsmith tinimete
tinsnips katikati tini
tint tae, kauruku
tintack pine whakairi
tiny tōitiiti
tip off (hint) whakamōhio(-tia)
tip (point) koi
tip (touch) tūtuki
tip, rubbish - putunga para
tiptoe hītekiteki
tired ngenge, hōhā, maea, ruhi
tireless kaha tonu
tissue, animal - kikokiko kararehe
tissue, human - kikokiko tangata
tissue paper papa muku, puka ngāwari, rauangiangi
tit (bird) miromiro
tit (nipple) kōmata
titbit kīnaki, whakapūwharu, horotai
title ingoa, taitara
to ki, kia
toad poroka taratara
toadstool waewae atua, tūtae ruru
toast (*n. and v.*) tōhi(-a)
toast rack tūnga tōhi, tītara tōhi
toaster whakatōhi, tāina parāoa
tobacco tupeka, torori
toboggan pānukunuku, reti, tōreherehe
today ināianei, tēnei rā, āianei
toddler kōhungahunga, pangore
toe matimati, koikara
toe, big - kōnui, koromatua, takonui, tokonui
toe, little - toiti, koroiti
toenail kotikara
toffee rare
together with hui atu ki
toil whakapau kaha
toilet (latrine) whare paku, heketua

T

toilet paper pepa heketua, pepa whēru
token tohu, maioha
token, love maimai aroha
tolerance ngāwaritanga, manawanui
tolerant (lenient) hāmārika, ngāwari, manawanui
tolerant (resistant) ārai mate
tolerate whakaae(-tia), tuku(-a), rata ki
toll call waea tawhiti, waea mamao, waea utu
tomahawk pātītī, pīau
tomato tōmato, tamato
tomb urupā
tomfoolery mahi heahea, mahi rorirori
tommy-gun pū tame
tomorrow āpōpō, auinaake
tomtit miromiro
ton tana, rua tekau hānarete
tone hā, reo
tone down whakamauru
tongs pīnohi, kuku
tongue arero
tonic rongoā whakakaha, wai rongoā
tonight ā te pō nei
tonne tana, mano kirokarama
tonsil miramira kakā, pūreke korokoro
tonsilitis miramira kakā
too hoki, anō, tino
tool taonga mahi, pāraha, utauta
tooth niho
toothache niho tunga
toothbrush parāhi
toothless ngore, niho more
top runga
top, bottle - taupoki
top (spinner) pōtaka
top-dressing rui(-a) manuia
topic kaupapa kōrero, kaupapa
topical o te wā
topknot tikitiki
topple hinga, whakahinga(-ia), tanuku
topsoil onemata, tātāhou
torch rama, kāpara, tōti
torment whakamamae(-tia), whakatoi(-a)
torn haehaea, pakaru, tīhaea, taretare, tītore
tornado āwha, tupuhi kaha
torpedo pohūwai
torrent hīrere
torrid wera, tūmāhoehoe, tūkaha, panapana noa
torso tikihope
tortoise honu whenua
tortuous kowiriwiri, whakairoiro
torture whakamamae, tūkino
toss whiu(-a), maka(-ia, -a, -ina), karawhiu(-a)
total kaute tōpū, hui katoa, tapeke
totalizator tiepī
totter turori, tapepa
touch whāwhā(-ria), pā(-ngia)
touchy āritarita
tough uaua, taikaha, pūioio
tour tāwhio, haereere
tourism tāpoi
tourist tūruhi, ruranga, wae tāpoi
tournament tātāwhāinga, tauwhāinga, whakataetae
tow (pull) tō(-ia), kukume (kumea), pārete(-tia)
towards ki, whaka (prefix to local noun)
towbar pōngere tō, pōngare tō
towel tauera, tauwera

towel rail rēra tauera, rōau tauera
tower pourewa
town tāone
toxic paihana, paitini, tāoke
toy taputapu tākaro, karetao, takawairore
trace (copy) whakaata, makenu
trace (vestige) pakuriki, tarapī
trachea pū hau ora, pū korokoro
track (pathway) ara, paparahi
track, racing - ara tuaoma, huarahi, ara tauwhāinga
tracks, bulldozer - mokamoka kōkō
tract of land takiwā whenua
tractable ngāwari, rata
tractor tarakihana
trade mahi-ā-rehe
trade union uniana, rōpū kaimahi
trademark waitohu, moko
tradition tikanga tuku iho, tikanga ā-iwi, kōrero tuku iho, ake kaupapa
traditional a ngā mātua tūpuna, mea tuku iho
traditional music pūoro-ā-iwi
traffic ngā waka
traffic lights rāiti ārahi
traffic service ratonga waka
trafficking hokohoko rongoā whakananu
tragedy aituā, kaupapa whiti
tragic kiriwetiweti, whakamate, hinapouri
trail (*n.*) ara
trail (*v.*) whai(-a), aru(-mia)
trailer waka kumea, tōanga, tauaru
trailing plant torotoro
train (teach) whakaako(-ngia), parakitihi, whakawai
train, railway - rerewhenua, tereina
trainer kaiwhakaako, kaiwhakangungu
training whakangungu, whakawai rākau
training programme mahi whakaako, whakahaere whakangungu
trait āhuatanga
traitor kūpapa, kaikaiwaiū
tram taramu
tramp (hobo) kaipaowe, tipiwhenua, kaihanu
tramp (plod) hīkoi, takahi(-a)
trample takahi(-a), takatakahī(-a)
trampoline papa tūpeke, papa hūpekepeke, papa tīrengirengi, tūraparapa
trance moemoeā
tranquillize miri(-a), whakarokiroki
transact kawe(-a), whakawhiti
transcend kei runga ake
transcript tuhinga kōrero
transfer whakawhiti
transferred riro i, tukua ki
transfix on a spit huki(-a)
transform whakaputa kē, whakarerekē, whakahou(-ngia), huri, panoni
transformation huringa kētanga
transformer whakamauru hiko
transfusion, blood - whāngai toto
transistor whitiārai
transit whakawhitinga
translate whakamāori, whakapākehā, whakawīwī, whakahuri(-hia)

T

translator kaiwhakamāori, kaiwhakapākehā, kaiwhakawīwī, etc.
transmit pānui(-tia), pāho, tukuoro, tare
transmitter tuku pāho, tare, tuku oro
transparency kiriata, pūataata, puata
transparent mārama kehokeho, purotu, puataata
transport (*n.*) waka hari
transport (*v.*) hari(-a), ikiiki
transverse tāpae
trap tāwhiti, rore, whakahei(-tia), kokoti
trapdoor taupoki, kōpani
trapeze tārere, mōari, mōrere
trappings tohu tūranga
trash (*n.*) para
trash (*v.*) whiu(-a), porowhiu(-a)
trauma ohonga ngaukino
travel haerere, haerenga, takahaere, tāwhe
traveller tangata haere
traveller's cheque tiēke tūruhi
traverse takataka(-hia), whakawhiti
trawl tō(-ia) kupenga, hiroi, koko kahawai
trawler waka koko
tray paepae, heri
treachery kōhuru(-tia)
treacle tirikara
tread takahi(-a)
tread, tyre - takahi taea
treadmill tawhiro, tīkeikei
treasure taonga
treasure house pātaka o ngā taonga tuku iho
treasurer kaitiaki moni
treat (entertain) taurima, manaaki(-tia)
treat (medicine) haumanu
treat badly tūkino(-tia)
treatment whakaora mate, manaaki, tiaki, whakamaimoa
treatment (care) maimoa
treatment, ill - tūkino, tutū
treaty tiriti
treble (x 3) tātoru
tree rākau
tree fern, black - mamaku, whekī, ponga, kātote
tree sap ware kauri, pia, taitea
tree, family - whakapapa, kāwai, tātai
treetop kāuru
trellis tāiki, taiepa tūwatawata, tītara
tremble wiriwiri, rurerure, hawa
tremendous nui whakaharahara, whakahirahira
tremor wiri, rure, wheoi
trench awakeri
trend ia, tikanga
trespass (err) hara, hē
trestle kaupae
trevally araara
trial (legal) whakawākanga
trial (test) whakamātautau(-ria)
triangle tapatoru
tribal ā-iwi
tribal authority mana ā-iwi
tribe iwi, hapū, mata ā-waka, mātāwaka
tribunal rūnanga, taraipiūnara
trick māminga(-tia), nuka, whakangaio, tinihanga, nukarau
trick, card - kohi
trickery tinihanga
trickle māturuturu

tricky uaua
tricycle taraihikara
tried whakamātauria
triennial ia toru tau
trifle mea noa iho, takunga, kanehe
trifle (dessert) taraiwhara
trigger keu
trim tahi(-a), whakatika, kaikawau
trinity terinita, tokotorutanga
trinket pōria, hanga noaiho
trio tokotoru, matengi
trip (journey) haere
trip up hīrau(-tia)
tripe puku kau
tripod toruwae, waetoru
trivial hauarea, hangahanga
trombone pū kumekume, toropona, pūhōkai
trophy paraihe, tohu toanga
Tropic of Cancer Kōpae Raro, Ara-a-Pūanga
Tropic of Capricorn Kōpae Runga, Ara-a-Whakaahu
trot toitoi
trotter (horse) hōiho toitoi
trotter, pigs - waepoaka
trouble raruraru, aituā, tūkino, pōrahu, hē
trouble, don't - kaua e māharahara
troubleshooting raparongoā
troublesome haututū, hōhā, mārehe
trough kumete, ngao
trough of wave awaawa
trounce pīti, patu(-a)
trousers tarau
trout taraute, tarautete
trowel pani, kōpaku
truant tamaiti ngaro i te kura, tamaiti takē
truce rongoawatea
truck taraka
trudge takahi haere, hawengenge, māngaingai
true pono, tika
truly pono, tika tonu
trump tānapu, hai
trumps! hai, kua – !
trumpet tētere, kaea, pūtātara, pūtara, pūawanui
truncated poro, koimutu, popore
trundler tokanga whai wira, tokanga kawe
trunk, tree - tinana, tīwai, kātua, kohiwi
trust whakapono(-hia)
trust board poari kaitiaki moni
trustee kaitiaki, tarahiti, kaiaupaki, matapopore
truth te pono, te tika
truthful tika tonu, pono mārika
try (rugby) piro, paneke
try hard ngana, whakapau kaha, uaua
try on (dress) kuhu(-na)
try out whakamātau(-ria)
tub tāpu
tube kōrere, ngongo
tuberculosis mate kohi-ā-kiko, kohitū
Tuesday Tūrei, Rārua, Rātū
tuft purepure, puhipuhi, puia, rake
tug (*v.*) tō(-ia), kume(-a), kāhakihaki
tug-boat waka tō, waka kume
tuition whakaakoranga
tulip turipa

T

tumble takataka
tumbler (acrobat) kaitakapore
tumour puku
tumult rarī, ngangau
tune (musical) rangi
tunnel (*n.*) ara raro whenua, rōri arapoka
tunnel (*v.*) apu(-a) raro whenua
turbine pūrere āwhio
turf pātītī
turkey korukoru, kerukeru
turmoil rū, ueue, kōrawa, ngaruwhati
turn (rotate) porotiti, huri(hia)
turn aside peka, auraki
turn, at every - he piko he piko
turn back hoki
turn inside out huri kōaro
turn off (light etc.) whakaweto, whakapirau, meinga iho
turn on (light etc.) whakakā(-ngia), meinga ake
turn over tahuri, whiti-rārunga
turn over and over tītakataka, hurihuri(-hia)
turn the back huri kōtua
turn upside down huripoki, taupoki(-hia)
turning hurihanga
turnip tōnapi, nanī, kotami
turpentine rongoā makamakariri
turret pourewa, pōtārewa, huki
turtle honu
tusk niho rei, niho puta, niho roa
tussock pātītī
tutor tauira, kaiako, kaiwhakaako
tutorial ako tauira
twelfth te tekau mā rua
twice kia rua, tānga rua
twig peka, rarā, tākupu
twilight māhina, ririko
twine tuaina, aho
twinge kikini, konatu mamae
twinkle kapokapo, kōpura
twins māhanga
twist wiri(-a), miri(-a), kōwiri(-tia)
twisted (warped) hakoko, kōrapa, kōriri, takawiri
twitch tākiri(-tia), arawhiti
twitter pekī, tīhau
two rua
two at a time takirua, huirua
two edged matarua
twofold kikorua
type (*v.*) patopato, pātōtō kupu
type (species) momo, āhua, taru
typewriter pūrere patopato
typewriter ribbon rīpene patopato
typhoid taipō
typhoon huripari
tyre taea, rapa

U

udder ū
UFO rererangi tupua, ngārara
ugly weriweri, kino
ukelele ukarere
ulcer (external) mariao, keha
ulcer (internal) kopito
umbilical cord iho/uho, tāngaengae, takai, pito
umbrella amarara, marara, maru atawhai
umpire amapaea, kaiwawao, kaiwhakawā matua
unable kāore e taea, kāore e wātea
unaccustomed tauhou, aweke, mohoa, tahangoi
unaltered mau tonu, kita
unanimous kotahi te whakaaro, oropapa
unarmed ringakore, rākau kore
unauthorised kore mana
unbalanced tahatahi, tītaha, pōraruraru
unbearable kore e taea te kawe, taumaha rawa
unbiased rite te whakaaro
unbreakable kore e taea te pakaru
uncanny atua, tipua
uncertain rangirua, ngākaurua
uncertainty āwangawanga, warawara
unchanged ū, mau tonu
uncharacteristic rerekē
uncivilised mohoao
uncle matua, matua kēkē
unconscious warea, hemo, ngahemo, mauri moe
uncultivated tupu noa, papatua, toitū
undecided āwangawanga, matawaenga, taharangi
under a/i/ki/kei/ko raro
underarm serve tuku whakararo, tuku kaku
underclothes kahakaha
undercover hunahuna
undergraduate pia, ākonga
undergrowth huru, heuheu
underhand nanakia, tinihanga
underline (*v.*) tāraro, ruri(-tia)
underneath kei raro i
underpants tarau poto
underrate whakaiti(-tia)
underside taha raro, raro iho
understand mōhio(-tia), mātau(-ria), kite(-a)
undertake whakatau(-ria), whakamātau(-ria)
undertaker kaiwhakatakataka tūpāpaku, kaiwhakarite uhunga
underwater ruku wai, roto wai
underweight tino māmā, iti iho
underworld rarohenga, pō
undesirable houhou
undetected huna, ngaro, puku
undisciplined taringa turi, torere ki te kino
undisturbed rangimārie, ukiuki, toitū

undo whakamatara(-tia), wete(-kia), wetewete (-a)
undress (self) unu(-hia) kākahu
unearned homai noa mai, aroha, puta noa mai
uneasy āwangawanga, manawapā
unemployment kore mahi
unemployment benefit takuhe koremahi
unequal tītaha, tītaka
uneven surface pāhiwihiwi
unfasten wete(-a), whakamatara
unfavourable kōaro, hunu
unfeeling ngākau pakeke, ngākau maroke
unfinished kohuku, hukihuki, taurangi
unfit (unhealthy) ngoikore
unfit (unsuitable) karihika
unforgettable maumahara tonu
unforgivable hara mau tonu, kore rawa e muru
unfortunate aituā, mūhore
unfriendly pukuriri, whakakeke
unfruitful huakore, tīpā, waiika
unhappy pōuri
unhealthy matemate
uniform kākahu ōrite
unify whakakotahi(-tia), whakatōpū
unimportant iti, meamea, wenewene
uninhabited whakarerea, hāhā, mahue
union whakakotahitanga, hononga, tūtakitanga
union, trade - uniana, kotahitanga
unit wāhanga, wae, taonga tūtahi
unite whakakotahi(-tia), takahui
United Nations Pāremata Kotahitanga o ngā Iwi o te Ao
unity kotahitanga
universe taiao, ao nui, ao takiwā
university whare wānanga
unjust hē
unjustified ehara i te tika, hē tonu
unlawful waho o te ture, hē, ekore e tika
unless ki te kore, meikore, engari ia
unlike rerekē i, kāore i rite ki
unlikely ekore pea
unload tuku iho, whakapiako, tangotango
unlock huaki raka
unlucky aituā, whakarapa
unmarried takakau, kiritapu
unmoved ū tonu, whakamoroki
unnatural autaia
unoccupied wātea
unofficial kore mana, nā te tangata noa
unpaid tārewa, kore utu
unprofitable kāore he hua, huakore
unprovoked riri noa
unqualified kore tiwhikete, kore mana
unquestionable pono tūturu
unravel wewete (wetea), whakamatara
unripe mata, kaimata, ota, torouka
unsafe mōrearea, hīrokiroki
unsettled kōroiroi, hārangi kei te tārewa tonu
unshaken pūmau, taketake
unsound mind hinengaro tūramarama
unspeakable kore taea te kōrero, mōrikarika

unstable hurihuri, korikori, pāhekeheke
untidy pōrohe, tūheihei, karukaru
untie wetewete (wetekina), unu(-hia)
until kia . . . rāno, āpānoa, tae noa ki
untouched urutapu
untrue teka, tito, horihori, kōrero papahu
unusual rerekē
unveil hura(-hia)
unveiling ritual hurahanga kōhatu
unwelcome waingaio, whakahouhou, matangerengere
unwell māuiui
unwilling whakatete, whakatohetohe, mārō, kōroiroi
unwind matara, wetewete(-a)
up ki runga, ake
upgrade whakapai ake
upheaval hurihanga nui
uppercut meke whakarunga
uprising whakatū riri
uproot ranga(-a), ketu(-a)
upset porohuri(-hia), tahuri(-tia)
upside-down kōaro, kōwaro, porotēteke, huripoki(-a)
upstairs pā runga
upsurge waipuke(-tia), aranga ake
uptight manawa popore, pohopā
upwards ake, whakarunga
urge (*n.*) hiahia, pīrangi
urge (*v.*) āki(-na), ā(-ia), ngare(-a)
urgent kākari, tino kaikā, whāwhai
urinal whare mimi
urine mimi
us (dual) tāua (you & I), māua (he & I)
us (several) tātou (you & I), mātou (they & I)
U.S.A. Amerika ki te Tokerau
use (utilise) whakamahi(-a), tango(-hia), whakarite(-a)
use up whakapau, waiho mō ngā meatanga
used to (accustomed) waia, taunga
used to (often did) *verb* + ai
useful whai tikanga, whai painga, whai hua
useless koretake, korepai, hakihakiā
user kaiwhiwhi, kaiwhakamahi
usual māori, anō
usual thing tikanga
usually i ngā wā katoa, te nuinga, *verb* + tonu
utensil (kitchen) taputapu, taonga, hanga
uterus whare tangata, kōpū, takapū, taranga whānau
utilise whakamahi(-a), whakarite(-a)
utter kī te waha, puaki(-na), whākoakoa
u-turn whakamuri

U

V

vacancy tūranga kei te wātea
vacant wātea, takoto noa, hāhā
vacation hararei
vaccine kano ārai mate
vacuum korehau, mārua
vacuum cleaner horo puehu, mīhini hauhuti
vagina taiawa, puta, tene, tara
vague mōnehunehu, rehu(-a), hākirikiri
vain, in - noa, paraurehe
valet hāwini, tumau
valid pono, whai mana, whaitake, tika
valley riu, awaawa, tāwhārua, kōawaawa
valuable (*n.*) tino taonga
valuable (*adj.*) utunui, puiaki, kura
valuation wāriutanga, uaratanga, kaingākau
value (*n.*) uara, wāriu, utu, whai painga, hua
value (*v.*) uara(-tia), hiahia(-tia)
valve puru kōrere, puruhau
van wakakawe kōporo, wēne
vandal kaitakakino, tamariki wāwāhi tahā, kaiauru
vanish memeha, nunumi, ngaro
vanity whakahīhī, whakapehapeha, whakatāupe
vapour mamaoa, tākohu, rehuwai, korohū
variation rerekētanga, momo taurangi, āhuatanga
variety momo tikanga
various maha, tūmomo, taurangi
varnish whakamōhinu, whakapīrata, wānihi
vary puta kē, rerekē
vase ipu putiputi
vast nui whakaharahara, nui noa atu
vat kāho nui rawa
vault (jump) hūpeke, kōkiri
vault (tomb) urupā, pūwhenua
vegetable hua whenua, kai māra, otaota, raurēkau
vehicle waka
veil ārai, kōpare
vein iaia toto pango, uaua toto, ia auraki
velvet kahu maene, wereweti, mōnehu
vending machine pūrere hoko, mīhini hoko
venerate whakahōnore
vengeance rapunga utu, ngaki mate
venom hūwhare whakamate, ware ngau kino, paitini
vent puaretanga, aumanga
venue wāhi tūtaki, papa
Venus (star) Kōpū
verandah mahau, parani, rueke, hōpua
verb kupumahi
verbatim āna ake kupu, ā kupu
verdict whakatau, whakaoti tikanga

verify whakaū, whakatūturu, tautoko
vermin kutukutu, iroiro
verse whiti
version ki tā tētahi titiro, whakaaturanga, motuhake
vertebra (cervical) tuahiwi, tangai
vertex tihi, akitu
vertical tūtika, tūmāhoehoe, poutū
very tino, rawa, pū, e kī!
vest himi, hemi
veterinary rata kararehe
veto whakakāhore, aukatinga
via mā
viaduct ara runga
vibrate (*v. intr.*) wiri, rū, ngatari, oreore
vibrate (*v. tr.*) whakangāteriteri
vicar minita pāriha, kairīwhi
vice (evil) kino, whakakino
vice-president tēputi, perehetini-o-raro, tumuaki tuarua
vice (tool) purimau
vicinity takiwā
vicious ngākau kino, hīkaka
victim ika
victor toa
victory wikitōria
video ataata, pūrere whakaata
video-cassette rīpene ataata
video game tākaro ataata
video programme whakaari ataata
video-recorder pūrere ataata
view tirohanga, mātakitaki, mātai
vigorous mātātoa, hauora, tūkaha
vile weriweri, whakarihariha
village kāinga, nohonga iwi
vindictive kaikiko, mauāhara
vine aka waina
vinegar winika
vineyard māra waina
violate whakanoa(-tia), takahi(-a), tūkino(-tia)
violate woman pawhera, raweke
violence tūkino, whakarekereke
violin whira, wairingi, toiri
virgin puhi, takakau, wāhina
virginal urutapu
Virgo (zodiac) Puhi
virtue pai, tūkaha ki te pai
visa pane uruwhenua, kōkota uruwhenua
visible e kitea ana, mārama, ariari, ari
vision (eye-sight) kite
vision (ghost) kēhua, moemoeā, kitenga, matakite, tūrua pō
visit toro, whakatau, mātoro
visitor manuhiri, tūwaewae
vital taketake
vitality hau, mauriora
vitamin matū huaora, huaora, ranuranu
viz. arā
vocal (speech) ā-waha
vogue tikanga o te wā
voice reo
void (vacuum) te kore
volatile hurihuri, etoeto, tākohu
volcano puia, ahi tipua
volley of gunfire waipū, waipūpū, waiwaipū
volleyball poirewa, mekepōro
voluminous rahi rawa
voluntary ngākau aroha, tuku noa iho, i runga i te hiahia
volunteer kaitūao
voluptuous poaina e te kikokiko, whakaahuareka
vomit ruaki(-na)

voracious orotā
vortex ripo, āwhiowhio
vote pōti(-tia)
vow oati, whakatau, kī taurangi
vowel reta paoro, oro puare
voyage hekenga, haerenga, rerenga, wharaunga
vulnerable noho tūwhera, whakaraerae
vulture whatura

W

wadding whakapuru
waddle hōnekeneke, wāke rakiraki
wade kautū
waft whiuwhiu
wag whiuwhiu, pōwaiwai
wages utu-ā-wiki
wagon wākena
wail auē, tangi, tīkape, tīwēwē
waist hope
waistcoat kahakaha, wēkete
wait for tatari (tāria) ki, whanga, tiaki(-na)
wait patiently for whakamōmori
waiter kaitono, weita, hāwini, kaihari
waitress hāwini
walk haere(-mā-raro), wāke, hīkoi, haere ā-waewae
wall pātū, pakitara, tuakiri
wallet pāhi, kopa, pēke moni
wallpaper pepapātū, pīngore
walnut wōnati
waltz warihi
wander manene, parore, haereere, kōpiko
want (wish for) hiahia(-tia), pīrangi(-tia)
want, in - pōhara, rawakore
war pakanga, whawhai, riri
war dance peruperu, tūtūngārehu, tūtū waewae
war, declare - whakaara i te rau o te patu
ward, hospital - riu hohipere, takotoranga tūroro
ward off parepare (parea), ārai, karo, ripa(-ia)
warder tautiaki, kaihere
warehouse whare takotoranga taonga, whare utanga
warfare kawe riri, whakatū riri
warlike kaitaua
warm mahana, āhuru
warm down whakamakaka
warm oneself painaina, inaina
warn whakatūpato(-tia)
warped pikopoto, kōrapa
warrant whakamana, warati, whakahau nā te kōti
warrior toa, matākaikutu
warship manuao, waka taua
wart tona, kiritona, tonga
wary tūpato, matakana
wash horoi(-a)
washer (gasket) porotiti whakapuru, tiwha, mōria
wasp wāpi, wāpu, katipō, pī katipō, wāhipa
wasteful maumau
watch (*v.*) mātakitaki(-tia), tirotiro (tirohia)
watch (timepiece) wati
watchful mataara, hiwa, matakana, matatū
watchman kaitūtei, kaimatāra
water (*v.*) hāwaiwai
water, fresh wai māori
water skis papa retiwai

watercress wātakirihi
waterfall wairere, tāheke, hīrere, horowai, korohā
watermelon wātamerengi
watertight pihi, piri, whakapiri
watery waiwai, kūtere, kōtere
wave (gesture) pōwhiri, piupiu, pīoioi
wave (sea) ngaru, karekare
wavelength roa o te ngaru, roangaru
waver ngākaurua, pūwakawaka
wavy karekare, pūngarungaru
wax-eye (bird) iringatau, pihipihi
way ara, āhuatanga, huarahi, tikanga
way, in that - pērā, pēnā
way, in this - pēnei
way, no -! kore rawa
wayward hīanga, kotiti
we (you and I) tāua
we (he/she & I) māua
we (you & I, 3+) tātou
we (they & I) mātou
weak-willed hauwarea
weakness ngoikoretanga, mate
wealth putea taonga
wealthy whai taonga, whai rawa
weapon patu, rākau
wear clothes mau kākahu
wear (fray) taiākotikoti(-tia)
wearied hōhā, takeo
weariness māuiuitanga, hūhi
weary ngenge, māuiui, ruha, parohea
weather āhua o te rangi, huarere
weave garments whatu(-a)
weaver kairaranga, kaiwhatu
web tukutuku, whare pungāwerewere
wedding mārena, ritenga o te mārena
wedge mākahi, wēti
Wednesday Wenerei, Rātoru, Rāapa
weed (*n.*) otaota, tarutaru, heuheu
weed (*v.*) ngaki taru, perepere
week wiki, rāwhitu
weekend paunga o te wiki, paunga rāwhitu
weep tangi(-hia)
weft aho, tāhuhu
weigh pauna(-tia), ine taumaha
weight taimaha, taumaha
weird autaia, tipua, rerekē
welcome pōwhiri(-tia), maioha, whakatau(-ria)
welcome! haere mai!, nau mai!, whakatau mai!
weld hono maitai
welfare oranga, tautoko i te ora
well ora, pai
well balanced tōtika, tino tautika
well established ū, whakamau
well known rongonui
wend kōtiti haere
Wesleyan Wēteriana
west uru, taihauāuru, rā tō, toengi, torengitanga
west wind hauāuru, tāuru
wet mākū, haumākū, whakamākū
whale tohoraha, ika moana, wēra, papatī
whalebone hihi tohorā, pāhautea
wharf wāpu
what? he aha?
what a . . .! anō te . . .!, inā te
what about? pēhea?
what of it! hei aha!
what place? kei whea?
wheat wīti

wheel wīra, porohita, tōhita, porotiti
wheelbarrow huripara
when kia, inā, ua
when? āhea?, nō nahea?
when . . . then . . . ka . . ., ka . . .
where from? i hea?, nō hea?
where to? ko hea?, ki hea?
where? kei hea?
whether . . . or rānei . . . rānei, ahakoa . . . ahakoa
which? tēhea? (*pl.* ēhea?)
while i + *subj.* + e *verb* ana
while, in a - taro ake nei, āianei, ākuanei, inangeto
whip wepu(-a), whiu(-a)
whirl kōripo, pōwaiwai
whirlpool koripo, riporipo, āwhiowhio
whirlwind āwhiowhio
whisky wihiki, weheki
whisper hamumu, kōwhetewhete, kōhimi, kōhumuhumu
whistle (*n.*) wīhara, pūtini
whistle (*v.*) whio, korowhio, korowhiti
white mā, tea
white person keha, pākehā, kiritea
white pine kahikatea, kahika
white-eye (bird) tauhou
whitebait īnanga
whiteboard papamā
who (descriptive) *verb* + nei *or* nā *or* rā
who did . . . nāna (past), māna (future)
who did? nā wai?
whoever te tangata, ahakoa ko wai, ngāti wai whānui
whose? nā wai, nō wai?
why? nā te aha?, he aha . . . ai?, he aha te take . . .?
wide māhorahora, whānui, mōmona
widow pouaru
width te whānui, hōkai, whānuitanga
wilderness koraha
will (testament) wira, kupu ōhākī
will (want) hiahia(-tia)
willow wiro, whiro
win eke panuku, toa
win for . . . riro i a . . ., wini, toa
wind (blow) hau, matangi
wind, rainy - marangai
wind up takahuri
winding about kōpikopiko
windmill mirahau, titi pārere rā
window wini, matapihi, mataaho
window sill papa matapihi
windscreen wini motokā, matapihi mua, mataaho waka
windy hauhau, whakapūangi
wine waina
wing parirau, pākau, pakikau
winkle pūpū, pūpūrore
winter hōtoke, takurua, makariri
wipe miri(-a), muku(-a), muru(-a), ūkui(-a)
wire waea
wireless waerehe, rerio, reo irirangi
wisdom mātauranga, whakaaronui
wish tūmanako, hiahia(-tia), minamina, pīrangi, wawata
wish away pain whakamomori i te mamae
witchcraft mākutu(-ria), whaiwhaiā
with kei, i, i te taha o, me

withdraw tango(-hia), unu(-hia), maunu(-hia), kōunu
without horekau, kore
withstand tū atu, whawhai atu, tū kaha
witness, eye - kaiwhakaatu, kaititiro, kaipono, kaiwhakapae
witness (observe) kite(-a), āta kitea
wizard tohunga mākutu, tohunga ruanuku
wobble tītaka, wheta, hūkokikikoki
wolf wuruhi
womb kōpū, takotoranga tamariki
women wāhine
women's refuge rauhī kōkā, kāinga punanga
wonder at mīharo
wonderful whakamīharo, mīharo
wonderland whenua mīharo
wood rākau
wood-pigeon kūkupa, kererū
woodhen weka
woodpile wahie
wool wūru, huruhuru
wool shed wuruhēti
word kupu
work station papamahi, taupuni mahi
worker kaimahi
worker, hard - ihu oneone
working bee ohu
world ao, taiao
worldwide puta noa te ao
worm toke, noke
worm-eaten kurupopo
worn out ruha, ngawhewhe
worry māharahara
worse kino iho
worship (adore) koropiko, atorāhio(-tia)
worship (prayer) karakia, hui karakia
worth mana, wāriu, painga
worthless koretake
worthwhile whai tikanga, whai hua
wound, flesh - kai-ā-kiri
wounded tū, kai-ā-kiko, whara, taotū
woven whatu (ā-ringa), raranga(-tia), paranene
wrap up takai(-a), pūkai(-tia), kōpaki(-na), ruruki, tākaikai
wreath (*n.*) pare
wreathe (*v.*) tau(-ria)
wreck pakarutanga, paenga
wren kōtipatipa, pīwauwau
wrench (tool) wāwāhi, ngauhuri
wrestle momou(-tia), nonoke, whātōtō, mamau
wriggle korikori, okeoke, kowiri, tākiri, whēkokikoki
wring whakawiri(-a), kawiri
wringer whakawiri kākahu
wrinkled mene, kūreherehe, korukoru, whewhengi
wrist kawititanga o te ringa, whatīanga ringa
wristband pare kawiti, tākai kawiti
writ hāmene-ā-tuhi
write tuhituhi (tuhia)
write off whakakore(-a)
writhe kowheta, tāwheta, takawhetawheta, okeoke
wrong, be - hē, pōhēhē
wrong, do - takakino(-ngia), whakahē(-ngia)
wrongdoing hara, mahi kino
W.W.W. tukutukuao whānui

XYZ

x-ray whakaahua roto
xeno- tauiwi
xenophobia mataku i tauiwi
xylophone pūpūoru, pakakau
yacht iota, wakarā, pere rua
yam uwhi, uhi
Yank (of U.S.) Marikena
yank kume(-a), tō(-ia), huhuti (hutia)
yap ngawī, pahupahu
yard iāri
yawn kōwaha, kohera te waha
year tau
yearn koroingo, ingoingo, warawara
yeast rēwena, īhi, pokeīhi
yell tīwaha, hāparangi
yellow kōwhai, punga, mangaeke, pīngao
yellowhead mohua, mohoua
yelp ngauī, auere
yes āe, āna
yesterday inanahi, nō nanahi
yet anō, tētahi anō
yield (crop) hua
yield (give in) tuku(-a)
yoghurt waiūpupuru, miraka tepe
yoke ioka, hemi
yolk tōhua, tōua, hākari
you (one) koe
you (several) koutou
you (two) kōrua
young pūhou, taiohi, tamariki, kōhungahunga
young animal kūao, punua
your (one person) tāu (*pl.* āu), tōu (*pl.* ōu), tō (*pl.* ō)
yourself tōu ake
youth rangatahi, taiohi, hunga mātatahi
youth, time of - whanaketanga, taitamarikitanga
youth worker kaitiaki hunga taiohi
zap patu-ā-hiko
zeal kaha, hihiko
zebra hepapa
zenith tihi, kōmata o te Rangi
zero kore
zig-zag hikohiko, kōpekapeka, kōpiko
zinc konutea
zip fastener kumemau, kōtui, kakati
zone takiwā, wāhi, rohe
zoo rohe kararehe
zoom lens whatu whakanui, arotahi topa
Zulu Hūru